HISTORICAL ATLAS

OF

THE UNITED STATES

HISTORICAL ATLAS

OF

THE UNITED STATES

MARK C. CARNES

Cartography

Malcolm A. Swanston

ROUTLEDGE
A member of the Taylor & Francis Group
New York • London

Published in 2003 by
Routledge
29 West 35th Street
New York, NY 10001-2299
www.routledge-ny.com

and

Routledge
11 New Fetter Line
London EC4P 4EE
www.routledge.co.uk

A member of the Taylor & Francis Group

Text Copyright © 2003 by Mark C. Carnes
Maps and design © 2003 by Cartographica Limited

Printed in the United States of America

10 9 8 7 6 5 4 3 2 1

Library of Congress Cataloging-in-Publication Data

Historical atlas of the United States / edited by Mark C. Carnes.
    p. cm.
    Includes bibliographical references and index.
    ISBN 0-415-94111-3 (hb : alk. paper)
    1. United States—History—Maps.   I. Carnes, Mark C. (Mark Christopher), 1950–

G1201.S1 H5 2002
911'.73—dc21

2002031764

Printed on acid-free, 250-year-life paper

Contents

Introduction

TO UNDERSTAND a people and their culture, one must understand their geographical environment. This insight was propounded with considerable fanfare in the academic world a half century ago by Fernand Braudel, one of *les Annalistes*, a group of French scholars perched on the "cutting edge" of social and cultural history studies. (The group took its name from its journal, the *Annals of Social and Economic History*.)

I was born after Braudel's seminal pronouncement, and I did not learn of it until graduate school. But I never needed *les Annalistes* to teach me the centrality of geography—and thus of maps—to history. I loved historical maps because they "explained" with vividness and clarity the great battles that first excited my historical imagination; then I learned to appreciate how historical maps illustrated so many other aspects of American history: the polarization of the antebellum North and South; the spread of industry and the emergence of a national transportation network; the rise of the Democratic Party under Franklin D. Roosevelt; the recurrent waves of immigration that swept across the nation. Maps demonstrated, too, that history had "happened" in places where I had lived, traveled through, or hoped to visit. By the time I graduated from college, I would no more read a history book without looking at a historical map than I would go on a long car trip without a good road map.

But all maps can be misleading. From the car you see billboards and strip malls and construction equipment; your road map depicts none of these. You steer around the twists and turns of the road and veer to avoid potholes; the map shows a straight, ageless highway, no different from others of its type. Finding the exit ramp in driving rain at night is a navigational challenge worthy of Magellan; but the merge of one highway into another appears on the map as perfectly seamless. How many of us, befuddled by the discrepancy between the visual chaos beyond the windshield and the clarity of the map, toss it onto the floor—only to fret over how to fold it up for later use?

Such moments teach an important lesson. We need maps because they render the complexity of the world comprehensible. Their appeal is partly visual: they create a type of picture. But their explanatory power is achieved by omitting "extraneous" detail; by compressing huge amounts of information into a small space; and by using symbols to "condense" abstract concepts and inferences.

Historical maps impose order on the past; but this "order" is even more suspect than the tidy lines of the road map. Historical mapmakers rely on the vague reports of explorers of dubious literary skill; locational information based on the primitive implements of early surveyors; the inconsistently compiled records of government clerks and officials; and an enormous variety of incomplete, controversial, and missing information from myriad sources. Moreover, the past often defies the simplifying conventions of mapmaking. For example, a map of European exploration in the "New World" usually omits the native peoples who, though they did not know it, were being "discovered." How, indeed, is the "presence" of Indians to be shown? Many (but certainly not all) of the pre-Columbian peoples of what is now the United States moved from one region to another according to the vagaries of season, foliage, and fauna. For this reason, most maps of exploration of the North American interior omit the native peoples: the explorers travel along rivers and through mountains and into seemingly uninhabited regions.

Historical maps compress not only space but time. In this atlas, for example, maps chronicle the resistance of Native Americans and even of slaves to white authority; this shows that oppressed peoples were not relentlessly ground into submission, an important insight of modern scholarship. However, the compression of these acts of resistance, which occurred over several decades, within a single map provides a false sense of the matter. Most Native Americans never raised a weapon against a white settler, nor slaves against their master. But how is this supplemental truth to be conveyed in a map?

Another form of compression is statistical: the adding up of millions of people and their actions, manipulating the data mathematically to yield insights (percentages, averages, and the like), and converting the numbers to visual symbols. Thus we include statistical maps of settlement along the frontier; of Irish immigrants flocking to the cities in the industrial Northeast and Midwest; of slaves from the Old South being traded to the new cotton plantations in Louisiana and Texas in the 1840s and 1850s; of poor farmers abandoning the "Dust Bowl" of the Midwest during the 1930s; of elderly people moving to the South in the 1970s and 1980s. We map the percentages of people who belonged to various churches, by colony, during the 18th century, and the percentage of the population, by state, that belonged to the Ku Klux Klan in the early 1900s. Such maps generate useful insights. But this aggrega-

tion of human experience omits its full range. Many Irish immigrants, for example, on finding themselves marooned in tenements in New York and Boston, booked passage back to Ireland, where they could return to a farming life that, however difficult, was familiar to them. Similarly, Ku Klux Klan members in New York were less likely to affirm their affiliation than those in the South. Statistical data allow social historians (and mapmakers) to comprehend larger patterns, but this "statistical" truth conceals countless variations and complexities. The reality is always messy.

Historical maps employ a variety of symbols whose meanings are "explained" with terseness—unavoidable terseness—in the key of each map. Arrows show the migration of buffalo, the trails of cattlemen, and the movement of armies and navies, and so on; however, buffalo went pretty much where they wanted, as did many units in an army. (The common refrain of soldiers in diaries is that they are nearly always lost.) Symbols often convey the relative size of cities (big circles for the most populous, for example); symbols also denote clusters of activity (strikes, internment camps, riots) and indicate who won battles. However, condensation through symbols is itself an act of distortion. The physical size of a city often bears little relation to its population; and the victor in a battle is often difficult to determine. During the Tet Offensive of 1968, for example, the Viet Cong absorbed staggering losses and were virtually eliminated as a military force; yet most historians regard the Tet Offensive as the decisive battle because it persuaded Americans that the Vietnam War could not be won. Which side, then, should be indicated on the map as the victor?

Because symbols encapsulate so many powerful assumptions and assertions, we have tried to err on the side of caution. We have eschewed the razor-sharp representations and clean linearity of some graphical styles. The messiness of history is incompatible with such renderings. One example is the tendency in historical atlases to show the boundaries of the various Native American "nations," and then to color them in. This in effect equates the Iroquois, Creeks, and Sioux with the nation-states of France, England, and Spain. But few Indians regarded land as something that could be owned, and no Indian polity resembled the territorial nation-states of Europe. To symbolically represent the Indians in this fashion is to impose on them a notion at variance with their thinking.

This historical atlas, like any historical atlas, offers a set of strong and clear interpretations. Its many assertions, assumptions, omissions, compressions, and inferences are based on innumerable historical sources. Each map warrants inclusion of an explanatory book. But given the alternative of including more explanatory text or more maps, we chose the latter. Road maps might be more accurate if they had plenty of pictures and footnotes but how would one then make use of them?

This atlas has been structured for ease of use. The parts mostly proceed in chronological order, as do the maps within the parts. In a few instances, however, we have subverted chronology so as to cluster maps about a particular region (especially the South and the West) or topic (especially social and cultural matters).

Just as we have attempted to satisfy the history buff's love of maps by providing as many of them as possible, we have tried to cover a wide range of topics. Historians in the past three decades have greatly expanded the discipline, so that entirely new subspecializations have attained mature development; the most important of these are women's history, ethnic history, labor history, ethnic and racial borderlands, popular culture, and consumption. We have attempted to include maps on each of these, with maps on topics ranging from the development of Hollywood, to abortion patterns, AIDS, and the rise of the illegal drug trade in the 1970s and 1980s. But we have also focused on themes that are particularly susceptible to mapping. We had hoped to include a map on global conglomerates during the 1990s, but the immensity and complexity of such entities meant that they could not be mapped in a way one could make sense of.

An atlas is necessarily a collective enterprise, a fusion of the work of many different specialists. In addition to the countless historians and geographers whose work constitutes the foundation for all modern historical atlases, I cite especially Malcolm Swanston and his staff at Cartographica Limited, who executed the maps, and Mark Georgiev of Routledge, who provided expeditious and sure-handed guidance rare among editors these days.

Mark C. Carnes
Ann Whitney Olin Professor of History, Barnard College, New York

PART ONE   NORTH AMERICA: GEOGRAPHY, CLIMATE, TOPOGRAPHY

HUMAN BEINGS have always clung to the notion that the earth is "solid." We contrast its permanence with the churning seas of the oceans and the unfathomable void of the heavens. From time immemorial, to claim land as their own, farmers have fenced it off and statesmen have built walls around it. For over five centuries cartographers have inscribed lines of latitude and longitude upon the planet, translating its fixity into mathematical precision. The implicit message conveyed by these actions is that while time changes, and people live and die, the earth remains immovable.

But our commonsensical understanding of the "solid earth," like so many other seemingly incontrovertible verities, is a myth. Like so many other myths, it is a product of our myopia, our inability to see beyond the boundaries of our own time and place.

Scientists have proven, and fairly recently, that the earth beneath our feet is anything but solid. The crucial insights were an unanticipated consequence of World War II and its aftermath. Harry Hess, a Princeton geologist who had devised a machine to map the ocean floor, tried it out while commanding a U.S. troopship in the Pacific. As he ferried his men to and from battle, his machine charted the contours of the ocean floor. His data showed that beneath thousands of feet of water, hundreds of small volcanoes dotted the floor of the Pacific, their tops apparently lopped off by ocean currents. Why volcanoes were so common in the deep seas he could not say.

A decade later, geologists with even finer mapping tools, many of which had been developed to monitor nuclear explosions, discovered that the undersea volcanoes perforated the ocean floors along lines or arcs, which apparently constituted seams in the ocean floor. They soon perceived that these edges continued above ground as fault lines on the earth's surface. Thus was born the new science of plate tectonics. And it set scientists into fervent consultation.

The science of plate tectonics advanced the theory that the surface of the earth consists of nearly two dozen slabs, each about 60 miles thick. These slabs, or plates, float upon molten materials. When the plates were somehow heaved above the surface of the oceans, they constituted continents. These discoveries, combined with abundant archaeological findings of marine fossils in modern deserts or fossils of desert-creatures in stones drawn from the depths of the ocean, suggested not only that the earth moved but that it was always moving.

Plate tectonics modified the theory of Alfred Wegener, a German meteorologist who early in the 20th century had contended that over hundreds of millions of years the continents, once lumped in a single landmass, had drifted apart. While Wegener had failed to adequately explain the nature of the force behind continent drift, plate tectonics supplied the answer. The plates beneath the oceans, under tremendous stress from the weight of the water, crumbled along their edges. Molten materials pushed upward through the cracks. As these cooled and hardened, they functioned like giant wedges that forced the plates outward, like toothpaste being squeezed between ice cubes. As these plates collided with others, they would bend and buckle, or one would slide beneath another, forcing the latter upward.

Most scientists now believe that about 500 million years ago, much of the Northern Hemisphere—including what is now North America—was open ocean, though perhaps only a few feet deep, while the plates containing large landmasses were mostly conjoined south of the equator. During the next 100–150 million years, some of these plates fractured and were pushed northward. Around 100 million years ago, the plate that became North America had moved toward the Tropic of Cancer, and around 50 million years ago North America was nearly in its present position and shape.

As the plates of the eastern Pacific pushed farther east, they collided with the main plates holding the North American continent. The consequent buckling and lifting formed the mountain ranges of the Far West. These profoundly affected the climate of the continent, as westerly winds laden with water from the Pacific were forced higher, dumping rainfall on the Pacific Northwest and depriving the skies over the Rocky Mountain states and western plains of moisture. The extreme climate fluctuations of the United States are largely a consequence of its geology.

The climate has been influenced by other factors as well. The period ranging from 110,000 until 18,000 years ago was unusually cold, with temperatures worldwide perhaps 5°C lower than present. Most of what is now Canada was covered by glaciers. Eighteen thousand years ago the earth began to warm, probably due to a slight shift in the earth's orbit of the sun. By 9,000 years ago, the climate of the Northern Hemisphere was warmer than even today. In consequence, the glaciers receded, having gouged vast pits that became the Great Lakes, Finger Lakes, and other bodies of water.

The slowly evolving geology, and the vicissitudes of climate, show that while human beings make history, their actions are always impinged on by environmental factors over which they have little control.

MAPS

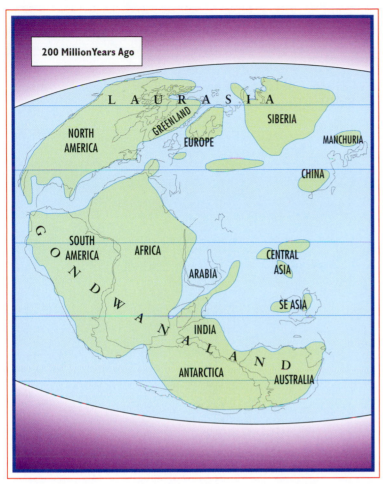

200 Million Years Ago

LAURASIA
NORTH AMERICA
GREENLAND
EUROPE
SIBERIA
MANCHURIA
CHINA
GONDWANALAND
SOUTH AMERICA
AFRICA
CENTRAL ASIA
ARABIA
SE ASIA
INDIA
ANTARCTICA
AUSTRALIA

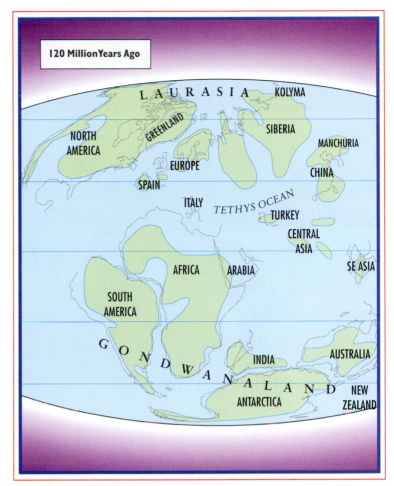

120 Million Years Ago

LAURASIA
KOLYMA
NORTH AMERICA
GREENLAND
EUROPE
SPAIN
SIBERIA
MANCHURIA
CHINA
ITALY
TETHYS OCEAN
TURKEY
CENTRAL ASIA
AFRICA
ARABIA
SE ASIA
SOUTH AMERICA
GONDWANALAND
INDIA
AUSTRALIA
ANTARCTICA
NEW ZEALAND

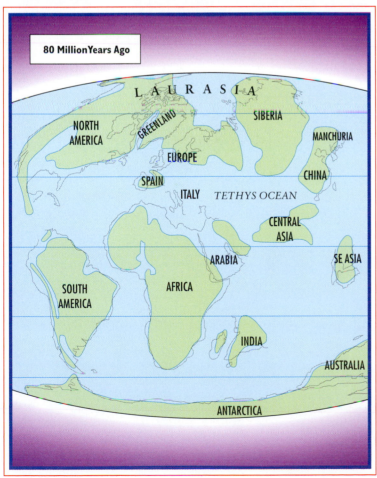

80 Million Years Ago

LAURASIA
NORTH AMERICA
GREENLAND
SIBERIA
EUROPE
MANCHURIA
SPAIN
ITALY
TETHYS OCEAN
CHINA
CENTRAL ASIA
ARABIA
SE ASIA
AFRICA
SOUTH AMERICA
INDIA
AUSTRALIA
ANTARCTICA

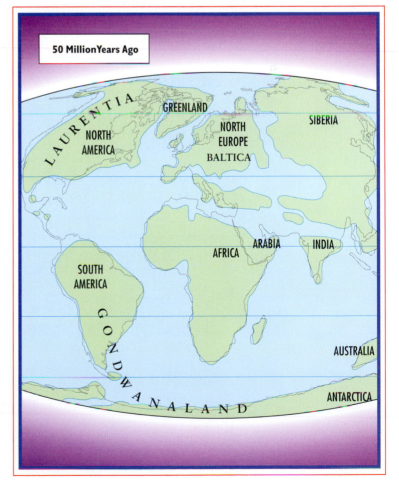

50 Million Years Ago

LAURENTIA
GREENLAND
SIBERIA
NORTH AMERICA
NORTH EUROPE
BALTICA
AFRICA
ARABIA
INDIA
SOUTH AMERICA
GONDWANALAND
AUSTRALIA
ANTARCTICA

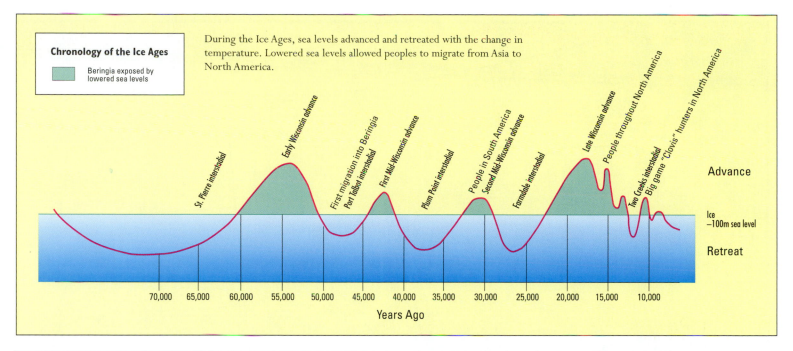

During the Ice Ages, sea levels advanced and retreated with the change in temperature. Lowered sea levels allowed peoples to migrate from Asia to North America.

Chronology of the Ice Ages

Beringia exposed by lowered sea levels

St. Pierre interstadial

Early Wisconsin advance

First migration into Beringia
Port Talbot interstadial

First Mid-Wisconsin advance

Plum Point interstadial

People in South America
Second Mid-Wisconsin advance

Farmdale interstadial

Late Wisconsin advance

People throughout North America

Two Creeks interstadial
Big game "Clovis" hunters in North America

Advance

Ice
–100m sea level

Retreat

70,000   65,000   60,000   55,000   50,000   45,000   40,000   35,000   30,000   25,000   20,000   15,000   10,000

Years Ago

18,000 Years Ago

- Ice sheet
- Northern forest
- Cool temperate forest
- Temperate forest
- Southern forest
- Steppe land
- Ancient coastline
- Modern coastline

AD 2000

- Ice sheet
- Tundra
- Northern forest
- Cool temperate forest
- Temperate forest
- Steppe
- Desert
- Tropical

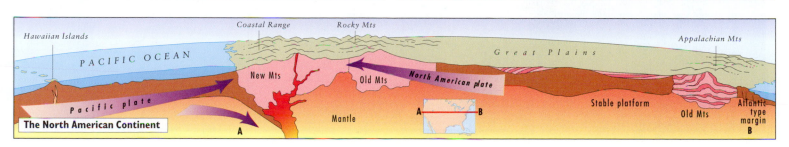

The North American Continent

Not to scale

The Importance of Topography in U.S. History

Native Vegetation c. AD 1620

0 400 km
0 400 miles

The topography of the United States has figured prominently in its history. The Appalachians long constituted a barrier to English settlers, who settled along the Atlantic coastal plain. In consequence, the original colonies were knit together by coastal shipping, along a north–south axis, with port cities such as New York, Boston, and Philadelphia serving as the focus of colonial life. Later the Mississippi River and its tributaries, which watered the nation's central plain, created another economic region, the nation's grainery; midwestern farmers floated their produce downriver to markets in New Orleans and beyond.

But the nation's earliest cities during the 19th century became its largest ones, and the demand for food in the cities of the Mid-Atlantic and New England provided the stimulus for the development of the railroads across the Appalachians, superimposing an east–west transport grid.

The Rocky Mountains constituted a yet more formidable barrier, accentuating California's cultural ties with Mexico. They were also a place of refuge. In the region around Salt Lake, the Mormons built an empire beyond ready interference by federal authorities of the United States; there, too, in remote mountains, Indian rebels for a time evaded reservation life, and desperadoes, the clutches of frontier lawmen.

PART TWO

FIRST AMERICANS

MERICAN HISTORY indeed, all human history—can perhaps be understood as a tension between a craving to be on the move and an equally powerful desire to set down roots. We seek the thrill of exploration and discovery as well as the comfort of repose and relaxation. We have a restless urge to be elsewhere; once there, we long to be home.

Unlike us, the earliest human beings were nearly always in motion. As hunters, they traveled constantly, following herds of large animals or attending to shifts in the seasons in search of fruits or edible nuts and plants. Their entire culture was predicated on swift movement. They fashioned light tools that could be readily carried. Seldom did they remain long enough in the same place to bother building habitations; they took shelter where they could find it, perhaps in caves or natural enclosures.

Insofar as the first human beings appeared over two million years ago, and sedentary communities did not appear more than 8,000 years ago, the history of 99.9 percent of all human generations has been the story of small hunting and foraging bands. Thus the human species adapted itself to a peripatetic existence. Women walked throughout pregnancy, and they carried infants. Elderly persons and the disabled, who contributed little to a hunting economy, were left behind. Hunting bands were necessarily small, well adapted to limited food supplies.

One set of maps in this section shows instances of this venturesome impulse: the initial map indicates the likely routes by which human beings in northern China and western Siberia migrated to the northeastern tip of Asia, crossed a land bridge into Alaska nearly 15,000 years ago (perhaps far earlier), ventured south between two vast glaciers, and eventually spread through much of what is now the United States and South America. These earliest human settlers of North America were probably hunting woolly mammoths and mastodons, huge lumbering beasts that had evolved in the absence of human predators. These hunters are identified as Clovis (for the long, multifaceted points on their spears that were first found by archaeologists near Clovis, New Mexico). Clovis hunting implements have been found throughout the United States.

By 8,800 years ago, most of the species of large mammals had become extinct. Perhaps the Clovis hunters had killed them off, or perhaps the heavily furred animals proved ill suited to the warmer climate of the era. In any case, the peoples of the Americas, deprived of the big game, were now obliged to look for new food sources. They learned to hunt smaller and more skittish animals, such as rabbits, deer and beaver, and they devised lines, hooks, and nets with which to catch fish; they learned as well which plants could be eaten and where to find them. Their lives were precarious, with starvation a constant threat. When food proved scarce in one place, they set out for another. Their survival depended on their ability to move quickly and without encumbrance.

But over time these peoples, known as Archaic, learned to satisfy most of their needs within a single region. They increasingly identified with a particular locality. They strengthened their association with that place by burying their dead in clearly identified mounds, often marked with elaborate "grave goods"—translucent mica figures, shiny copper statuettes, obsidian blades, or beds of seashells. The Archaic peoples represented a transitional stage between the nomadic existence of earlier hunters and foragers and the settled lives of agricultural peoples.

Some Archaic peoples had learned to cultivate edible plants, such as sumpweed, but none of these provided much sustenance. This changed when corn cultivation, practiced by Aztecs and Incas, spread north of the Rio Grande about 2,000 years ago. Over the next millennium, corn cultivation supplanted hunting and foraging economies, first in the lower Mississippi valley and then in the upper Mississippi and the southeastern United States. Corn cultivation, too, caused a shift from peripatetic cultures to sedentary ones. By AD 1000, major settled communities—the Hohokam, Anasazi, and Mogollon—had been carved into the cliffs of the arid hills and mountains, or along the rivers, of what is now the southwestern United States. In the Mississippi and Ohio valleys, as well as the Southeast, scores of communities appeared that were characterized by the cultivation of corn and the construction of mounds, some consisting of millions of cubic yards of earth, on which sat wooden fortifications and houses. The largest of these moundbuilding communities was located at Cahokia, Illinois, with a population at its peak of perhaps 15,000.

But if corn-cultivation generated settled communities throughout much of what is now the United States, these communities did not endure. By AD 1400, many of the towns and cliffdwellings of the Southwest had been abandoned, as were nearly all of the mound-cities of the Mississippi valley. The remaining peoples reverted to the hunting and foraging existence of their forebears.

During these years, too, the tension between peripatetic and sedentary life was not limited to North America. In Europe, a shortage of farmland forced thousands of young men to look for new opportunities; many of the boldest of them looked to the sea, where strong winds and currents could take them on far-flung adventures. One of these was a venturesome Italian named Christopher Columbus.

MAPS

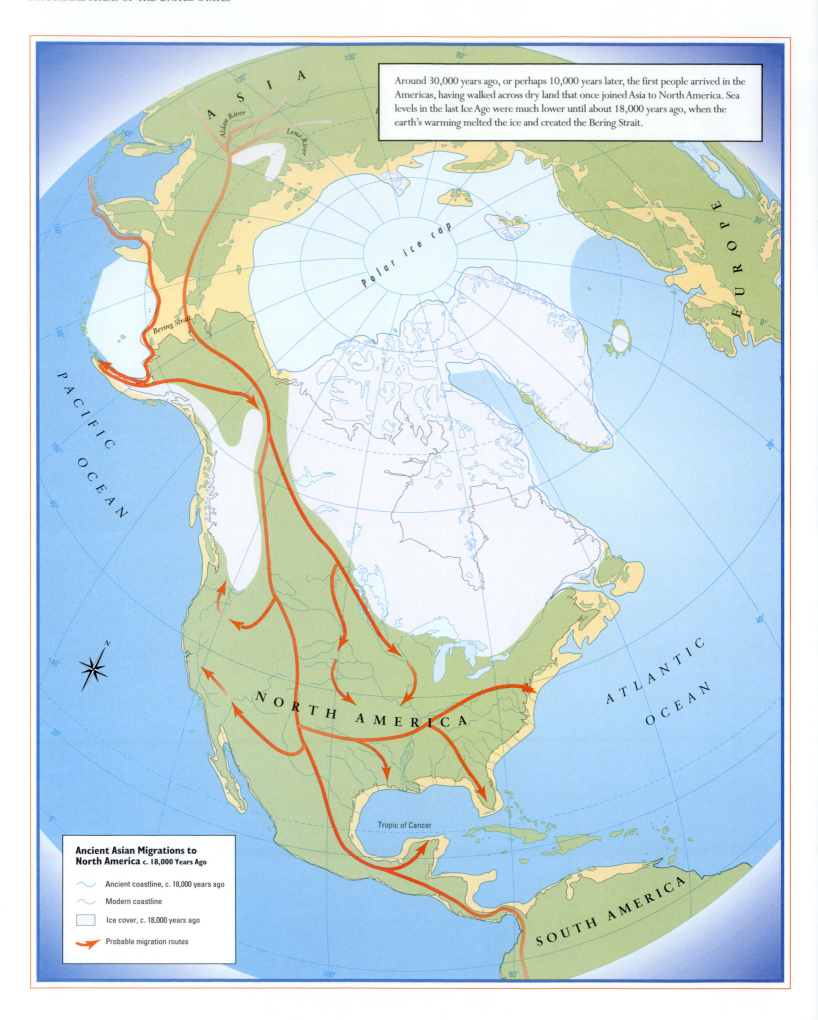

Around 30,000 years ago, or perhaps 10,000 years later, the first people arrived in the Americas, having walked across dry land that once joined Asia to North America. Sea levels in the last Ice Age were much lower until about 18,000 years ago, when the earth's warming melted the ice and created the Bering Strait.

Ancient Asian Migrations to North America c. 18,000 Years Ago

〜〜 Ancient coastline, c. 18,000 years ago

〜〜 Modern coastline

▢ Ice cover, c. 18,000 years ago

➤ Probable migration routes

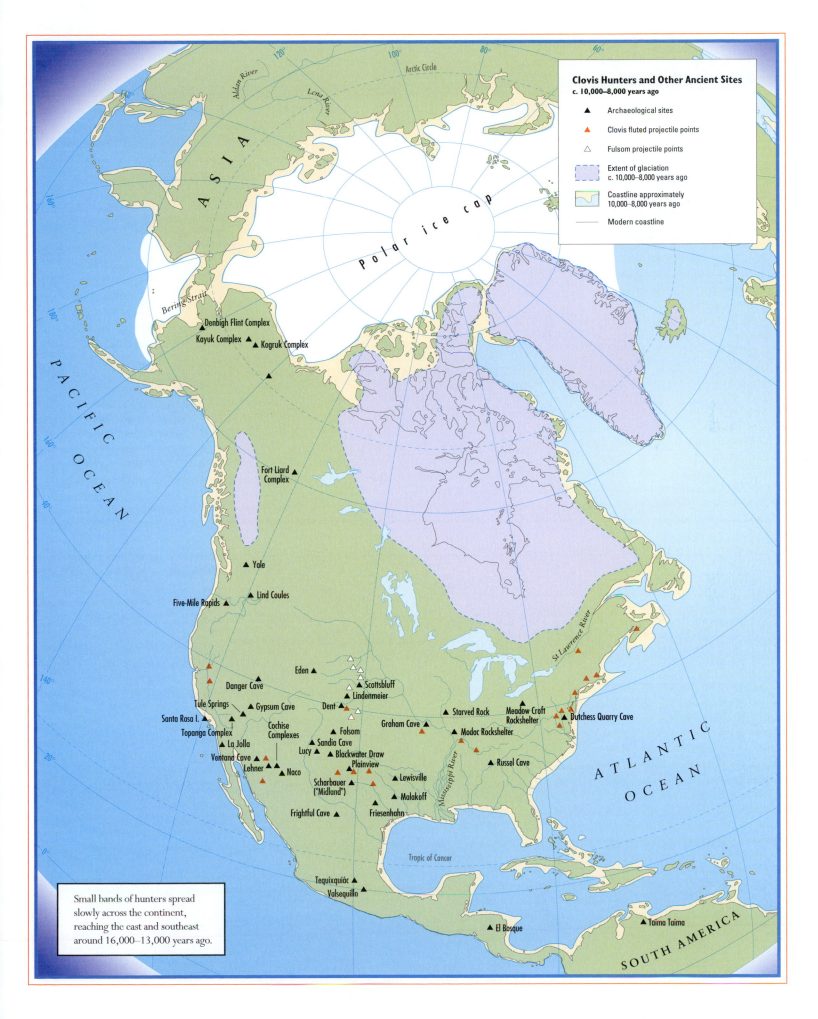

Clovis Hunters and Other Ancient Sites
c. 10,000–8,000 years ago

▲ Archaeological sites

▲ Clovis fluted projectile points

△ Fulsom projectile points

Extent of glaciation
c. 10,000–8,000 years ago

Coastline approximately
10,000–8,000 years ago

Modern coastline

ASIA

Aldan River

Lena River

Arctic Circle

Polar ice cap

Bering Strait

PACIFIC OCEAN

Denbigh Flint Complex

Kayuk Complex ▲ ▲ Kogruk Complex

▲

Fort Liard Complex ▲

▲ Yale

Five-Mile Rapids ▲ ▲ Lind Coules

Eden ▲

△ △
△ Scottsbluff
Danger Cave ▲ △ Lindenmeier

Tule Springs ▲ Gypsum Cave
Santa Rosa I. ▲ Dent ▲ △ Graham Cave ▲ ▲ Starved Rock
Topanga Complex ▲ Cochise △ ▲ Folsom Modoc Rockshelter ▲
La Jolla ▲ Complexes ▲ Sandia Cave
Ventana Cave ▲ ▲ Lucy ▲ Blackwater Draw
Lehner ▲ ▲ ▲ Naco Plainview
Scharbauer ▲ ▲ Lewisville ▲ Russel Cave
("Midland") ▲ Malakoff
Frightful Cave ▲ ▲ Friesenhahn

Meadow Croft Rockshelter ▲ ▲ Dutchess Quarry Cave

St Lawrence River

Mississippi River

ATLANTIC OCEAN

Tropic of Cancer

Tequixquiác ▲
Valsequillo ▲

Small bands of hunters spread slowly across the continent, reaching the east and southeast around 16,000–13,000 years ago.

El Bosque ▲

▲ Taima Taima

SOUTH AMERICA

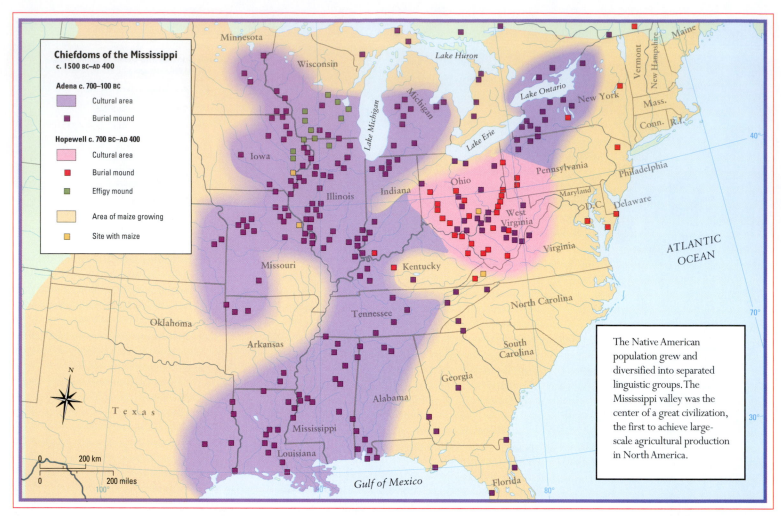

Chiefdoms of the Mississippi
c. 1500 BC–AD 400

Adena c. 700–100 BC

▨ Cultural area

■ Burial mound

Hopewell c. 700 BC–AD 400

▨ Cultural area

■ Burial mound

■ Effigy mound

▨ Area of maize growing

■ Site with maize

The Native American population grew and diversified into separated linguistic groups. The Mississippi valley was the center of a great civilization, the first to achieve large-scale agricultural production in North America.

0 — 200 km

0 — 200 miles

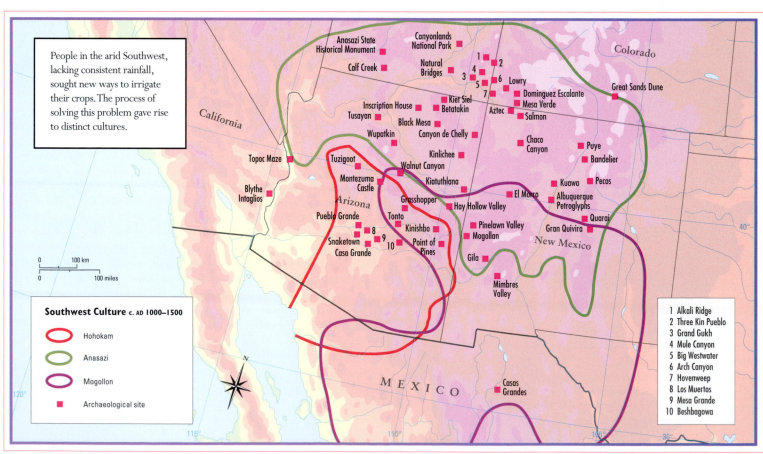

People in the arid Southwest, lacking consistent rainfall, sought new ways to irrigate their crops. The process of solving this problem gave rise to distinct cultures.

0 — 100 km

0 — 100 miles

Southwest Culture c. AD 1000–1500

◯ Hohokam

◯ Anasazi

◯ Mogollon

■ Archaeological site

1 Alkali Ridge
2 Three Kin Pueblo
3 Grand Gukh
4 Mule Canyon
5 Big Westwater
6 Arch Canyon
7 Hovenweep
8 Los Muertos
9 Mesa Grande
10 Beshbagowa

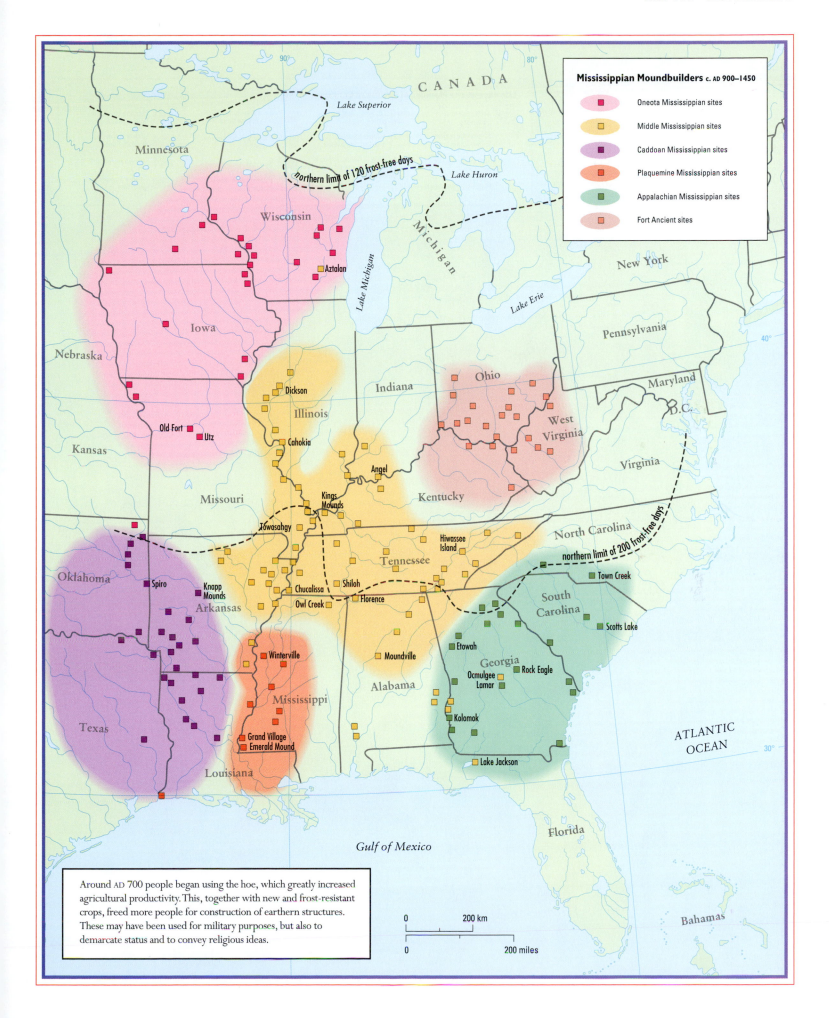

Mississippian Moundbuilders c. AD 900–1450

- Oneota Mississippian sites
- Middle Mississippian sites
- Caddoan Mississippian sites
- Plaquemine Mississippian sites
- Appalachian Mississippian sites
- Fort Ancient sites

CANADA

Lake Superior

Minnesota

northern limit of 120 frost-free days

Lake Huron

Wisconsin

Michigan

Aztalan

New York

Lake Michigan

Lake Erie

Iowa

Pennsylvania

Nebraska

Maryland

Old Fort   Utz

Dickson

Illinois

Indiana

Ohio

West Virginia

D.C.

Kansas

Cahokia

Angel

Virginia

Missouri

Kings Mounds

Kentucky

northern limit of 200 frost-free days

North Carolina

Towosahgy

Hiwassee Island

Oklahoma

Spiro

Knapp Mounds

Chucalissa   Shiloh

Tennessee

Town Creek

South Carolina

Arkansas

Owl Creek   Florence

Etowah

Scotts Lake

Texas

Winterville

Moundville

Georgia

Ocmulgee   Rock Eagle
Lamar

Mississippi

Alabama

Grand Village
Emerald Mound

Kolomok

ATLANTIC OCEAN

Louisiana

Lake Jackson

Florida

Gulf of Mexico

Bahamas

Around AD 700 people began using the hoe, which greatly increased agricultural productivity. This, together with new and frost-resistant crops, freed more people for construction of earthern structures. These may have been used for military purposes, but also to demarcate status and to convey religious ideas.

0   200 km

0   200 miles

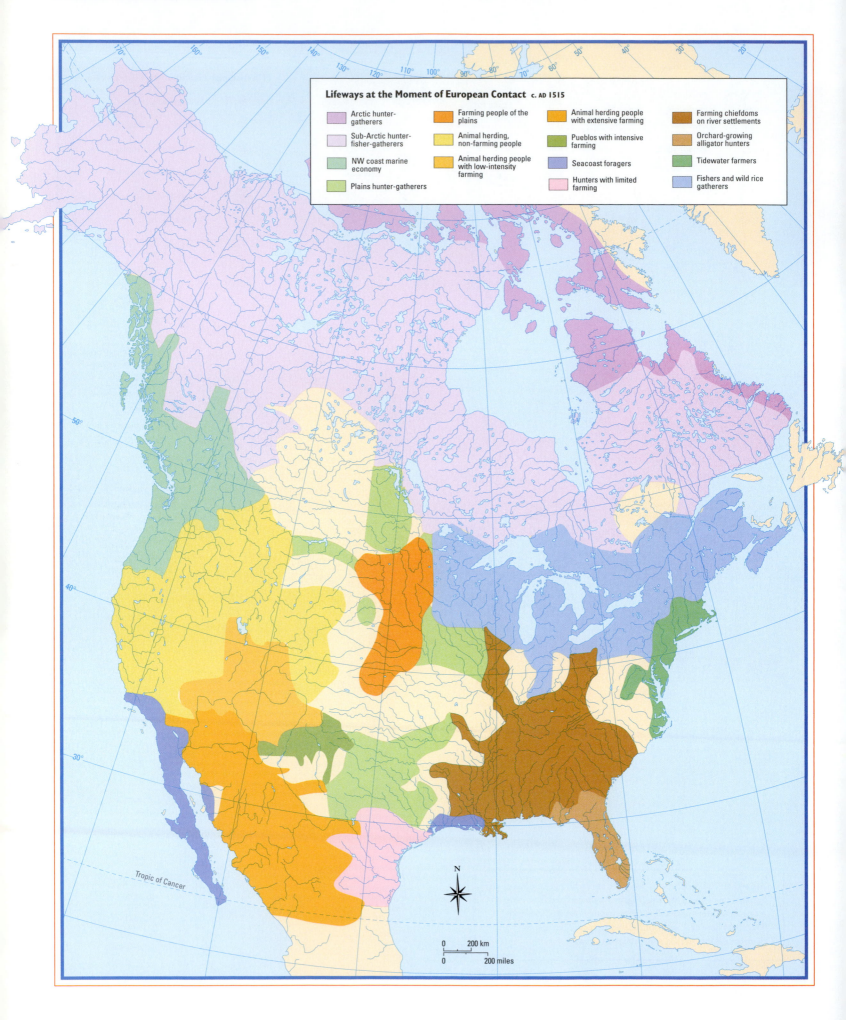

Lifeways at the Moment of European Contact c. AD 1515

- Arctic hunter-gatherers
- Sub-Arctic hunter-fisher-gatherers
- NW coast marine economy
- Plains hunter-gatherers
- Farming people of the plains
- Animal herding, non-farming people
- Animal herding people with low-intensity farming
- Animal herding people with extensive farming
- Pueblos with intensive farming
- Seacoast foragers
- Hunters with limited farming
- Farming chiefdoms on river settlements
- Orchard-growing alligator hunters
- Tidewater farmers
- Fishers and wild rice gatherers

Tropic of Cancer

N

0   200 km
0   200 miles

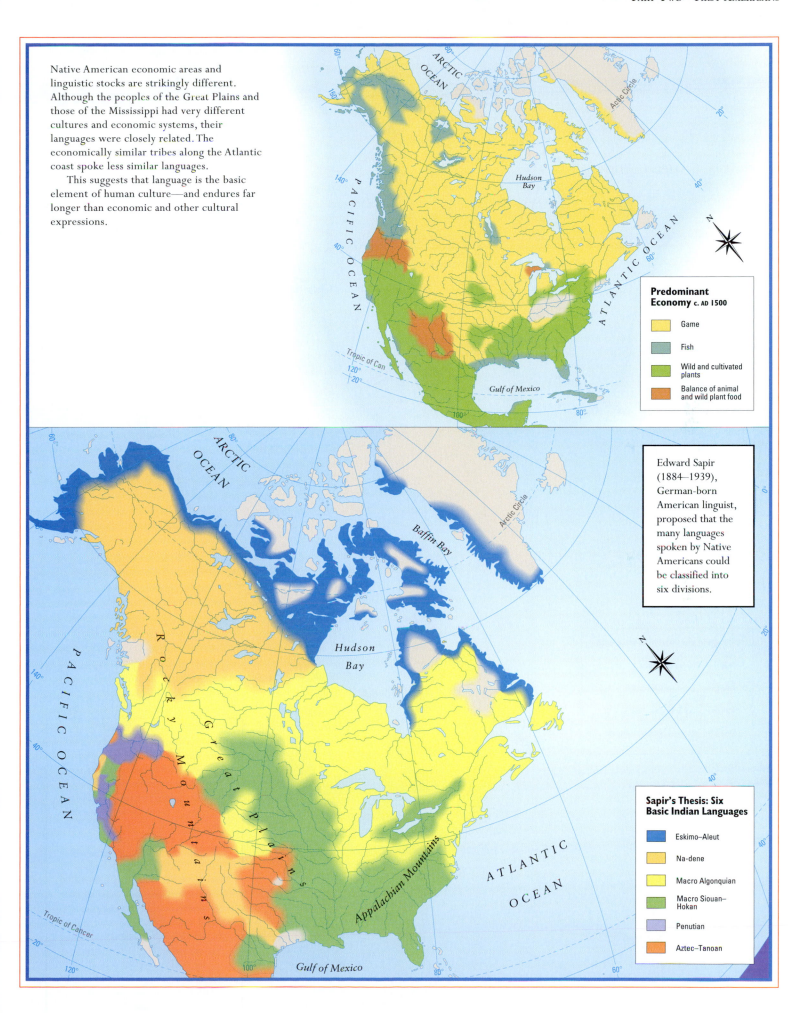

Native American economic areas and linguistic stocks are strikingly different. Although the peoples of the Great Plains and those of the Mississippi had very different cultures and economic systems, their languages were closely related. The economically similar tribes along the Atlantic coast spoke less similar languages.

This suggests that language is the basic element of human culture—and endures far longer than economic and other cultural expressions.

Predominant Economy c. AD 1500

- Game
- Fish
- Wild and cultivated plants
- Balance of animal and wild plant food

Edward Sapir (1884–1939), German-born American linguist, proposed that the many languages spoken by Native Americans could be classified into six divisions.

Sapir's Thesis: Six Basic Indian Languages

- Eskimo–Aleut
- Na-dene
- Macro Algonquian
- Macro Siouan–Hokan
- Penutian
- Aztec–Tanoan

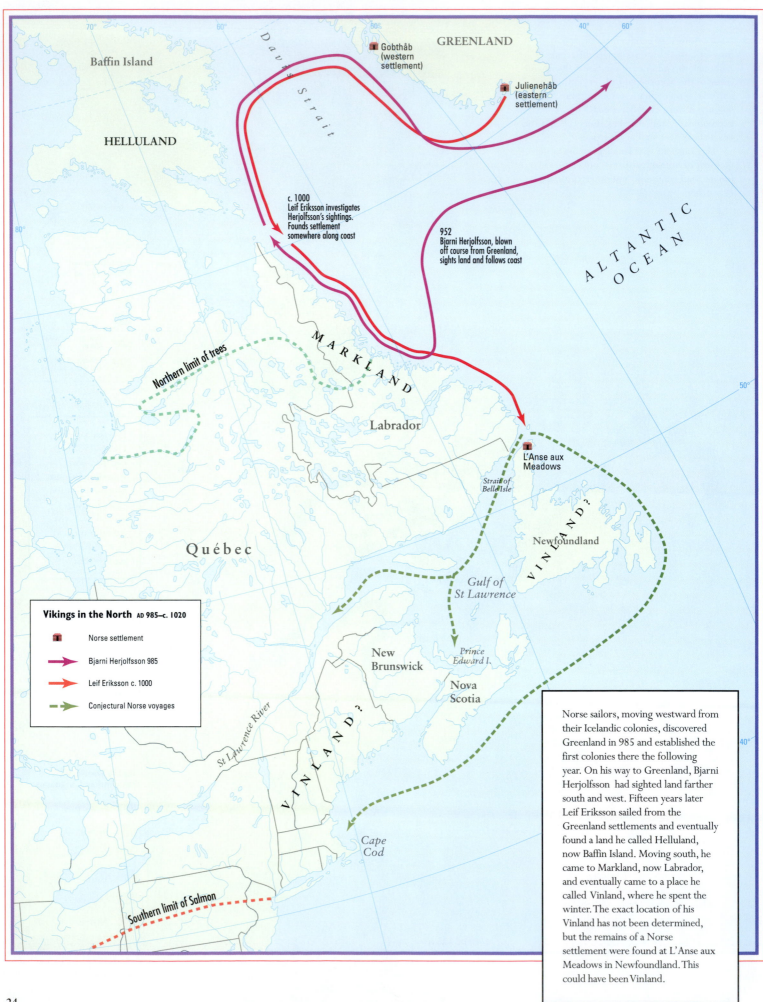

Baffin Island

Gobthåb
(western
settlement)

GREENLAND

Julienehåb
(eastern
settlement)

HELLULAND

Davis Strait

ALTANTIC
OCEAN

c. 1000
Leif Eriksson investigates
Herjolfsson's sightings.
Founds settlement
somewhere along coast

952
Bjarni Herjolfsson, blown
off course from Greenland,
sights land and follows coast

Northern limit of trees

MARKLAND

Labrador

L'Anse aux
Meadows

Strait of
Belle Isle

Québec

VINLAND?

Newfoundland

VINLAND?

Gulf of
St Lawrence

Vikings in the North AD 985–c. 1020

Norse settlement

Bjarni Herjolfsson 985

Leif Eriksson c. 1000

Conjectural Norse voyages

New
Brunswick

Prince
Edward I.

Nova
Scotia

St Lawrence River

VINLAND?

Cape
Cod

Southern limit of Salmon

Norse sailors, moving westward from
their Icelandic colonies, discovered
Greenland in 985 and established the
first colonies there the following
year. On his way to Greenland, Bjarni
Herjolfsson had sighted land farther
south and west. Fifteen years later
Leif Eriksson sailed from the
Greenland settlements and eventually
found a land he called Helluland,
now Baffin Island. Moving south, he
came to Markland, now Labrador,
and eventually came to a place he
called Vinland, where he spent the
winter. The exact location of his
Vinland has not been determined,
but the remains of a Norse
settlement were found at L'Anse aux
Meadows in Newfoundland. This
could have been Vinland.

In every part of North America the native peoples developed crafts, which they traded with near and distant tribes—forming a network that extended throughout much of the continent.

Native Trade Networks c. AD 1450

— Trade routes

● Major trade centers

Corn — Food for trade gatherings

Hides — Trade goods from area

ENO — Tribe

ARCTIC OCEAN

Labrador Sea

Hudson Bay

PACIFIC OCEAN

ATLANTIC OCEAN

Gulf of Mexico

ATHAPASCANS

MACKENZIE ESKIMO

Iron

Amber

Furs
Copper

EVAK

Marine Shells
Sea Mammal Oil

TUNGIT

Furs

HAIDA

Cedar Canoes
Slaves

NOOTKA

MAKAH

CHINOOK

The Dalles

Salmon

Slaves

WASCO
WISHRAM

CREE

Skins
Furs

ASSINIBOINE

Corn

MANDAM

ARIKARA

Maize

Flint
Tobacco
Skins

Copper

Whitefish

Alumette I.

OJIBWA

HURON

NEUTRAL

Tobacco
Pottery
Meat
Dried fish
Copper

IROQUOIS

SHOSHONE

Shoshone
Rendezvous
(moveable)

DAKOTA

Birch
bark
Canoe

WINNEBAGO

Hides

PISCATAWAY

CHICACOANS

RAPPAHANNOCK

Susquehanna

PAIUTE

Corn
Beans
Squash

Marine
Shells

CHUMASH

SOUTHERN
PAIUTE

Salt
Turquoise

Obsidian
Maize

Taos

Cohokia

Flint

Mica
Copper
Red pigment

Pearls
Dried fish

MOHAVE

Hopi

Cloth

Zia

Maize

APACHEANS

Hides
Jerky

Bison
hides

ENO

Maize

PANYA

Pottery

Zuni
PUEBLOS

Pecos

CADDO

QUECHAN

Cotton

PIA

PIMA

Maize

COCOPA

HIATATH O'ODHAM

OPATA

Casas
Grandes

Corazones

Mineral
pigments

La Junta

Pueblo
de los

Maize

Salt

Caddo
Villages

NATCHEZ

MOBILE

Mauvila

WARRING
CHIEFDOMS

APALACREE

Corn
Shellfish

Marine shells
Gourds
Racoon skin
Nets

Woodpecker
beaks

TIMUANCUANS

CALUSA

Marine shells

Bear oil
Feathers

Feathers
(from Mexico)

Tropic of Cancer

Hides
Jerky

N

0   200 km

0   200 miles

25

PART THREE   ACROSS THE WATERS: EXPLORATIONS AND OUTPOSTS

BY THE late 15th century, Europeans had become the finest sailors in the world. They viewed large bodies of water much as we view highways; sailing vessels were their automobiles. Thus the history of the early European exploration and settlement of North America is largely the story of men who spent much of their lives in boats and felt most comfortable when they were on water or near it.

But the generation of Europeans that came of age in the late 15th and early 16th centuries were sailors of a different type. Unlike their predecessors, who hugged the coastlines for fear of losing their way, this new generation dared to sail directly into the open sea and to strike out far from land. Partly this was due to improvements in navigational devices, such as the sextant and the astrolabe, and also to greater knowledge of distant waters through publication of navigational information, such as maps (see the simplified reproduction of Johan Ruysch's map of 1507).

Christopher Columbus's fateful voyage of 1492 was the best example of this new sensibility, though scholars have long debated whether he made use of sophisticated navigational technologies of the day. (Columbus, despite his advanced knowledge, committed the great navigational error of the century, perhaps even of the millennium, in assuming—and then persisting in the error after multiple voyages to the West Indies—that he had found a route to China.)

When it became clear to others that Columbus had instead happened upon a "Mundus Novus" (New World), the seafaring nations of Europe commenced an extravagant landgrab. In 1497 King Henry VII of England authorized John Cabot to explore and establish English "right, title, and jurisdiction" to whatever new lands he could discover. Several decades later King Francis I of France dispatched Giovanni da Verrazana (1524) and Jacques Cartier (1534) to the New World to find gold, spices, and a route to China.

The Paris Map c. 1490

*The vastness of the Atlantic Ocean remained a challenge for European cartographers. Most imagined a possible route to China and based their maps on this idea. The Paris Map (*above*) shows the Island of Brazil and the Island of the Seven Cities west of Ireland.*

*Two years later Behaim's globe (*below*) shows the rectangular island of Antilia halfway between Europe and Cipangu (Japan). Columbus's voyage of 1492, for some time after, confirmed to most, if not all, that they had found a route to the Indies.*

But these explorers, and those who followed them, seldom wandered much beyond sight of their ships. They sailed along the Atlantic coast, from Hudson Bay to the mouth of the Amazon, and up major rivers as long as they were navigable. When they laid out the first settlements, they preferred deep-sea harbors or those that were located on islands (New Amsterdam, Roanoke, Port Royal) or protected by bays (Plymouth, Boston). They abandoned their ships and ventured inland rarely—and usually then only to attend to rumors of extravagant treasure. And when they did so, they proved vulnerable to Indian attack and infectious diseases.

Spanish exploration and settlement of what is now the United States usually commenced as naval expeditions mounted from Spanish island possessions in the Caribbean. In 1513 Ponce de León, after exploring Puerto Rico, led an expedition that landed at St. Augustine, and then sailed southward, through the Florida Keys, and up the west coast to Florida. In 1528 Pánfilo de Narváez, commissioned to colonize northern Florida and the lands to the west, landed with a force of 400 men near Tampa Bay and marched inland, where his party was harassed by Indians. In July they returned to the coast and built five ships that carried them westward along the Gulf of Mexico. Eventually all of the ships were lost, and with them Narváez; only four survived the journey. One of them, Cabeza de Vaca, after being shipwrecked near Galveston, Texas, was held prisoner by Karankawa Indians for two years; then he journeyed across Texas, through northern Mexico until reaching Mexico City.

In 1539 Hernando de Soto, in search of precious metals and other treasure, sailed with 10 ships and 700 men from Cuba to Florida. Then began a remarkable overland trek through much of the southeastern United States. In 1541 he crossed the Mississippi River and wandered through Arkansas and east Texas. Although de Soto died of fever the next year, the expedition, having lost half its men, eventually made it back to the Gulf of Mexico.

The English colonies were originally founded by trading companies that plied the oceans. Although they operated under royal charters that alluded to missionary activities, such as bringing "the Infedels and Savages to human civility," the main purpose of such ventures was "to dig, mine, and search for all Manner of Mines of Gold, Silver, and Copper." English settlement, which commenced in earnest somewhat later, also focused on islands and coastal areas. In 1584 Captains Philip Amadas and Arthur Barlowe, acting under the orders of Sir Walter Raleigh to found an English colony in the North Carolina region, settled upon Roanoke Island. They reasoned that it could be supplied by sea and that it could be more readily defended from Indian attack.

English settlers, too, preferred islands and coastal areas. Puritan emigrants themselves sailed

1492 by Martin Behaim

from the ports of Yarmouth, Ipswich, and Southampton, and they settled in coastal areas that could readily be supplied by seagoing vessels. Plymouth and Boston were selected in the Massachusetts region partly because they could readily accommodate large ships. Few of the first two generations of English settlers lived more than five or six miles from navigable rivers or from the Atlantic Ocean itself.

French explorers penetrated the New World via the waterways leading to the Great Lakes and the Mississippi River and its tributaries. As they made their way deeper into the woodlands of the upper Midwest, they built canoes much like those used by the Indians. The Dutch colony of New Netherland was centered at New Amsterdam, a settlement on the southern tip of Manhattan Island, and Dutch settlement along the banks of the Hudson River to the north. The Dutch and the Swedes planted competing colonies along the banks of the Delaware River.

The next stage of settlement obliged these Europeans to shift their gaze from the seas and toward the interior, where lurked in immense forests a type of human being very different from themselves.

MAPS

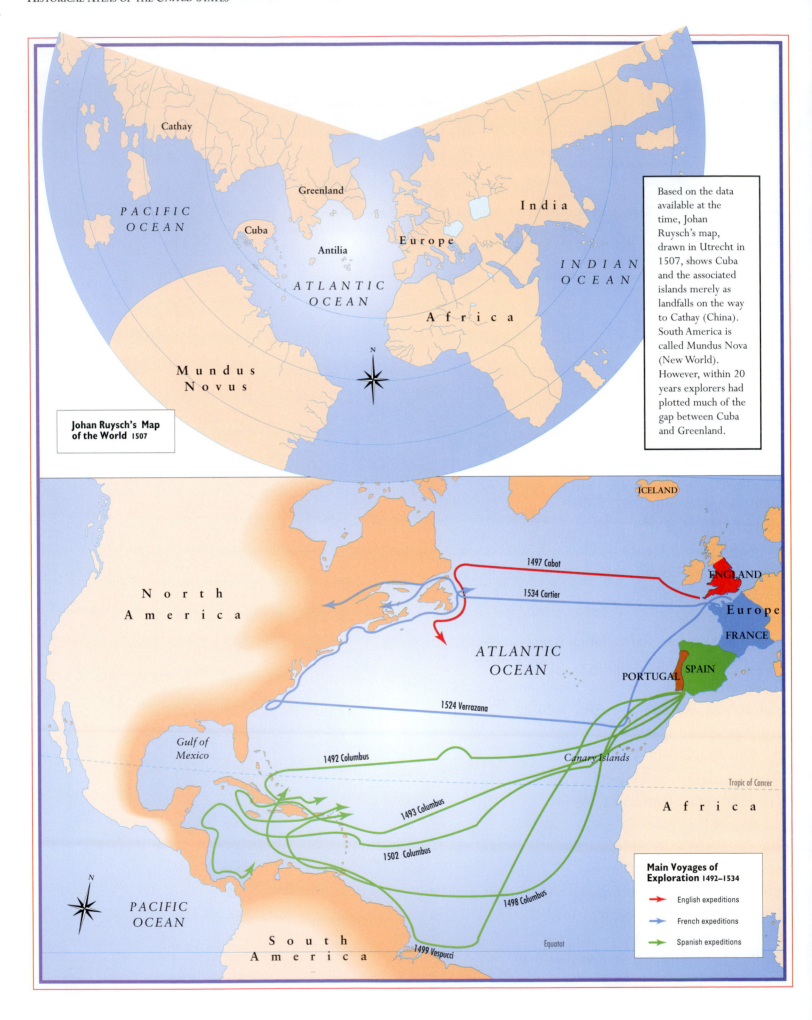

Cathay

PACIFIC
OCEAN

Greenland

Cuba

Antilia

ATLANTIC
OCEAN

Europe

India

INDIAN
OCEAN

Africa

M u n d u s
N o v u s

N

**Johan Ruysch's Map
of the World** 1507

Based on the data
available at the
time, Johan
Ruysch's map,
drawn in Utrecht in
1507, shows Cuba
and the associated
islands merely as
landfalls on the way
to Cathay (China).
South America is
called Mundus Nova
(New World).
However, within 20
years explorers had
plotted much of the
gap between Cuba
and Greenland.

ICELAND

1497 Cabot

ENGLAND

1534 Cartier

Europe

FRANCE

N o r t h
A m e r i c a

ATLANTIC
OCEAN

PORTUGAL SPAIN

1524 Verrazana

Gulf of
Mexico

1492 Columbus

Canary Islands

Tropic of Cancer

A f r i c a

1493 Columbus

1502 Columbus

1498 Columbus

**Main Voyages of
Exploration** 1492–1534

N

PACIFIC
OCEAN

S o u t h
A m e r i c a

1499 Vespucci

Equator

→ English expeditions

→ French expeditions

→ Spanish expeditions

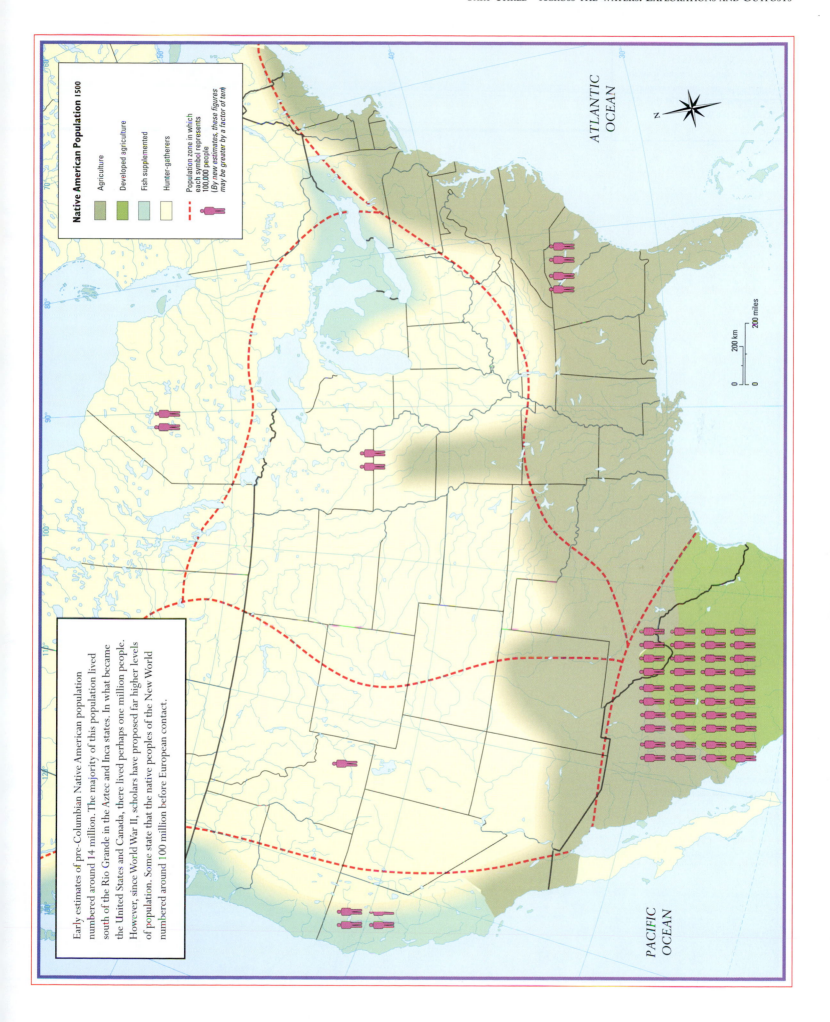

Native American Population 1500

Agriculture

Developed agriculture

Fish supplemented

Hunter-gatherers

Population zone in which each symbol represents 100,000 people
(By new estimates, these figures may be greater by a factor of ten)

Early estimates of pre-Columbian Native American population numbered around 14 million. The majority of this population lived south of the Rio Grande in the Aztec and Inca states. In what became the United States and Canada, there lived perhaps one million people. However, since World War II, scholars have proposed far higher levels of population. Some state that the native peoples of the New World numbered around 100 million before European contact.

ATLANTIC OCEAN

PACIFIC OCEAN

200 km

200 miles

Between 1513 and 1544 explorers working for the Spanish crown explored and understood the geography of much of the South and the West.

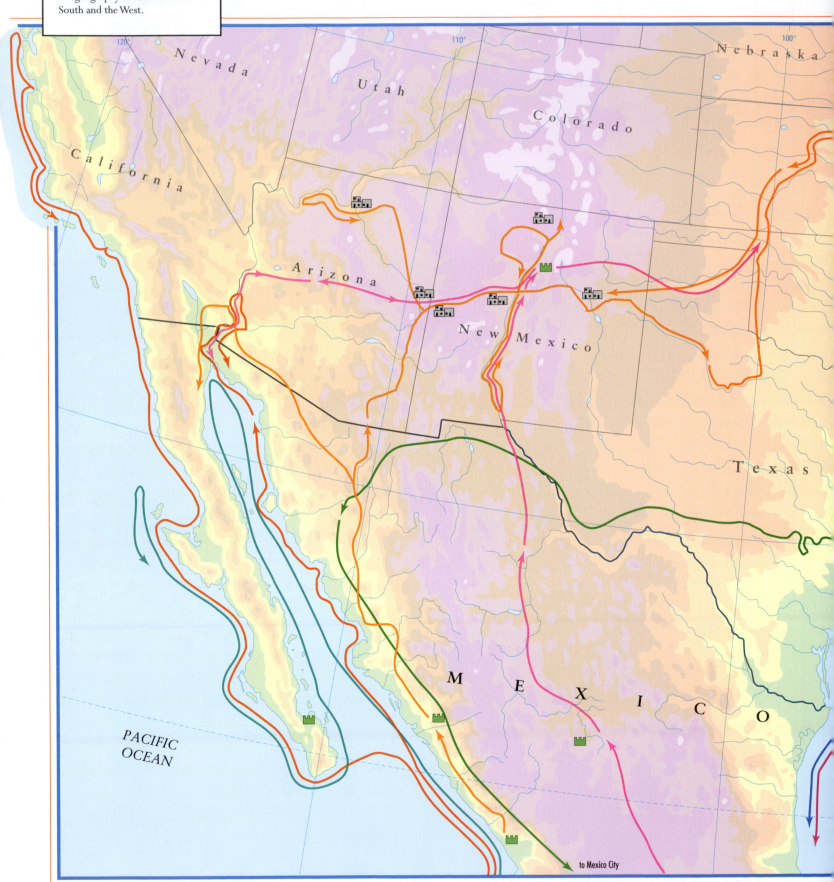

PACIFIC OCEAN

to Mexico City

Quivira

Iowa

Illinois   Indiana   Ohio   Pennsylvania

New Jersey

Kansas   Missouri   West Virginia   Maryland   D.C.   Delaware

Virginia

Oklahoma   Kentucky   North Carolina

Arkansas   Tennessee   South Carolina

Alabama   Georgia

Mississippi

Louisiana   ATLANTIC OCEAN

Gulf of Mexico   Florida

Spanish Explorations 1513–1605

→ Ponce de León 1513

→ Pineda 1519

→ Gordillo and Quexos 1521

→ Ayllón 1526

→ Narváez 1526

→ Cabeza de Vaca 1528–36

→ de Ulloa 1539–40

→ de Soto 1539–44

→ Alarcón 1540

→ de Coronado 1540–42

→ Oñate 1598–1605

— Modern borders

⛺ Native American settlements

🏰 Spanish forts/settlements

🏛 Pueblos

CUBA

Tropic of Cancer

31

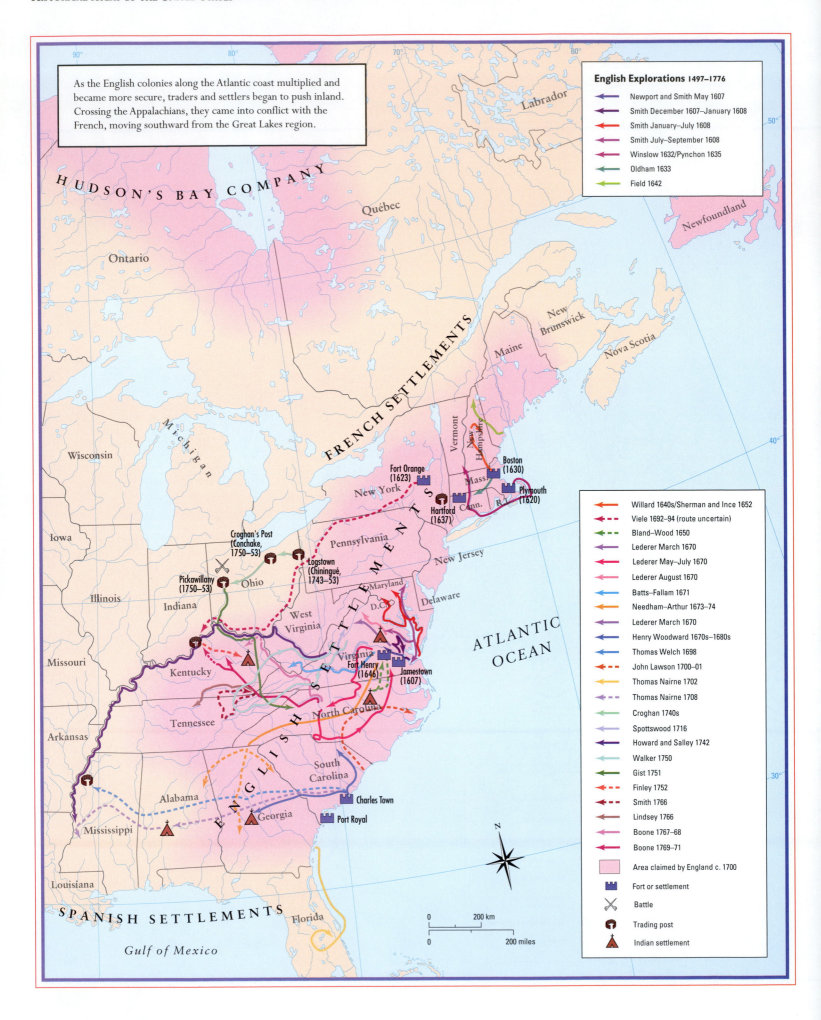

As the English colonies along the Atlantic coast multiplied and became more secure, traders and settlers began to push inland. Crossing the Appalachians, they came into conflict with the French, moving southward from the Great Lakes region.

English Explorations 1497–1776

- Newport and Smith May 1607
- Smith December 1607–January 1608
- Smith January–July 1608
- Smith July–September 1608
- Winslow 1632/Pynchon 1635
- Oldham 1633
- Field 1642

- Willard 1640s/Sherman and Ince 1652
- Viele 1692–94 (route uncertain)
- Bland–Wood 1650
- Lederer March 1670
- Lederer May–July 1670
- Lederer August 1670
- Batts–Fallam 1671
- Needham–Arthur 1673–74
- Lederer March 1670
- Henry Woodward 1670s–1680s
- Thomas Welch 1698
- John Lawson 1700–01
- Thomas Nairne 1702
- Thomas Nairne 1708
- Croghan 1740s
- Spottswood 1716
- Howard and Salley 1742
- Walker 1750
- Gist 1751
- Finley 1752
- Smith 1766
- Lindsey 1766
- Boone 1767–68
- Boone 1769–71

- Area claimed by England c. 1700
- Fort or settlement
- Battle
- Trading post
- Indian settlement

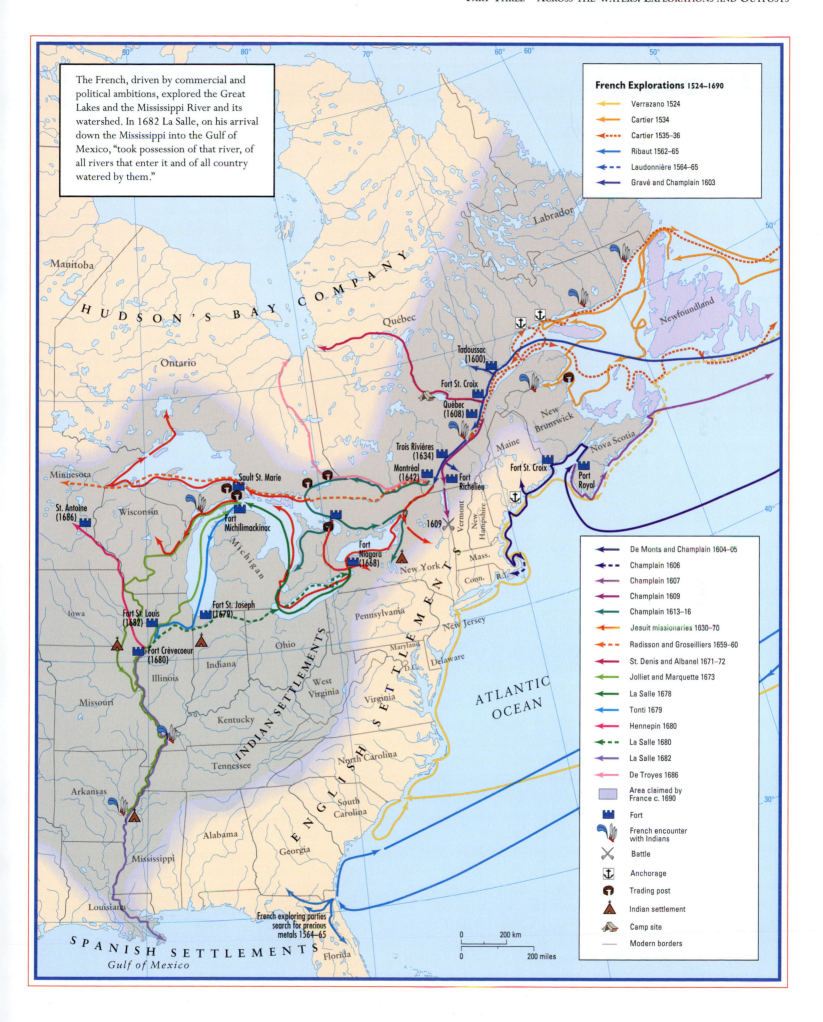

The French, driven by commercial and political ambitions, explored the Great Lakes and the Mississippi River and its watershed. In 1682 La Salle, on his arrival down the Mississippi into the Gulf of Mexico, "took possession of that river, of all rivers that enter it and of all country watered by them."

French Explorations 1524–1690

→ Verrazano 1524
→ Cartier 1534
→ Cartier 1535–36
→ Ribaut 1562–65
→ Laudonnière 1564–65
→ Gravé and Champlain 1603

← De Monts and Champlain 1604–05
← Champlain 1606
← Champlain 1607
← Champlain 1609
← Champlain 1613–16
← Jesuit missionaries 1630–70
← Radisson and Groseilliers 1659–60
← St. Denis and Albanel 1671–72
← Jolliet and Marquette 1673
← La Salle 1678
← Tonti 1679
← Hennepin 1680
← La Salle 1680
← La Salle 1682
← De Troyes 1686

Area claimed by France c. 1690

🏰 Fort

French encounter with Indians

✕ Battle

⚓ Anchorage

Trading post

⛺ Indian settlement

Camp site

Modern borders

HUDSON'S BAY COMPANY

Manitoba

Ontario

Québec

Labrador

Newfoundland

New Brunswick

Nova Scotia

Maine

Minnesota

Wisconsin

Michigan

Iowa

Illinois

Indiana

Ohio

Missouri

Kentucky

Tennessee

Arkansas

Mississippi

Alabama

Georgia

Louisiana

New York

Vermont

New Hampshire

Mass.

Conn.

R.I.

Pennsylvania

New Jersey

Maryland

Delaware

D.C.

West Virginia

Virginia

North Carolina

South Carolina

Florida

Tadoussac (1600)

Fort St. Croix

Québec (1608)

Trois Rivières (1634)

Montréal (1642)

Fort Richelieu

Fort St. Croix

Port Royal

Sault St. Marie

St. Antoine (1686)

Fort Michilimackinac

Fort Niagara (1668)

Fort St. Louis (1682)

Fort St. Joseph (1679)

Fort Crèvecoeur (1680)

1609

INDIAN SETTLEMENTS

ENGLISH SETTLEMENTS

ATLANTIC OCEAN

French exploring parties search for precious metals 1564–65

SPANISH SETTLEMENTS

Gulf of Mexico

0   200 km
0   200 miles

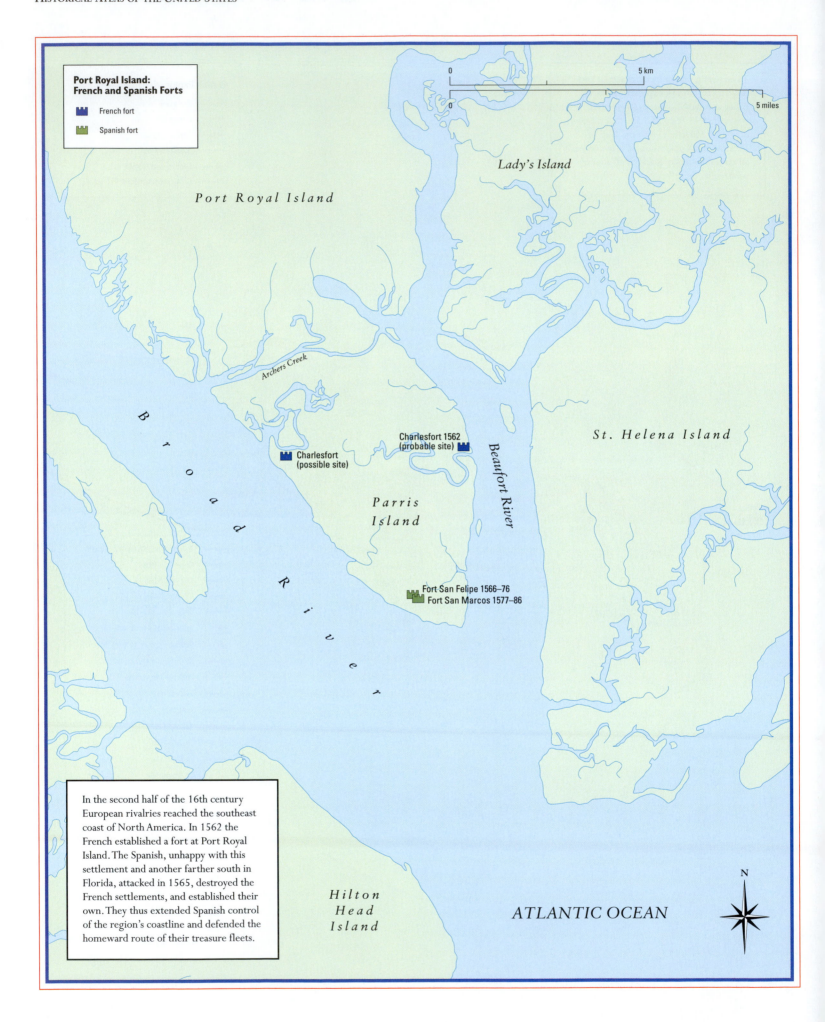

Port Royal Island:
French and Spanish Forts

■ French fort

■ Spanish fort

Lady's Island

Port Royal Island

0   5 km

0   5 miles

Archers Creek

Charlesfort 1562
(probable site)

■ Charlesfort
(possible site)

St. Helena Island

B r o a d R i v e r

*Parris
Island*

Beaufort River

Fort San Felipe 1566–76
Fort San Marcos 1577–86

In the second half of the 16th century
European rivalries reached the southeast
coast of North America. In 1562 the
French established a fort at Port Royal
Island. The Spanish, unhappy with this
settlement and another farther south in
Florida, attacked in 1565, destroyed the
French settlements, and established their
own. They thus extended Spanish control
of the region's coastline and defended the
homeward route of their treasure fleets.

*Hilton
Head
Island*

ATLANTIC OCEAN

N

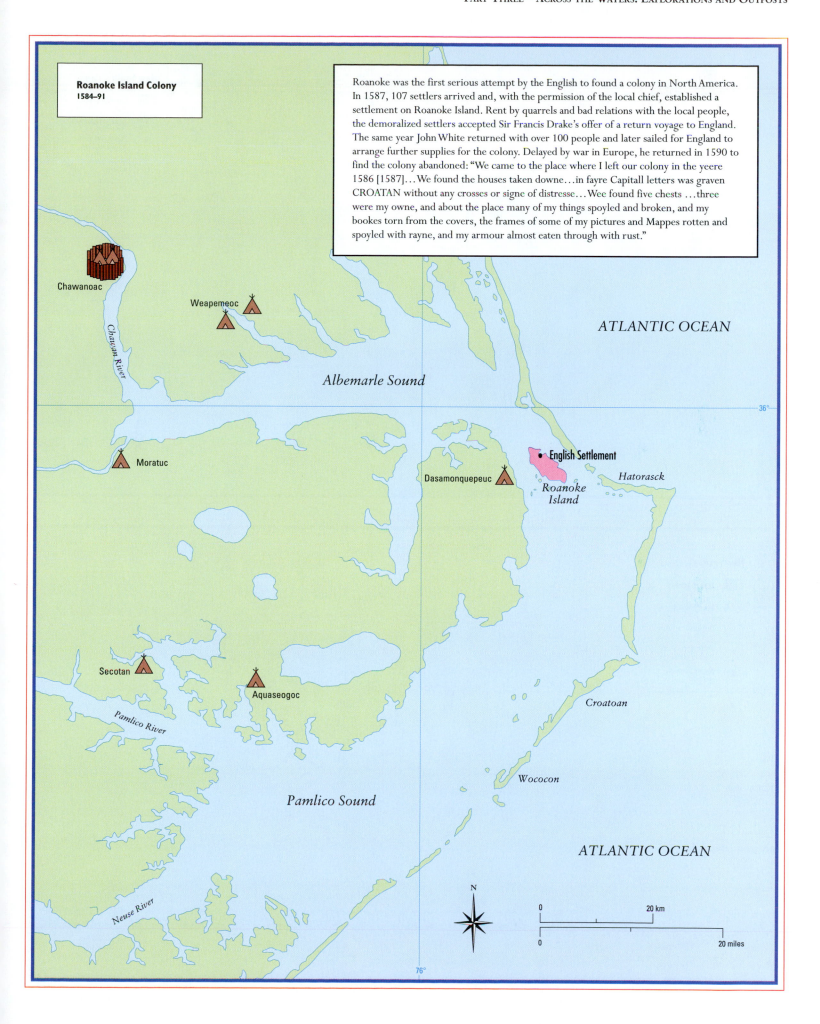

Roanoke Island Colony
1584–91

Roanoke was the first serious attempt by the English to found a colony in North America. In 1587, 107 settlers arrived and, with the permission of the local chief, established a settlement on Roanoke Island. Rent by quarrels and bad relations with the local people, the demoralized settlers accepted Sir Francis Drake's offer of a return voyage to England. The same year John White returned with over 100 people and later sailed for England to arrange further supplies for the colony. Delayed by war in Europe, he returned in 1590 to find the colony abandoned: "We came to the place where I left our colony in the yeere 1586 [1587]…We found the houses taken downe…in fayre Capitall letters was graven CROATAN without any crosses or signe of distresse…Wee found five chests …three were my owne, and about the place many of my things spoyled and broken, and my bookes torn from the covers, the frames of some of my pictures and Mappes rotten and spoyled with rayne, and my armour almost eaten through with rust."

Chawanoac

Chawan River

Weapemeoc

ATLANTIC OCEAN

Albemarle Sound

36°

Moratuc

English Settlement

Dasamonquepeuc

Roanoke Island

Hatorasck

Secotan

Aquaseogoc

Croatoan

Pamlico River

Wococon

Pamlico Sound

ATLANTIC OCEAN

N

Neuse River

0   20 km

0   20 miles

76°

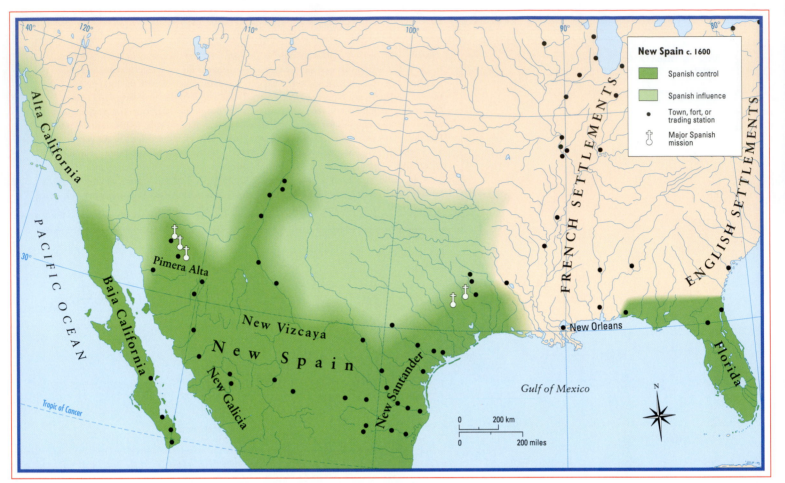

New Spain c. 1600

- Spanish control
- Spanish influence
- • Town, fort, or trading station
- ✝ Major Spanish mission

Alta California

PACIFIC OCEAN

Baja California

Pimera Alta

New Vizcaya

N e w   S p a i n

New Galicia

New Santander

Tropic of Cancer

Gulf of Mexico

New Orleans

FRENCH SETTLEMENTS

ENGLISH SETTLEMENTS

Florida

0   200 km

0   200 miles

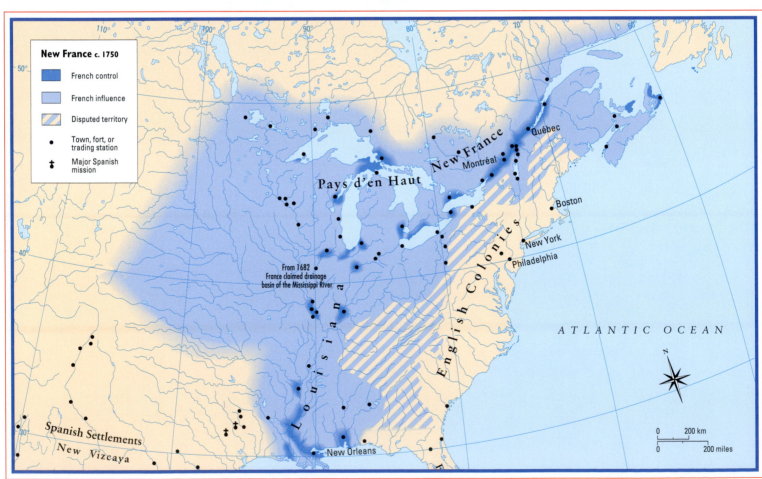

New France c. 1750

- French control
- French influence
- Disputed territory
- • Town, fort, or trading station
- ✝ Major Spanish mission

Pays d'en Haut

New France

Québec

Montréal

Boston

New York

Philadelphia

From 1682 France claimed drainage basin of the Mississippi River

L o u i s i a n a

E n g l i s h   C o l o n i e s

ATLANTIC OCEAN

Spanish Settlements

New Vizcaya

New Orleans

0   200 km

0   200 miles

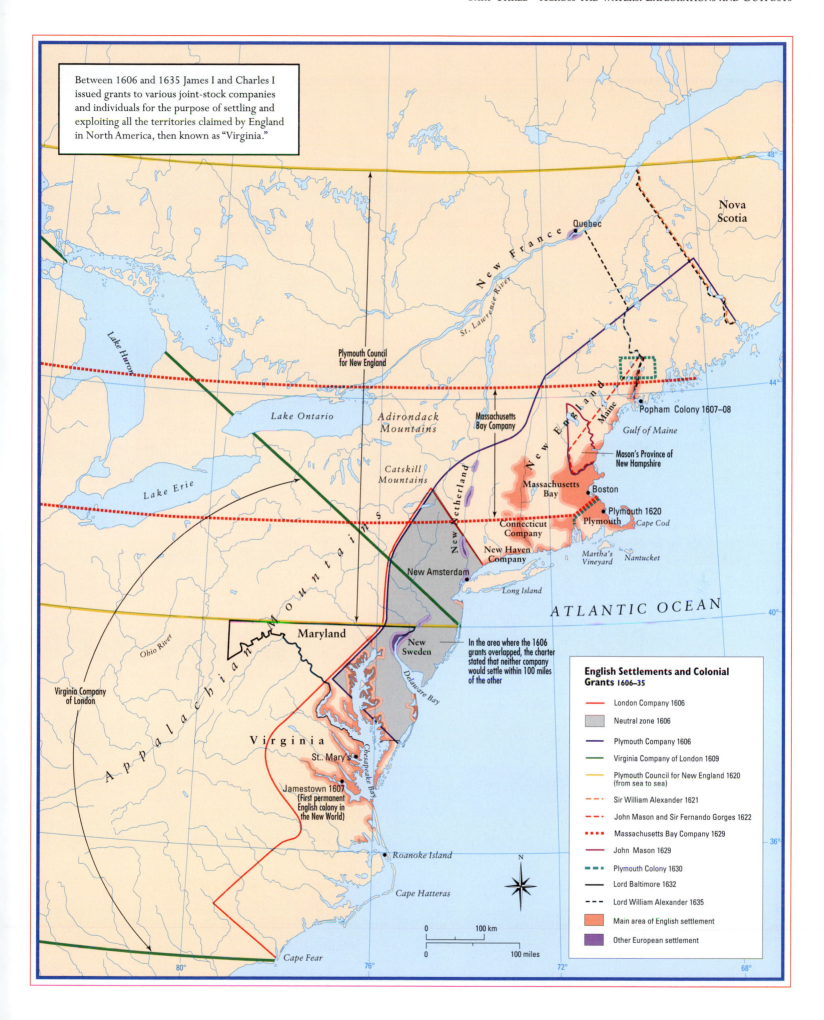

Between 1606 and 1635 James I and Charles I issued grants to various joint-stock companies and individuals for the purpose of settling and exploiting all the territories claimed by England in North America, then known as "Virginia."

Nova Scotia

Quebec

New France

St. Lawrence River

Plymouth Council for New England

Lake Huron

Lake Ontario

Adirondack Mountains

Maine

Massachusetts Bay Company

Popham Colony 1607–08

Gulf of Maine

Mason's Province of New Hampshire

Lake Erie

Catskill Mountains

New England

New Netherland

Massachusetts Bay

Boston

Plymouth 1620

Plymouth

Cape Cod

Connecticut Company

New Haven Company

New Amsterdam

Martha's Vineyard

Nantucket

Long Island

ATLANTIC OCEAN

Ohio River

Maryland

New Sweden

Delaware Bay

In the area where the 1606 grants overlapped, the charter stated that neither company would settle within 100 miles of the other

Virginia Company of London

Appalachian Mountains

Virginia

St. Mary's

Chesapeake Bay

Jamestown 1607 (First permanent English colony in the New World)

Roanoke Island

Cape Hatteras

Cape Fear

English Settlements and Colonial Grants 1606–35

— London Company 1606
▨ Neutral zone 1606
— Plymouth Company 1606
— Virginia Company of London 1609
— Plymouth Council for New England 1620 (from sea to sea)
--- Sir William Alexander 1621
--- John Mason and Sir Fernando Gorges 1622
···· Massachusetts Bay Company 1629
— John Mason 1629
▪▪▪ Plymouth Colony 1630
— Lord Baltimore 1632
--- Lord William Alexander 1635
▨ Main area of English settlement
▨ Other European settlement

N

0   100 km

0   100 miles

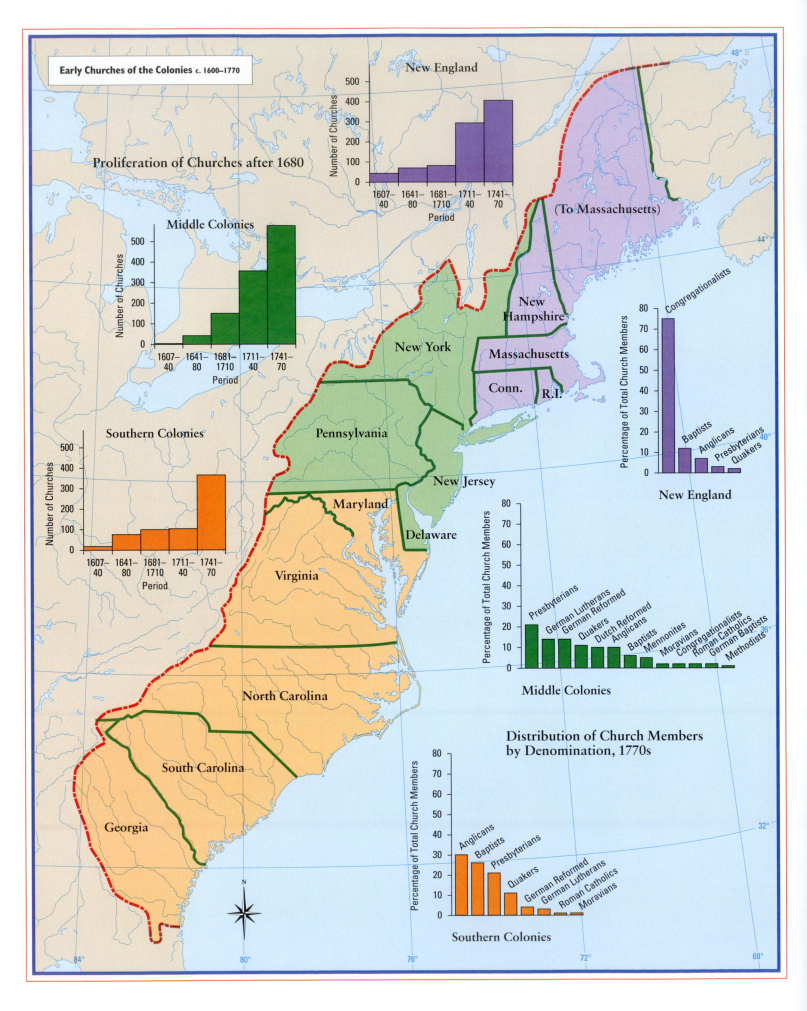

Early Churches of the Colonies c. 1600–1770

New England

Proliferation of Churches after 1680

Middle Colonies

Southern Colonies

Distribution of Church Members by Denomination, 1770s

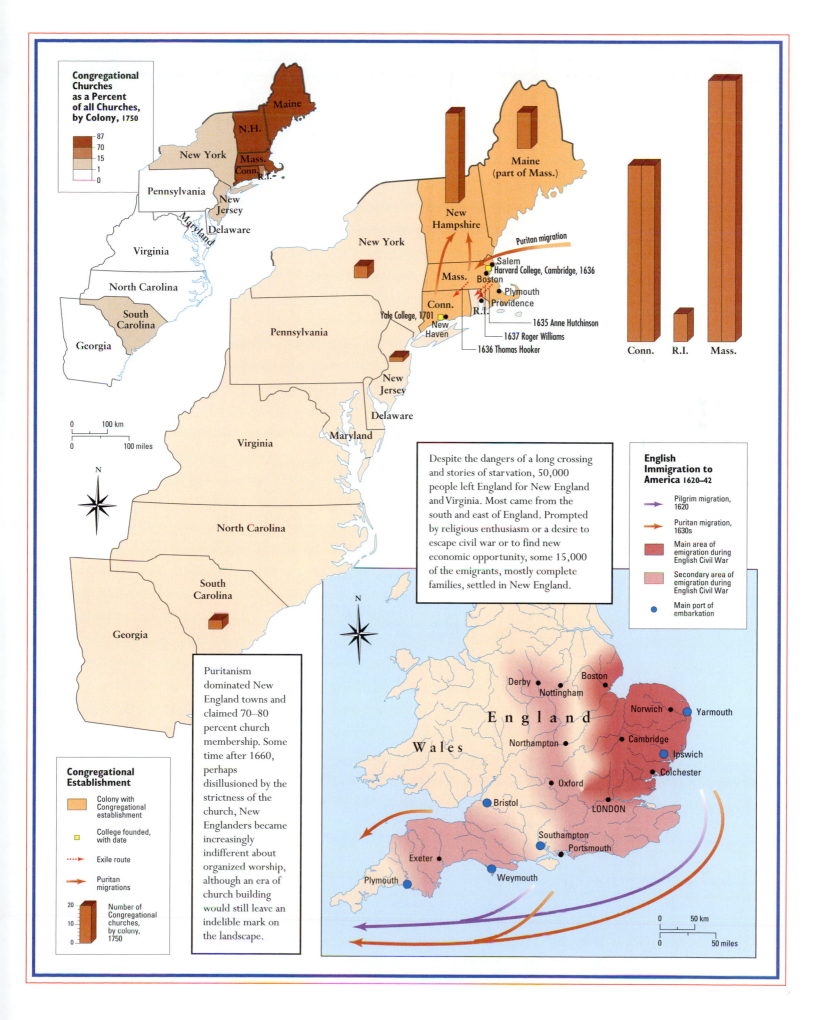

Congregational Churches as a Percent of all Churches, by Colony, 1750

87
70
15
1
0

Harvard College, Cambridge, 1636

Puritan migration

Salem
Boston
Plymouth
Providence
1635 Anne Hutchinson
1637 Roger Williams
1636 Thomas Hooker

Yale College, 1701
New Haven

Conn.   R.I.   Mass.

0   100 km
0   100 miles

N

Despite the dangers of a long crossing and stories of starvation, 50,000 people left England for New England and Virginia. Most came from the south and east of England. Prompted by religious enthusiasm or a desire to escape civil war or to find new economic opportunity, some 15,000 of the emigrants, mostly complete families, settled in New England.

English Immigration to America 1620–42

Pilgrim migration, 1620

Puritan migration, 1630s

Main area of emigration during English Civil War

Secondary area of emigration during English Civil War

Main port of embarkation

Congregational Establishment

Colony with Congregational establishment

College founded, with date

Exile route

Puritan migrations

20
10
0
Number of Congregational churches, by colony, 1750

Puritanism dominated New England towns and claimed 70–80 percent church membership. Some time after 1660, perhaps disillusioned by the strictness of the church, New Englanders became increasingly indifferent about organized worship, although an era of church building would still leave an indelible mark on the landscape.

England

Wales

Derby
Nottingham
Boston
Norwich   Yarmouth
Northampton
Cambridge
Ipswich
Colchester
Oxford
Bristol
LONDON
Southampton
Portsmouth
Exeter
Weymouth
Plymouth

N

0   50 km
0   50 miles

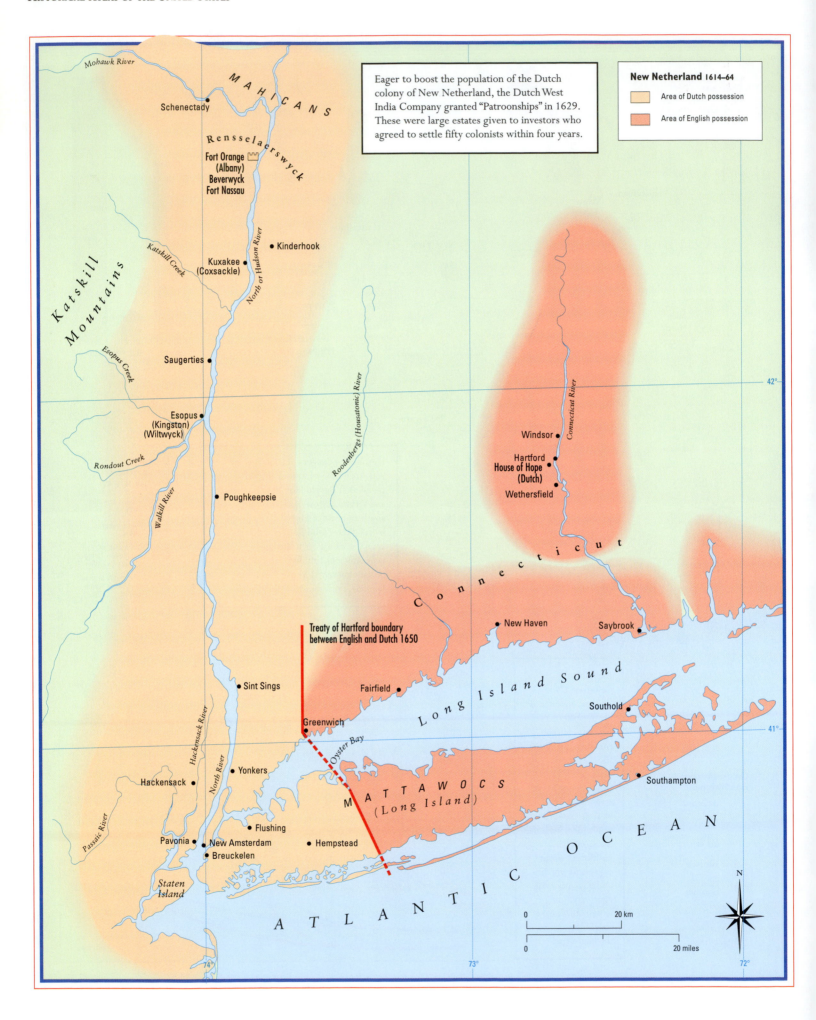

Eager to boost the population of the Dutch colony of New Netherland, the Dutch West India Company granted "Patroonships" in 1629. These were large estates given to investors who agreed to settle fifty colonists within four years.

New Netherland 1614–64

Area of Dutch possession

Area of English possession

Mohawk River

MAHICANS

Schenectady

Rensselaerswyck

Fort Orange
(Albany)
Beverwyck
Fort Nassau

Katskill Creek

North or Hudson River

Kinderhook

Kuxakee
(Coxsackle)

Katskill Mountains

Esopus Creek

Saugerties

42°

Esopus
(Kingston)
(Wiltwyck)

Roodenbergs (Housatonic) River

Windsor

Connecticut River

Rondout Creek

Hartford
House of Hope
(Dutch)

Walkill River

Poughkeepsie

Wethersfield

C o n n e c t i c u t

Treaty of Hartford boundary
between English and Dutch 1650

New Haven

Saybrook

L o n g   I s l a n d   S o u n d

Sint Sings

Fairfield

Southold

Hackensack River

Greenwich

41°

North River

Oyster Bay

Yonkers

Hackensack

M A T T A W O C S
(L o n g   I s l a n d)

Southampton

Passaic River

Flushing

Pavonia
New Amsterdam
Breuckelen

Hempstead

Staten
Island

A T L A N T I C   O C E A N

N

0   20 km

0   20 miles

74°   73°   72°

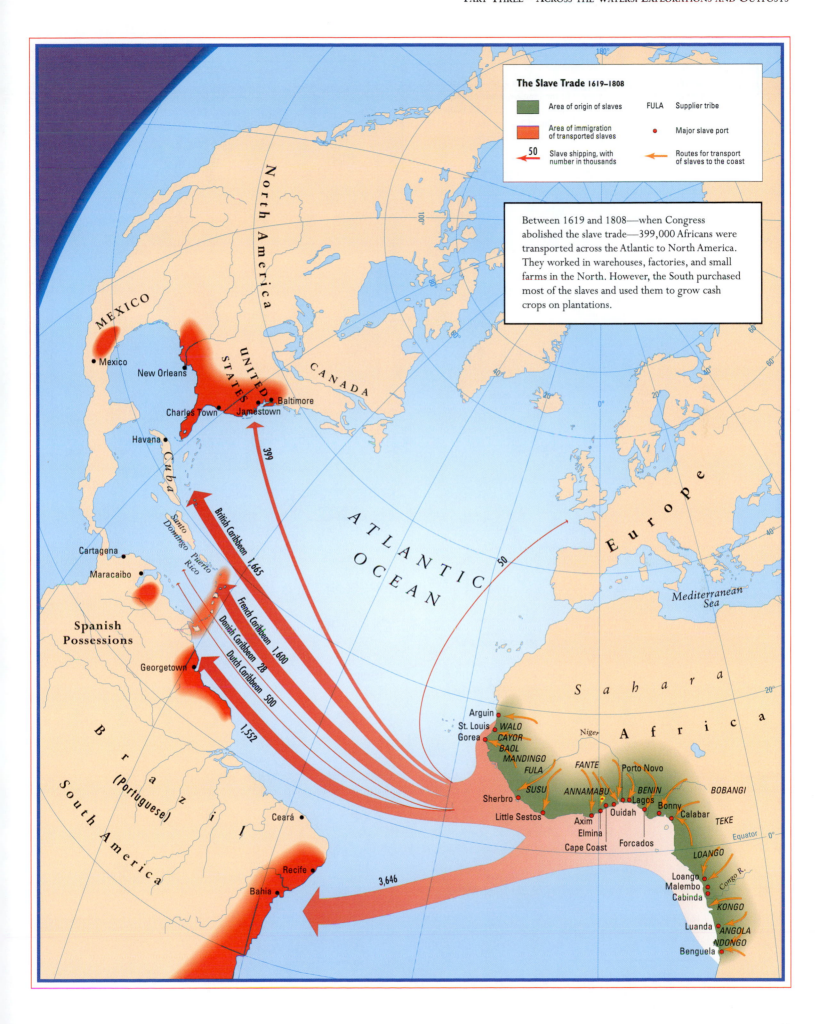

The Slave Trade 1619–1808

Area of origin of slaves

Area of immigration of transported slaves

50 ← Slave shipping, with number in thousands

FULA Supplier tribe

● Major slave port

→ Routes for transport of slaves to the coast

Between 1619 and 1808—when Congress abolished the slave trade—399,000 Africans were transported across the Atlantic to North America. They worked in warehouses, factories, and small farms in the North. However, the South purchased most of the slaves and used them to grow cash crops on plantations.

North America

MEXICO

Mexico

New Orleans

UNITED STATES

Baltimore

Charles Town

Jamestown

CANADA

Havana

Cuba

399

Cartagena

Maracaibo

Santo Domingo

Puerto Rico

British Caribbean 1,665

French Caribbean 1,600

Danish Caribbean 28

Dutch Caribbean 500

Spanish Possessions

Georgetown

ATLANTIC OCEAN

50

Europe

Mediterranean Sea

1,552

B r a z i l (Portuguese)

South America

Ceará

Recife

Bahia

3,646

Sahara

Africa

Arguin

St. Louis

Gorea

WALO

CAYOR

BAOL

MANDINGO

FULA

Niger

SUSU

FANTE

ANNAMABU

Porto Novo

BENIN

Lagos

Bonny

Calabar

BOBANGI

TEKE

Sherbro

Little Sestos

Axim

Elmina

Cape Coast

Ouidah

Forcados

Equator

LOANGO

Loango

Malembo

Cabinda

Congo R.

KONGO

Luanda

ANGOLA

NDONGO

Benguela

41

The *Mayflower*'s intended destination, according to an agreement with the Virginia Company, was near the mouth of the Hudson River on the northern edge of that company's grant. However, the *Mayflower* made its American landfall to the north, arriving in Cape Cod Bay on 21 November 1620. Unwilling to travel onward in a stormy winter season, they opted to remain where they were.

Winslow House

Rouses Hummock

Cape Cod Bay

Duxbury R

Powder Pt.

Blue River

Duxbury Beach

Duxbury Bay

High Pines

Eagles Nest

Captains Hill

Clark I.

Brewster Point

Saquish Cave

The Gurnet

Saquish Head

Jones River

Rocky Nook

Nathans Brook

Browns Bank

Goose Point

Dotens Cliff

Plymouth Harbor

Long Beach

Smelt Pond

Plymouth
Exploration party landed
21 December, Pilgrims
landed 28 December

The Rock

Billington Sea

Warrens Cove

Manomet Hill

0 — 2 km

0 — 2 miles

Nauinkeag
(Salem)

Massachusetts

Massachusetts Bay

ATLANTIC OCEAN

Mount Wollaston

Wessagusset

Cohasset
(northern boundary claimed
by Plymouth Plantation)

Plymouth

Clark's Island

Provincetown
(first landing of
the *Mayflower*
21 November 1620)

Pamet River
(Truro Village)

42°

PLYMOUTH

Cape Cod

Namassakett
(Wampanoag Village)

Cape Cod Bay

Manonscussett

Eastham
(first Indian encounter)

Manomet

Manamoiak
(Nauser Indian Village)

Rhode Island

Buzzards Bay

Vineyard Sound

Nantucket Sound

N

Capawack
(Martha's Vineyard)

Plymouth Plantation
1620–30

→ Route of the *Mayflower*

▲ Indian settlement

Nantucket

0 — 10 km

0 — 10 miles

70°

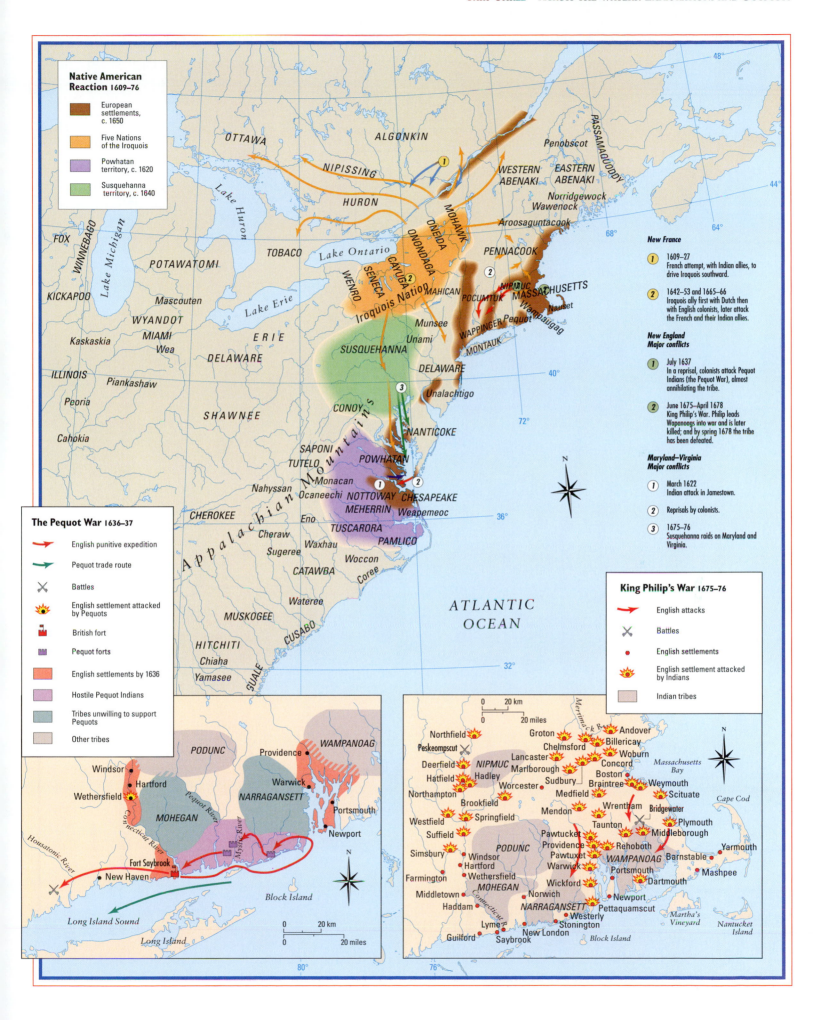

Native American Reaction 1609–76

- European settlements, c. 1650
- Five Nations of the Iroquois
- Powhatan territory, c. 1620
- Susquehanna territory, c. 1640

The Pequot War 1636–37

- English punitive expedition
- Pequot trade route
- Battles
- English settlement attacked by Pequots
- British fort
- Pequot forts
- English settlements by 1636
- Hostile Pequot Indians
- Tribes unwilling to support Pequots
- Other tribes

King Philip's War 1675–76

- English attacks
- Battles
- English settlements
- English settlement attacked by Indians
- Indian tribes

New France

1. 1609–27 French attempt, with Indian allies, to drive Iroquois southward.
2. 1642–53 and 1665–66 Iroquois ally first with Dutch then with English colonists, later attack the French and their Indian allies.

New England Major conflicts

1. July 1637 In a reprisal, colonists attack Pequot Indians (the Pequot War), almost annihilating the tribe.
2. June 1675–April 1678 King Philip's War. Philip leads Wapanoags into war and is later killed; and by spring 1678 the tribe has been defeated.

Maryland–Virginia Major conflicts

1. March 1622 Indian attack in Jamestown.
2. Reprisals by colonists.
3. 1675–76 Susquehanna raids on Maryland and Virginia.

ATLANTIC OCEAN

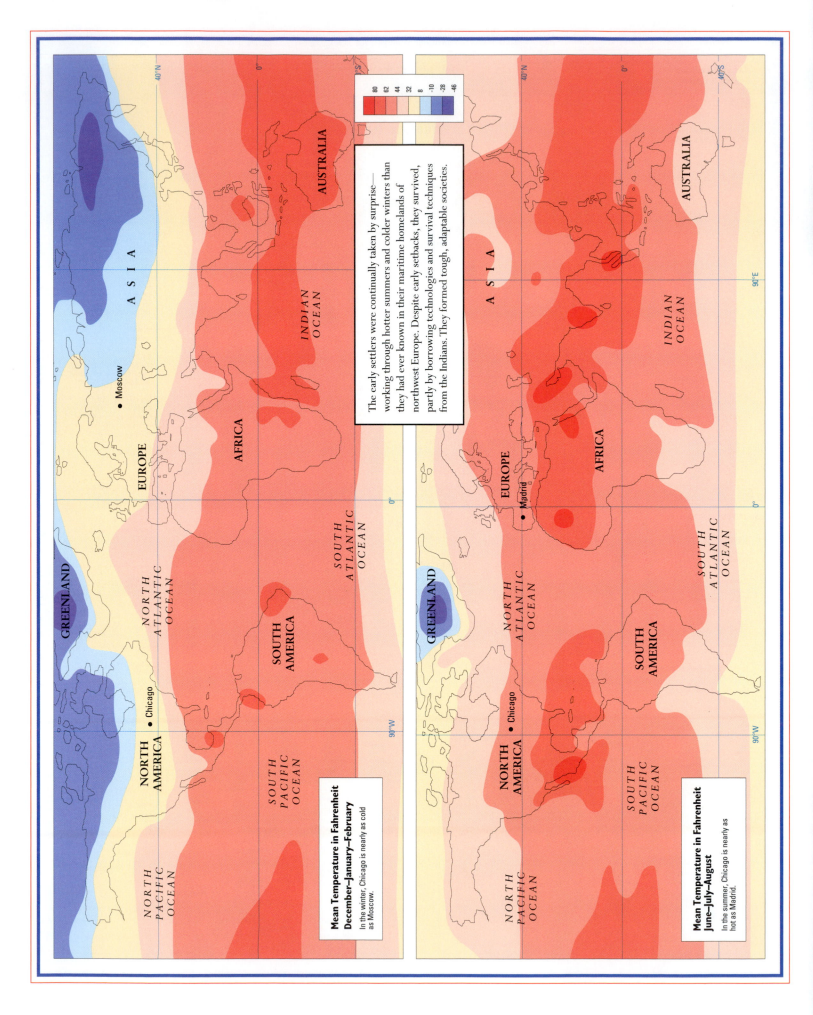

The early settlers were continually taken by surprise—working through hotter summers and colder winters than they had ever known in their maritime homelands of northwest Europe. Despite early setbacks, they survived, partly by borrowing technologies and survival techniques from the Indians. They formed tough, adaptable societies.

Mean Temperature in Fahrenheit December–January–February

In the winter, Chicago is nearly as cold as Moscow.

Mean Temperature in Fahrenheit June–July–August

In the summer, Chicago is nearly as hot as Madrid.

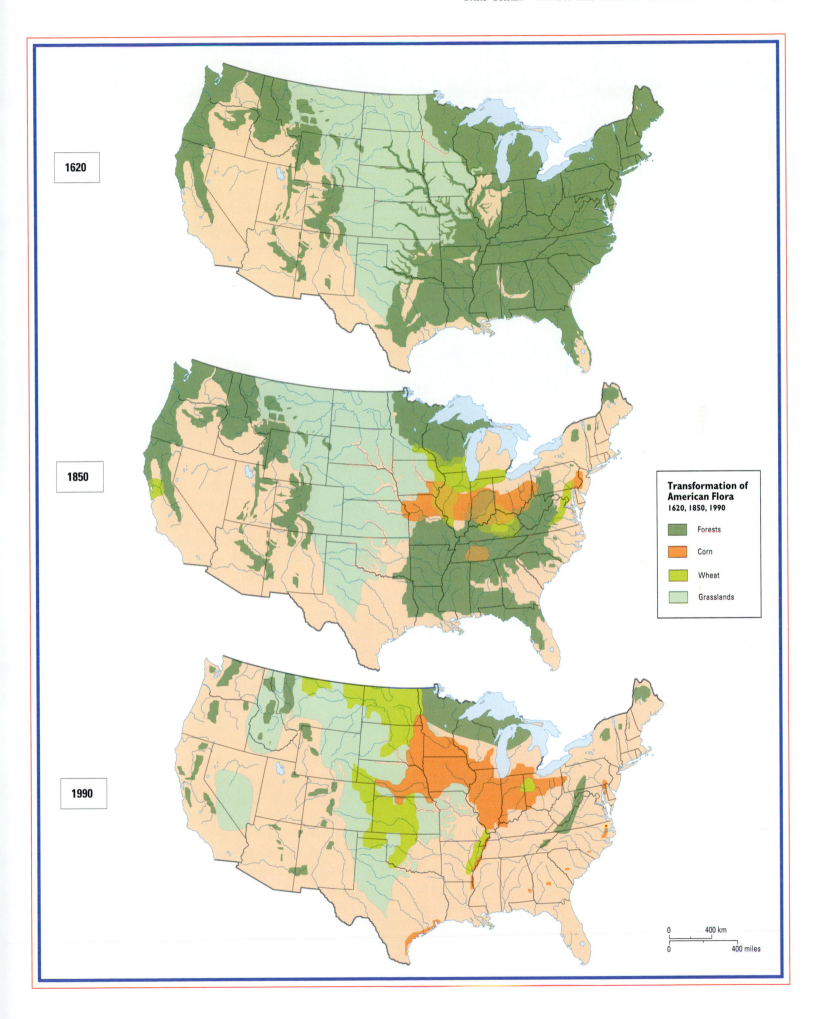

1620

1850

1990

Transformation of American Flora
1620, 1850, 1990

- Forests
- Corn
- Wheat
- Grasslands

0 — 400 km
0 — 400 miles

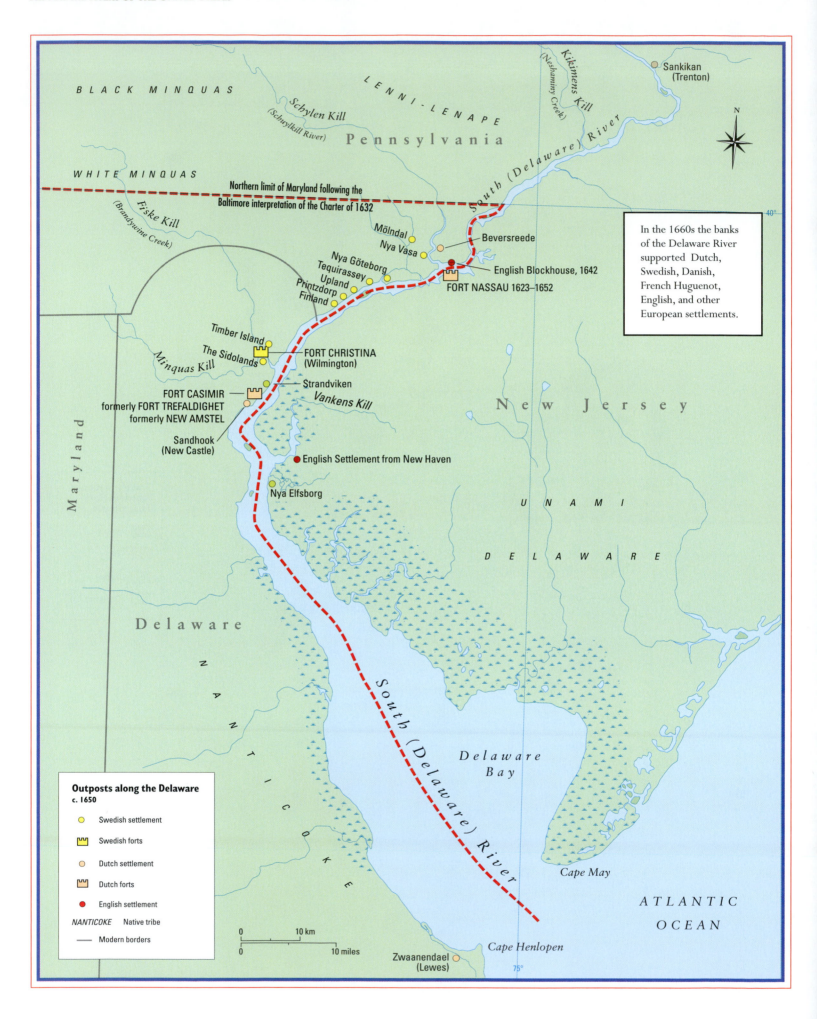

BLACK MINQUAS

LENNI-LENAPE

Sankikan (Trenton)

Schylen Kill (Schuylkill River)

Pennsylvania

(Neshaminy Creek)

Kikimens Kill

South (Delaware) River

N

WHITE MINQUAS

Northern limit of Maryland following the Baltimore interpretation of the Charter of 1632

Fiske Kill (Brandywine Creek)

40°

Mölndal
Nya Vasa

Beversreede

Nya Göteborg
Tequirassey
Upland
Printzdorp
Finland

English Blockhouse, 1642
FORT NASSAU 1623–1652

In the 1660s the banks of the Delaware River supported Dutch, Swedish, Danish, French Huguenot, English, and other European settlements.

Timber Island

The Sidolands

Minquas Kill

FORT CHRISTINA (Wilmington)

Strandviken
Vankens Kill

New Jersey

FORT CASIMIR
formerly FORT TREFALDIGHET
formerly NEW AMSTEL

Sandhook (New Castle)

English Settlement from New Haven

Nya Elfsborg

U N A M I

D E L A W A R E

M a r y l a n d

D e l a w a r e

N A N T I C O K E

South (Delaware) River

D e l a w a r e B a y

Cape May

Outposts along the Delaware
c. 1650

○ Swedish settlement

🏰 Swedish forts

○ Dutch settlement

🏰 Dutch forts

● English settlement

NANTICOKE Native tribe

— Modern borders

ATLANTIC OCEAN

0   10 km

0   10 miles

Cape Henlopen

75°

Zwaanendael (Lewes)

In the 1660s New Amsterdam overlooked the anchorage and jetties on the East River. Its commercial hub was Pearle Straet with its weigh house and offices. When plans of the town were sent to the directors in Amsterdam, Director General Peter Stuyvesant was criticized for allowing too much land for use as gardens. In 1664, when the city became English New York, its population was 1,500.

Bowerie No. 6

The Pond

Tavern of Wolfert Webber

Bowerie of Annetje Jans

Bowerie No. 5

Common Land

Public Cow Pasture

Jan Teunizer

Heerewegh Straet

Hudson River

Dutch West India Company Farm

The Common

Wolfherts Marsh

Bowerie Lane

Henry Brazier

The Swamp

Mill

Thomas Hall

Cornelius van Tienhoven

Ferry to Long Island

Jan Jansen Damen

T'Maagde Staatje

Abraham Verplanck

Smits Vly

Peter Stoutenberg

New Cemetery

Cornelius Aertzen

Jan Vinje

East River

Gate

Het Cingle

Garden of the West India Company

Heere Dwars Straet

Tuyn Straet

Smee Straet

Old Church Yard

De Heere Straet

Prince Straet

Hoogh Straet

Beaver Gracht

Slyck Steegh

The Wall

The Market Place

Marckvelt Straet

Heere Gracht

Common Road

Public Mill

Browers Straet

Stadt Huys

Fort Amsterdam

Governor's House

Brugh Straet

N

Pearle Straet

The Waterside

Peter Stuyvesant's White Hall

New Amsterdam c. 1660

Main buildings where known

Gardens

Orchards

Defensive works

Jan Vinje — Major landowner where known

Farmland and pasture

Common land

0 — 1/4 km

0 — 1/4 miles

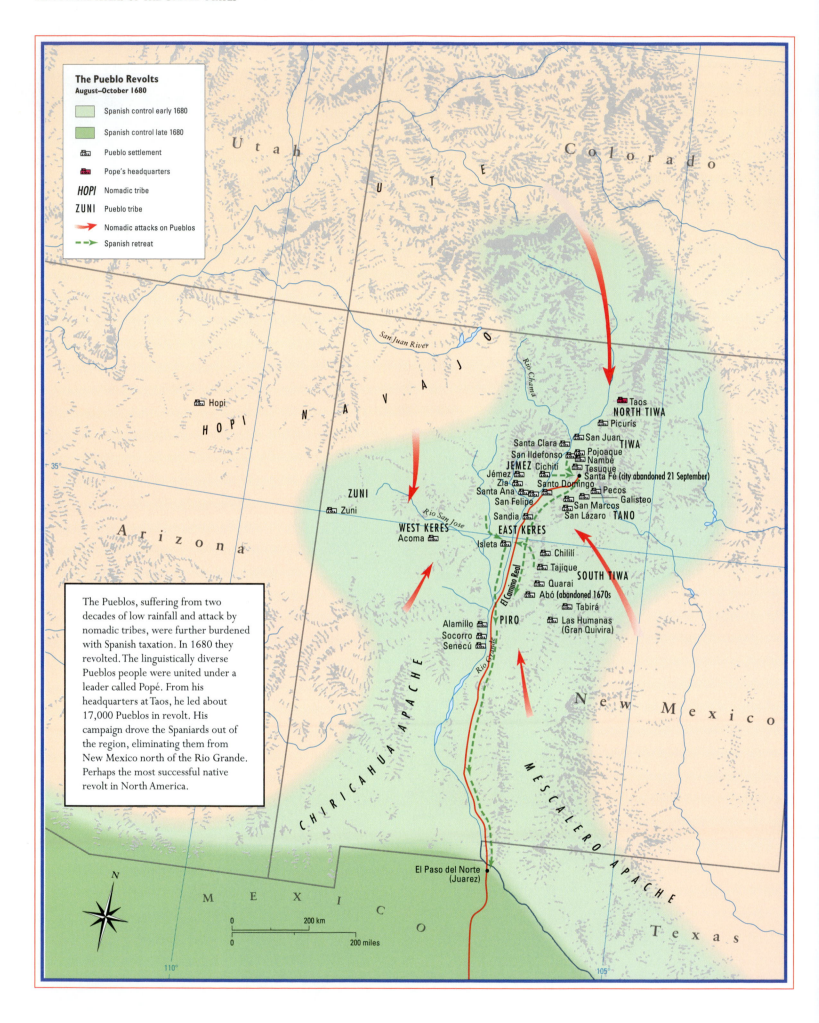

The Pueblo Revolts
August–October 1680

- Spanish control early 1680
- Spanish control late 1680
- Pueblo settlement
- Pope's headquarters
- *HOPI* Nomadic tribe
- *ZUNI* Pueblo tribe
- Nomadic attacks on Pueblos
- Spanish retreat

The Pueblos, suffering from two decades of low rainfall and attack by nomadic tribes, were further burdened with Spanish taxation. In 1680 they revolted. The linguistically diverse Pueblos people were united under a leader called Popé. From his headquarters at Taos, he led about 17,000 Pueblos in revolt. His campaign drove the Spaniards out of the region, eliminating them from New Mexico north of the Rio Grande. Perhaps the most successful native revolt in North America.

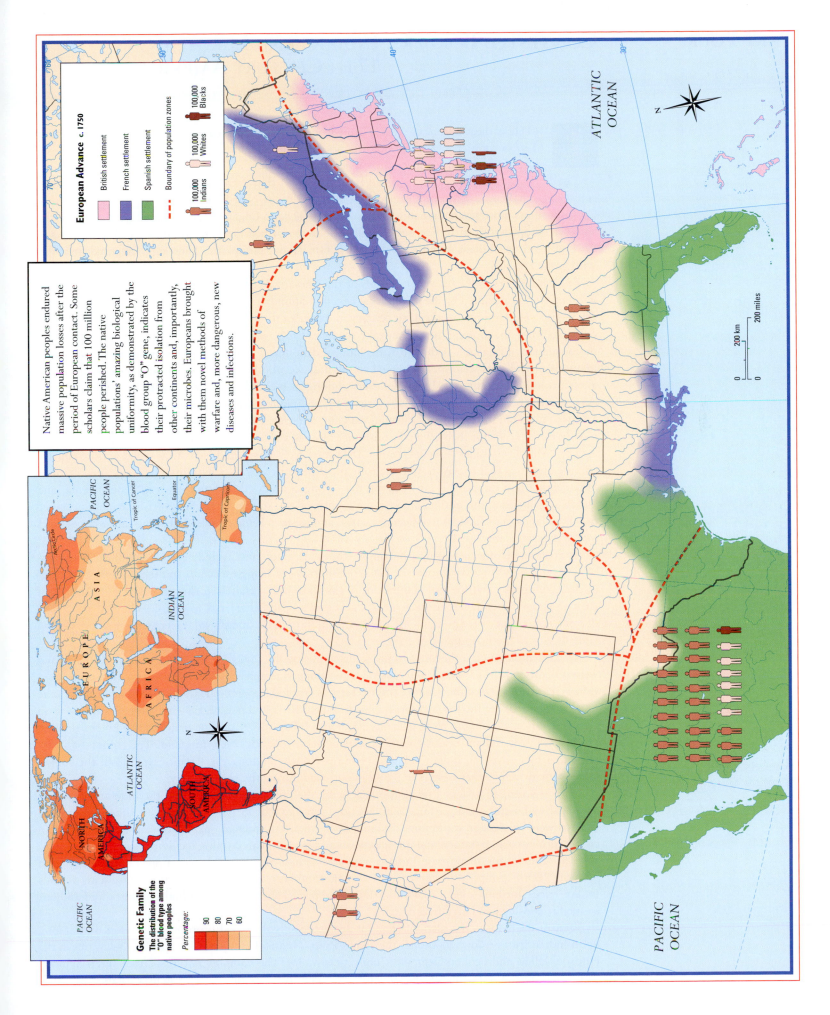

ATLANTIC OCEAN

European Advance c. 1750

British settlement	
French settlement	
Spanish settlement	
Boundary of population zones	

100,000 Blacks
100,000 Whites
100,000 Indians

Native American peoples endured massive population losses after the period of European contact. Some scholars claim that 100 million people perished. The native populations' amazing biological uniformity, as demonstrated by the blood group "O" gene, indicates their protracted isolation from other continents and, importantly, their microbes. Europeans brought with them novel methods of warfare and, more dangerous, new diseases and infections.

PACIFIC OCEAN
PACIFIC OCEAN
Tropic of Cancer
Equator
Tropic of Capricorn
INDIAN OCEAN
EUROPE
ASIA
AFRICA
ATLANTIC OCEAN
NORTH AMERICA
SOUTH AMERICA
PACIFIC OCEAN

Genetic Family
The distribution of the "O" blood type among native peoples
Percentage:
90 80 70 60

ATLANTIC OCEAN

200 km
200 miles

PACIFIC OCEAN

PART FOUR

CONTESTED BORDERS: INDIANS AND EUROPEANS IN 17TH CENTURY AMERICA

F THE earliest European settlers came from the sea and gazed on it with fondness, their point of view soon changed. Agriculture, not gold and treasure, would prove to be the colonists' chief source of sustenance and, on occasion, wealth.

The Puritans of New England learned from the outset that if they did not raise crops, they would starve. The challenges of survival were compounded by rocky New England soil, by early killing frosts, and by winters more severe than any they had experienced in England. Of necessity, the Puritans cultivated the crops with which they were familiar—barley (for beer), rye, oats, and vegetables. They also learned from the Indians how to grow corn, potatoes, and pumpkins. They supplemented their diet with game and fish.

English farmers in the tidewater regions of the Chesapeake, though spared the harsh New England winters, were confronted by the debilitating heat and humidity that gave rise to malaria, dysentery, and other diseases. Throughout the 17th century, the death rate was unusually high. What prevented the colonists from abandoning the Chesapeake region entirely was tobacco, an Indian crop that appealed to consumers in England. Although King James I denounced smoking as a "vile and stinking habit," many of his subjects were soon addicted to the practice. As the price of tobacco soared, Chesapeake and Carolina planters scraped together every shilling they could find or borrow to buy every available acre of land, burn away the trees and overgrowth, and plant it with tobacco. In South Carolina, farmers also cultivated indigo, used for dyeing woolens, and rice. Unlike the farmers of New England, who mostly raised crops for their own consumption, those in the South produced them for export.

The "Middle Colonies"—Pennsylvania, Delaware, New Jersey, and New York—had a more equable climate and soils that proved hospitable to many different crops. German immigrants poured through Philadelphia and established farms along the rolling countryside of southeastern Pennsylvania, and Dutch settled along the fertile banks of the Hudson River to the north. Scots-Irish farmers occupied marginal lands in the distant frontiers of central and western Pennsylvania and along the eastern slopes of the Appalachians.

As farming became increasingly profitable, the demand for land proved nearly insatiable. This resulted in several important developments. First, the shortage of labor, especially in the tobacco plantations in the Chesapeake and the rice plantations in the Carolinas, resulted in the wholesale importation of African slaves; second, the various colonial governments and chartered companies claimed vast tracts of land—and often the same land—to the west; and third, land-hungry colonists increasingly settled on lands occupied by the Indians.

An early indication of the latter trend occurred during the 1630s, when the Pequots of Rhode Island were squeezed by the growing English settlements along Narragansett Bay and those in the Connecticut valley. Tensions between the Pequots and the settlers erupted in open warfare in 1636. The Pequots were quickly subdued, but further encroachments prompted King Philip, leader of the Wampanoags, to form a confederation of tribes to resist the colonists. From 1675 to 1676, during what became known as King Philip's War, the Indians raided countless settlements throughout New England. The colonial militias retaliated by destroying Indian villages. Here, as elsewhere along the Atlantic seaboard, the Indian tribes were driven farther west. The pattern continued during the next century.

But it is wrong to assume that relations between the European colonists and the Indians were characterized by hostility and warfare. Scholars now perceive that for long stretches of time, settlers and Indians were engaged in continuous and mostly harmonious interactions. Europeans exploited Indian crops, such as corn, potatoes, and pumpkins, and adopted Indian farming techniques and technologies, such as canoes; for their part, Indians took advantage of European iron-tipped implements and weapons. Both groups also entered into complex military and political relationships, with various Indian tribes forming alliances with various European states, and individual colonists and Indians formed friendships and even intermarried.

Some of the maps in this section represent this process by showing European settlements overlapping upon Indian tribes—Powhatans near the James River, Nanticokes in the Chesapeake, Delawares in the Hudson valley, and Pequots near the Connecticut valley. The complex nature of that intersection—sometimes hostile, sometimes wary, sometimes cooperative—continues to intrigue scholars.

Maps

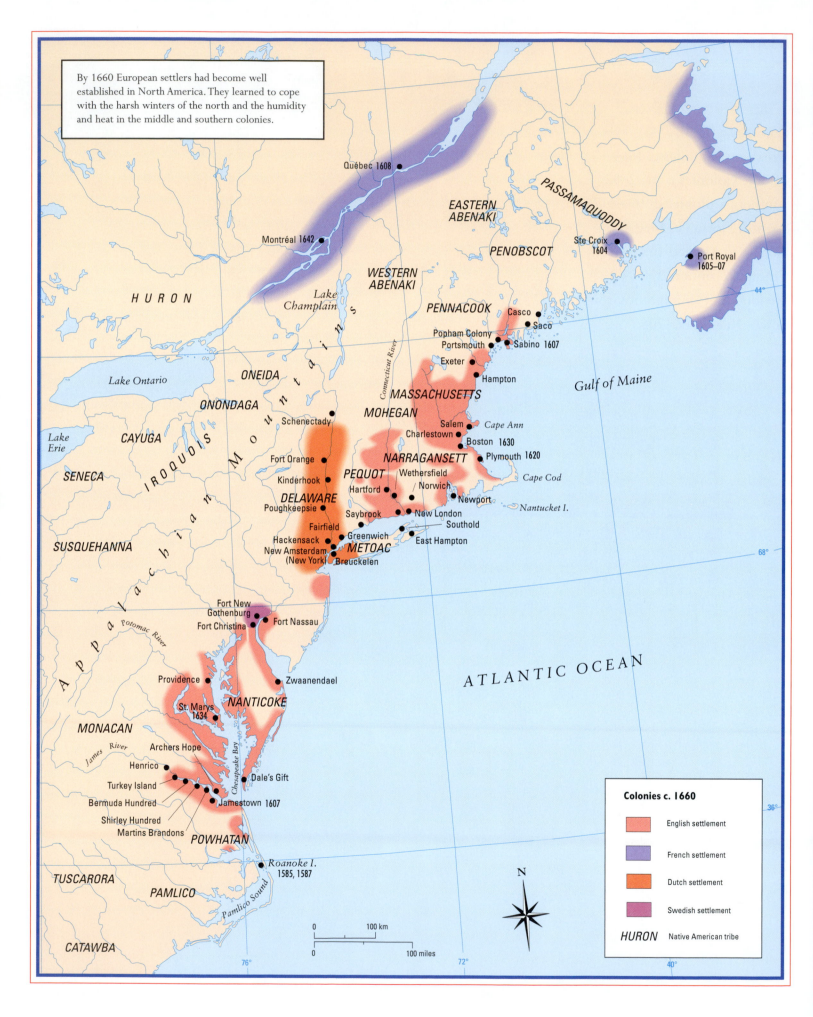

By 1660 European settlers had become well established in North America. They learned to cope with the harsh winters of the north and the humidity and heat in the middle and southern colonies.

Québec 1608

Montréal 1642

Ste Croix 1604

Port Royal 1605–07

EASTERN ABENAKI

PASSAMAQUODDY

PENOBSCOT

HURON

Lake Champlain

WESTERN ABENAKI

PENNACOOK

Casco

Saco

Popham Colony

Portsmouth

Sabino 1607

Exeter

Hampton

Gulf of Maine

Lake Ontario

ONEIDA

ONONDAGA

MASSACHUSETTS

MOHEGAN

CAYUGA

Lake Erie

SENECA

Schenectady

Salem

Cape Ann

Charlestown

Boston 1630

Plymouth 1620

Connecticut River

Fort Orange

Kinderhook

NARRAGANSETT

PEQUOT

Wethersfield

Norwich

Cape Cod

DELAWARE

Hartford

Poughkeepsie

Saybrook

New London

Newport

Nantucket I.

SUSQUEHANNA

Fairfield

Greenwich

Southold

East Hampton

Hackensack

New Amsterdam
(New York)

METOAC

Breuckelen

Fort New Gothenburg

Fort Christina

Fort Nassau

Potomac River

Providence

Zwaanendael

ATLANTIC OCEAN

St. Marys 1634

NANTICOKE

MONACAN

Archers Hope

James River

Henrico

Turkey Island

Bermuda Hundred

Shirley Hundred

Martins Brandons

Chesapeake Bay

Dale's Gift

Jamestown 1607

POWHATAN

TUSCARORA

Roanoke I.
1585, 1587

Pamlico Sound

PAMLICO

CATAWBA

IROQUOIS Mountains

Appalachian Mountains

N

Colonies c. 1660

	English settlement
	French settlement
	Dutch settlement
	Swedish settlement
HURON	Native American tribe

0   100 km

0   100 miles

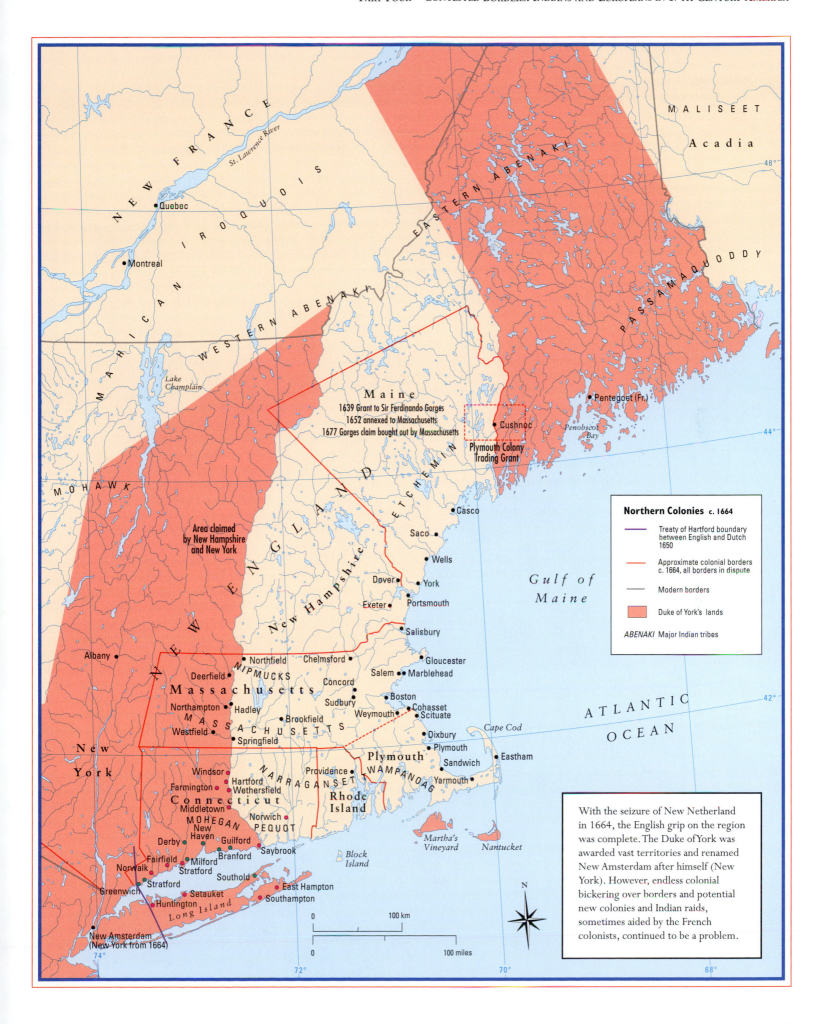

MALISEET

Acadia

NEW FRANCE

St. Lawrence River

MAHICAN IROQUOIS

• Quebec

EASTERN ABENAKI

PASSAMAQUODDY

• Montreal

WESTERN ABENAKI

Lake Champlain

Maine
1639 Grant to Sir Ferdinando Gorges
1652 annexed to Massachusetts
1677 Gorges claim bought out by Massachusetts

• Pentegoet (Fr.)

• Cushnoc
Penobscot Bay

Plymouth Colony
Trading Grant

MOHAWK

ETCHEMIN

Area claimed
by New Hampshire
and New York

• Casco

• Saco

• Wells

Gulf of Maine

• Dover • York

Exeter • • Portsmouth

• Salisbury

• Albany

• Gloucester

New Hampshire

NIPMUCKS

• Northfield • Chelmsford

Salem • • Marblehead

Deerfield •

Massachusetts

• Concord

Northampton • • Hadley

• Sudbury   • Boston

ATLANTIC OCEAN

MASSACHUSETTS

• Brookfield

Weymouth • • Cohasset
• Scituate

Westfield • • Springfield

• Dixbury

New York

Windsor •

Providence •

• Plymouth

Cape Cod

• Plymouth • Sandwich • Eastham

Connecticut

Farmington • Hartford •
• Wethersfield

Plymouth

WAMPANOAG

• Yarmouth

NARRAGANSET

Middletown •

MOHEGAN
New •
Haven

• Norwich

Rhode Island

Derby • • Guilford

PEQUOT

Fairfield • • Branford
• Milford • Saybrook

Martha's Vineyard

Nantucket

Norwalk • • Stratford

• Stratford

Greenwich •

• Setauket
Huntington • • Southampton

• East Hampton

Long Island

New Amsterdam
(New York from 1664)

Northern Colonies c. 1664

— Treaty of Hartford boundary between English and Dutch 1650

— Approximate colonial borders c. 1664, all borders in dispute

— Modern borders

▨ Duke of York's lands

ABENAKI Major Indian tribes

With the seizure of New Netherland in 1664, the English grip on the region was complete. The Duke of York was awarded vast territories and renamed New Amsterdam after himself (New York). However, endless colonial bickering over borders and potential new colonies and Indian raids, sometimes aided by the French colonists, continued to be a problem.

0   100 km

0   100 miles

N

Middle Colonies c. 1632–82

Maryland border according to Baltimore's interpretation of the 1632 Charter
New Netherland c. 1654
Granted to William Penn 1681
New Jersey Quintipartite Deed division line 1676
New Sweden c. 1654
Grant to the Duke of York in 1664
Grant by the Duke of York to Lord Berkeley and Sir George Carteret in 1664
Grant to William Penn by the Duke of York in 1682
Quaker towns

HURON

Lake Ontario

Lake Erie

ONEIDA

ONONDAGA

CAYUGA

SENECA

ERIE

MOHAWK

MAHIGAN

Schenectady
Albany
Kinderhook
Coxsackle

New York (New Netherland) to 1664

Kingston

Pokeepsie

P e n n s y l v a n i a
1681

MUNSEE

Sint Sings

East Jersey

Yonkers

Hackensack

Newark
Elizabethtown
New York (New Amsterdam)

ONAMI

Spotswood
Cranbury
Middletown
Shrewsbury

S U S Q U E H A N A

Lancaster

Burlington
Bordentown
Mount Holly
Bridgeton

Philadelphia
Gloucester
Paulsboro
Woodbury

West Jersey

Little Egg Harbor

Maryland

New Castle
Salem

Joppa
Bohemia Manor
Greenwich
Bridgeton

Baltimore

Dover

C O N O Y

Arundelton
D.C.

Chesapeake Bay

Delaware Bay

Cape Island

Delaware

Lewes

N

C H I C K A H O M I N Y

NANTICOKE

V i r g i n i a

ATLANTIC OCEAN

0   100 km
0   100 miles

St. Marys

Maryland

Delaware

Fairfax Propriety

V i r g i n i a

James River

• St. Marys

Williamsburg •
• Jamestown

Albemarle
(Durant's Neck)

• Norfolk

Northern boundary of Carolina
according to the Charter of 1665

Roanoke River

C H E R O K E E

Northern boundary of Carolina
according to the Charter of 1663

North Carolina
Royal Province from 1729

Neuse River

• New Berne

T U S C A R O R A

C A T A W B A

Cape Fear River

Separation 1712

Cape Lookout

South Carolina
Royal Province from 1729

G
e
o
r
g
i
a

Savannah River

Ogeechee River

Brunswick •
Cape Fear •

Augusta •

Y A M A S E E

Santee River

• Jamestown

C
R
E
E
K

Ocmulgee River

Goose Creek •
• Charles Town

Limit of Spanish claim
Treaty of Madrid 1670

Beaufort •
• Stuart's Town
Port Royal

Altamaha River

Savannah •

Fort George

A T L A N T I C   O C E A N

A P A L A C H E

F
L
O
R
I
D
A

S E M I N O L E

St. Mary's River

Southern boundary of Carolina
according to the Charter of 1663

• St Augustine

St. John's River

N

Southern Colonies c. 1664–1735

⎯⎯ Extent of the Carolina Charter 1663

⎯⎯ Extent of the Carolina Charter 1665

⎯⎯ Northern limit of the Spanish claim
Treaty of Madrid 1670

▢ Grant to James Oglethorpe in 1732

⎯ Modern borders

▨ Maximum extent of Spanish claim

Southern boundary of Carolina
according to the Charter of 1665

0 ⎯⎯ 100 km
0 ⎯⎯ 100 miles

C R E E K

Coosa River

Tallapoosa River

Ocmulgee River

Oconee River

Ogeechee River

Savannah River

Georgia

Carolina

CUSABO

Fort Toulouse
(French)

Coweta Town

Northern line of Spanish claim

Santa Elena

Port Royal

Spanish Fort

Savacola

MIDDLE
CREEK

Alabama River

Tombigbee River

Perdido River

Escambia River

Apalachicola River

Choctawhatchee River

Chattahoochee River

Pedernales (Flint) River

LOWER CREEK

Santa-Cruz de Savacola

Oclockonee River

Aucilla River

Savannah

Altamaha River

Satilla River

Santa Catalina

Frederica

San Pedro

ATLANTIC
OCEAN

Southern boundary of Carolina
under Charter of 1663

Mobile
(French)

Pensacola
(San Carlos de Austria)

APALACHE

San Pedro

San Luis

San Marcos

Conception

Ayubale
Massacre

TIMUCUA

St. Marys River

Santa Fe

FLORIDA

Suwannee River

Fort San Mateo
Fort Diego
Santa Cruz
Port Mooas

Fort Picolata
Fort St. Francis

St. Augustine
Fort San Marco
Fort Matanzas
Matonzan Inlet

30°

St. Johns River

Southern limit of English claim
(Carolina Charter of 1665)

Gulf of Mexico

N

ACUERA

F
L
O
R
I
D
A

Cape
Canaval

AIS

MOCOZO

Lake
Okeechobee

10 km

0

0   10 miles

San Carlos

Ponce de
Leon Bay

Caloosahatchee
River

CALOOSA

San Ignacio

25°

Spanish Florida c. 1660

Spanish claims

English claims

Disputed territory

Fort

Mission

TEKESTA

Spain, England, and France all
attempted to control the
strategic Southeast. Despite
conflicting claims and the
construction of forts and
settlements, the Southeast
remained in Spanish hands until
after the Seven Years' War when,
in 1763, it was ceded to Britain
in return for Cuba.

85°

80°

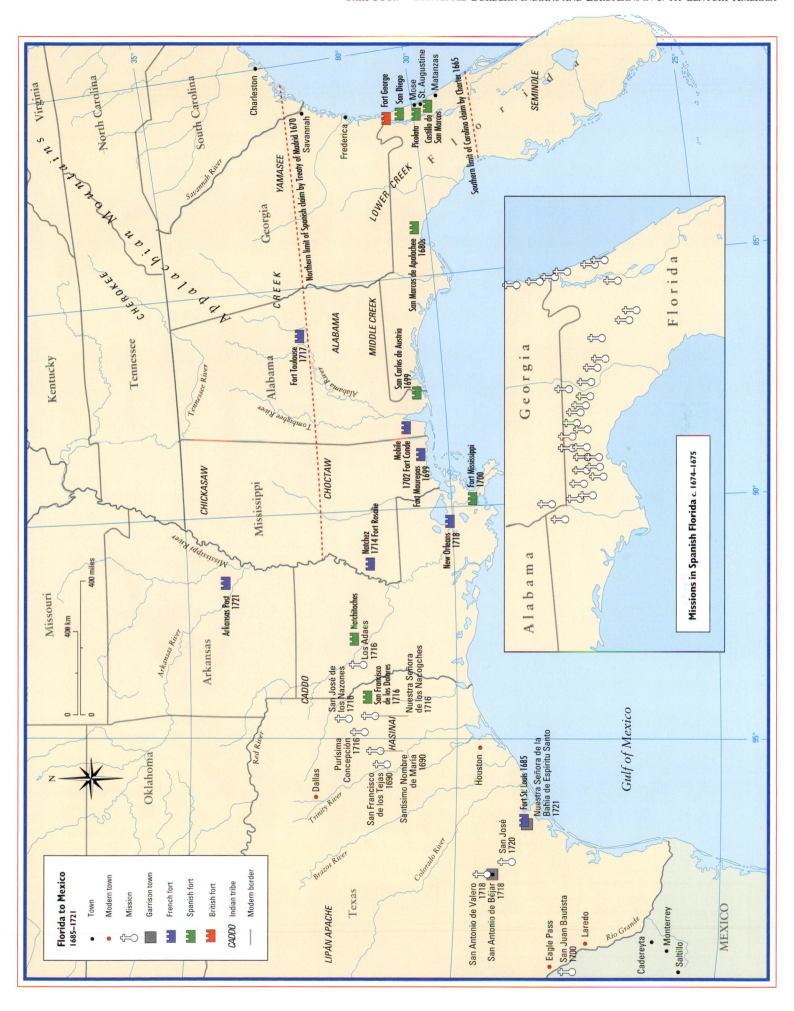

Missions in Spanish Florida c. 1674–1675

Florida to Mexico
1685–1721

- • Town
- • Modern town
- ⚲ Mission
- ▪ Garrison town
- ▪ French fort
- ▪ Spanish fort
- ▪ British fort
- *CADDO* Indian tribe
- — Modern border

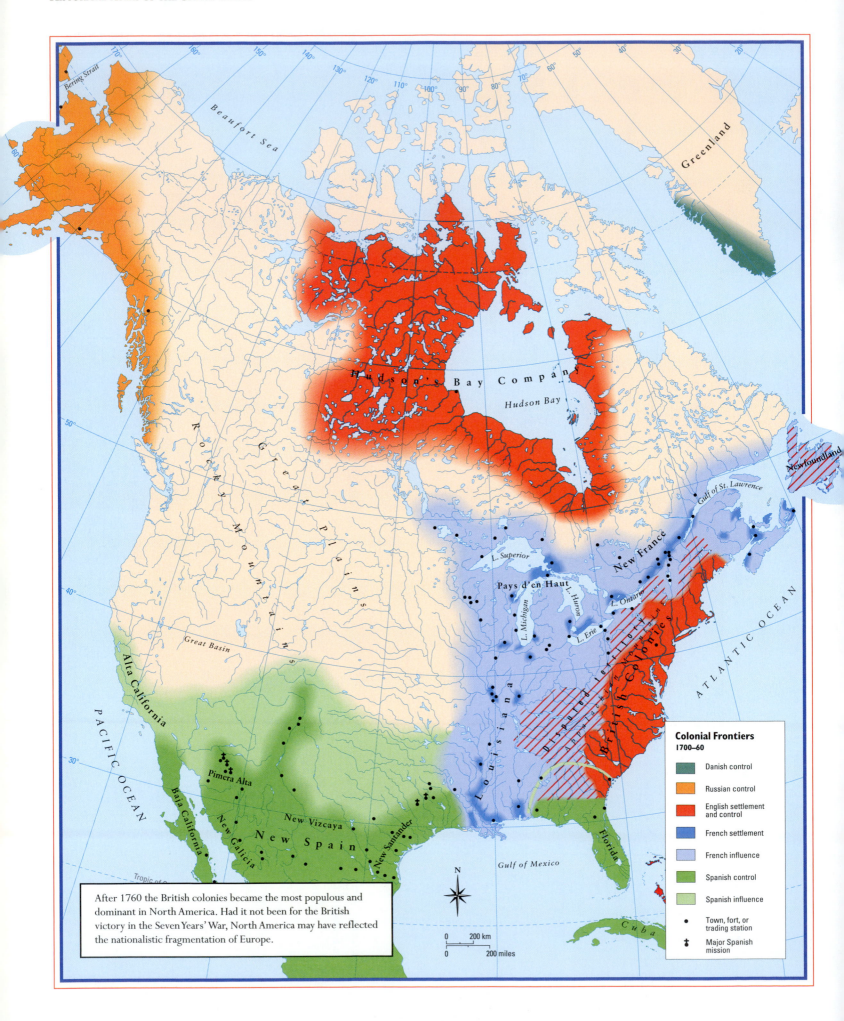

Beaufort Sea

Greenland

Bering Strait

Hudson's Bay Company

Hudson Bay

Newfoundland

Gulf of St. Lawrence

Rocky Mountains

Great Plains

Great Basin

L. Superior

New France

Pays d'en Haut

L. Michigan

L. Huron

L. Ontario

L. Erie

British Colonies

Disputed Territory

Appalachian Mountains

ATLANTIC OCEAN

Alta California

PACIFIC OCEAN

Pimera Alta

New Vizcaya

New Galicia

Baja California

NEW SPAIN

New Santander

Louisiana

Florida

Gulf of Mexico

Cuba

Tropic of C

N

After 1760 the British colonies became the most populous and dominant in North America. Had it not been for the British victory in the Seven Years' War, North America may have reflected the nationalistic fragmentation of Europe.

0   200 km
0   200 miles

Colonial Frontiers
1700–60

- Danish control
- Russian control
- English settlement and control
- French settlement
- French influence
- Spanish control
- Spanish influence
- ● Town, fort, or trading station
- ✝ Major Spanish mission

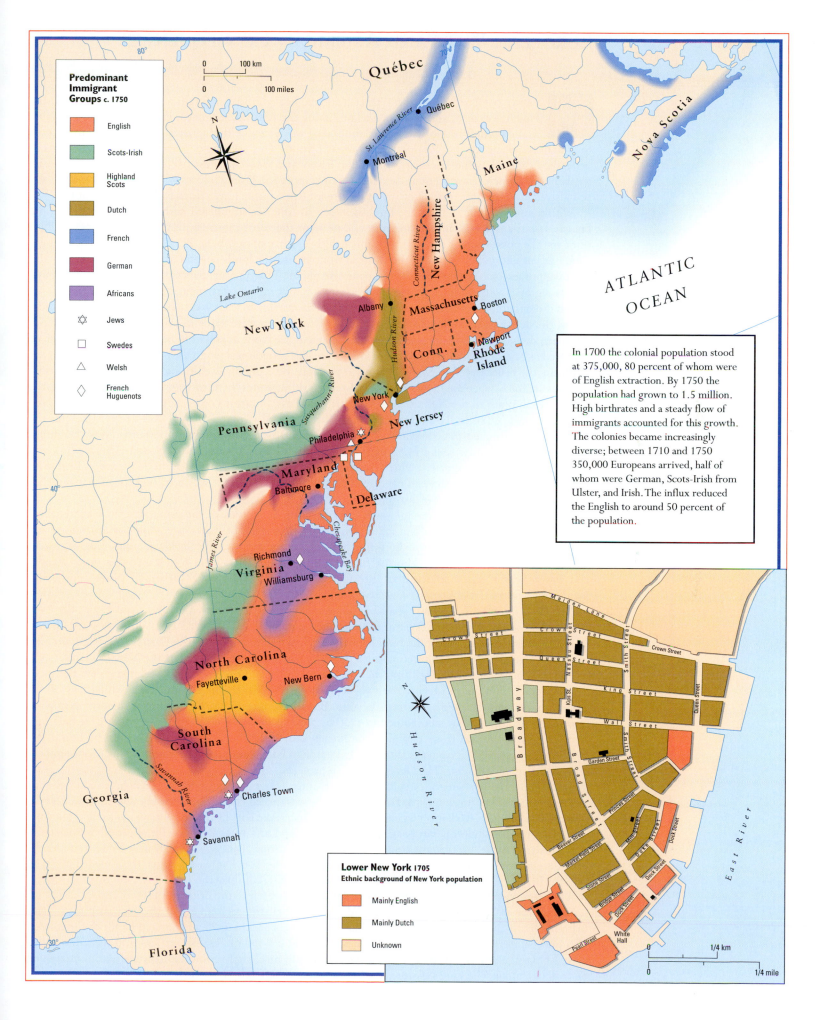

Predominant Immigrant Groups c. 1750

- English
- Scots-Irish
- Highland Scots
- Dutch
- French
- German
- Africans
- ✡ Jews
- ▢ Swedes
- △ Welsh
- ◇ French Huguenots

In 1700 the colonial population stood at 375,000, 80 percent of whom were of English extraction. By 1750 the population had grown to 1.5 million. High birthrates and a steady flow of immigrants accounted for this growth. The colonies became increasingly diverse; between 1710 and 1750 350,000 Europeans arrived, half of whom were German, Scots-Irish from Ulster, and Irish. The influx reduced the English to around 50 percent of the population.

Lower New York 1705
Ethnic background of New York population

- Mainly English
- Mainly Dutch
- Unknown

PART FIVE

EUROPEAN WARS AND AMERICAN CONSEQUENCES

D URING THE last half of the 17th century, the heavy influx of English settlers overwhelmed the Dutch, Swedish, and Spanish enclaves along the Atlantic seaboard. From the shores of Maine to the borders of Florida, the Atlantic coast was awash with English settlers. The Atlantic coast thus readily fell under the domination of Great Britain. The vast region beyond the Appalachians, a watershed drained by the Mississippi and Ohio Rivers and their countless tributaries, was claimed insistently by the French crown, though held loosely by trappers and missionaries who inhabited isolated outposts stretching from the mouth of the St. Lawrence River to the lower reaches of the Mississippi.

Within another half century the English in North America numbered perhaps 1.5 million, and the French, less than 90,000. In the long run, and perhaps the short one as well, the English appeared destined to take possession of the continent through sheer force of numbers. The English colonists, though, were not patient. They regarded the western frontier and the lands beyond as up for grabs; if they did not take possession of those lands, someone else might. That various tribes of Indians occupied much of this region was considered by most Europeans a temporary inconvenience.

But if demographic pressure foreordained English supremacy in what was to become much of the United States, the decisions that dictated British control of the region were made in London, Paris, and Madrid. European monarchs and their courts regarded colonial possessions as pawns to be exchanged, sacrificed, or advanced as best suited strategic objectives in Europe. This geopolitical pragmatism was consistent with mercantilism, the belief that the colonies existed to promote the economic well-being of the mother country.

Thus in 1689, when England, Spain, and several other states went to war with France, most of the fighting took place in the Netherlands. But the boundless ambitions of certain colonial leaders caused this "European war" to flare up in the New World as well (King William's War 1689–97). After the French had attacked Schenectady and raided outposts throughout northern New England, Massachusetts colonists sent a naval expedition that seized Port Royal, Nova Scotia. There followed a handful of more engagements, widely scattered and generally inconclusive. In 1697, when European statesmen negotiated a peace, all captured territory in the Americas was returned to the nations that possessed them at the outset of hostilities.

War resumed in Europe several years later, igniting hostilities in the Americas. In what became known there as Queen Anne's War (1702–13), Indians from the St. Lawrence, supplied and supported by the French, staged raids throughout northern New England and the Mohawk valley. English forces from the Carolinas attacked and burned St. Augustine, while others from New England invaded Acadia and Nova Scotia, again taking Port Royal. The Peace of Utrecht (1713) ceded Nova Scotia and Newfoundland to Great Britain.

In 1739 a third European war sparked Indian raids in northern New England. And again, the New England colonists dispatched a naval force to the north. In 1745 it seized Louisburg on Cape Breton Island, a major fort guarding the mouth of the St. Lawrence. But when the European powers decided on peace, Louisburg was again returned to the French, much to the dismay of the New Englanders.

Despite these recurrent hostilities, the English colonists and the French had relatively few points of acute contact. For the most part the two peoples were separated by the trackless wilderness of the Appalachians and the immense forests beyond. But by the late 1740s, English fur traders were moving into the Ohio valley; they were joined in 1750 by land speculators who received a grant of a half million acres in the region from Virginia. The French shored up their claims to the region by building a string of forts stretching from the shores of Lake Erie to Fort Duquesne, at the fork of the Monongahela and the Allegheny Rivers. They ignored British protests.

In 1754 George Washington, a young Virginia planter, was sent to dislodge the French. After a few skirmishes near what became known as Fort Necessity, he was turned back. The following year General Edward Braddock led some 1,400 British regulars on a campaign to take Fort Duquesne. He was killed and his army defeated. British assaults on Fort Niagara, near the falls, and on Crown Point, on the approach to Montreal, also ended in failure. By 1756 the conflict had spread to Europe. Two years later King George II, under the brilliant guidance of William Pitt, threw another force against Fort Duquesne, which this time fell; the next year the British seized both Fort Niagara and Crown Point. Fresh from these victories, the British attempted a multi-pronged offensive against Montreal, which at last fell to the British in 1760.

The Peace of Paris of 1763 ceded Canada and most of the region east of the Mississippi to Great Britain. "Half the continent," wrote the historian Francis Parkman, "had changed hands at the scratch of a pen." Later that year King George III, fearful that a flood of English settlers into the Ohio valley would inflame the Indians, established a "proclamation line" that prohibited colonists from infringing on Indian claims. The king's words did not constitute an effective boundary.

MAPS

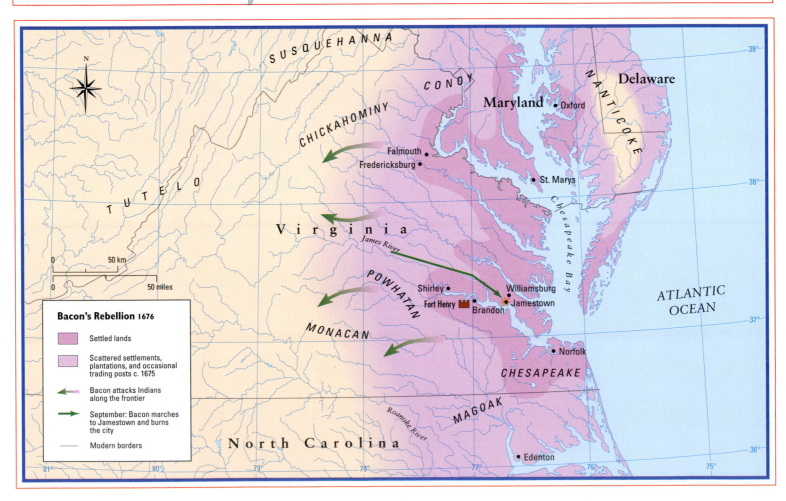

New England
1621–82

Land granted to Massachusetts
Bay Company 1629

Land granted to Connecticut
Colony Company 1662

Nova Scotia
To Sir William Alexander
1621

Isle
Madeleine

Cape Breton
Island

Isle St. Jean

Gaspé Peninsula

New France

Québec

Trois Rivière

Montréal

St. Lawrence River

Ottawa River

Lake
Nipissing

Lake
Attigonautan

Lake
aux Claies

Lake Ontario

Lake Erie

Grant to
Sir William Alexander
1635,
Duke of York
1664

Grand Pré

Port Royal

Halifax

Plymouth Colony
1630

Maine
Grant to Gorges
1639

Falmouth

New Hamphire
To Mason
1629

Portsmouth

Salem

Boston

Massachusetts

Plymouth Colony
1630

Rhode Island and
Providence Plantations
1663

Connecticut

New York
Grant to Duke of York
1664

Albany

Connecticut River

Hudson River

Pennsylvania
Grant to William Penn
1681

Delaware River

New York

Harry's Ferry

Raystown

Maryland
Grant to Lord Baltimore
1632

New Jersey
Grant by Duke of York
to Lord Berkeley
and Sir George Carteret
1664

ATLANTIC
OCEAN

N

0   100 km
0   100 miles

Bacon's Rebellion 1676

Settled lands

Scattered settlements,
plantations, and occasional
trading posts c. 1675

Bacon attacks Indians
along the frontier

September: Bacon marches
to Jamestown and burns
the city

Modern borders

N

0   50 km
0   50 miles

SUSQUEHANNA

CONOY

CHICKAHOMINY

TUTELO

POWHATAN

MONACAN

MAGOAK

NANTICOKE

CHESAPEAKE

Delaware

Maryland

Oxford

St. Marys

Falmouth

Fredericksburg

Virginia

James River

Shirley

Fort Henry

Brandon

Williamsburg

Jamestown

Norfolk

Chesapeake Bay

ATLANTIC
OCEAN

Roanoke River

North Carolina

Edenton

62

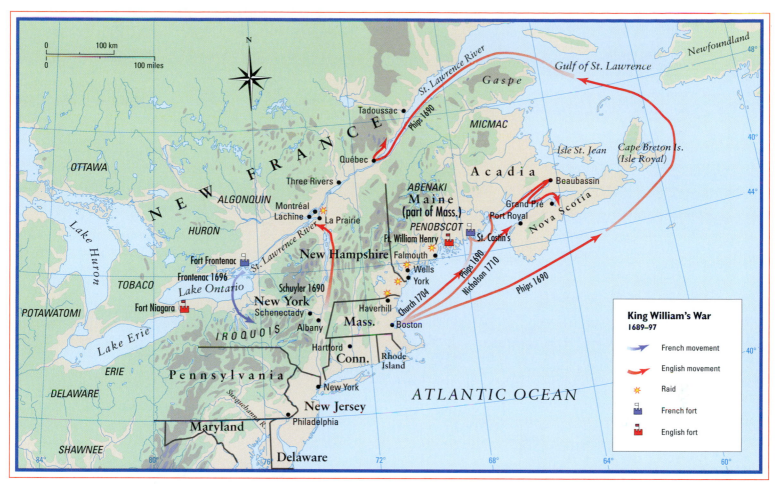

King William's War
1689–97

- French movement
- English movement
- Raid
- French fort
- English fort

King George's War 1743–48

- French movement
- British movement
- Raid
- Battle
- French fort
- British fort

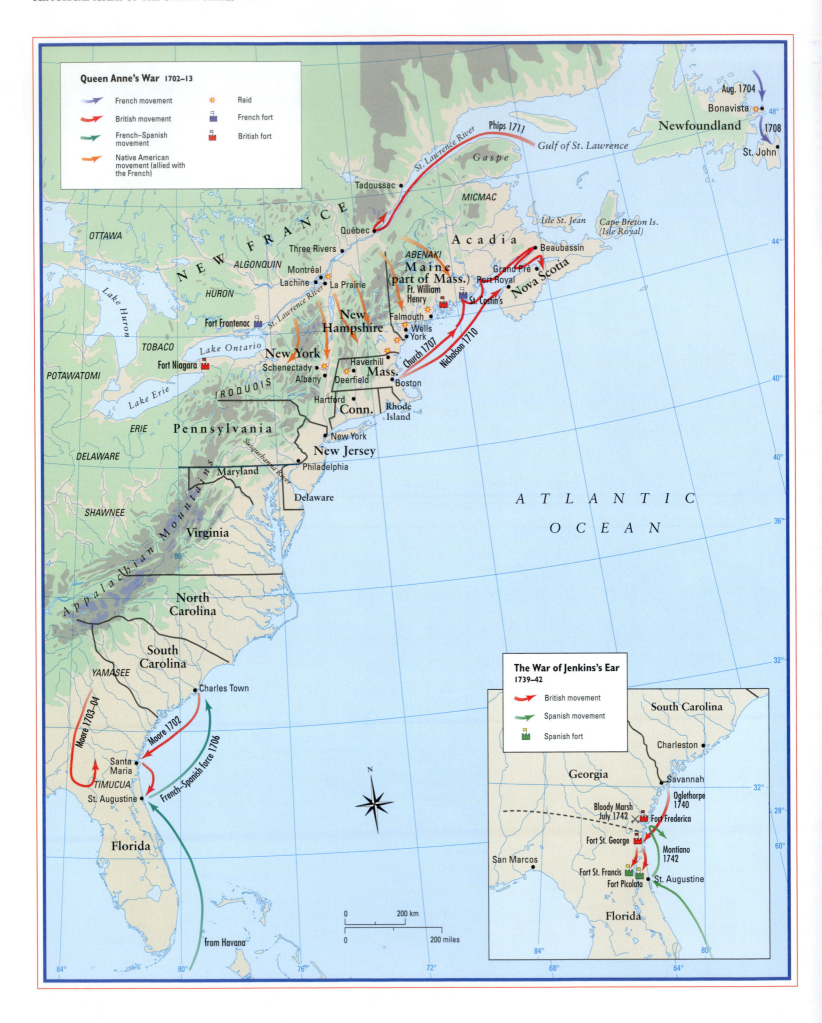

Queen Anne's War 1702–13

→ French movement
→ British movement
→ French–Spanish movement
→ Native American movement (allied with the French)

✷ Raid
▪ French fort
▪ British fort

The War of Jenkins's Ear 1739–42

→ British movement
→ Spanish movement
▪ Spanish fort

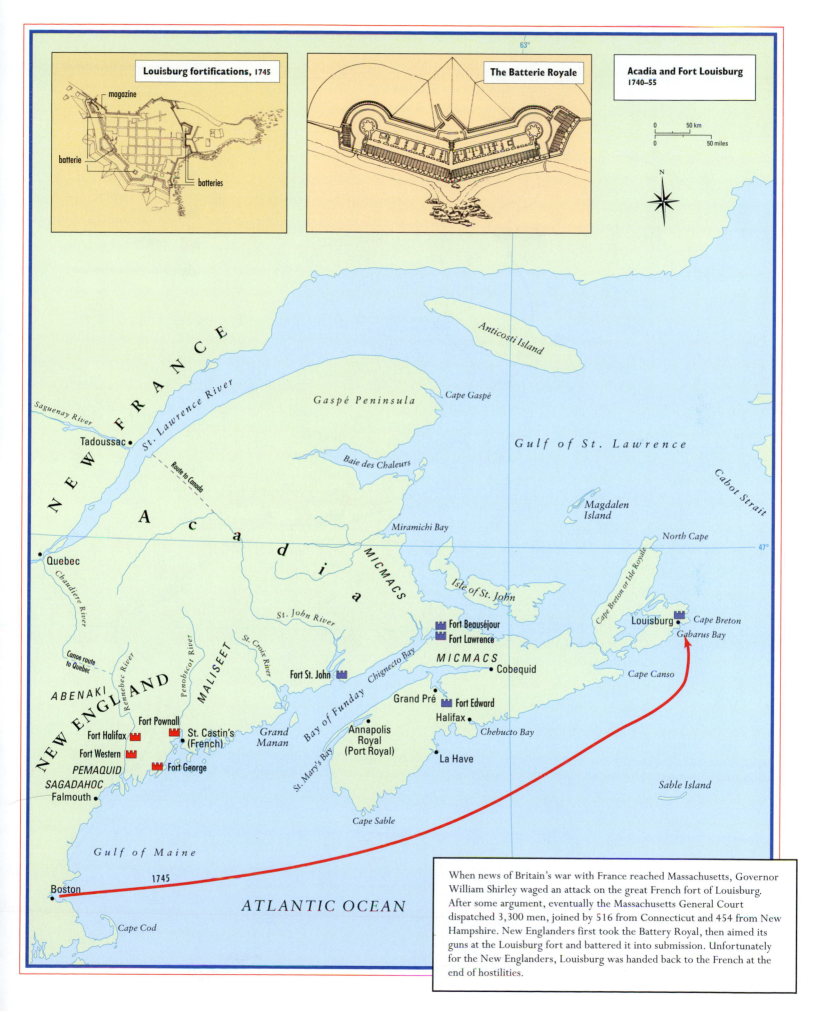

Louisburg fortifications, 1745

magazine

batterie

batteries

The Batterie Royale

Acadia and Fort Louisburg
1740–55

0   50 km
0   50 miles

N

NEW FRANCE

Saguenay River

Tadoussac

St. Lawrence River

Route to Canada

Quebec

Chaudiere River

Canoe route to Quebec

ABENAKI

NEW ENGLAND

Fort Halifax

Fort Western

PEMAQUID

SAGADAHOC

Falmouth

Fort Pownall

St. Castin's (French)

Fort George

Kennebec River

Penobscot River

MALISEET

St. Croix River

St. John River

Gaspé Peninsula

Cape Gaspé

Baie des Chaleurs

Miramichi Bay

MICMACS

Fort St. John

Chignecto Bay

Fort Beauséjour

Fort Lawrence

MICMACS

Cobequid

Grand Pré

Fort Edward

Halifax

Chebucto Bay

La Have

Grand Manan

Bay of Funday

St. Mary's Bay

Annapolis Royal (Port Royal)

Cape Sable

ATLANTIC OCEAN

Gulf of Maine

1745

Boston

Cape Cod

Anticosti Island

Gulf of St. Lawrence

Magdalen Island

Cabot Strait

North Cape

47°

63°

Isle of St. John

Cape Breton or Isle Royale

Louisburg

Cape Breton

Gabarus Bay

Cape Canso

Sable Island

Acadia

When news of Britain's war with France reached Massachusetts, Governor William Shirley waged an attack on the great French fort of Louisburg. After some argument, eventually the Massachusetts General Court dispatched 3,300 men, joined by 516 from Connecticut and 454 from New Hampshire. New Englanders first took the Battery Royal, then aimed its guns at the Louisburg fort and battered it into submission. Unfortunately for the New Englanders, Louisburg was handed back to the French at the end of hostilities.

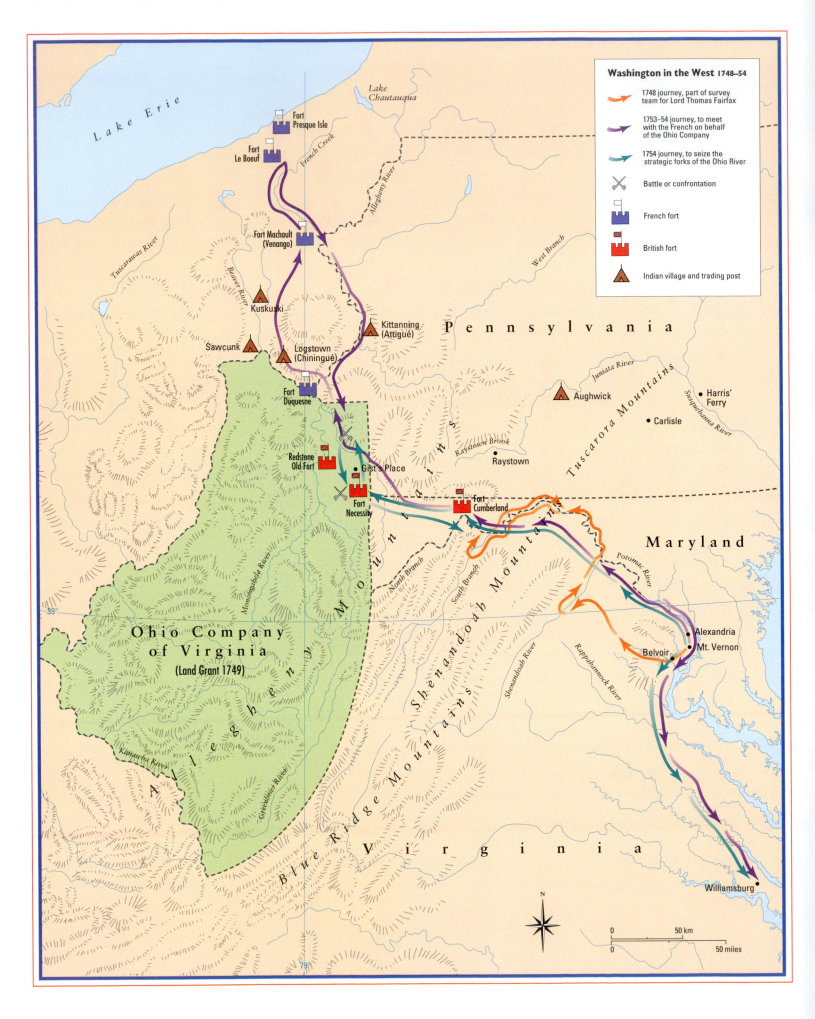

Lake Erie

Lake Chautauqua

Fort Presque Isle

Fort Le Boeuf

French Creek

Allegheny River

Washington in the West 1748–54

- 1748 journey, part of survey team for Lord Thomas Fairfax
- 1753–54 journey, to meet with the French on behalf of the Ohio Company
- 1754 journey, to seize the strategic forks of the Ohio River
- ✕ Battle or confrontation
- ◻ French fort
- ◼ British fort
- ▲ Indian village and trading post

Tuscarawas River

Fort Machault (Venango)

Beaver River

Kuskuski

Sawcunk

Kittanning (Attigué)

Logstown (Chiningué)

P e n n s y l v a n i a

West Branch

Juniata River

Aughwick

Harris' Ferry

Carlisle

Susquehanna River

Fort Duquesne

Redstone Old Fort

Gist's Place

Raystown Brook

Raystown

Tuscarora Mountains

Fort Necessity

Fort Cumberland

M a r y l a n d

Monongahela River

North Branch

South Branch

A l l e g h e n y   M o u n t a i n s

Potomac River

Ohio Company of Virginia

(Land Grant 1749)

S h e n a n d o a h   M o u n t a i n s

Shenandoah River

Alexandria

Mt. Vernon

Belvoir

Rappahannock River

39°

Kanawha River

Greenbrier River

B l u e   R i d g e   M o u n t a i n s

V i r g i n i a

Williamsburg

79°

N

0   50 km

0   50 miles

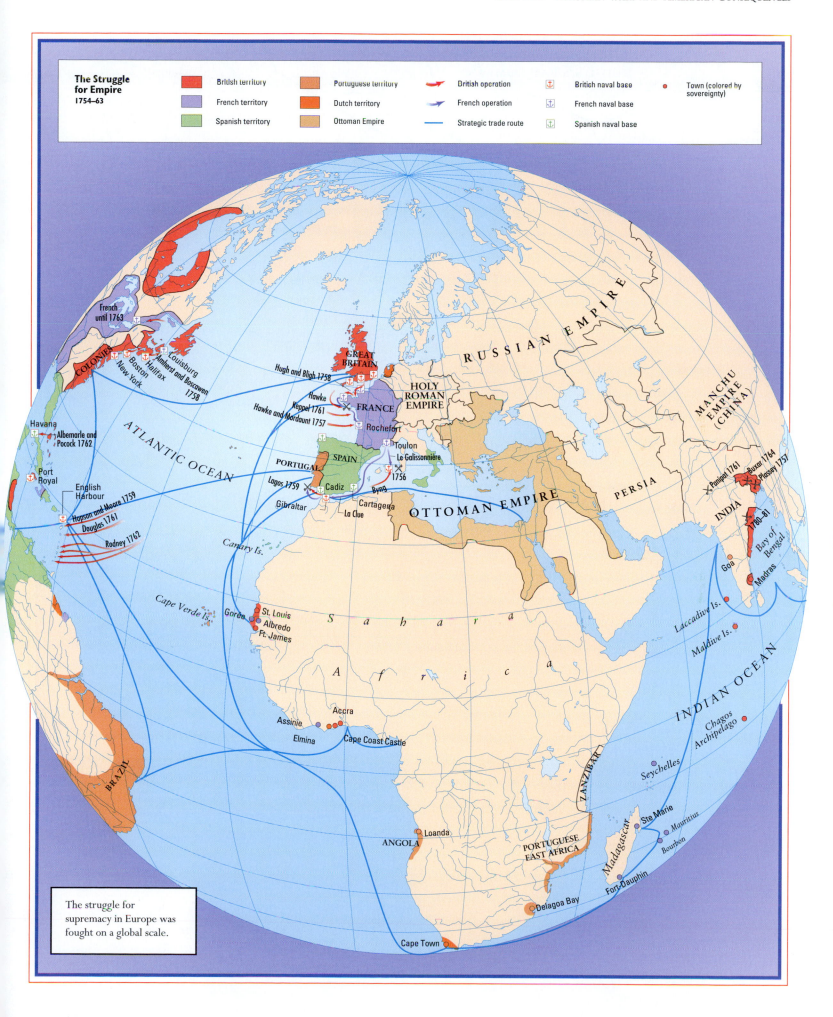

The Struggle for Empire 1754–63

British territory
French territory
Spanish territory
Portuguese territory
Dutch territory
Ottoman Empire
British operation
French operation
Strategic trade route
British naval base
French naval base
Spanish naval base
Town (colored by sovereignty)

French until 1763

COLONIES
Louisburg
Amherst and Boscawen 1758
Boston
Halifax
New York

Havana
Albemarle and Pocock 1762
Port Royal
English Harbour
Hopson and Moore 1759
Douglas 1761
Rodney 1762

ATLANTIC OCEAN

GREAT BRITAIN
Hugh and Bligh 1758
Hawke
Keppel 1761
Hawke and Mordaunt 1757
FRANCE
Rochefort

HOLY ROMAN EMPIRE

RUSSIAN EMPIRE

MANCHU EMPIRE (CHINA)

PORTUGAL
SPAIN
Lagos 1759
Cadiz
Gibraltar
Cartagena
La Clue
Byng

Toulon
Le Galissonnière
1756

OTTOMAN EMPIRE

PERSIA

INDIA
Panipat 1761
Buxar 1764
Plassey 1757
1780–81
Bay of Bengal
Goa
Madras

Canary Is.

Cape Verde Is.
Gorée
St. Louis
Albredo
Ft. James

Laccadive Is.
Maldive Is.

INDIAN OCEAN

S a h a r a

A f r i c a

Accra
Assinie
Elmina
Cape Coast Castle

Chagos Archipelago

Seychelles

ZANZIBAR

ANGOLA
Loanda

PORTUGUESE EAST AFRICA

Madagascar
Ste Marie
Mauritius
Bourbon

Fort-Dauphin

BRAZIL

Delagoa Bay

Cape Town

The struggle for supremacy in Europe was fought on a global scale.

The 1763 Proclamation Line

▬ ▪ ▬ Proclamation Line of 1763, preventing settlement west of the Appalachians except for the new Royal Colonies of Québec and East and West Florida. It created an Indian Reserve west to Spanish Louisiana, north to the Hudson's Bay Company Reserve

▬ ▬ ▬ Mason-Dixon Line 1763–67 defining northern border of Maryland

▮ Settled area

🏰 Fort

CREEK Indian tribe

The Treaty of Paris was signed on 10 February 1763. Britain received Canada, Nova Scotia, and Cape Breton Island from France and, in exchange, restored fishing rights on the Newfoundland banks and the St. Lawrence. France held on to St. Pierre and Miquelon Islands. Britain received Florida from Spain in exchange for Cuba and fishing rights off Newfoundland. In a second treaty France ceded Louisiana to Spain, and, for the time being, France retreated from North America.

Hudson Bay

Labrador

H u d s o n ' s   B a y   C o m p a n y

🏰 Fort Winnipeg
🏰 Fort St. Charles
🏰 Fort William
🏰 Fort Nippigon
Fort Albany 🏰
Moose Factory 🏰
🏰 Fort Rupert

Newfoundland

St. Pierre
et Miquelon 🏳️

Lake Superior

🏰 Sault Ste. Marie

QUÉBEC

St. Lawrence River

Québec •

Montréal •

Nova Scotia

• Halifax

Lake Michigan

Lake Huron

Lake Ontario

🏰 Fort Pontchartrain

Lake Erie

Boston •

New York •

I N D I A N   R E S E R V E

🏰 Fort Vincennes

**SPANISH-
LOUISIANA**

🏰 Fort Kaskaskia

Philadelphia •

T H E   T H I R T E E N   C O L O N I E S

Norfolk •

A T L A N T I C   O C E A N

Bermuda

Charles Town •

Savannah •

West Florida

• New Orleans

St. Augustine •

**East
Florida**

Gulf of Mexico

Bahamas

1762–63
British occupied

N

British North America
1764–76

■ Original thirteen colonies

■ Other British territories

▨ Spanish Louisiana, secretly ceded by France in 1763

🏳️ Only French possession after Treaty of Paris, 1763

🏰 Fort

0   300 km

0   300 miles

PART SIX

18TH CENTURY AMERICAN SOCIETY

T HE FATEFUL decision of the colonies to break away from Great Britain was partly a response to taxation policies adopted in London, a subject considered in the following section. Equally important, though far less obvious, was the emergence of a cluster of institutions and orientations that marked the beginnings of a national culture. As the English colonists began to think of themselves as a distinct society, as "Americans," they found it easier to imagine themselves as a nation.

Religion constituted one important "nationalizing" force. This observation goes against conventional thinking, which has long regarded the 18th century as a period of diminished religious enthusiasm. As farmers took increasing satisfaction from their full barns, and merchants, their well-stocked shops, they were less inclined to direct their attention heavenward, or so the argument goes. But during the 18th century the practice of religion acquired, if not more intensity, more sustained support. As several maps in this section suggest, from 1741 to 1770 nearly all denominations experienced a tremendous growth in membership, as manifested by the surge in church construction.

Moreover, congregations not only contributed to the maintenance of their new and larger church buildings; they also proved peculiarly susceptible to itinerant evangelists. Jonathan Edwards, a congregationalist minister, initiated what became known as the Great Awakening in Connecticut. His sermons evoked a sterner, more demanding God that drew a fervent response among many New England listeners. To carry on this work, he invited several English ministers to rekindle religion throughout the colonies. George Whitefield, the most successful, arrived in Philadelphia in 1739. Benjamin Franklin, himself no religious zealot, was impressed with Whitefield's sermons. "I silently resolved he should get nothing from me," he wrote.

> I had in my Pocket a Handful of Copper Money, three or four silver Dollars, and five Pistoles in Gold. As he proceeded I began to soften and concluded to give the Coppers. Another Stroke of his Oratory . . . determin'd me to give the Silver; and he finish'd so admirably that I empty'd my Pocket wholly into the Collector's Dish.

Over the next fourteen months, Whitefield spoke in scores of cities throughout English America, often to huge audiences. During a three-day visit to Boston, he attracted some 19,000 listeners. Frederick Frelinghuysen (Dutch Reformed Church), Gilbert Tennent, Samuel Davies, and James Davenport (Presbyterian), and Nikolaus von Zinzendorf (Lutheran) were among the other important itinerant ministers of the era.

As religious leaders moved throughout the colonies, and denominational networks became more elaborate, the intellectual horizons of the colonists widened. Their attachments to their own village or town or colony were supplemented by identification with like-minded members of their faith throughout the Atlantic seaboard.

The maturation of the colonial economies further contributed to the emergence of an "American" identity. The development of shipbuilding in the Northeast and of various industries in the Middle Atlantic states portended a time when the American colonies would not be dependent on British factories and craftsmen. The situation was different in the South. Tobacco farmers in Maryland, Delaware, Virginia, and North Carolina, and rice and indigo planters in South Carolina, were becoming increasingly enmeshed in financial obligations with creditors and suppliers in Great Britain. But familiarity with one's creditors commonly bred resentment; many planters longed to be free from their dependence on British capital.

At the same time, the British government, having acquired a vast empire in the Americas in 1763, now resolved to collect from its American subjects the money to administer it. Parliament's adoption the following year of the Sugar Act, which taxed sugar, wine, and coffee imports to America, generated considerable opposition. "If our Trade may be taxed why not our lands?" asked a meeting of outraged Bostonians. "Why not the produce of our Lands and every Thing we possess or make use of?" Then, as if in response, came a drumbeat of new British revenue measures: the Stamp Act (1765), the Declaratory Act (1766), the Townshend Acts (1767), and the Coercive Acts (1774).

Although the new sugar tax generated considerable revenue, and helped fund the expansion of the British administrative and military presence in the Americas, the other taxes were mostly evaded or ignored; they also generated increasing tensions and soon spawned clandestine organizations, such as the Sons of Liberty, that staged riots and organized protests against the British.

MAPS

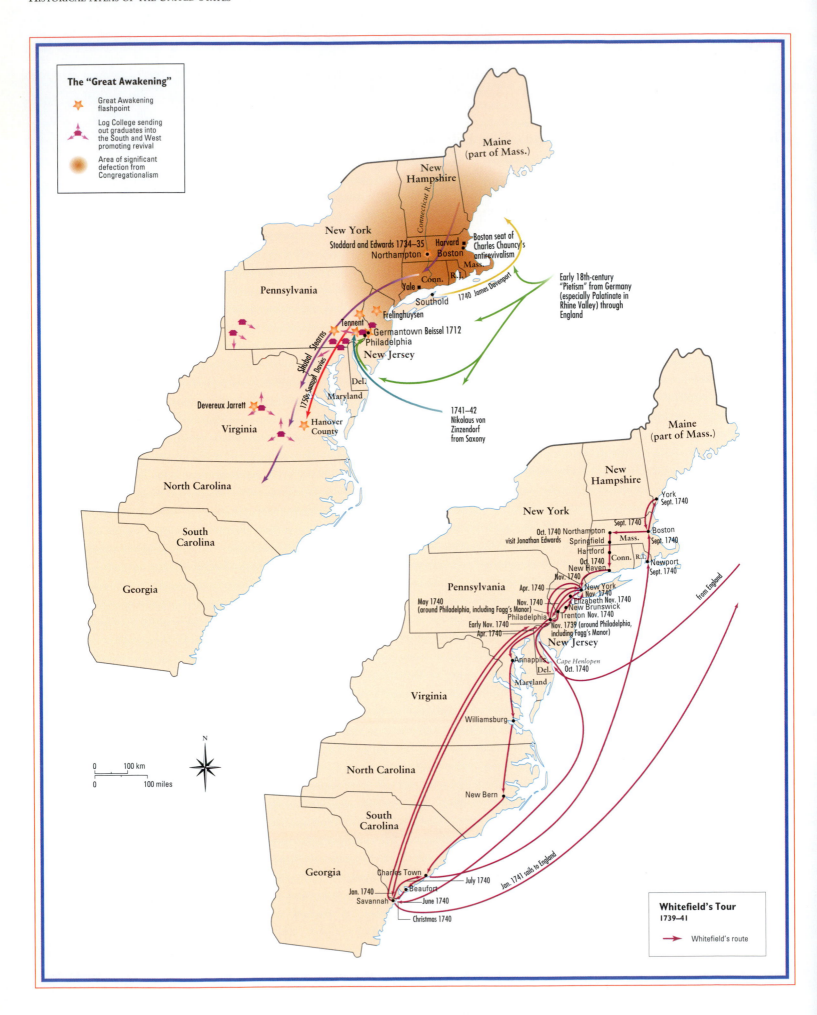

The "Great Awakening"

⭐ Great Awakening flashpoint

🔺 Log College sending out graduates into the South and West promoting revival

🟠 Area of significant defection from Congregationalism

Maine (part of Mass.)

New Hampshire

New York

Stoddard and Edwards 1734–35
Northampton

Harvard
Boston Boston seat of Charles Chauncy's antirevivalism

Yale Conn. R.I.

Pennsylvania

Southold 1740 James Davenport

Frelinghuysen

Tennent
Germantown Beissel 1712
Philadelphia

New Jersey

Shubal Stearns

Del.

Maryland

Devereux Jarrett

1750s Samuel Davies

Virginia Hanover County

North Carolina

South Carolina

Georgia

Early 18th-century "Pietism" from Germany (especially Palatinate in Rhine Valley) through England

1741–42 Nikolaus von Zinzendorf from Saxony

0   100 km
0   100 miles

N

Maine (part of Mass.)

New Hampshire

New York

Oct. 1740 Northampton
visit Jonathan Edwards Springfield
Hartford Mass.
Oct. 1740 Conn. R.I.
New Haven Newport
Nov. 1740 Sept. 1740

York
Sept. 1740

Sept. 1740 Boston
Sept. 1740

Pennsylvania

Apr. 1740 New York
Nov. 1740
May 1740
(around Philadelphia, including Fagg's Manor) Nov. 1740 Elizabeth Nov. 1740
New Brunswick
Philadelphia Trenton Nov. 1740
Early Nov. 1740 Nov. 1739 (around Philadelphia, including Fagg's Manor)
Apr. 1740

New Jersey

Annapolis Cape Henlopen
Del. Oct. 1740

Maryland

Virginia

Williamsburg

from England

North Carolina

New Bern

South Carolina

Georgia

Charles Town
July 1740
Beaufort Jan. 1741 sails to England
Jan. 1740 June 1740
Savannah
Christmas 1740

Whitefield's Tour
1739–41

→ Whitefield's route

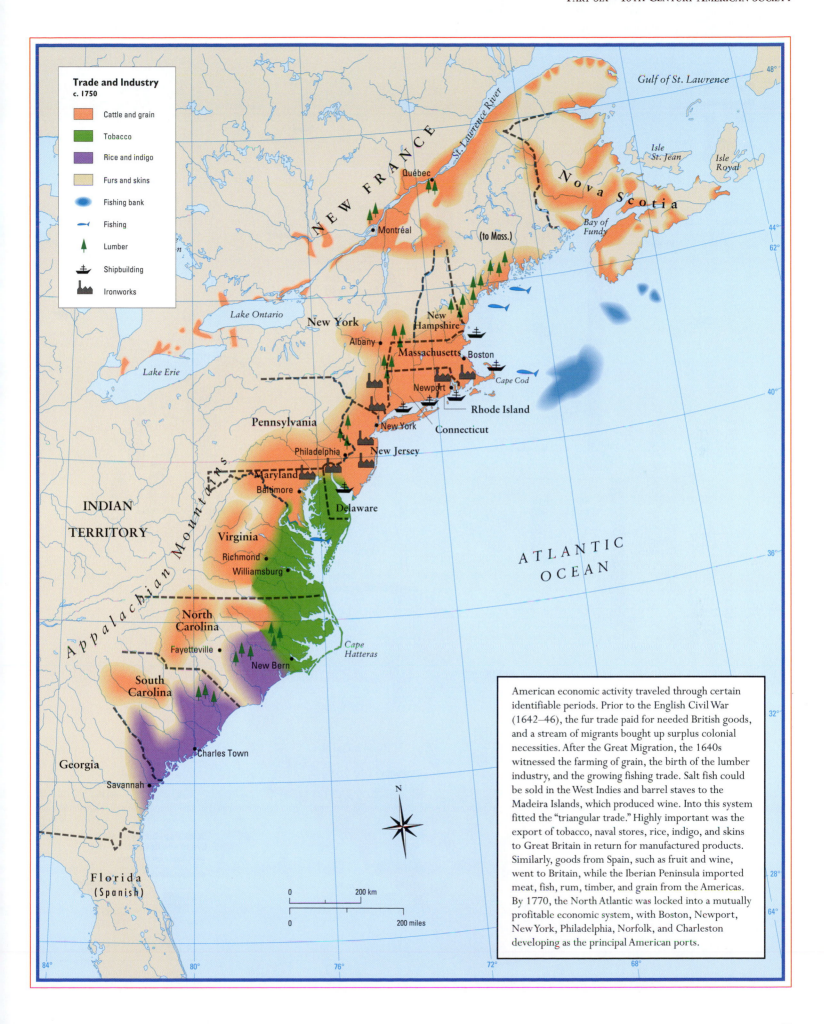

Trade and Industry
c. 1750

- Cattle and grain
- Tobacco
- Rice and indigo
- Furs and skins
- Fishing bank
- Fishing
- Lumber
- Shipbuilding
- Ironworks

Gulf of St. Lawrence

NEW FRANCE

St. Lawrence River

Québec

Nova Scotia

Montréal

Isle St. Jean

Isle Royal

(to Mass.)

Bay of Fundy

Lake Ontario

New York

Albany

New Hampshire

Massachusetts

Boston

Lake Erie

Newport

Cape Cod

Rhode Island

Pennsylvania

New York

Connecticut

Philadelphia

New Jersey

INDIAN TERRITORY

Maryland

Baltimore

Delaware

Virginia

Richmond

Williamsburg

Appalachian Mountains

ATLANTIC OCEAN

North Carolina

Fayetteville

Cape Hatteras

New Bern

South Carolina

Georgia

Charles Town

Savannah

Florida (Spanish)

N

0   200 km

0   200 miles

American economic activity traveled through certain identifiable periods. Prior to the English Civil War (1642–46), the fur trade paid for needed British goods, and a stream of migrants bought up surplus colonial necessities. After the Great Migration, the 1640s witnessed the farming of grain, the birth of the lumber industry, and the growing fishing trade. Salt fish could be sold in the West Indies and barrel staves to the Madeira Islands, which produced wine. Into this system fitted the "triangular trade." Highly important was the export of tobacco, naval stores, rice, indigo, and skins to Great Britain in return for manufactured products. Similarly, goods from Spain, such as fruit and wine, went to Britain, while the Iberian Peninsula imported meat, fish, rum, timber, and grain from the Americas. By 1770, the North Atlantic was locked into a mutually profitable economic system, with Boston, Newport, New York, Philadelphia, Norfolk, and Charleston developing as the principal American ports.

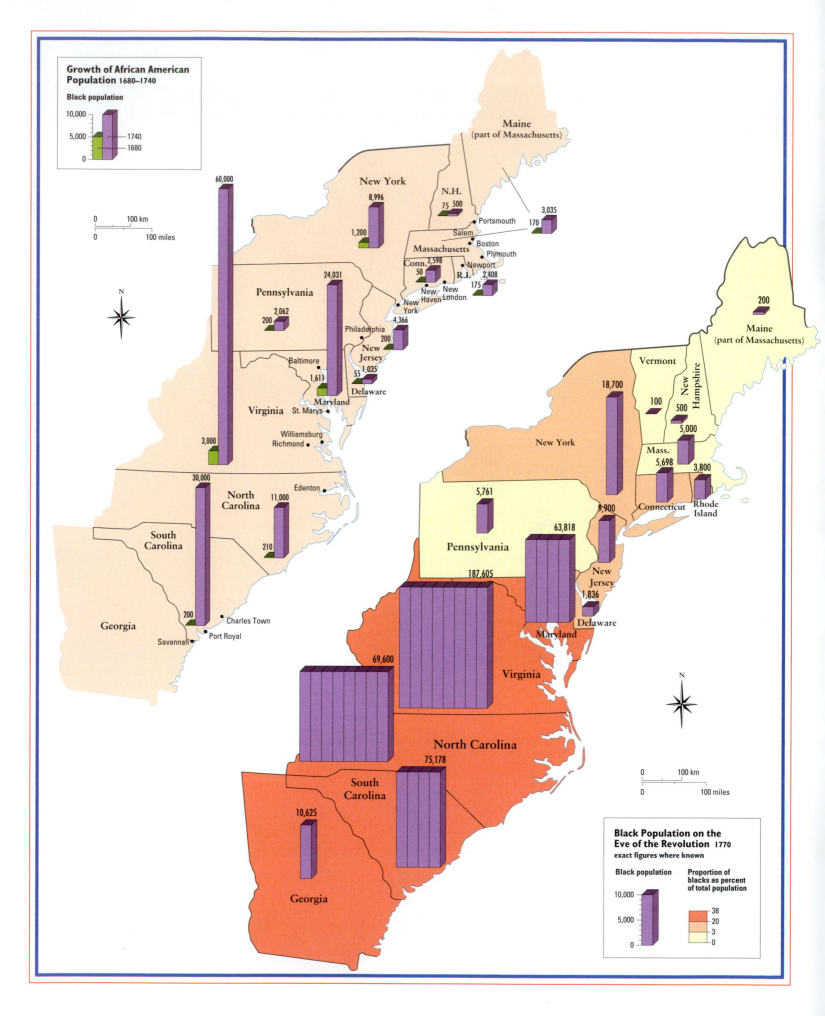

Growth of African American Population 1680–1740

Black population

10,000

5,000 — 1740

0 — 1680

0 100 km

0 100 miles

New York
8,996
1,200

N.H.
75 500

Maine
(part of Massachusetts)

Portsmouth
3,035
170

Salem
Boston
Plymouth

Massachusetts

Conn. 2,598
50
New Haven
New London
R.I.
2,408
175
Newport

Pennsylvania
24,031
2,062
200

New York

Philadelphia
New Jersey
200
4,366

Baltimore
1,611
Delaware
55 1,035

Maryland
St. Marys

Virginia
Williamsburg
Richmond
3,000

60,000

North Carolina
11,000
Edenton

South Carolina
30,000
210

Georgia
200
Charles Town
Savannah
Port Royal

Black Population on the Eve of the Revolution 1770
exact figures where known

Maine
(part of Massachusetts)
200

Vermont
100

New Hampshire
500
5,000

New York
18,700

Mass.
5,698

Connecticut
5,000

Rhode Island
3,800

Pennsylvania
5,761

New Jersey
9,900
1,836

Maryland
63,818

Delaware

Virginia
187,605

North Carolina
69,600

South Carolina
75,178

Georgia
10,625

0 100 km

0 100 miles

Black population

10,000

5,000

0

Proportion of blacks as percent of total population

38
20
3
0

74

Hudson Bay

LABRADOR

HUDSON'S BAY COMPANY

Newfoundland

Lake Superior

St. Pierre et Miquelon

PROVINCE OF QUÉBEC

Québec

Lake Michigan

Lake Huron

Montréal

Nova Scotia

PROVINCE OF QUÉBEC

Lake Ontario

Lake Erie

Boston

SPANISH LOUISIANA

Vandalia

New York

Philadelphia

Transylvania

THE THIRTEEN COLONIES

ATLANTIC OCEAN

Norfolk

Indian Reserve

Bermuda

Charles Town

Savannah

West Florida (formerly Spanish)

St. Augustine

East Florida

Gulf of Mexico

Bahamas

The Québec Act, passed in June 1774, set up an unrepresentative government in the Canadian colony designed to deal with people of French origin within a British colony. The act placed within Québec Territory land north of the Ohio River long claimed by Connecticut, Virginia, and Pennsylvania.

The Québec Act
1774

- Original province of Québec
- Province of Québec after 1774
- The thirteen colonies and British possessions
- Indian reservation open for settlers of the thirteen colonies 1767–71
- Spanish Louisiana, secretly ceded by France in 1763
- Only French possession after Treaty of Paris, 1763

London and the American colonies increasingly wrangled over measures to raise revenue. Various acts, passed between 1763 and 1765, intended to solve matters had the opposite effect. Secret societies were formed, one being the Sons of Liberty, and demonstrations and riots ensued.

HUDSON'S BAY COMPANY

Lake Superior

Lake Michigan

Lake Huron

St. Lawrence Rivers

Québec

Charlottetown

Nova Scotia

To Mass.

HALIFAX

Q U E B E C

L. Ontario

Lake Erie

New York

New Hampshire

Portsmouth

Mass.

Boston

Conn.

Newport

RI

New Haven

Pennsylvania

New York City

Philadelphia

Burlington

New Jersey

Md.

Annapolis

Delaware

Virginia

Williamsburg

A T L A N T I C
O C E A N

Mississippi River

INDIAN
RESERVE

North Carolina

New Bern

South Carolina

Charles Town

L
O
U
I
S
I
A
N
A

West Florida

Georgia

Savannah

Pensacola

St. Augustine

Florida

Gulf of Mexico

N

Bahama Islands

Discontent in the Colonies on the Eve of War 1764–76

British territory

Army garrison, 1766

HALIFAX   Vice-Admiralty Court, 1764–68

Boston   Additional Vice-Admiralty Court, 1768

New Bern   Colonial capital

Anti-customs riot, 1764–74

Spanish territory

88° 84° C U B A 80° 76° 72° 68°

48° 44° 40° 36° 32° 64° 28° 24°

British military strategy envisioned control of all the southern approaches, East and West Florida, the Bahamas, and the Georgia and South Carolina coastlines. In the north, a chain of army garrisons held a firm grip on the provinces of Québec, Newfoundland, and Nova Scotia.

A major army would be based in New York aimed at controlling the Hudson valley up to Lake Champlain, splitting the fractious New England colonies from any potential support from farther east and south. This pivotal position would give the British maximum control over all the major commercial centers.

HUDSON'S BAY COMPANY

Lake Superior

Lake Michigan

Lake Huron

L. Ontario

Lake Erie

Québec

Q U É B E C

NEWFOUNDLAND

Charlottetown

NOVA SCOTIA

To Mass.

HALIFAX

New Hampshire
Portsmouth

New York

Mass.
Boston

Conn.
Newport

R.I.
New Haven

Pennsylvania

New York City

Philadelphia

Burlington

New Jersey

Md.
Annapolis

Delaware

Virginia

Williamsburg

LOUISIANA

Mississippi River

INDIAN
RESERVE

North
Carolina

New Bern

South
Carolina

Charles Town

Georgia

Savannah

West Florida

Pensacola

St. Augustine

East
Florida

A T L A N T I C   O C E A N

Gulf of Mexico

Bahama Islands

New Providence

CUBA

The British Military Presence in the Colonies
1764–76

British territory

Army garrison, 1766

Army headquarters, 1764

Naval headquarters

HALIFAX Vice-Admiralty Court, 1764–68

Boston Additional Vice-Admiralty Court, 1768

Formal port of entry, 1768

Spanish territory

N

52°
48°
44°
60°
40°
64°
68°
36°
32°
28°
24°

88° 84° 80° 76° 72°

PART SEVEN WAR AND REVOLUTION, 1775–1783

THE BRITISH government mostly ignored the protests and petitions of colonial leaders and legislatures. In America, resentments mounted, and protests became violent. New York City and Boston especially became centers of agitation. On 5 March 1770, a mob of young men in Boston pelted a company of British soldiers with snowballs, and then rocks. The soldiers panicked and fired their muskets into the crowd, killing five. Passions then subsided, as if all recoiled from the immense implications of further violence. But new British measures, and a gradually awakening sense of common cause among colonists, caused new hostilities to flare up. In 1773, after British customs officials threatened to impound a huge shipment of tea in Boston harbor to force payment of an import tax, colonists disguised as Indians rowed out to the ships and dumped the tea overboard.

This crime the British government could not tolerate. It closed Boston harbor to commerce until someone paid for the tea, and dispatched more troops to Boston, who camped in Boston Common to the west of the harbor. On the evening of 18 April 1775, some 700 Redcoats slipped by boat across the Charles River basin and proceeded to march to Lexington, where they hoped to capture Patriot leaders and supplies. At Lexington Common they encountered a contingent of Patriot militia; a skirmish left eight Patriots dead. The British then marched to Concord. Meanwhile, colonial militia and partisans streamed toward the road from Concord to Cambridge. No sooner had the British seized North Bridge, near Concord, than withering fire from the colonists forced their withdrawal. Then ensued a bizarre battle. The British soldiers formed ranks and marched back to Boston while snipers harassed them at every turn. Only the arrival of a column of reinforcements ensured their escape. Now war was on.

Massachusetts, though it confronted the British Empire, immediately took the offensive. Its forces seized Fort Ticonderoga and moved north along Lake Champlain, threatening British positions in Canada. More Massachusetts soldiers took positions around Boston, keeping watch on the British garrison in the city. When a contingent of colonists moved across the Charlestown neck and took positions on Breed's Hill, just to the east of Bunker Hill and overlooking Boston, the British commander, General Thomas Gage, was alarmed. From Breed's Hill, Patriot artillery could blast the British positions in the city.

On 17 June, 2,500 British solders were ferried across the Charles River. They formed ranks and marched up Breed's Hill. Twice they were repulsed, but eventually they overwhelmed the Patriots, who had run out of ammunition. But during the misnamed "Battle of Bunker Hill," the British lost nearly 1,000 men, a staggering number. King George III declared the colonies "in open rebellion." The Continental Congress, containing representatives from most of the colonies, made open preparations for war against Britain. When the colonists learned that the British had hired soldiers from the German state of Hesse and were sending them to fight, the Patriots' nerve hardened. In early July 1776, the Continental Congress declared the "United Colonies" to be "free and independent States, absolved from all allegiance to the British Crown."`

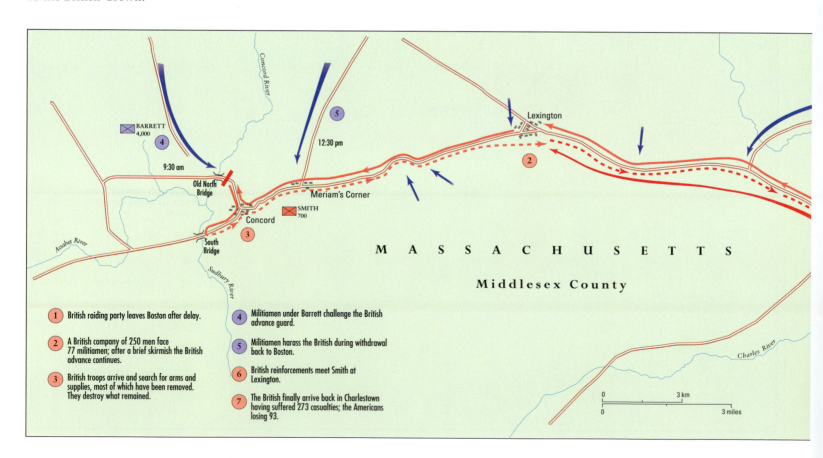

1. British raiding party leaves Boston after delay.

2. A British company of 250 men face 77 militiamen; after a brief skirmish the British advance continues.

3. British troops arrive and search for arms and supplies, most of which have been removed. They destroy what remained.

4. Militiamen under Barrett challenge the British advance guard.

5. Militiamen harass the British during withdrawal back to Boston.

6. British reinforcements meet Smith at Lexington.

7. The British finally arrive back in Charlestown having suffered 273 casualties; the Americans losing 93.

Not everyone agreed. Many people—they became known as Tories and Loyalists—regarded a rupture with Britain as foolish or downright treasonous. Loyalist sentiment was most pronounced in rural New York, especially the large holdings east of the Hudson, in backcountry North Carolina, and among many merchants in New York and even Boston.

Even as Congress was declaring independence, Sir William Howe, who had succeeded Gage as commander of British armies in the Americas, evacuated Boston and struck New York City, hoping to drive a wedge between the "United Colonies." George Washington, commander of the army of the Continental Congress, had anticipated this move and moved to block it. But when the British landed in force on Staten Island, Washington was unprepared. The British won one battle after another, forcing Washington to abandon Long Island and Manhattan. As the British occupied New York City, Washington slipped across the Hudson River to New Jersey and retreated into Pennsylvania. That winter, Washington's men staged several morale-building attacks, including one on Christmas night at Trenton, New Jersey, that led to the surrender of 900 Hessians.

The following spring the British commenced their great campaign to take control of the entire Hudson valley, thereby severing the colonies. Three separate British armies would converge on Albany, forcing its surrender. But this complicated offensive required perfect timing and coordination; in this, the British failed. Colonial armies defeated the first two armies, forcing the surrender of some 5,700 British soldiers at Saratoga, north of Albany; the third army made a halfhearted threat up the Hudson and then turned back. The colonists were elated. This victory prompted King Louis XVI of France to provide vital military support to the Continental Congress.

The British regrouped and headed south, hoping to exploit ties with Loyalists in Charleston and the backcountry of North Carolina. In 1780 Sir Henry Clinton, the new British commander, seized Charleston, capturing more than 3,000 colonists. Throughout that year and into the next, Clinton's forces moved northward, where they were harassed by guerrilla bands and colonial militia led by men such as Francis Marion, the "Swamp Fox," Daniel Morgan, and Nathaniel Greene.

Although the main campaigns focused on the moves of the large British forces along the Atlantic coast, many actions were fought in western Pennsylvania, the frontier of New York, the Ohio valley, and even the remote Indiana Territory.

What ended the war, however, was the fate of the 7,000-man British army in the South. Led by General Cornwallis, the British had taken up a defensive position at Yorktown, on the Chesapeake Bay, expecting to be supplied by sea. But when the French navy, commanded by Admiral François de Grasse, drove off the British relief squadron, Cornwallis's army was doomed. Its surrender, on 17 October 1781, effectively ended hostilities. The Treaty of Paris confirmed the independence of the American colonies.

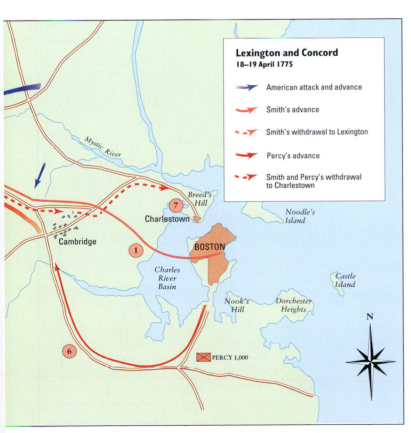

Lexington and Concord
18–19 April 1775

→ American attack and advance
→ Smith's advance
-→ Smith's withdrawal to Lexington
→ Percy's advance
-→ Smith and Percy's withdrawal to Charlestown

MAPS

Boston June 1775

American lines

British lines

By 10 May, British-held Boston was under siege by the Massachusetts militia. Later the militia would be joined by the American forces who captured Fort Ticonderoga that same day—dragging 60 captured cannons overland to reinforce the siege lines around Boston. The Americans also began to fortify Breed's Hill, overlooking the towns of Charlestown and Boston. Meanwhile British reinforcements arrived.

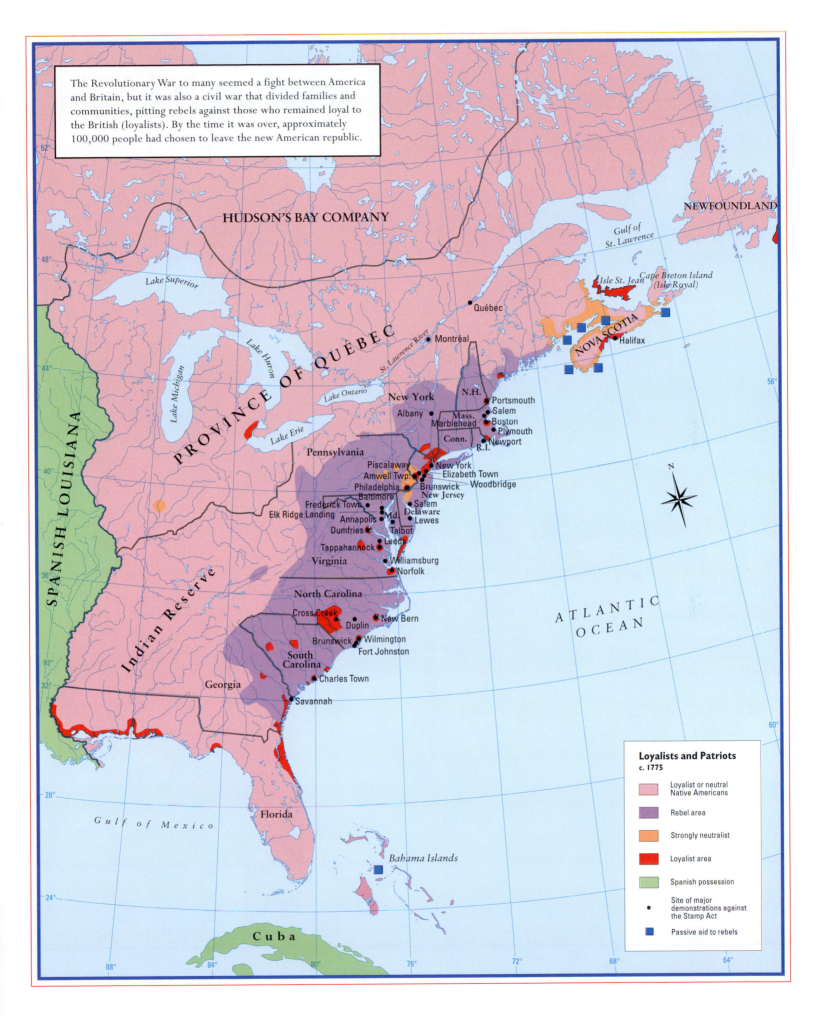

The Revolutionary War to many seemed a fight between America and Britain, but it was also a civil war that divided families and communities, pitting rebels against those who remained loyal to the British (loyalists). By the time it was over, approximately 100,000 people had chosen to leave the new American republic.

HUDSON'S BAY COMPANY

NEWFOUNDLAND

Gulf of St. Lawrence

Lake Superior

Québec

Isle St. Jean   Cape Breton Island (Isle Royal)

Lake Huron

Montréal

St. Lawrence River

NOVA SCOTIA

Halifax

PROVINCE OF QUÉBEC

Lake Michigan

Lake Ontario

Lake Erie

New York   N.H.

Albany   Portsmouth
Salem
Mass.   Boston
Marblehead   Plymouth
Conn.   Newport
R.I.

Pennsylvania

Piscataway   New York
Amwell Twp.   Elizabeth Town
Philadelphia   Brunswick   Woodbridge
Baltimore   New Jersey
Frederick Town   Salem
Elk Ridge Landing   Delaware
Annapolis   Md.   Lewes
Dumfries   Talbot
Leeds
Tappahannock   Williamsburg
Virginia   Norfolk

SPANISH LOUISIANA

North Carolina

Cross Creek   New Bern
Duplin
Brunswick   Wilmington
Fort Johnston
South Carolina

Georgia   Charles Town

Savannah

Indian Reserve

ATLANTIC OCEAN

N

Gulf of Mexico

Florida

Bahama Islands

C u b a

Loyalists and Patriots
c. 1775

Loyalist or neutral Native Americans

Rebel area

Strongly neutralist

Loyalist area

Spanish possession

• Site of major demonstrations against the Stamp Act

■ Passive aid to rebels

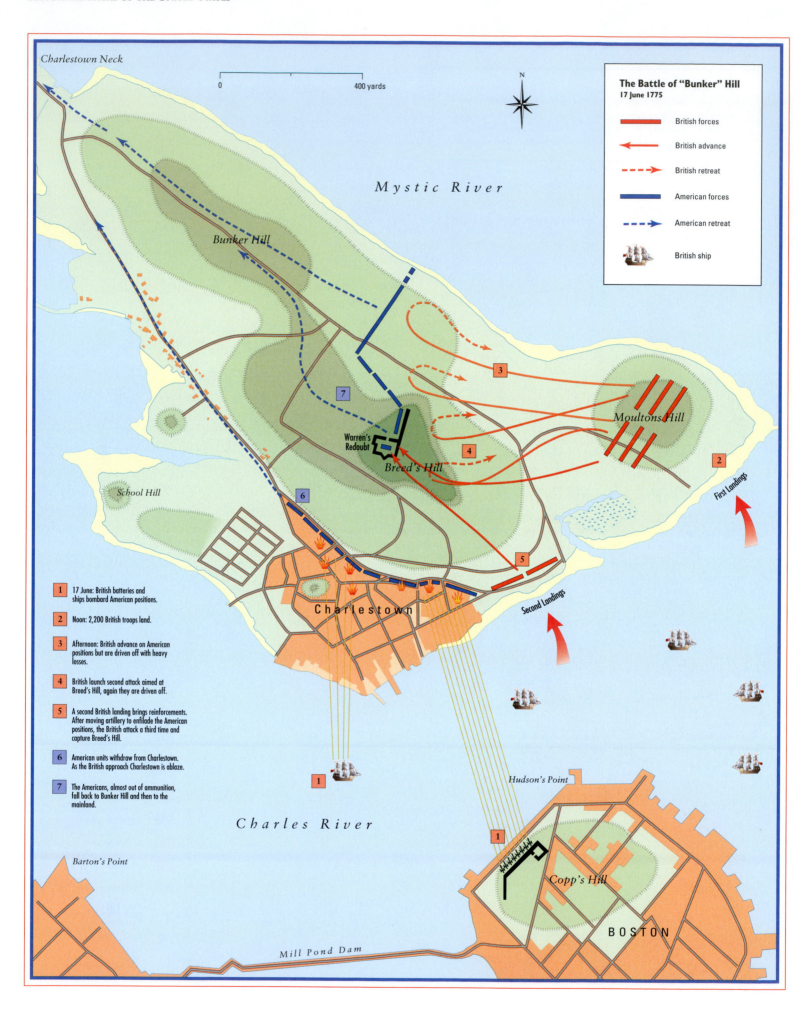

The Battle of "Bunker" Hill
17 June 1775

British forces
British advance
British retreat
American forces
American retreat
British ship

Charlestown Neck

0   400 yards

Mystic River

Bunker Hill

7

Moultons Hill

Warren's Redoubt

3

4

Breed's Hill

2

School Hill

First Landings

6

5

Charlestown

Second Landings

1 17 June: British batteries and ships bombard American positions.

2 Noon: 2,200 British troops land.

3 Afternoon: British advance on American positions but are driven off with heavy losses.

4 British launch second attack aimed at Breed's Hill, again they are driven off.

5 A second British landing brings reinforcements. After moving artillery to enfilade the American positions, the British attack a third time and capture Breed's Hill.

6 American units withdraw from Charlestown. As the British approach Charlestown is ablaze.

7 The Americans, almost out of ammunition, fall back to Bunker Hill and then to the mainland.

Charles River

Hudson's Point

1

Barton's Point

1

Copp's Hill

BOSTON

Mill Pond Dam

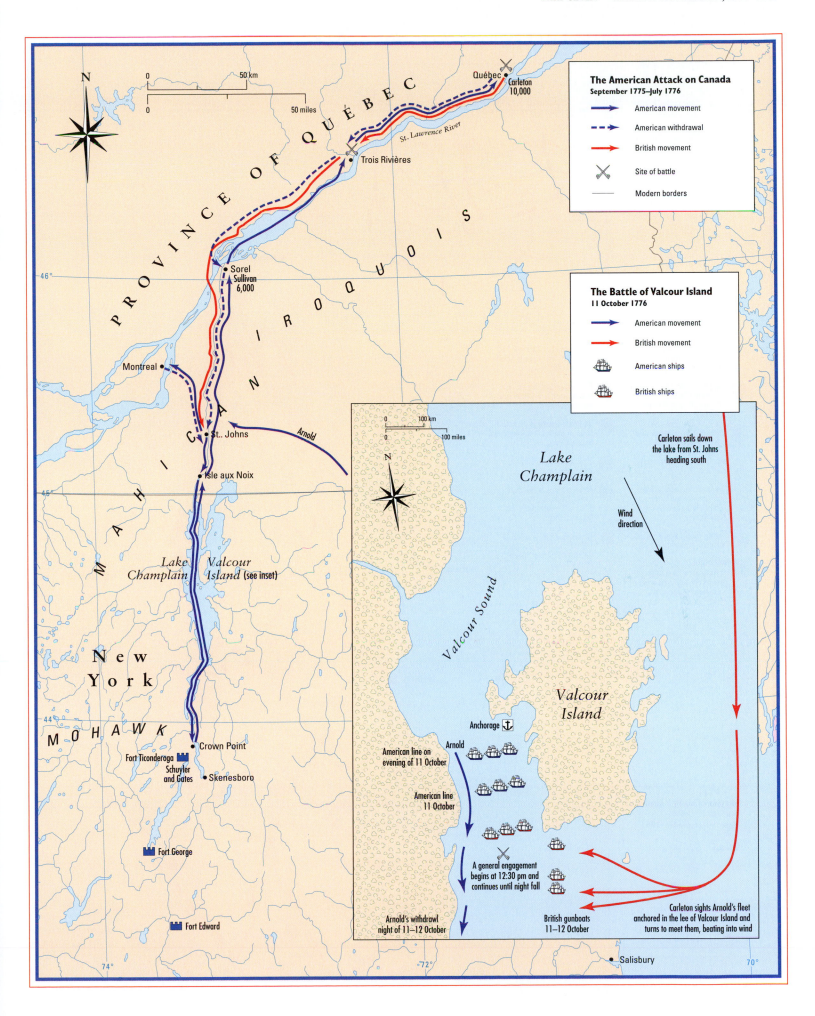

The American Attack on Canada
September 1775–July 1776

→ American movement

⇢ American withdrawal

→ British movement

✕ Site of battle

— Modern borders

The Battle of Valcour Island
11 October 1776

→ American movement

→ British movement

🚢 American ships

🚢 British ships

0   100 km
0   100 miles

Lake Champlain

Carleton sails down the lake from St. Johns heading south

Wind direction

Valcour Sound

Valcour Island

Anchorage ⚓

Arnold

American line on evening of 11 October

American line 11 October

A general engagement begins at 12:30 pm and continues until night fall

Arnold's withdrawl night of 11–12 October

British gunboats 11–12 October

Carleton sights Arnold's fleet anchored in the lee of Valcour Island and turns to meet them, beating into wind

Salisbury

0   50 km
0   50 miles

N

P R O V I N C E   O F   Q U É B E C

Québec ✕

Carleton 10,000

St. Lawrence River

Trois Rivières

Sorel
Sullivan 6,000

Montreal

St.. Johns

Arnold

Isle aux Noix

Lake Champlain

Valcour Island (see inset)

M A H I C A N

I R O Q U O I S

New York

M O H A W K

Crown Point

Fort Ticonderoga
Schuyler and Gates

Skenesboro

Fort George

Fort Edward

46°

45°

44°

74°   72°   70°

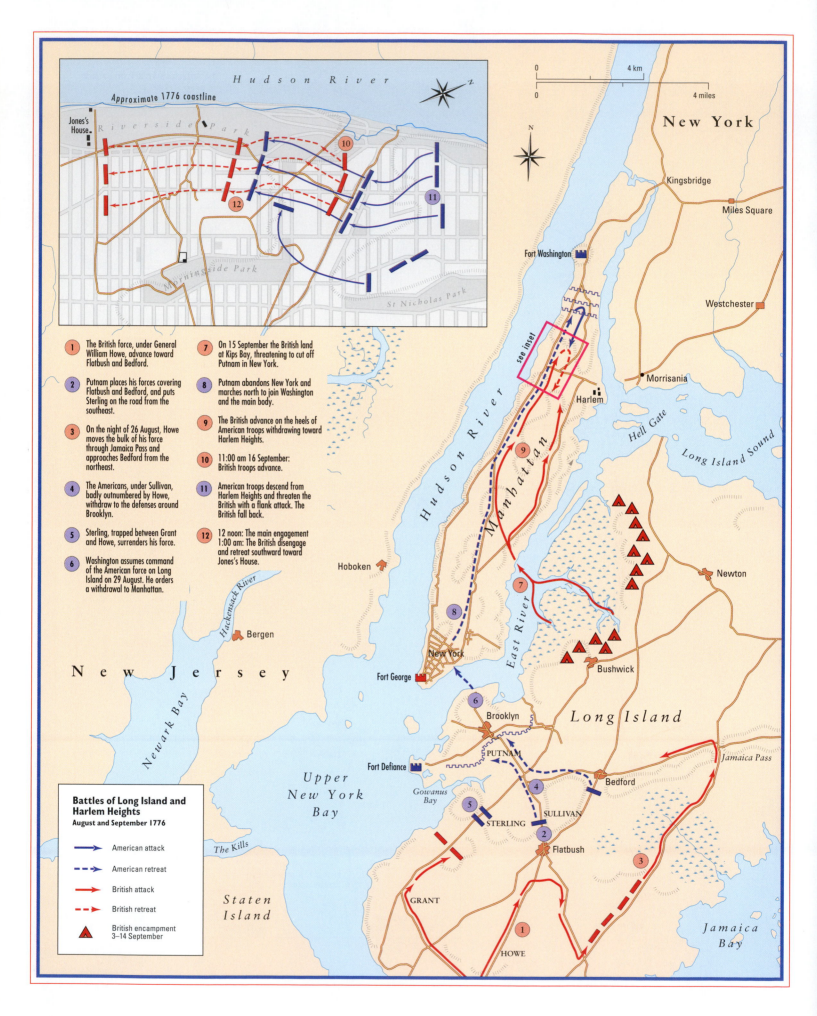

1 The British force, under General William Howe, advance toward Flatbush and Bedford.

2 Putnam places his forces covering Flatbush and Bedford, and puts Sterling on the road from the southeast.

3 On the night of 26 August, Howe moves the bulk of his force through Jamaica Pass and approaches Bedford from the northeast.

4 The Americans, under Sullivan, badly outnumbered by Howe, withdraw to the defenses around Brooklyn.

5 Sterling, trapped between Grant and Howe, surrenders his force.

6 Washington assumes command of the American force on Long Island on 29 August. He orders a withdrawal to Manhattan.

7 On 15 September the British land at Kips Bay, threatening to cut off Putnam in New York.

8 Putnam abandons New York and marches north to join Washington and the main body.

9 The British advance on the heels of American troops withdrawing toward Harlem Heights.

10 11:00 am 16 September: British troops advance.

11 American troops descend from Harlem Heights and threaten the British with a flank attack. The British fall back.

12 12 noon: The main engagement 1:00 am: The British disengage and retreat southward toward Jones's House.

Battles of Long Island and Harlem Heights
August and September 1776

→ American attack
⇢ American retreat
→ British attack
⇢ British retreat
▲ British encampment 3–14 September

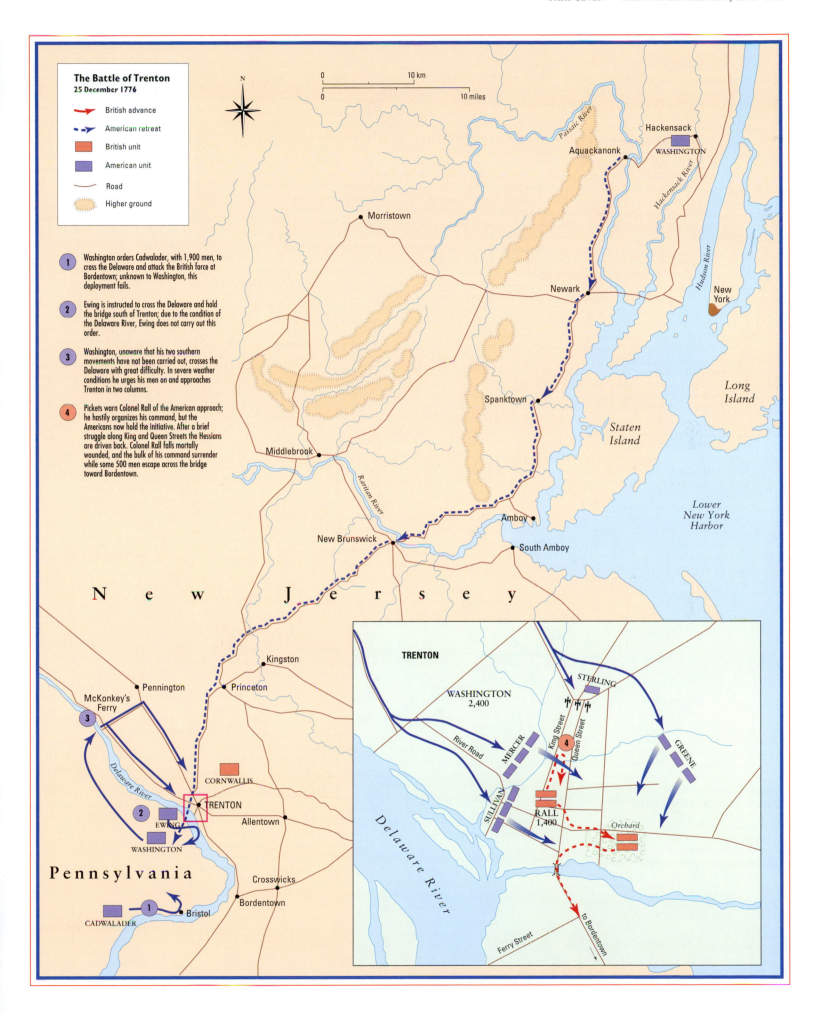

The Battle of Trenton
25 December 1776

- ➤ British advance
- ➤ American retreat
- 🟧 British unit
- 🟪 American unit
- ⟋ Road
- Higher ground

1 Washington orders Cadwalader, with 1,900 men, to cross the Delaware and attack the British force at Bordentown; unknown to Washington, this deployment fails.

2 Ewing is instructed to cross the Delaware and hold the bridge south of Trenton; due to the condition of the Delaware River, Ewing does not carry out this order.

3 Washington, unaware that his two southern movements have not been carried out, crosses the Delaware with great difficulty. In severe weather conditions he urges his men on and approaches Trenton in two columns.

4 Pickets warn Colonel Rall of the American approach; he hastily organizes his command, but the Americans now hold the initiative. After a brief struggle along King and Queen Streets the Hessians are driven back. Colonel Rall falls mortally wounded, and the bulk of his command surrender while some 500 men escape across the bridge toward Bordentown.

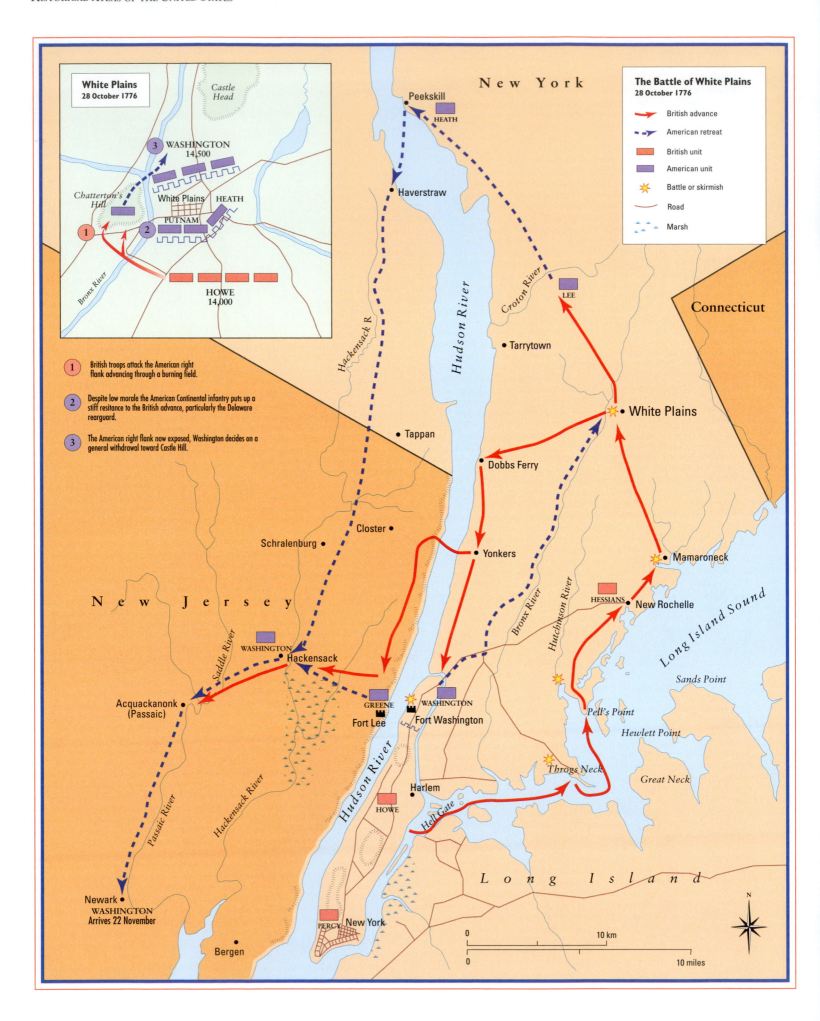

White Plains
28 October 1776

Castle
Head

3 WASHINGTON
14,500

*Chatterton's
Hill*

White Plains   HEATH

PUTNAM

1   2

HOWE
14,000

Bronx River

The Battle of White Plains
28 October 1776

→ British advance

⇠ American retreat

British unit

American unit

✷ Battle or skirmish

Road

Marsh

1 British troops attack the American right
flank advancing through a burning field.

2 Despite low morale the American Continental infantry puts up a
stiff resistance to the British advance, particularly the Delaware
rearguard.

3 The American right flank now exposed, Washington decides on a
general withdrawal toward Castle Hill.

New York

Peekskill
HEATH

Connecticut

Haverstraw

Croton River

LEE

Hackensack R.

Tarrytown

Hudson River

Tappan

Dobbs Ferry

White Plains

Closter

Schralenburg

Yonkers

Mamaroneck

New Jersey

Bronx River

Hutchinson River

HESSIANS

New Rochelle

Long Island Sound

Saddle River

WASHINGTON

Hackensack

Sands Point

Acquackanonk
(Passaic)

GREENE

WASHINGTON

Pell's Point

Hewlett Point

Fort Lee

Fort Washington

Hackensack River

Throgs Neck

Great Neck

Harlem

Hell Gate

HOWE

Passaic River

Newark
WASHINGTON
Arrives 22 November

Long Island

PERCY   New York

Hudson River

Bergen

N

0   10 km

0   10 miles

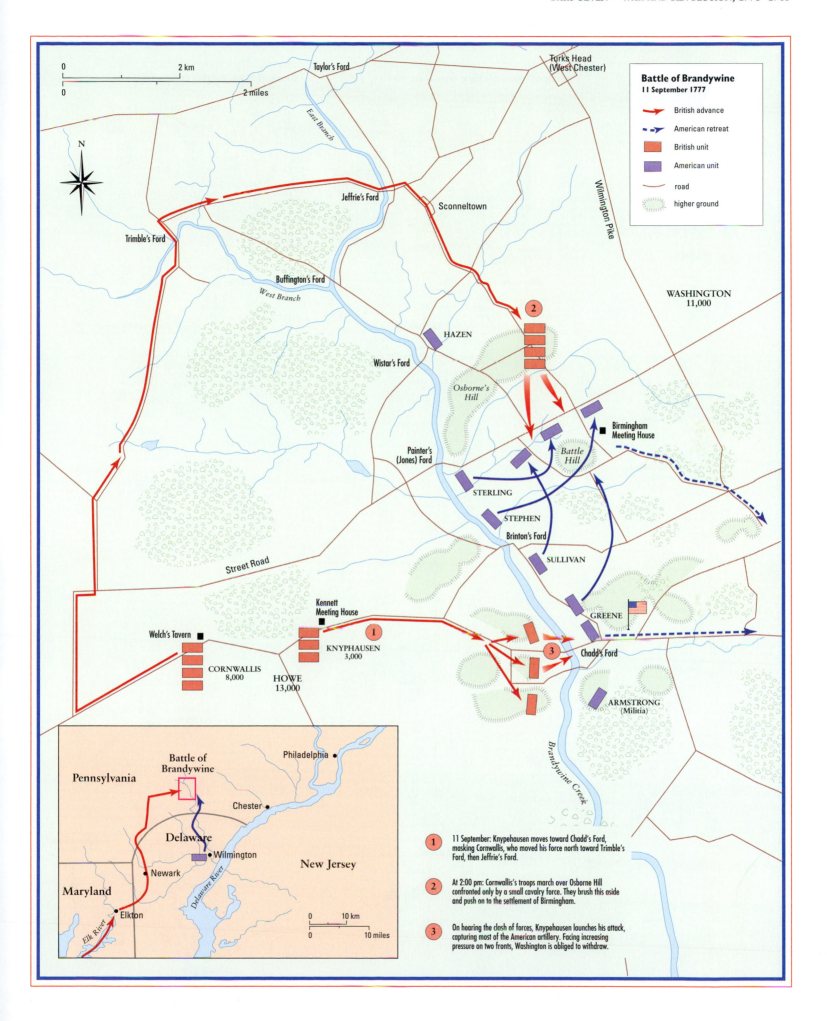

Battle of Brandywine
11 September 1777

- British advance
- American retreat
- British unit
- American unit
- road
- higher ground

0   2 km
0   2 miles

N

WASHINGTON
11,000

Taylor's Ford

East Branch

Turk's Head
(West Chester)

Jeffrie's Ford

Sconneltown

Wilmington Pike

Trimble's Ford

Buffington's Ford

West Branch

HAZEN

Wistar's Ford

Osborne's Hill

2

Birmingham
Meeting House

Battle Hill

Painter's
(Jones) Ford

STERLING

STEPHEN

Brinton's Ford

SULLIVAN

GREENE

Street Road

Kennett
Meeting House

KNYPHAUSEN
3,000

1

3

Chadd's Ford

Welch's Tavern

CORNWALLIS
8,000

HOWE
13,000

ARMSTRONG
(Militia)

Brandywine Creek

Inset map:

Pennsylvania

Battle of
Brandywine

Philadelphia

Chester

Delaware

Wilmington

New Jersey

Delaware River

Maryland

Newark

Elkton

Elk River

0   10 km
0   10 miles

1 11 September: Knypehausen moves toward Chadd's Ford, masking Cornwallis, who moved his force north toward Trimble's Ford, then Jeffrie's Ford.

2 At 2:00 pm: Cornwallis's troops march over Osborne Hill confronted only by a small cavalry force. They brush this aside and push on to the settlement of Birmingham.

3 On hearing the clash of forces, Knypehausen launches his attack, capturing most of the American artillery. Facing increasing pressure on two fronts, Washington is obliged to withdraw.

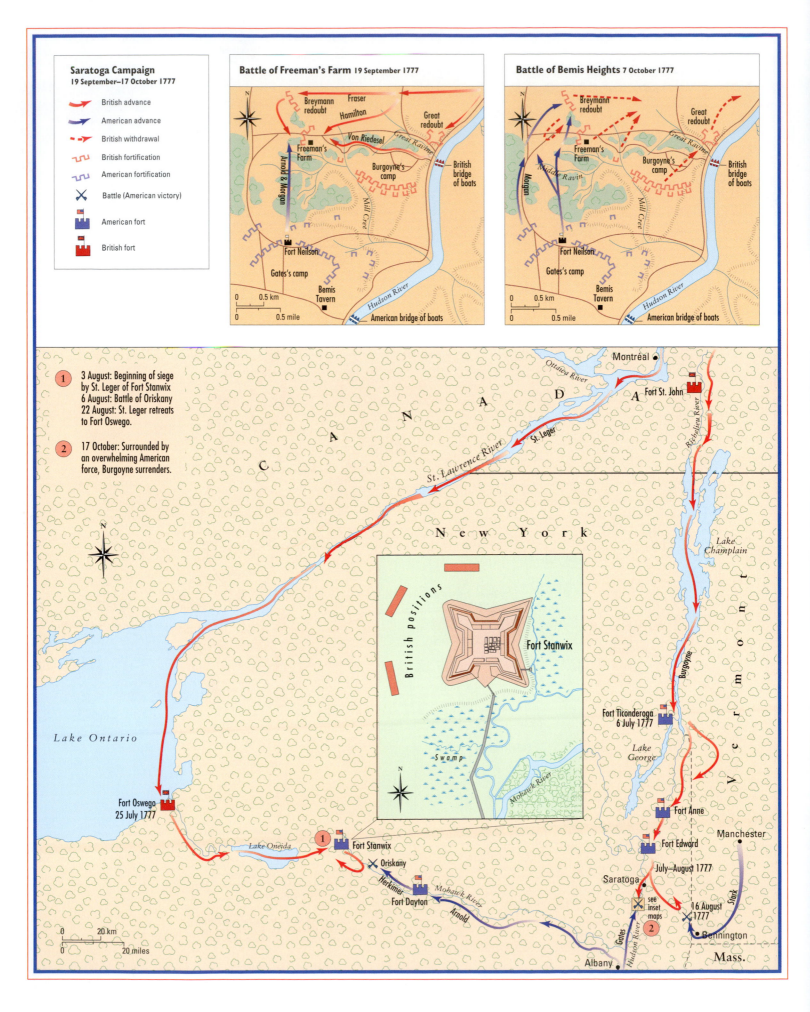

Saratoga Campaign
19 September–17 October 1777

- British advance
- American advance
- British withdrawal
- British fortification
- American fortification
- Battle (American victory)
- American fort
- British fort

Battle of Freeman's Farm 19 September 1777

N

Breymann redoubt
Fraser
Hamilton
Freeman's Farm
Von Riedesel
Great redoubt
Great Ravine
Arnold & Morgan
Burgoyne's camp
British bridge of boats
Mill Creek
Fort Neilson
Gates's camp
Bemis Tavern
Hudson River
0   0.5 km
0   0.5 mile
American bridge of boats

Battle of Bemis Heights 7 October 1777

N

Breymann redoubt
Freeman's Farm
Great redoubt
Great Ravine
Morgan
Middle Ravine
Burgoyne's camp
British bridge of boats
Mill Creek
Fort Neilson
Gates's camp
Bemis Tavern
Hudson River
0   0.5 km
0   0.5 mile
American bridge of boats

1 3 August: Beginning of siege by St. Leger of Fort Stanwix
6 August: Battle of Oriskany
22 August: St. Leger retreats to Fort Oswego.

2 17 October: Surrounded by an overwhelming American force, Burgoyne surrenders.

Montréal
Ottawa River
Fort St. John
Richelieu River
St. Leger
St. Lawrence River

C A N A D A

N E W   Y O R K

Lake Champlain

British positions

Fort Stanwix

Swamp
Mohawk River

V e r m o n t

Lake Ontario

Fort Ticonderoga
6 July 1777
Lake George
Burgoyne

Fort Oswego
25 July 1777

Fort Anne

Manchester

1 Fort Stanwix
Lake Oneida
Oriskany
Herkimer
Fort Dayton
Mohawk River
Arnold

Fort Edward
July–August 1777

Saratoga
Gates
see inset maps
2
16 August 1777
Stark

Bennington

Albany
Hudson River

Mass.

0   20 km
0   20 miles

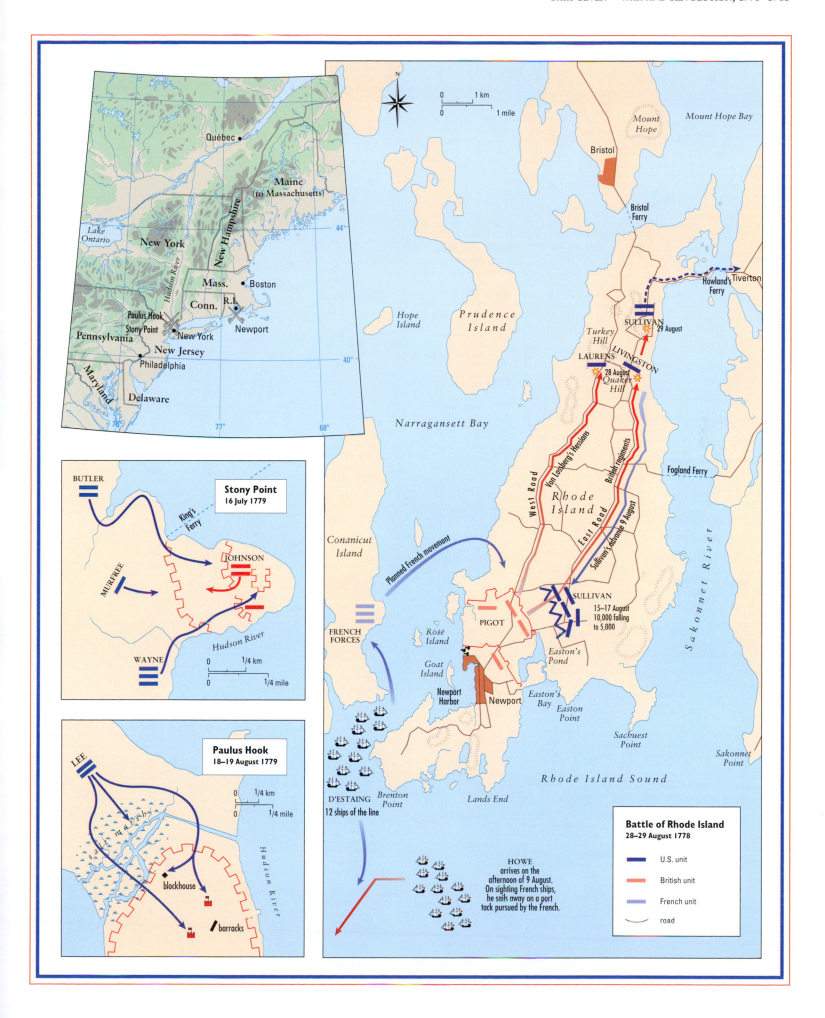

Stony Point
16 July 1779

BUTLER

King's Ferry

MURFREE

JOHNSON

WAYNE

Hudson River

0   1/4 km
0   1/4 mile

Paulus Hook
18–19 August 1779

LEE

salt marsh

blockhouse

barracks

Hudson River

0   1/4 km
0   1/4 mile

Québec

Lake Ontario

New York

New Hampshire

Maine (to Massachusetts)

Hudson River

Mass.   Boston

Conn.   R.I.

Paulus Hook
Stony Point
New York   Newport

Pennsylvania

New Jersey

Philadelphia

Maryland

Delaware

44°

40°

76°   72°   68°

N

0   1 km
0   1 mile

Mount Hope Bay

Mount Hope

Bristol

Bristol Ferry

Howland's Ferry   Tiverton

Hope Island

Prudence Island

Turkey Hill

SULLIVAN   29 August

LAURENS   LIVINGSTON

28 August
Quaker Hill

Narragansett Bay

Van Loosberg's Hessians

British regiments

West Road

Rhode Island

East Road

Sullivan's advance 9 August

Fogland Ferry

Sakonnet River

Conanicut Island

Planned French movement

FRENCH FORCES

Rose Island

PIGOT

SULLIVAN   15–17 August
10,000 falling to 5,000

Goat Island

Newport Harbor   Newport

Easton's Pond

Easton's Bay

Easton Point

Sachuest Point

Sakonnet Point

Rhode Island Sound

Brenton Point

Lands End

D'ESTAING
12 ships of the line

HOWE
arrives on the afternoon of 9 August. On sighting French ships, he sails away on a port tack pursued by the French.

Battle of Rhode Island
28–29 August 1778

U.S. unit
British unit
French unit
road

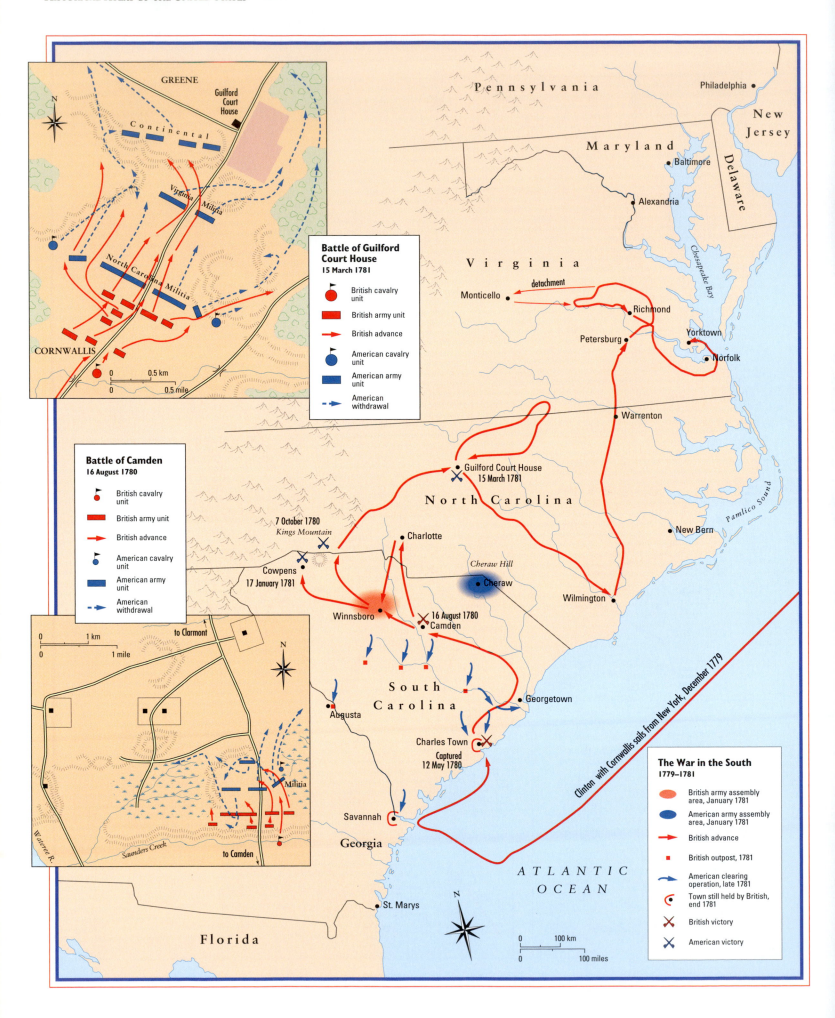

Battle of Guilford Court House
15 March 1781

- ● British cavalry unit
- ▬ British army unit
- → British advance
- ⚑ American cavalry unit
- ▬ American army unit
- ⇢ American withdrawal

Battle of Camden
16 August 1780

- ● British cavalry unit
- ▬ British army unit
- → British advance
- ● American cavalry unit
- ▬ American army unit
- ⇢ American withdrawal

The War in the South
1779–1781

- British army assembly area, January 1781
- American army assembly area, January 1781
- → British advance
- ■ British outpost, 1781
- → American clearing operation, late 1781
- ◖ Town still held by British, end 1781
- ✕ British victory
- ✕ American victory

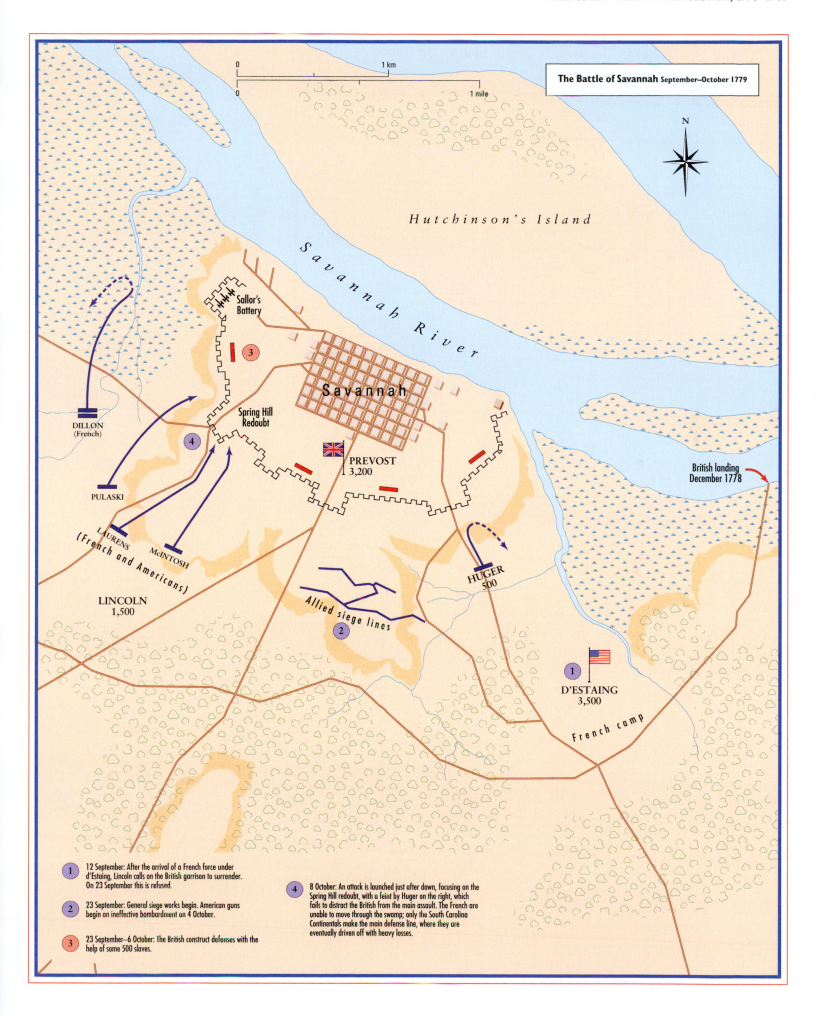

The Battle of Savannah September–October 1779

Hutchinson's Island

Savannah River

Sallor's Battery

Savannah

3

4

Spring Hill Redoubt

PREVOST 3,200

DILLON (French)

PULASKI

LAURENS (French and Americans)

McINTOSH

LINCOLN 1,500

Allied siege lines

2

HUGER 500

British landing December 1778

1

D'ESTAING 3,500

French camp

1. 12 September: After the arrival of a French force under d'Estaing, Lincoln calls on the British garrison to surrender. On 23 September this is refused.

2. 23 September: General siege works begin. American guns begin an ineffective bombardment on 4 October.

3. 23 September–6 October: The British construct defenses with the help of some 500 slaves.

4. 8 October: An attack is launched just after dawn, focusing on the Spring Hill redoubt, with a feint by Huger on the right, which fails to distract the British from the main assault. The French are unable to move through the swamp; only the South Carolina Continentals make the main defense line, where they are eventually driven off with heavy losses.

The Battle of Chesapeake Bay
5 September 1781

- French ship
- French advance
- British ship
- British advance

wind direction

From New York

flagship
London
Admiral Graves

Main body and
rear becalmed

Chesapeake Bay

Lynnhaven Bay

Cape Henry

flagship
Ville de Paris
Admiral de Grasse

0   10 km
0   10 miles

Chester

Wilmington

New Castle

Elkton

P e n n s y l v a n i a

Susquehanna River

Delaware River

N e w   J e r s e y

Baltimore

M a r y l a n d

Dover

Delaware Bay

Cape May

Cape Henlopen

Annapolis

Alexandria

Mount Vernon

*Eastern
Bay*

Delaware

Indian River Inlet

Nanticoke River

Remington

Port Tobacco

Potomac River

Tangier Sound

Assateague Island

Fredericksburg

Bowling Green

Rappahannock River

Hanover

*Tangier
Island*

*Pocomoke
Sound*

Chesapeake Bay

Richmond

V i r g i n i a

Hood en route to New York
(14 ships of the line)

*Parramore
Island*

**A T L A N T I C
O C E A N**

Hog Island

Petersburg

Williamsburg

York River

Yorktown

LAFAYETTE   CORNWALLIS

WASHINGTON

ROCHAMBEAU

James River

*Smith
Island*

Cape Charles

30 August de Grasse arrives
(28 ships of the line)

Cape Henry

Portsmouth   Norfolk

Virginia Beach

Chesapeake

0   50 km
0   50 miles

Chesapeake Bay
1781

- American movement
- British movement
- French army
- British army

In the siege of Yorktown on 28 September 1781, General Washington, with 9,000 Americans and 7,800 well-equipped French regulars, faced Cornwallis's 8,000 troops. The British prepared their defenses to receive fire from the new French Gribeauval artillery, with its great accuracy, mobility, and punch. Washington also sent a force under de Choissey to Gloucester Point to observe Tarleton's 700 men positioned there. Cornwallis believed that reinforcements would relieve his troops and preferred to give up his outer fortifications than fight. On 14 October, as Franco-American forces advanced parallel trenches, they successfully stormed two defensive positions, extending to the American second parallel. The British counterattacked (16 October) under General Abercromby, took a few prisoners, and destroyed six guns, but this action was ineffective. Cornwallis was faced with the destruction of his fortifications, smallpox, and heavy casualties. A plan to evacuate some troops to Gloucester Point came to naught when his boats were scattered in a storm. Surrounded, outgunned, and short of food and ammunition,

Cornwallis surrendered his 8,000 men and 240 guns on 19 October 1781. Five days later, Clinton arrived at the Chesapeake with 7,000 British reinforcements, but the presence of de Grasse's fleet sent him back to New York. Meanwhile, Cornwallis and his troops marched out of Yorktown to the tune of "The World Turned Upside Down" and were imprisoned in the Virginia interior. Washington then returned to New York.

On 27 February 1782, after the defeat at Yorktown, the British House of Commons voted against continuing the war.

The Treaty of Paris was eventually signed on 3 September 1783. This recognized the independence of the United States, with a western border resting on the Mississippi. The northern and southern borders left problems that would have to be sorted out at a later date. Meanwhile, Florida went to the Spanish crown; in the north Britain held on to territories claimed by the United States.

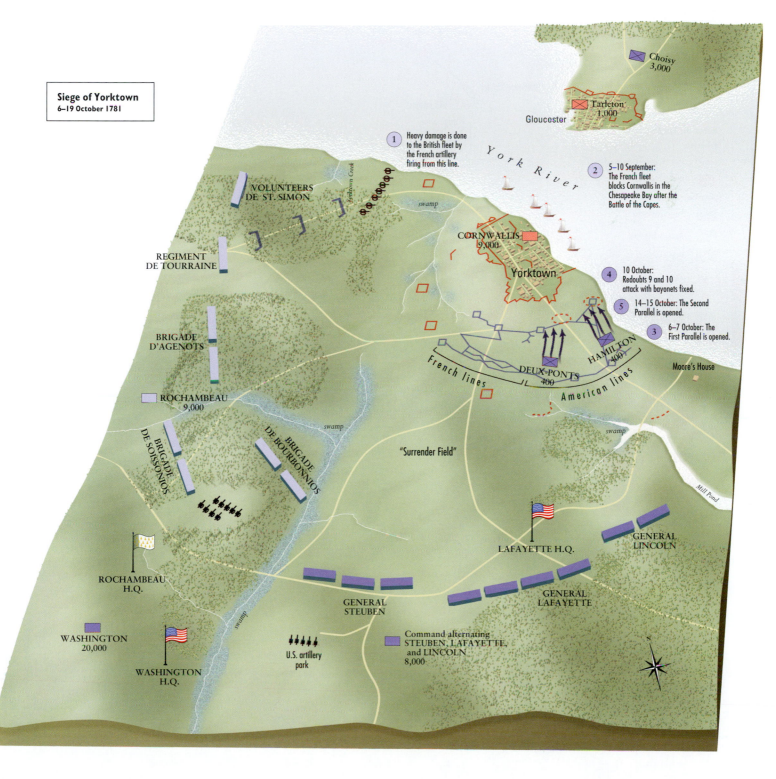

Siege of Yorktown
6–19 October 1781

1 Heavy damage is done to the British fleet by the French artillery firing from this line.

2 5–10 September: The French fleet blocks Cornwallis in the Chesapeake Bay after the Battle of the Capes.

4 10 October: Redoubts 9 and 10 attack with bayonets fixed.

5 14–15 October: The Second Parallel is opened.

3 6–7 October: The First Parallel is opened.

Choisy 3,000

Tarleton 1,000

Gloucester

York River

CORNWALLIS 9,000

Yorktown

Moore's House

VOLUNTEERS DE ST. SIMON

REGIMENT DE TOURRAINE

BRIGADE D'AGENOTS

ROCHAMBEAU 9,000

BRIGADE DE SOISSONIOS

BRIGADE DE BOURBONNIOS

HAMILTON 400

DEUX-PONTS 400

French lines

American lines

"Surrender Field"

Mill Pond

ROCHAMBEAU H.Q.

WASHINGTON 20,000

WASHINGTON H.Q.

U.S. artillery park

GENERAL STEUBEN

Command alternating STEUBEN, LAFAYETTE, and LINCOLN 8,000

LAFAYETTE H.Q.

GENERAL LAFAYETTE

GENERAL LINCOLN

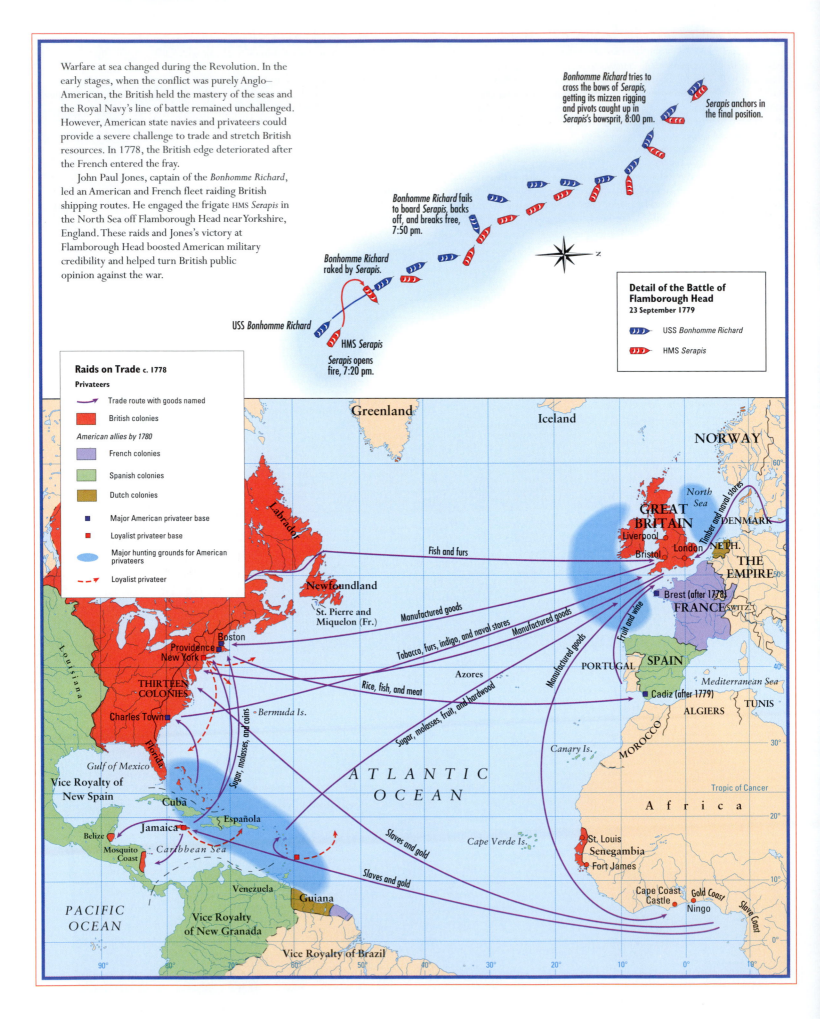

Warfare at sea changed during the Revolution. In the early stages, when the conflict was purely Anglo–American, the British held the mastery of the seas and the Royal Navy's line of battle remained unchallenged. However, American state navies and privateers could provide a severe challenge to trade and stretch British resources. In 1778, the British edge deteriorated after the French entered the fray.

John Paul Jones, captain of the *Bonhomme Richard*, led an American and French fleet raiding British shipping routes. He engaged the frigate HMS *Serapis* in the North Sea off Flamborough Head near Yorkshire, England. These raids and Jones's victory at Flamborough Head boosted American military credibility and helped turn British public opinion against the war.

Bonhomme Richard tries to cross the bows of *Serapis*, getting its mizzen rigging and pivots caught up in *Serapis's* bowsprit, 8:00 pm.

Serapis anchors in the final position.

Bonhomme Richard fails to board *Serapis*, backs off, and breaks free, 7:50 pm.

Bonhomme Richard raked by *Serapis*.

USS *Bonhomme Richard*

HMS *Serapis*

Serapis opens fire, 7:20 pm.

Detail of the Battle of Flamborough Head
23 September 1779

USS *Bonhomme Richard*

HMS *Serapis*

Raids on Trade c. 1778

Privateers

Trade route with goods named

British colonies

American allies by 1780

French colonies

Spanish colonies

Dutch colonies

Major American privateer base

Loyalist privateer base

Major hunting grounds for American privateers

Loyalist privateer

Greenland

Iceland

NORWAY

North Sea

GREAT BRITAIN

Liverpool

London   DENMARK

Bristol   NETH.

THE EMPIRE

FRANCE   SWITZ.

Labrador

Newfoundland

St. Pierre and Miquelon (Fr.)

Fish and furs

Timber and naval stores

Brest (after 1778)

Fruit and wine

Manufactured goods

Manufactured goods

Manufactured goods

Manufactured goods

Tobacco, furs, indigo, and naval stores

PORTUGAL   SPAIN

Azores

Mediterranean Sea

Providence

Boston

New York

Rice, fish, and meat

Cadiz (after 1779)

TUNIS

ALGIERS

THIRTEEN COLONIES

Louisiana

Charles Town

Bermuda Is.

Sugar, molasses, fruit, and hardwood

MOROCCO

Canary Is.

Florida

Sugar, molasses, and coins

Gulf of Mexico

Vice Royalty of New Spain

Cuba

Española

ATLANTIC OCEAN

Tropic of Cancer

Africa

Jamaica

Belize

Mosquito Coast

Caribbean Sea

Slaves and gold

Cape Verde Is.

St. Louis

Senegambia

Fort James

Slaves and gold

Venezuela

PACIFIC OCEAN

Guiana

Vice Royalty of New Granada

Vice Royalty of Brazil

Cape Coast Castle

Ningo

Gold Coast

Slave Coast

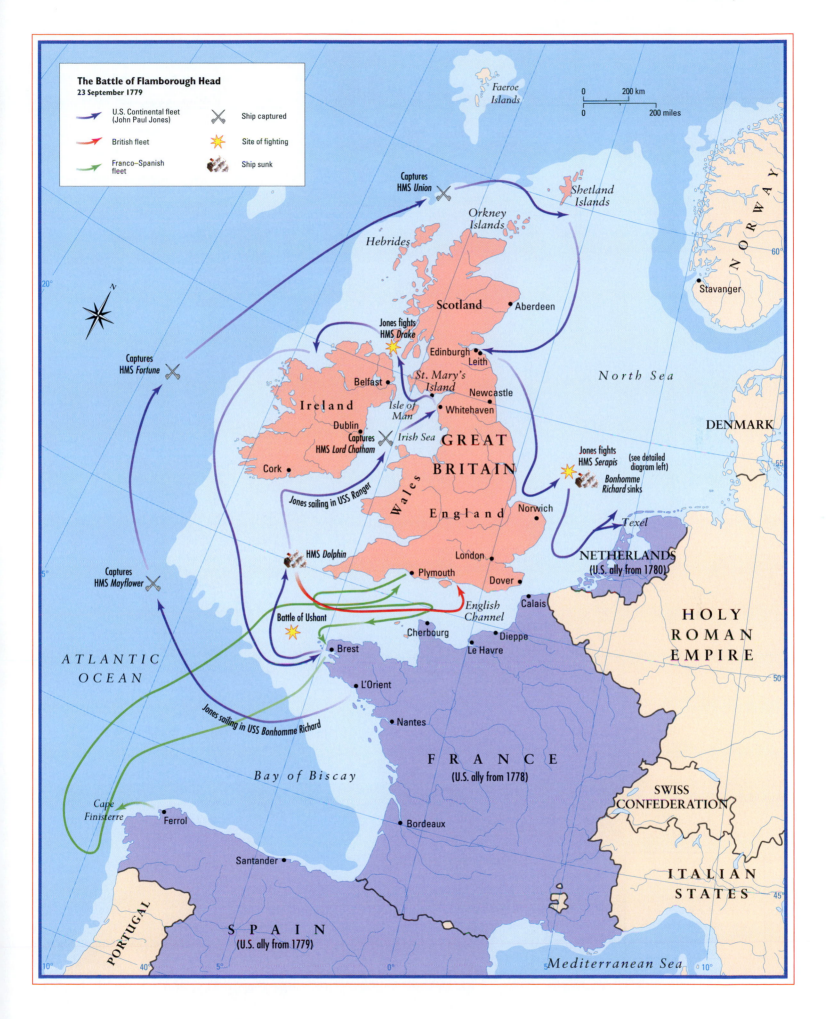

The Battle of Flamborough Head
23 September 1779

- U.S. Continental fleet (John Paul Jones)
- British fleet
- Franco–Spanish fleet
- ✕ Ship captured
- ✦ Site of fighting
- Ship sunk

0   200 km
0   200 miles

Faeroe Islands

Shetland Islands

Orkney Islands

Hebrides

Scotland
- Aberdeen

N O R W A Y

- Stavanger

Captures HMS *Union* ✕

Jones fights HMS *Drake* ✦

- Edinburgh
- Leith

St. Mary's Island

North Sea

Captures HMS *Fortune* ✕

- Belfast

Isle of Man

- Newcastle
- Whitehaven

Ireland

- Dublin

Captures HMS *Lord Chatham* ✕

Irish Sea

GREAT BRITAIN

DENMARK

- Cork

Wales

Jones fights HMS *Serapis* ✦ (see detailed diagram left)

Bonhomme Richard sinks

England

- Norwich

Jones sailing in USS *Ranger*

HMS *Dolphin*

- London

Texel

Captures HMS *Mayflower* ✕

- Plymouth

- Dover

- Calais

NETHERLANDS (U.S. ally from 1780)

A T L A N T I C O C E A N

Battle of Ushant ✦

English Channel

- Cherbourg
- Dieppe
- Le Havre

H O L Y R O M A N E M P I R E

- Brest

Jones sailing in USS *Bonhomme Richard*

- L'Orient

- Nantes

F R A N C E
(U.S. ally from 1778)

- Bordeaux

SWISS CONFEDERATION

Bay of Biscay

Cape Finisterre

- Ferrol

PORTUGAL

- Santander

S P A I N
(U.S. ally from 1779)

I T A L I A N S T A T E S

Mediterranean Sea

North America c. 1780

- British territory
- Spanish territory
- Disputed by Spain and Great Britain
- Disputed by Spain, Great Britain, and Russia
- Russian Empire
- French possessions

0   200 km
0   200 miles

RUSSIAN EMPIRE

Alaska

Northwest Territories

Vancouver I.

Hudson Bay

Rupert's Land (Hudson's Bay Company)

Newfoundland

Nova Scotia

Québec

Montréal

York

Detroit

Fort St. Joseph

Thirteen Colonies

Boston

New York

Philadelphia

Williamsburg

New Bern

Charles Town

Savannah

St. Augustine

San Francisco

N e w   S p a i n

L o u i s i a n a

St. Louis

Louisville

New Madrid

Nashville

Los Angeles

San Diego

Santa Fe

Tucson

El Paso

Nacogdoches

Fort Panmure

Fort Bute

New Orleans

Fort Charlotte

Pensacola

Monterey

PACIFIC OCEAN

Gulf of Mexico

ATLANTIC OCEAN

Bahama Islands

Tropic of Cancer

N

Léon

Guadalajara

MEXICO CITY

Havana

Cuba

Despite the fact that some of Britain's colonies were in revolt, on the map it seemed that Britain and Spain were the inheritors of North America.

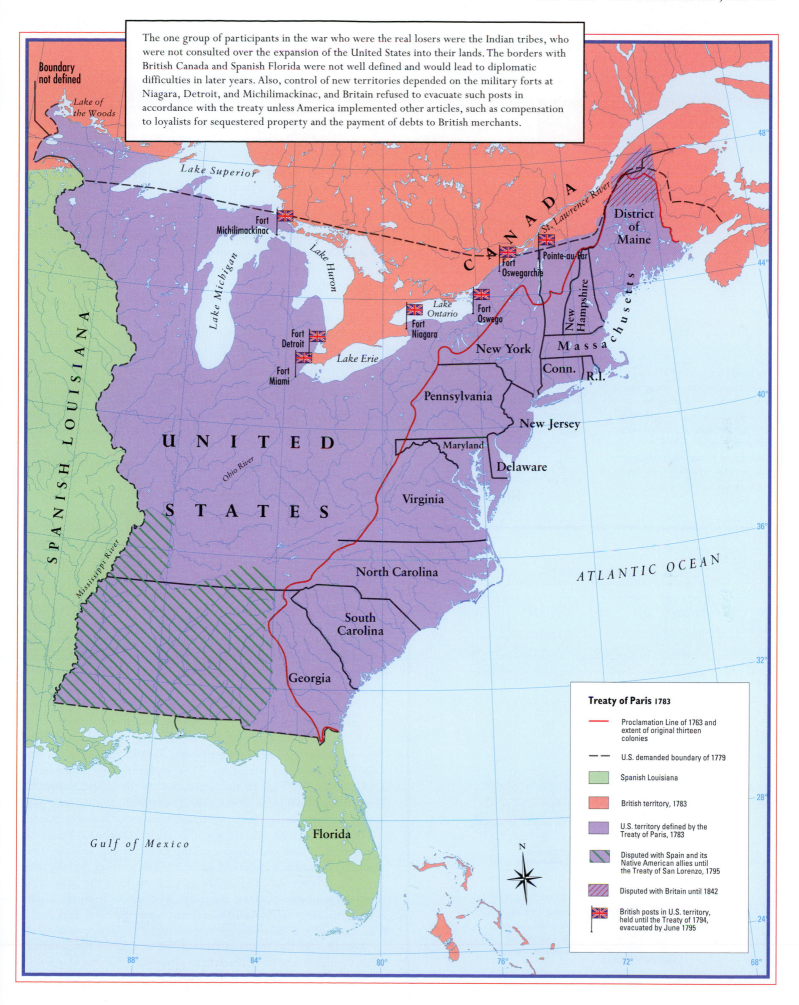

The one group of participants in the war who were the real losers were the Indian tribes, who were not consulted over the expansion of the United States into their lands. The borders with British Canada and Spanish Florida were not well defined and would lead to diplomatic difficulties in later years. Also, control of new territories depended on the military forts at Niagara, Detroit, and Michilimackinac, and Britain refused to evacuate such posts in accordance with the treaty unless America implemented other articles, such as compensation to loyalists for sequestered property and the payment of debts to British merchants.

Boundary not defined

Lake of the Woods

Lake Superior

CANADA

St. Lawrence River

Fort Michilimackinac

Lake Michigan

Lake Huron

Fort Oswegarchie

Pointe-au-Fer

District of Maine

Fort Detroit

Fort Niagara

Lake Ontario

Fort Oswego

New Hampshire

Massachusetts

Fort Miami

Lake Erie

New York

Conn.

R.I.

SPANISH LOUISIANA

Pennsylvania

New Jersey

Maryland

Delaware

UNITED STATES

Ohio River

Virginia

Mississippi River

North Carolina

ATLANTIC OCEAN

South Carolina

Georgia

Florida

Gulf of Mexico

N

Treaty of Paris 1783

— Proclamation Line of 1763 and extent of original thirteen colonies

– – U.S. demanded boundary of 1779

Spanish Louisiana

British territory, 1783

U.S. territory defined by the Treaty of Paris, 1783

Disputed with Spain and its Native American allies until the Treaty of San Lorenzo, 1795

Disputed with Britain until 1842

British posts in U.S. territory, held until the Treaty of 1794, evacuated by June 1795

PART EIGHT

FORGING THE NEW NATION

NATIONS ARE not created; they develop over time. By the late 18th century, the British political system had been the product of five centuries of evolution, as the growing power of noblemen and merchants became institutionalized in Parliament, which provided a countervailing force to the monarchy. That political system was projected across the Atlantic, where colonial legislatures functioned almost like miniature Parliaments, and sometimes were so regarded by colonists.

Thus when the thirteen American states separated from Britain, they were heirs to a highly evolved political system. But that system was tainted by its association with a "tyrant" monarch and an implacable Parliament. Some American statesmen (and especially military officers) could think of no alternative and proposed that George Washington become "king" of the new American polity. Washington squelched this idea, which doubtless would have received little support in Congress. But in the absence of a monarchy, American statesmen were forced to invent a new political system.

In 1777 the Continental Congress proposed a confederation of the thirteen original states for the prosecution of the war. In 1781 Maryland ratified the Confederation, the last state to do so. According to the "articles" of confederation, each state retained "its sovereignty, freedom, and independence." The Confederation itself possessed few real powers or the capacity to enforce those allotted to it. The pressures of war disguised the defects of the Confederation, as individual states willingly relinquished their rights to ensure their survival.

Thus the young nation progressed. In 1780 Congress persuaded the states to cede to the national government their claims to western lands. The Confederation would form the new regions "into distinct republican States" with the "same rights" as the original states. The Land Ordinance of 1785 regularized procedures to survey and sell this land, and the Northwest Ordinance of 1787 created the means for establishing state governments there.

But the inadequacies of the Confederation were painfully obvious. It had no powers to establish tariffs or regulate international trade, and tariffs established by states could be easily evaded; if Rhode Island established an import tax and Connecticut did not, shippers could evade the former by importing goods to the latter and then reshipping them.

Moreover, state legislatures, in an attempt to fulfill all of the duties of a government, were obliged to impose high taxes. In Massachusetts in the 1780s, the average farmer paid about one-third of his income in state taxes. Those who could not pay lost their farms; some were thrown into prison as debtors. In 1786, Daniel Shays, a veteran of the Revolutionary War, persuaded farmers in western Massachusetts to take up arms against the state government. When Massachusetts raised a militia in opposition, Shays's men attacked the state arsenal in Springfield. Massachusetts dispersed the farmers, but sober statesmen were persuaded that the absence of a strong national authority was giving rise to lawlessness and chaos. This led to calls for a convention to consider a new form of national government, which Congress reluctantly convened.

On 25 May 1787, delegates from every state except Rhode Island, which declined to participate, met in Philadelphia, with George Washington presiding. That summer they produced the Constitution that became the framework of the United States. The Constitution featured a strong executive branch, headed by a president, counterbalanced by a two-house legislature and a judiciary.

The Constitution was to go into effect when nine states had approved it. Those who supported the Constitution, and the strong central government it endorsed, were called Federalists, and the opponents, Anti-Federalists. Federalists were mostly from the more settled and prosperous areas along the coast, while those from the interior were more likely to be Anti-Federalists. When the New York legislature voted 30 to 27 in favor, ratification was a foregone conclusion.

According to the Treaty of Paris (1783) ending the Revolutionary War, Congress was to "earnestly recommend" that the states reimburse British loyalists whose lands and properties had been confis-

---

The Land Ordinance of 1785 was enacted by Congress to set up an orderly system for settling the Northwest Territory. Land would be surveyed and divided into townships. Each township would be 6 miles square divided into 36 one-square-mile sections. One section in every township was to be set aside to support public schools.

Land Ordinance of 1785

Grid pattern of a township (6 miles by 6 miles)
36 sections of 640 acres each (1 square mile each)

36	30	24	18	12	6
35	29	23	17	11	5
34	28	22	16	10	4
33	27	21	15	9	3
32	26	20	14	8	2
31	25	19	13	7	1

16 — Income of one section reserved for the support of public education

(1 mile by 1 mile)
A Half-section — 320 acres
B Quarter-section — 160 acres
C Eighth-section — 80 acres
D Sixteenth-section — 40 acres

cated; indeed, the harassment of such individuals had precipitated an exodus of tens of thousands of loyalists from the United States to British Canada, especially Nova Scotia and Acadia, and to British possessions in the Caribbean.

The failure of most states to make such payments provided justification for the British to renege on their promise to withdraw their troops from American soil—which included all lands south of the Great Lakes, east of the Mississippi River, and north of Florida—"with all convenient speed." As American settlers poured through the Cumberland Gap into the Northwest Territory, the Indians chose to drive them off. From 1790 to 1792 Little Turtle, chief of the Miami, staged a series of devastating attacks north of the Ohio River. Claiming that the Indians had received assistance from the British, settlers of the region called on Congress and President Washington to force the British to relinquish the "illegal" forts. For a time, this proved impossible.

Although the new nation hoped to develop free from the complications of European rivalries, and be rid of the vexing problem of the Indians, this proved impossible. European statesmen were loath to relinquish an entire continent, and Indians persisted in claiming a right to the lands they occupied. Both issues long bedeviled American statesmen.

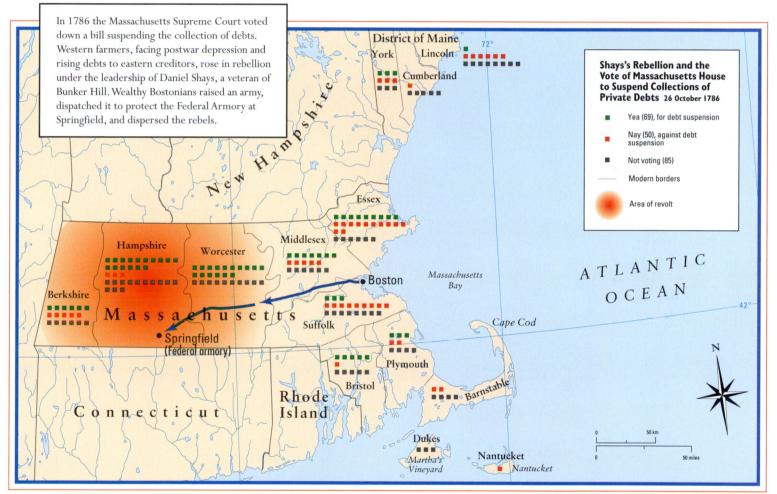

In 1786 the Massachusetts Supreme Court voted down a bill suspending the collection of debts. Western farmers, facing postwar depression and rising debts to eastern creditors, rose in rebellion under the leadership of Daniel Shays, a veteran of Bunker Hill. Wealthy Bostonians raised an army, dispatched it to protect the Federal Armory at Springfield, and dispersed the rebels.

Shays's Rebellion and the Vote of Massachusetts House to Suspend Collections of Private Debts 26 October 1786

- Yea (69), for debt suspension
- Nay (50), against debt suspension
- Not voting (85)
- Modern borders
- Area of revolt

MAPS

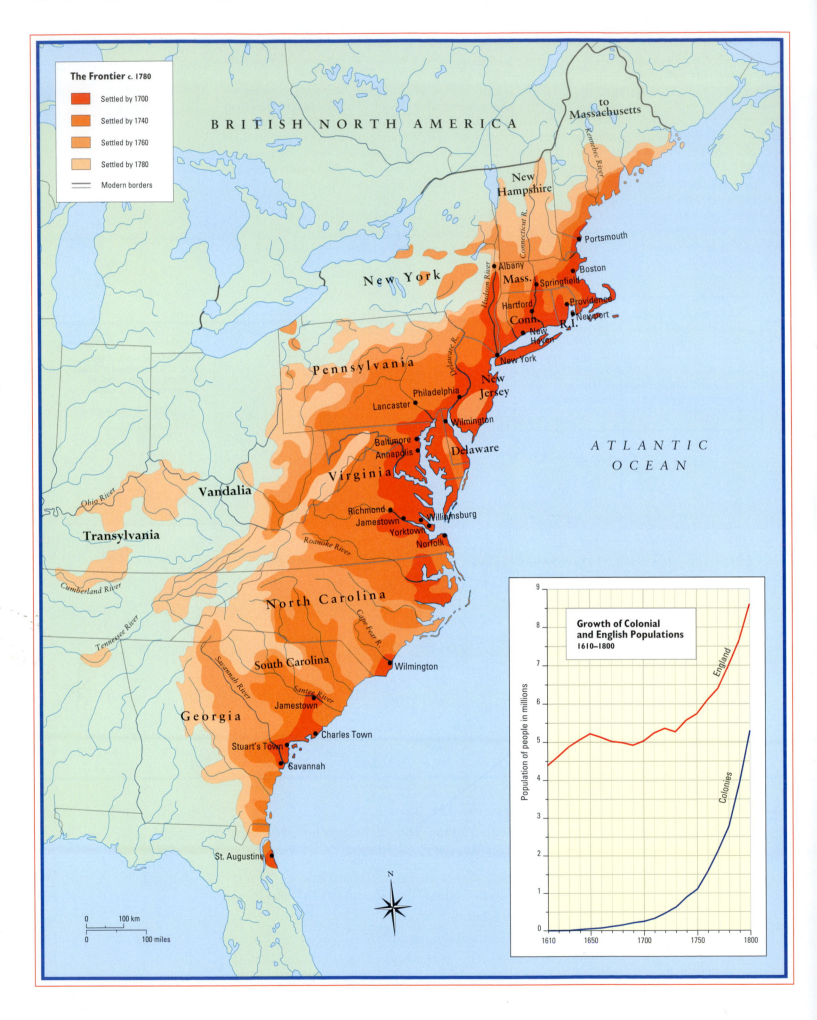

The Frontier c. 1780

- Settled by 1700
- Settled by 1740
- Settled by 1760
- Settled by 1780
- Modern borders

BRITISH NORTH AMERICA

to Massachusetts

New Hampshire

New York

Portsmouth

Albany
Boston
Mass.
Springfield
Hartford
Providence
Conn.
R.I.
Newport
New Haven
New York

Pennsylvania

Philadelphia
Lancaster
New Jersey

Wilmington

Baltimore
Annapolis
Delaware

Virginia

Vandalia

ATLANTIC OCEAN

Richmond
Jamestown
Williamsburg
Yorktown
Norfolk

Transylvania

Roanoke River

Ohio River

Cumberland River

North Carolina

Tennessee River

Cape Fear R.

South Carolina
Wilmington

Savannah River

Santee River
Georgia
Jamestown

Stuart's Town
Charles Town
Savannah

St. Augustine

N

0   100 km

0   100 miles

Growth of Colonial and English Populations
1610–1800

Population of people in millions

England

Colonies

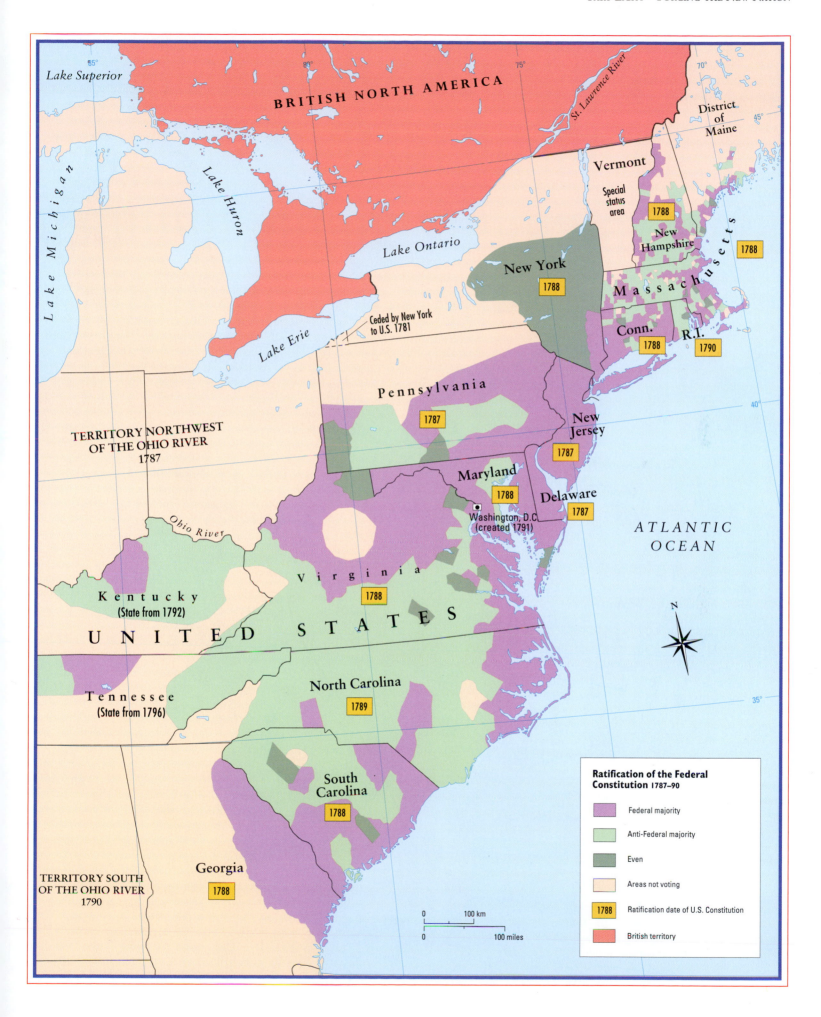

BRITISH NORTH AMERICA

Lake Superior

Lake Michigan

Lake Huron

Lake Ontario

Lake Erie

St. Lawrence River

District of Maine

Vermont

Special status area

1788

New Hampshire

1788

M a s s a c h u s e t t s

New York

1788

Conn.

1788

R.I.

1790

Ceded by New York to U.S. 1781

Pennsylvania

1787

New Jersey

1787

TERRITORY NORTHWEST OF THE OHIO RIVER 1787

Maryland

1788

Delaware

1787

Washington, D.C. (created 1791)

Ohio River

ATLANTIC OCEAN

Virginia

1788

Kentucky (State from 1792)

U N I T E D   S T A T E S

N

Tennessee (State from 1796)

North Carolina

1789

South Carolina

1788

TERRITORY SOUTH OF THE OHIO RIVER 1790

Georgia

1788

Ratification of the Federal Constitution 1787–90

- Federal majority
- Anti-Federal majority
- Even
- Areas not voting
- 1788 Ratification date of U.S. Constitution
- British territory

0   100 km

0   100 miles

British Possessions

Lower Canada

Lake of
the Woods

Lake Superior

Mississippi River

Claimed by until 1784

Lake Michigan

Lake Huron

Upper Canada

Montreal

St. Lawrence River

Disputed
with
Britain

Maine
(Massachusetts)

Also claimed by Massachusetts
until 1785

Lake Ontario

New York

Claimed by
N.Y. and
N.H.

Vermont

New
Hampshire

Boston

Also claimed by Connecticut
until 1786

Virginia

Claimed by
Mass.
(ceded to
N.Y. 1786)

Lake Erie

Claimed
by
Conn.

(to Pa.
1782)

Mass.

Conn.   R.I.

Missouri River

Ohio River

Pennsylvania

Philadelphia

New Jersey

Baltimore

Maryland

New York

Delaware

Virginia

District of
Kentucky

Washington

Williamsburg

SPANISH
POSSESSIONS

North
Carolina

Claimed by North Carolina
until 1790

Tennessee River

Arkansas River

Claimed by South Carolina until 1787

South
Carolina

ATLANTIC
OCEAN

Claimed by Georgia,
also claimed by
South Carolina until 1787

Georgia

Charles Town

Mississippi River

Claimed by Georgia,
also claimed by Spain

Savannah

N

Florida

St. Augustine

Gulf of Mexico

Western Land Claims
1782–90

0   100 km

0   100 miles

•••• Claimed by New York,
until 1782

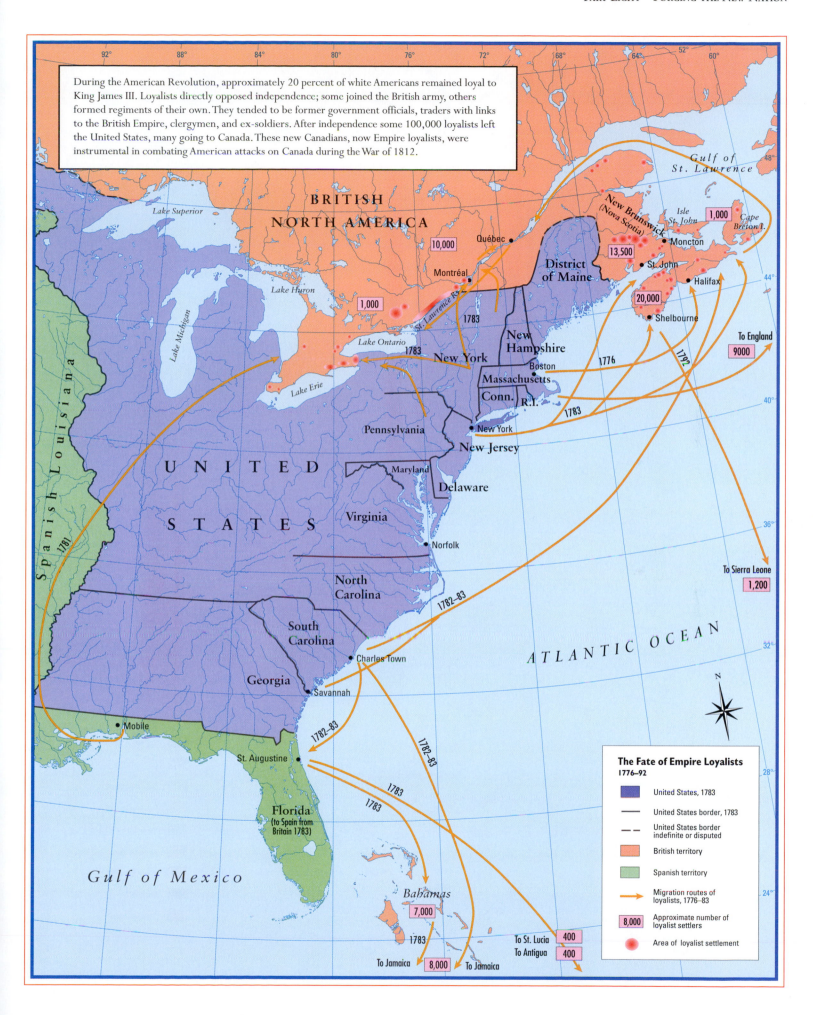

During the American Revolution, approximately 20 percent of white Americans remained loyal to King James III. Loyalists directly opposed independence; some joined the British army, others formed regiments of their own. They tended to be former government officials, traders with links to the British Empire, clergymen, and ex-soldiers. After independence some 100,000 loyalists left the United States, many going to Canada. These new Canadians, now Empire loyalists, were instrumental in combating American attacks on Canada during the War of 1812.

BRITISH NORTH AMERICA

Gulf of St. Lawrence

Lake Superior

Lake Huron

Lake Michigan

Lake Ontario

Lake Erie

10,000

Québec

Montréal

1,000

St. Lawrence R.

1783

New York

District of Maine

New Brunswick (Nova Scotia)

Isle St. John

1,000

Cape Breton I.

Moncton

13,500

St. John

20,000

Halifax

Shelbourne

New Hampshire

Boston

Massachusetts

Conn.

R.I.

1776

1792

To England

9000

1783

Pennsylvania

New York

New Jersey

Maryland

Delaware

S p a n i s h   L o u i s i a n a

1781

U N I T E D   S T A T E S

Virginia

Norfolk

North Carolina

South Carolina

Charles Town

Georgia

Savannah

Mobile

St. Augustine

Florida (to Spain from Britain 1783)

1782–83

1782–83

1782–83

1783

1783

To Sierra Leone

1,200

ATLANTIC OCEAN

N

Gulf of Mexico

Bahamas

7,000

1783

To Jamaica

8,000

To Jamaica

To St. Lucia

400

To Antigua

400

The Fate of Empire Loyalists
1776–92

- United States, 1783
- United States border, 1783
- United States border indefinite or disputed
- British territory
- Spanish territory
- Migration routes of loyalists, 1776–83
- 8,000 Approximate number of loyalist settlers
- Area of loyalist settlement

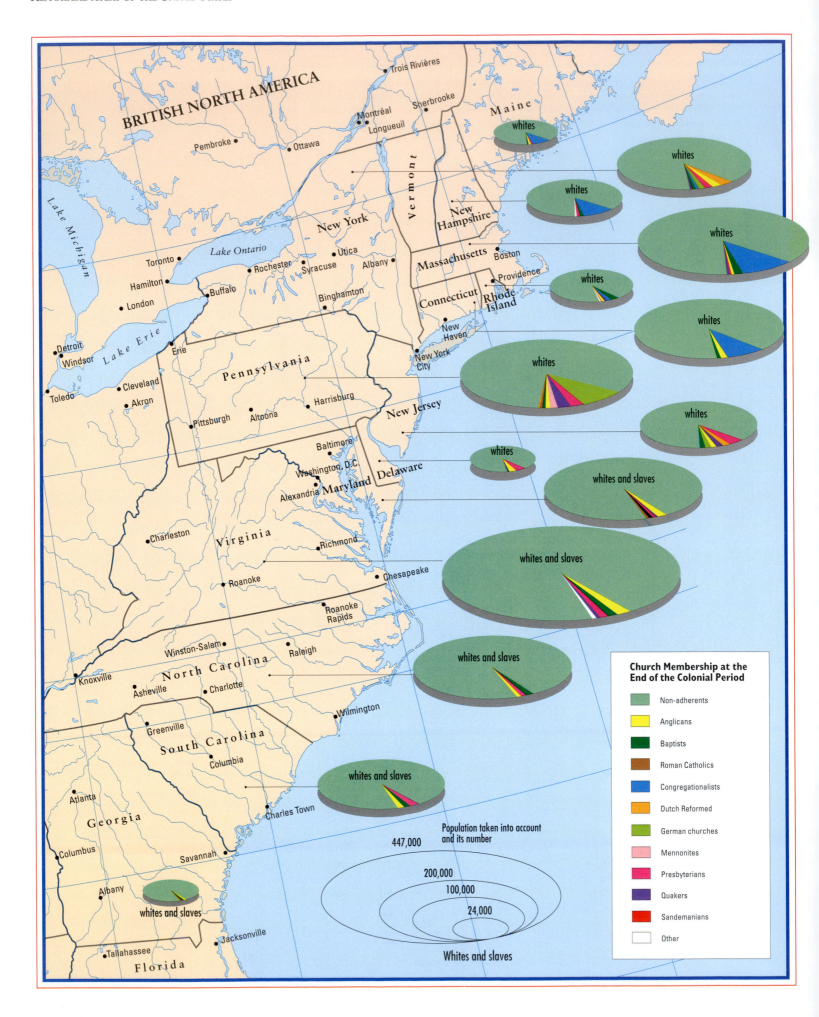

Church Membership at the End of the Colonial Period

- Non-adherents
- Anglicans
- Baptists
- Roman Catholics
- Congregationalists
- Dutch Reformed
- German churches
- Mennonites
- Presbyterians
- Quakers
- Sandemanians
- Other

Population taken into account and its number

447,000
200,000
100,000
24,000

Whites and slaves

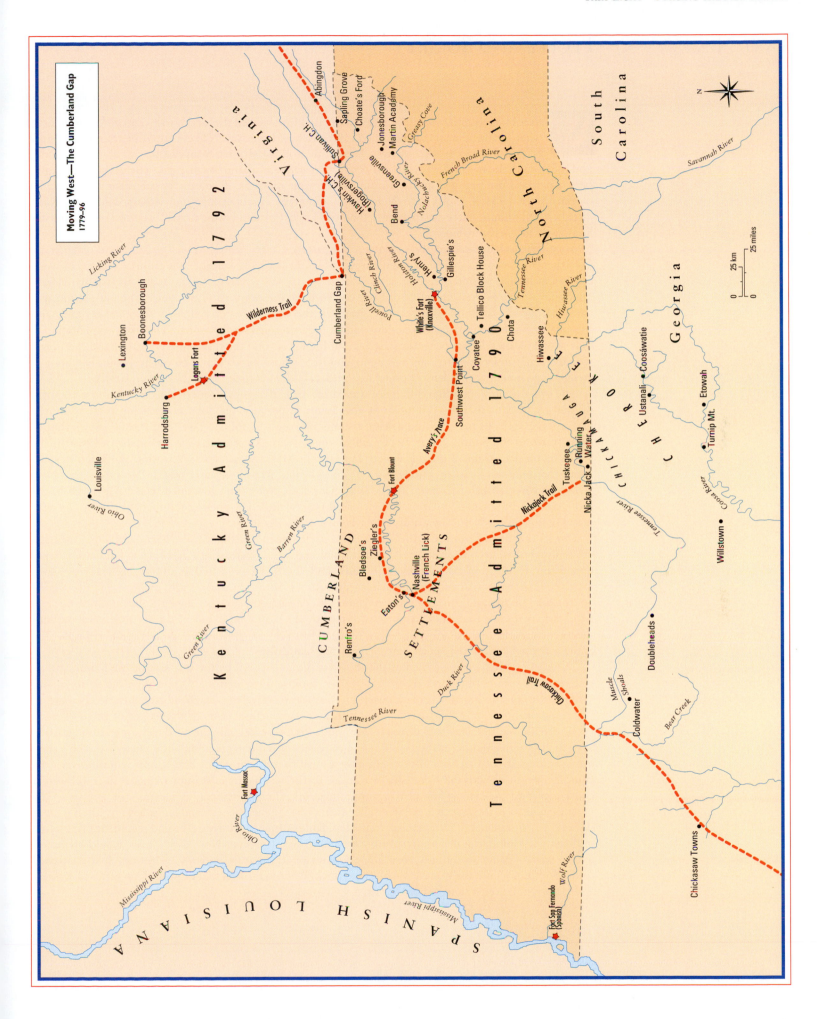

Moving West—The Cumberland Gap
1779–96

PART NINE   PEOPLE AND SOCIETY

WHEN JAMES Smith, a wealthy Virginia planter, first viewed the land northwest of the Ohio, near what is now Cincinnati, he called it "the richest I ever saw." There could be found "the most beautiful level that ever my eyes beheld; the soil is rich, free from swampy or marshy ground, and the growth mostly hickory… If you desire to raise great quantities of corn, wheat, or other grain, here is perhaps the best soil in the world, inviting your industry. If you prefer the raising of cattle or deeding large flocks of sheep, here the beautiful and green *parara* excites your wonder and claims your attention." Thomas Jefferson imagined that such rich farmland would yield a sturdy—and mostly homogeneous—citizenship.

Yet differences in the land and climate of the eastern United States, as well as historical divergences in settlement, created a variety of population profiles. In 1790, for example, the frontier regions of western Pennsylvania, western Virginia, and western North and South Carolina had a disproportionately high number of children. In many of the same regions, the proportion of men in the population was considerably in excess of 50 percent. Conversely, the coastal regions of New York, Maryland, and Virginia had a low population of children and a high proportion of women. The likely explanation is that women were relatively unenthusiastic about life far beyond the reach of civilization and that those who did settle in frontier regions had many children, whose hands could be put to profitable labor at an early age. In cities and densely populated areas, children constituted a drain on resources.

The other main population difference was racial. In 1790 African Americans constituted a majority of the population in many counties of the South, especially the tobacco-growing regions of the Chesapeake and the rice-growing coastal regions of South Carolina. The 1800 census shows that in most states in the South, about 95 percent of the African Americans were slaves. In the North, the status of blacks exhibited greater variety by state. In Massachusetts and Vermont, the small African American populations were entirely free; in Pennsylvania, 90 percent were free. In New York and New Jersey, however, three-quarters of the African American population remained in slavery. By 1830, the total African American population had increased significantly. The greatest numbers of free blacks were now found in New York, Maryland, Pennsylvania, and Virginia.

During the antebellum years, the slave system itself was in transformation. Farmland along the eastern seaboard had become exhausted from years of cotton cultivation, and fertile new lands were being opened up in Alabama, Mississippi, Louisiana, and Texas. This resulted in an internal trade of slaves from the east to the new, and often much larger, cotton plantations to the south and west. It also ripped apart slave families and generated new tensions that caused slaves to challenge the authority of masters and, with increasing frequency, to run away. All of these factors—the shift of slavery westward and into the territories; the flight of more slaves to freedom; the weakening economy of the coastal region of the South—contributed to the South's increasingly strident defense of slavery.

The geographical particularism of the people was underscored by the vast size of the nation and its rudimentary means of inland travel. In 1800, it took a traveler from New York a week to sail to Wilmington, on the North Carolina coast, and as long to travel the much shorter distance by land to Pittsburgh, Pennsylvania. The development during the antebellum years of thousands of miles of turnpikes, canals, and railroads was driven by economic forces—especially the need to ship western grain to eastern (and transatlantic) markets. But it had the effect of reducing regional differences. By 1860 a traveler who departed from New York could have a meal that afternoon in Pittsburgh; within a week, he could be venturing into the Nebraska or Kansas Territory. The greatest improvements in travel were a consequence of the elaboration of the railroad network, though regional variations still persisted. The most obvious was the fact that the width between rails—the gauge—varied considerably, forcing long-distance consignments to be repeatedly reloaded. For example, a westward-bound shipment originating in Portland, Maine, traveled along a train fitted for 4' 8½" track; in New York City it would be put on a train with 6' gauge to Buffalo. From there to Cincinnati the train had a 4' 10" gauge. If it continued to the South, it would likely travel on 5' gauge track. Although travel had improved, an efficient nation-wide transportation system did not yet exist.

MAPS

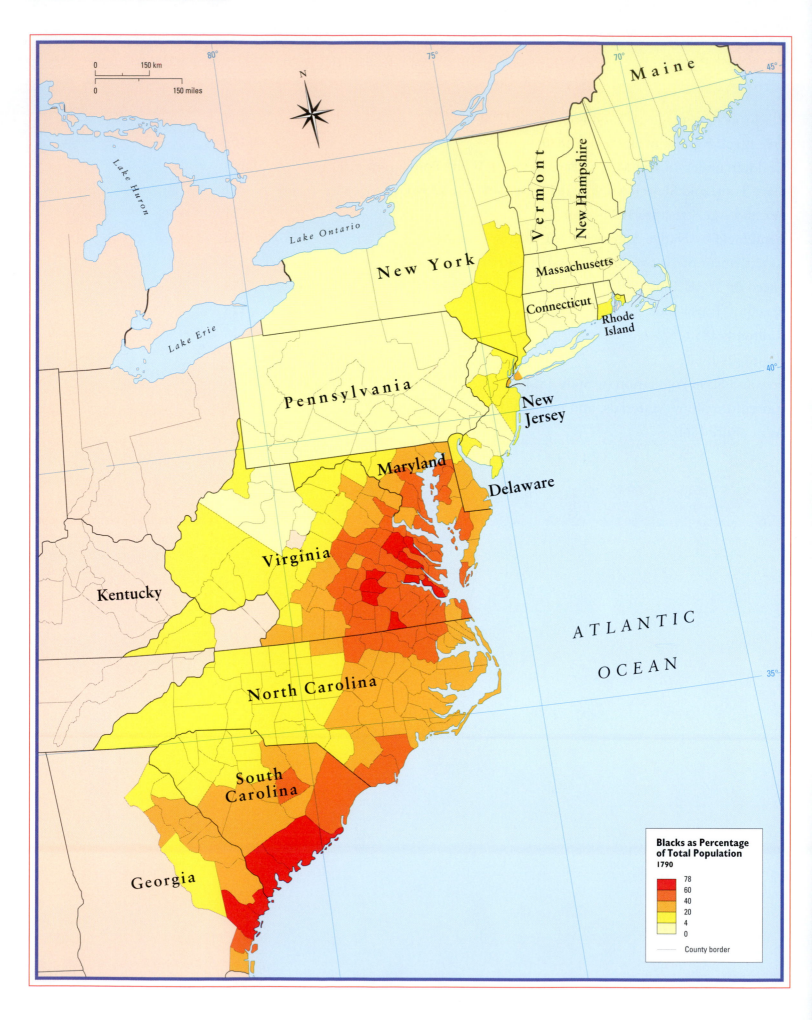

Blacks as Percentage
of Total Population
1790

78
60
40
20
4
0

County border

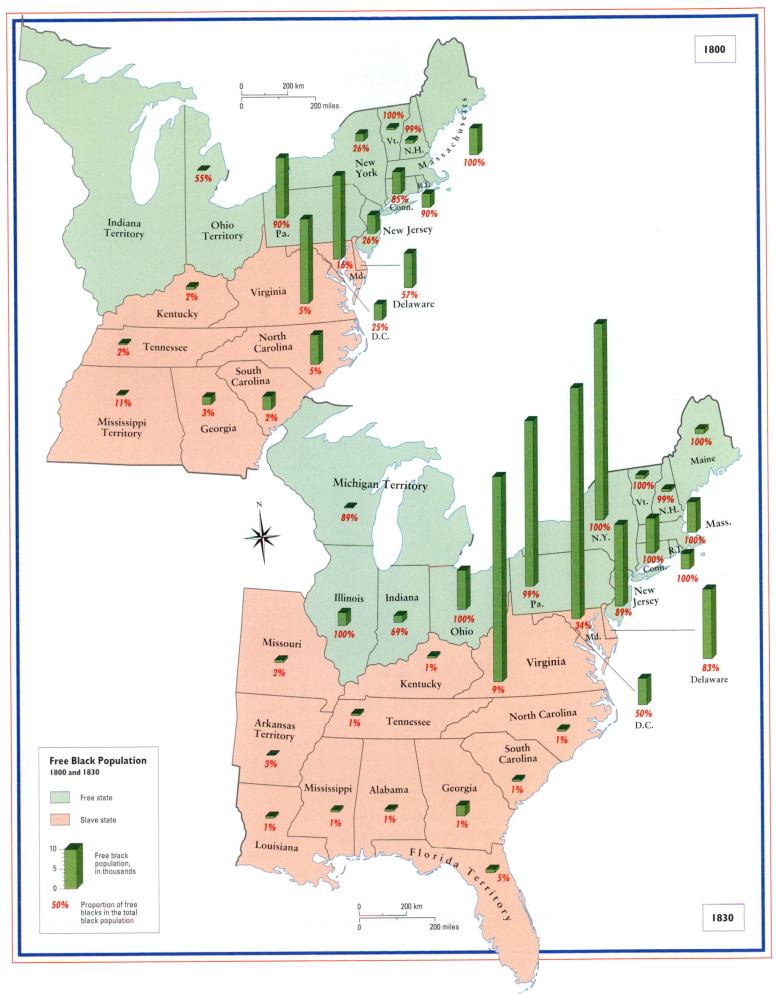

1800

1830

Free Black Population
1800 and 1830

Free state

Slave state

Free black population, in thousands

50% Proportion of free blacks in the total black population

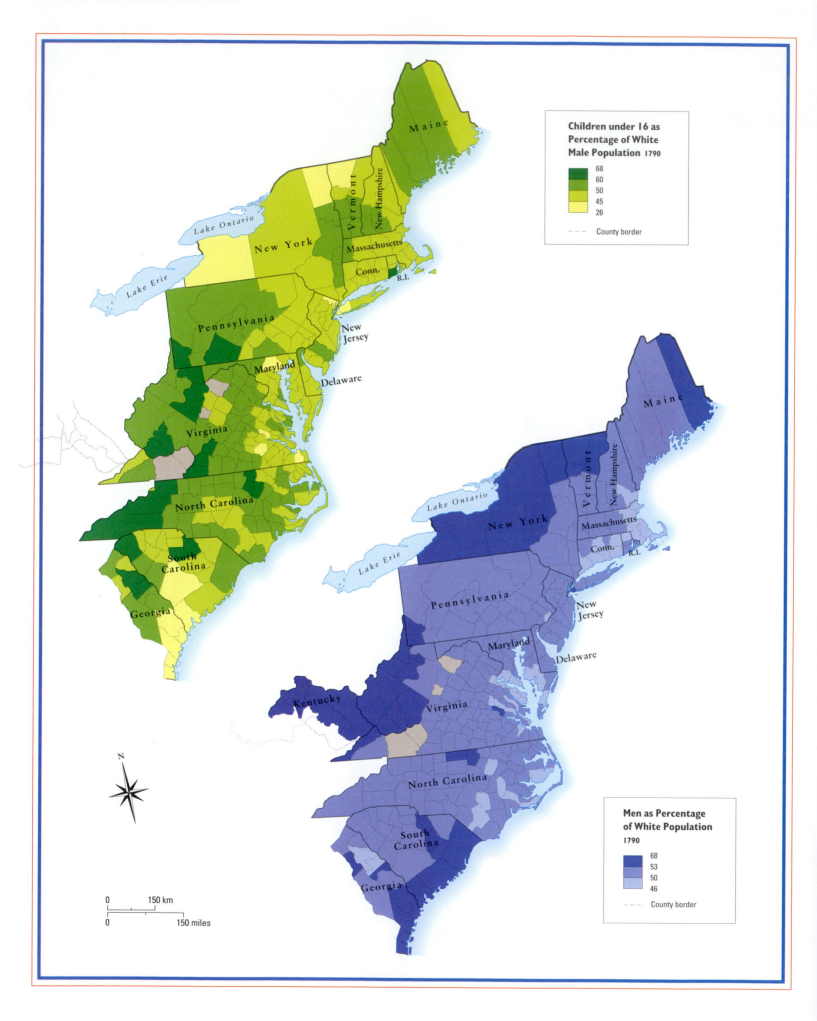

Children under 16 as Percentage of White Male Population 1790

- 68
- 60
- 50
- 45
- 26

--- County border

Maine

Lake Ontario

New York

Lake Erie

Vermont

New Hampshire

Massachusetts

Conn.

R.I.

Pennsylvania

New Jersey

Maryland

Delaware

Virginia

North Carolina

South Carolina

Georgia

Maine

Lake Ontario

New York

Lake Erie

Vermont

New Hampshire

Massachusetts

Conn.

R.I.

Pennsylvania

New Jersey

Maryland

Delaware

Kentucky

Virginia

North Carolina

South Carolina

Georgia

N

0   150 km

0   150 miles

Men as Percentage of White Population

1790

- 68
- 53
- 50
- 46

--- County border

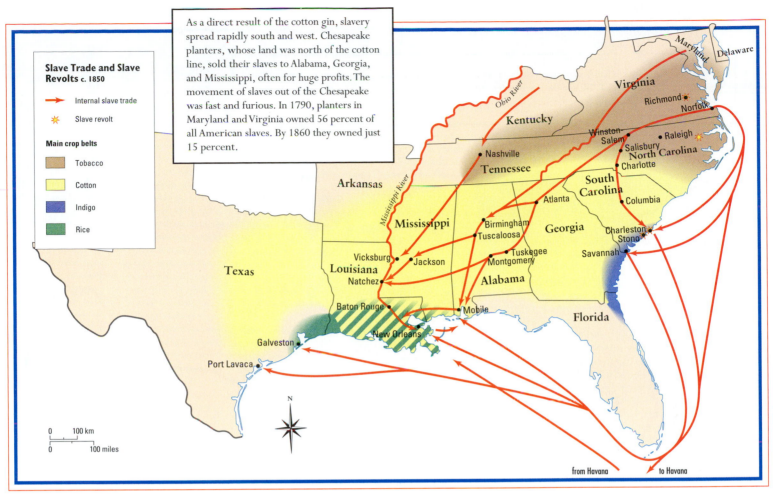

Slave Trade and Slave Revolts c. 1850

→ Internal slave trade

✴ Slave revolt

Main crop belts

- Tobacco
- Cotton
- Indigo
- Rice

As a direct result of the cotton gin, slavery spread rapidly south and west. Chesapeake planters, whose land was north of the cotton line, sold their slaves to Alabama, Georgia, and Mississippi, often for huge profits. The movement of slaves out of the Chesapeake was fast and furious. In 1790, planters in Maryland and Virginia owned 56 percent of all American slaves. By 1860 they owned just 15 percent.

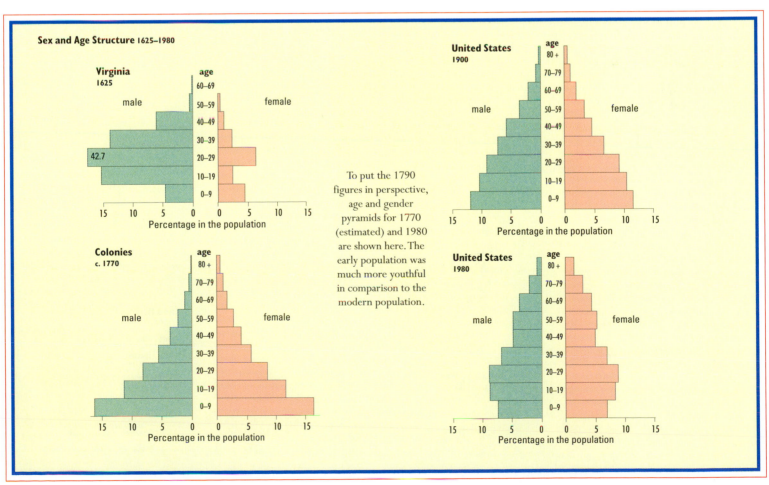

Sex and Age Structure 1625–1980

Virginia 1625

Colonies c. 1770

United States 1900

United States 1980

To put the 1790 figures in perspective, age and gender pyramids for 1770 (estimated) and 1980 are shown here. The early population was much more youthful in comparison to the modern population.

111

Some Native Americans had been dispossessed or fled before the steady advance of the whites. Land had been ceded between 1768 and 1774, and the newly independent United States then began a series of negotiations to secure further territories for settlement, recognizing a movement that was already under way.

BRITISH NORTH AMERICA

Lake Superior

Lake Huron

Lake Michigan

Lake Ontario

Maine
(Massachusetts)

Vt.

Lake Erie

N.H.

• Portland

Fort Poutchartrain
(Detroit)

New York

Albany •

Mass.

Salem •

• Haverhill

• Boston

Claimed by
Connecticut

Territory Northwest
of Ohio River

⚔ Harman's Battle
September 1790
⚔ St. Clair's Battle
November 1791

Providence •
Conn.

• Taunton
• New Bedford
R.I.

Pennsylvania

• New York

St. Louis •
• Cahokia

• Cincinnati

Brooklyn •

New
Jersey

Ohio River
• Louisville

Baltimore •

Washington • Md.

Delaware

Kaskaskia •

Ceded by Virginia
1789

V i r g i n i a

Nashville •

• Richmond

Territory South
of Ohio River

North Carolina

Arkansas
Post

A T L A N T I C
O C E A N

Claimed by Georgia

South Carolina

Georgia

Augusta •

Disputed with Spain

• Charleston

Mobile •

• Pensacola

Savannah •

New
Orleans

Land Held by Native Americans
c. 1790

━━━ Border of United States 1790

▨ Largely occupied or controlled
by Native Americans

▢ Ceded by Native Americans
1768–74

▢ Ceded by Native Americans
1790

▨ Settled by or controlled by
Europeans/descendants

• St. Augustine

Gulf of Mexico

Florida

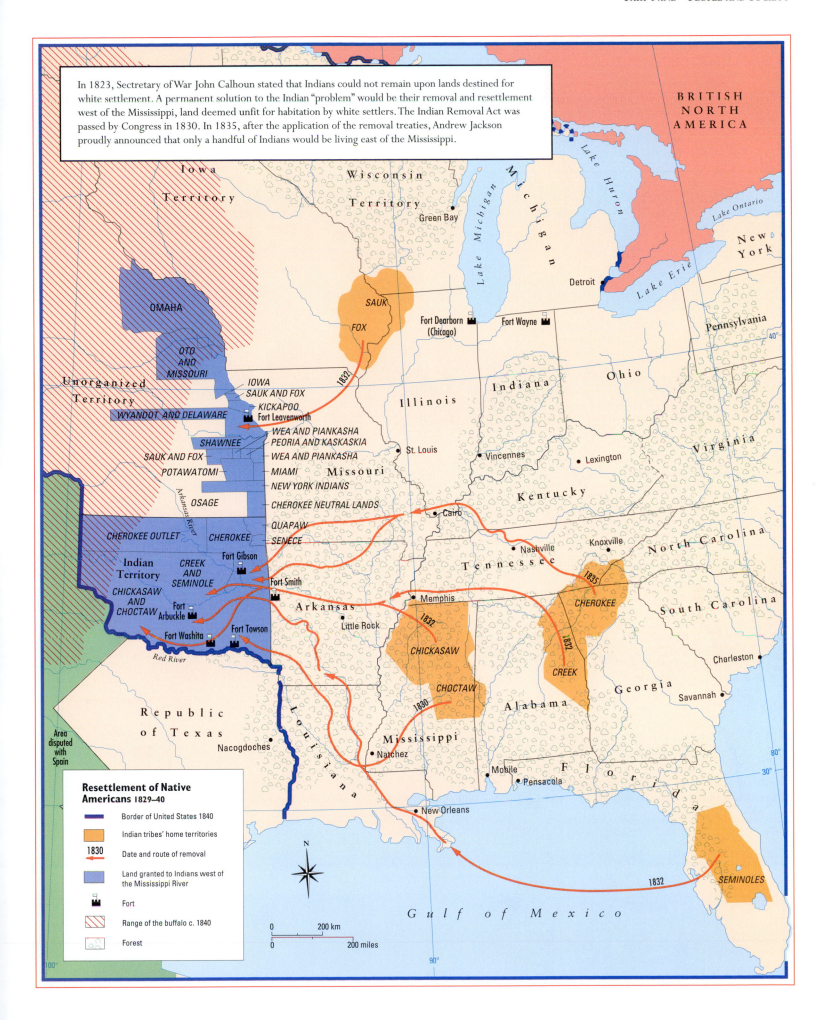

In 1823, Secretary of War John Calhoun stated that Indians could not remain upon lands destined for white settlement. A permanent solution to the Indian "problem" would be their removal and resettlement west of the Mississippi, land deemed unfit for habitation by white settlers. The Indian Removal Act was passed by Congress in 1830. In 1835, after the application of the removal treaties, Andrew Jackson proudly announced that only a handful of Indians would be living east of the Mississippi.

BRITISH NORTH AMERICA

Iowa Territory

Wisconsin Territory

Green Bay

Lake Michigan

Michigan

Lake Huron

Lake Ontario

New York

Detroit

Lake Erie

Pennsylvania

SAUK FOX

Fort Dearborn (Chicago)

Fort Wayne

OMAHA

OTO AND MISSOURI

Unorganized Territory

IOWA SAUK AND FOX

KICKAPOO Fort Leavenworth

WYANDOT AND DELAWARE

WEA AND PIANKASHA PEORIA AND KASKASKIA

WEA AND PIANKASHA

SHAWNEE

SAUK AND FOX

POTAWATOMI

MIAMI

NEW YORK INDIANS

OSAGE

CHEROKEE NEUTRAL LANDS

QUAPAW

CHEROKEE OUTLET

CHEROKEE

SENECE

Indian Territory

CREEK AND SEMINOLE

Fort Gibson

CHICKASAW AND CHOCTAW

Fort Arbuckle

Fort Washita

Fort Towson

Red River

Fort Smith

Arkansas

Little Rock

Memphis

Illinois

Indiana

Ohio

St. Louis

Vincennes

Lexington

Virginia

Missouri

Kentucky

Nashville

Knoxville

North Carolina

Tennessee

CHEROKEE

South Carolina

Cairo

1835

1832

Charleston

CHICKASAW

1832

CREEK

Georgia

Savannah

Republic of Texas

Area disputed with Spain

Nacogdoches

Louisiana

CHOCTAW

1830

Mississippi

Natchez

Alabama

Mobile

Pensacola

Florida

New Orleans

1832

Gulf of Mexico

SEMINOLES

Resettlement of Native Americans 1829–40

Border of United States 1840

Indian tribes' home territories

1830   Date and route of removal

Land granted to Indians west of the Mississippi River

Fort

Range of the buffalo c. 1840

Forest

0   200 km
0   200 miles

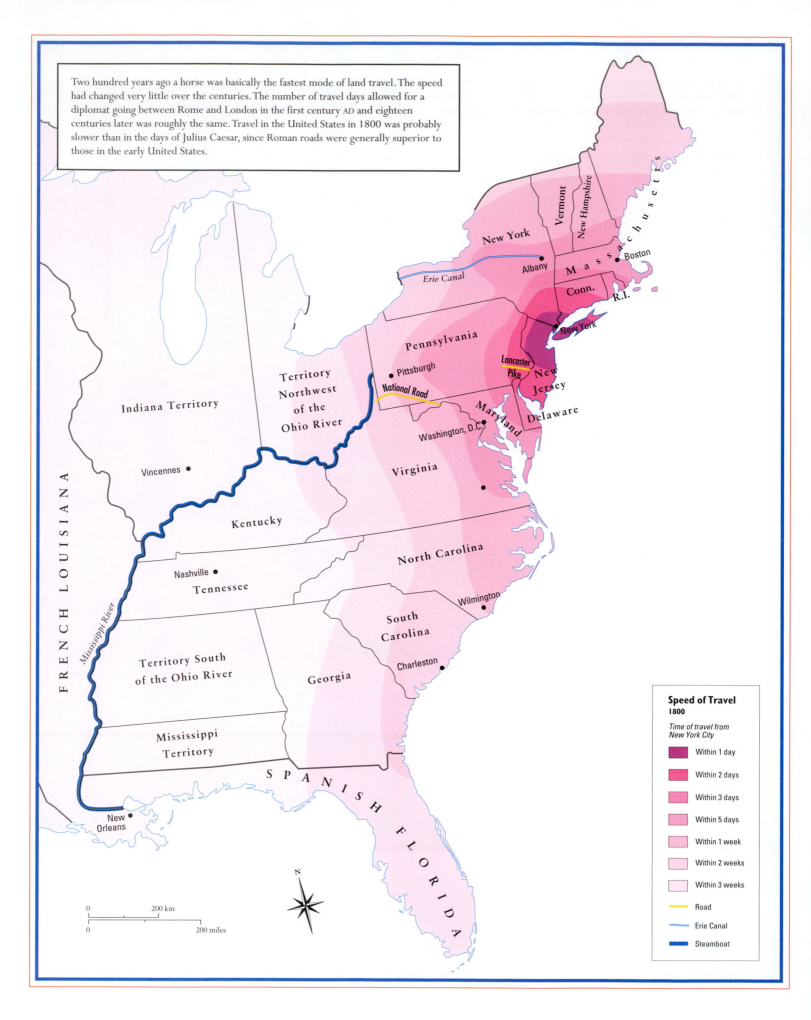

Two hundred years ago a horse was basically the fastest mode of land travel. The speed had changed very little over the centuries. The number of travel days allowed for a diplomat going between Rome and London in the first century AD and eighteen centuries later was roughly the same. Travel in the United States in 1800 was probably slower than in the days of Julius Caesar, since Roman roads were generally superior to those in the early United States.

Speed of Travel
1800

Time of travel from New York City

Within 1 day
Within 2 days
Within 3 days
Within 5 days
Within 1 week
Within 2 weeks
Within 3 weeks
Road
Erie Canal
Steamboat

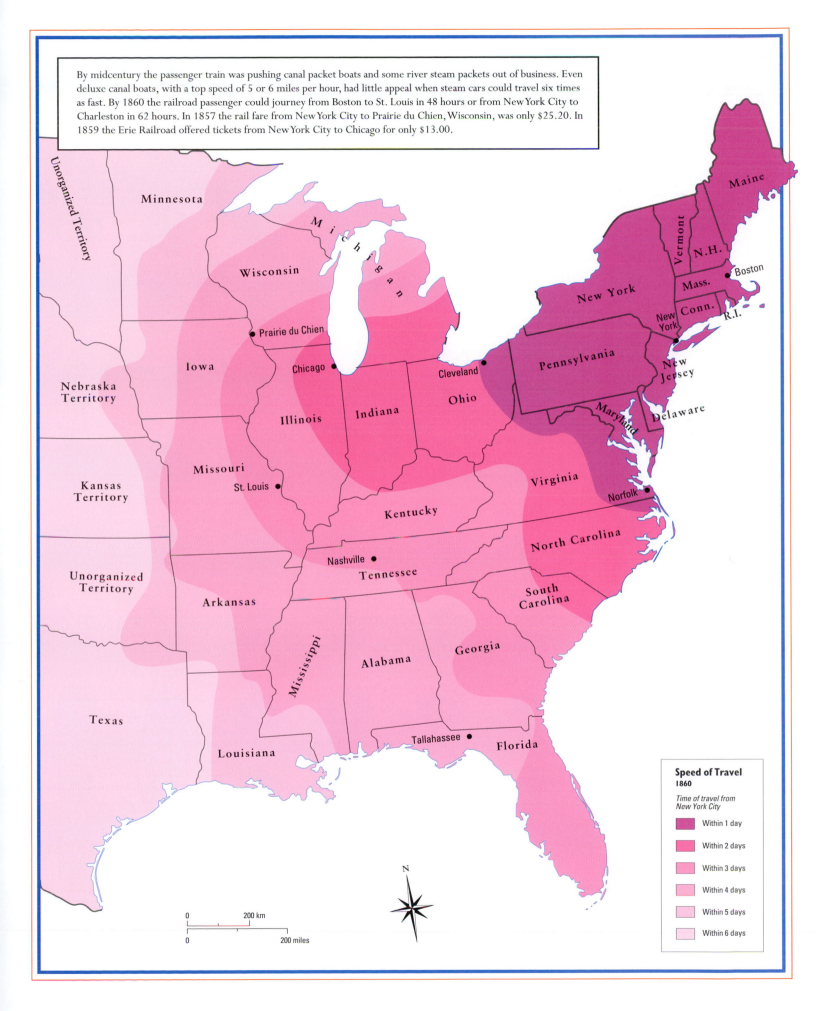

By midcentury the passenger train was pushing canal packet boats and some river steam packets out of business. Even deluxe canal boats, with a top speed of 5 or 6 miles per hour, had little appeal when steam cars could travel six times as fast. By 1860 the railroad passenger could journey from Boston to St. Louis in 48 hours or from New York City to Charleston in 62 hours. In 1857 the rail fare from New York City to Prairie du Chien, Wisconsin, was only $25.20. In 1859 the Erie Railroad offered tickets from New York City to Chicago for only $13.00.

Speed of Travel
1860

Time of travel from New York City

- Within 1 day
- Within 2 days
- Within 3 days
- Within 4 days
- Within 5 days
- Within 6 days

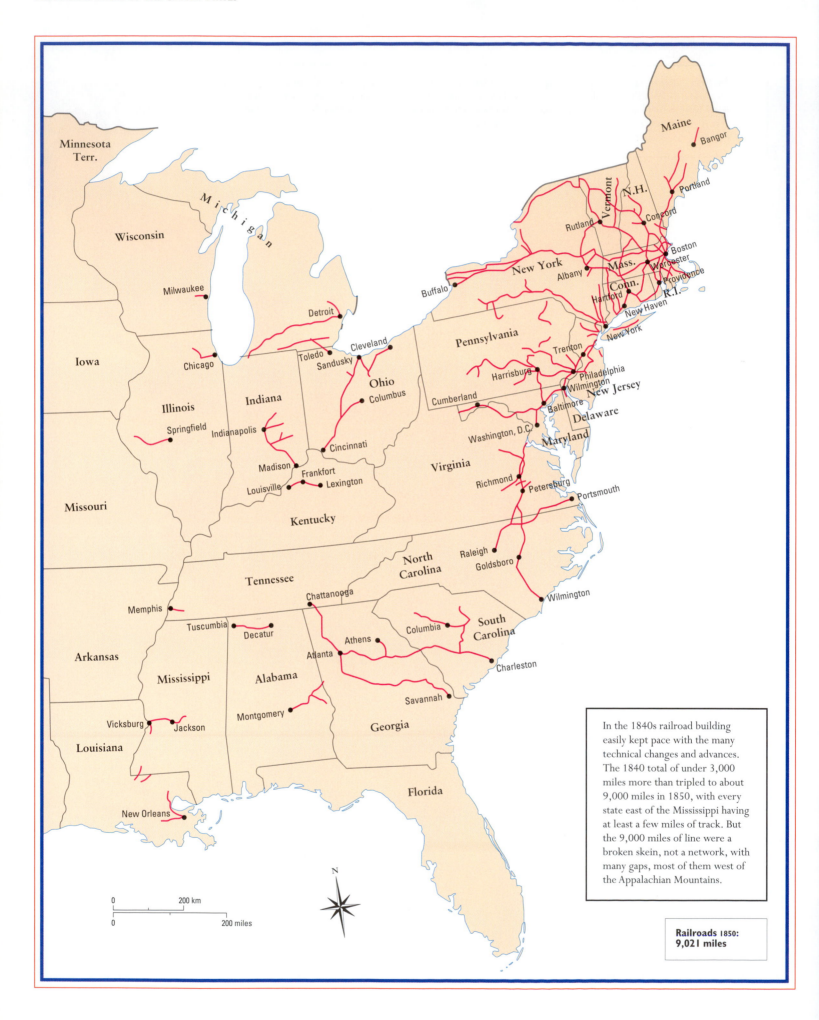

In the 1840s railroad building easily kept pace with the many technical changes and advances. The 1840 total of under 3,000 miles more than tripled to about 9,000 miles in 1850, with every state east of the Mississippi having at least a few miles of track. But the 9,000 miles of line were a broken skein, not a network, with many gaps, most of them west of the Appalachian Mountains.

Railroads 1850: 9,021 miles

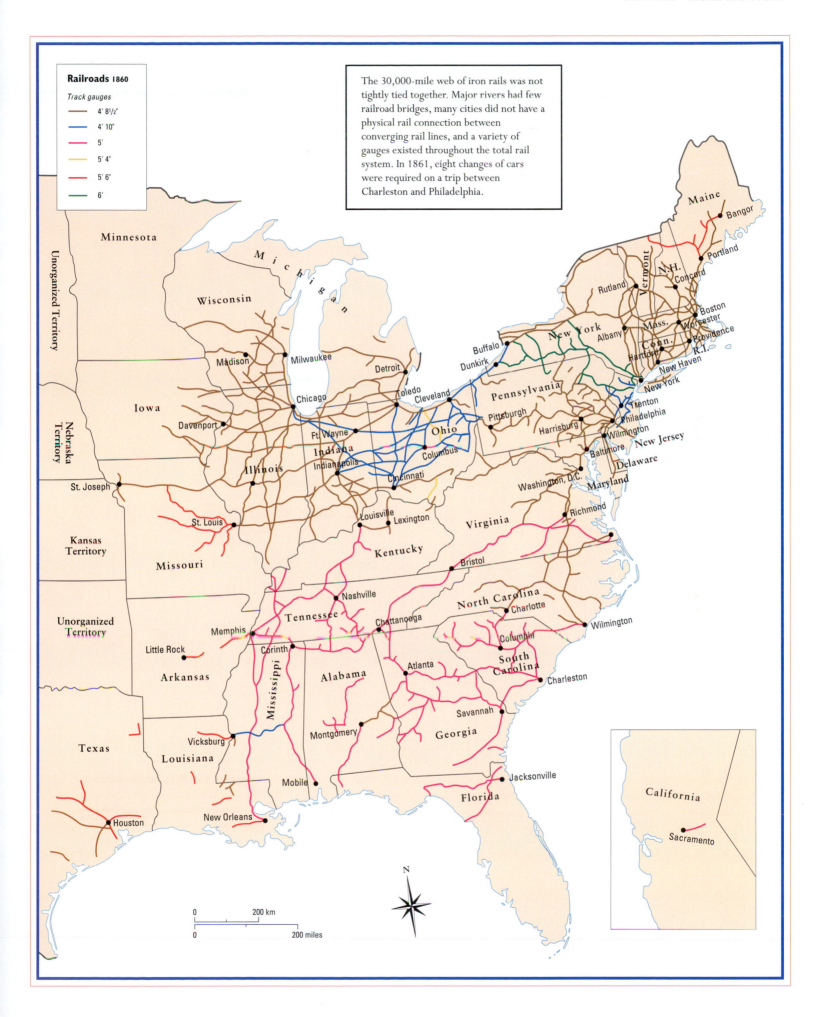

Railroads 1860

Track gauges

— 4' 8½"
— 4' 10"
— 5'
— 5' 4"
— 5' 6"
— 6'

The 30,000-mile web of iron rails was not tightly tied together. Major rivers had few railroad bridges, many cities did not have a physical rail connection between converging rail lines, and a variety of gauges existed throughout the total rail system. In 1861, eight changes of cars were required on a trip between Charleston and Philadelphia.

0   200 km
0   200 miles

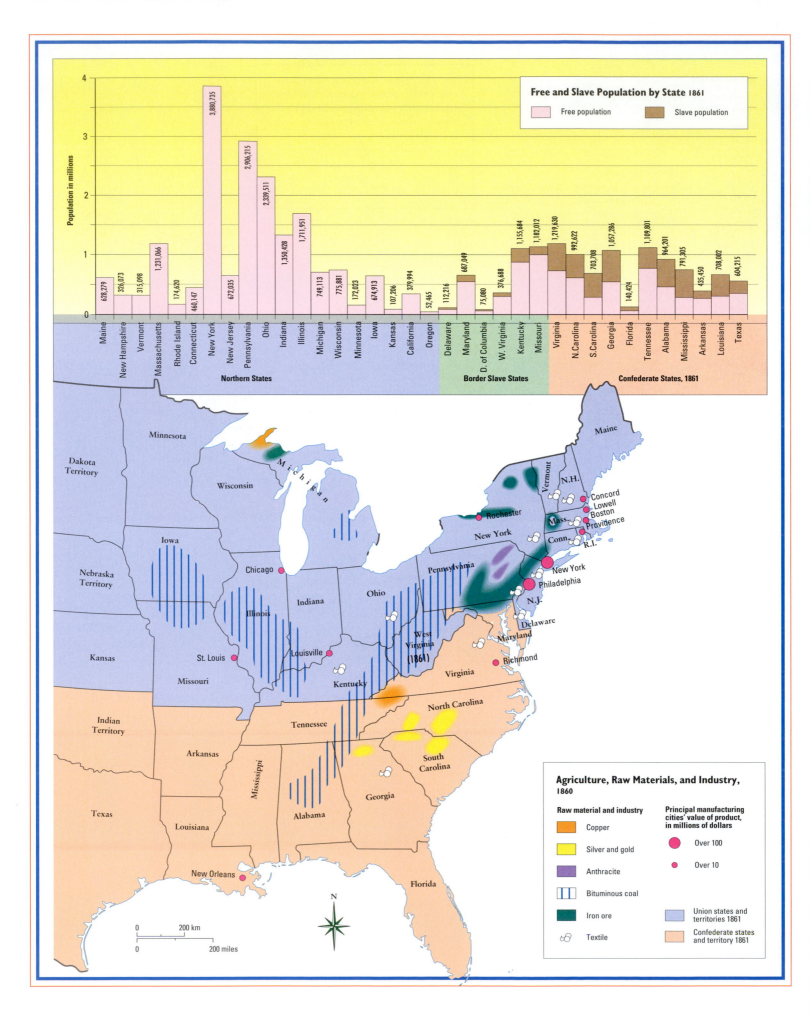

Free and Slave Population by State 1861

Free population
Slave population

Population in millions

4
3
2
1
0

628,279 Maine
326,073 New Hampshire
315,098 Vermont
1,231,066 Massachusetts
174,620 Rhode Island
460,147 Connecticut
3,880,735 New York
672,035 New Jersey
2,906,215 Pennsylvania
2,339,511 Ohio
1,350,428 Indiana
1,711,951 Illinois
749,113 Michigan
775,881 Wisconsin
172,023 Minnesota
674,913 Iowa
107,206 Kansas
379,994 California
52,465 Oregon

112,216 Delaware
687,049 Maryland
75,080 D. of Columbia
376,688 W. Virginia
1,155,684 Kentucky
1,182,012 Missouri

1,219,630 Virginia
992,622 N. Carolina
703,708 S. Carolina
1,057,286 Georgia
140,424 Florida
1,109,801 Tennessee
964,201 Alabama
791,305 Mississippi
435,450 Arkansas
708,002 Louisiana
604,215 Texas

Northern States
Border Slave States
Confederate States, 1861

Minnesota
Dakota Territory
Wisconsin
Michigan
Maine
Vermont
N.H.
Concord
Lowell
Boston
Providence
Rochester
Iowa
New York
Mass.
Conn.
R.I.
Nebraska Territory
Chicago
Pennsylvania
New York
Philadelphia
N.J.
Indiana
Ohio
Kansas
St. Louis
Louisville
West Virginia (1861)
Delaware
Maryland
Missouri
Kentucky
Virginia
Richmond
Indian Territory
Tennessee
North Carolina
Arkansas
Mississippi
South Carolina
Texas
Georgia
Alabama
Louisiana
New Orleans
Florida

N

0   200 km
0   200 miles

Agriculture, Raw Materials, and Industry, 1860

Raw material and industry

Copper
Silver and gold
Anthracite
Bituminous coal
Iron ore
Textile

Principal manufacturing cities' value of product, in millions of dollars

Over 100
Over 10

Union states and territories 1861
Confederate states and territory 1861

These maps convey the great disparity in human resources, industrial development, and raw materials between northern and southern states prior to the Civil War.

The North enjoyed an immediately apparent superiority in men and resources. Even if the divided border states are excluded, almost 20 million Yankees faced only 9 million Southerners. Since the Confederacy would not arm its 3.5 million slaves, the Union advantage in available military manpower was even greater. Union armies through the war would maintain about a 2.5:1 numerical superiority. American industry had been nurtured in the North, and the raw materials, skilled labor, and manufacturing facilities necessary to outfit large armies were concentrated there. Northern states accounted for over 90

percent of the pig iron, firearms, cloth, and footwear the United States produced in 1860.

The Confederate government also cultivated its war industry. Southern firms succeeded in limiting shortages of arms and ammunition. Yet Confederate failures more than balanced successes. The Confederacy could not exploit the world's dependence on cotton as much as it hoped, being hindered by the Union blockade and its own muddled policies. Though the Confederacy increased its food production, it could not ensure that food reached areas of greatest need. Failing to establish its financial independence, the South relied on printed money. It suffered 9,000 percent inflation, compared with the North's inflation of 80 percent.

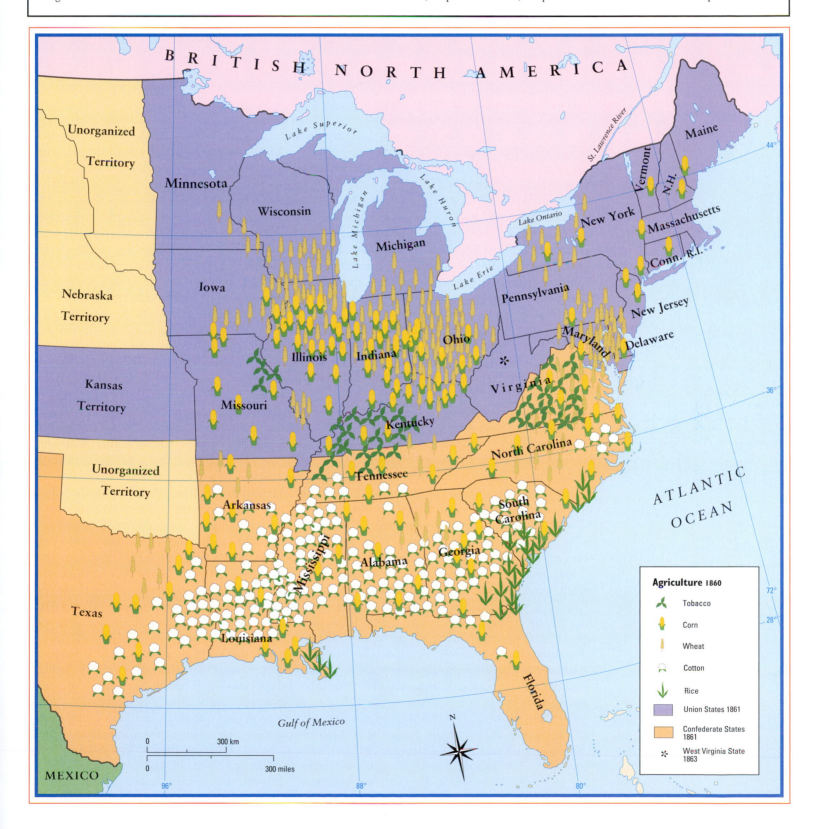

Agriculture 1860

- Tobacco
- Corn
- Wheat
- Cotton
- Rice
- Union States 1861
- Confederate States 1861
- West Virginia State 1863

PART TEN

GROWTH OF THE NATION THROUGH THE WAR OF 1812

T HE NATIONAL government followed the settlers westward. In 1795, after the Battle of Fallen Timbers, a dozen Indian tribes "signed" the Treaty of Greenville, surrendering huge tracts of land. These cessions, however, did not satisfy the land hunger of the settlers. "I believe scarcely anything short of a Chinese Wall or a line of Troops will restrain the Incroachment of Settlers upon Indian Territory," President Washington observed in 1796. Kentucky, admitted as a state in 1792, was followed by Tennessee in 1796. Two years later, the Mississippi Territory was organized. Indian resentments smoldered, as before. Although most Indians were pushed steadily westward, many Cherokee, Creek, and Chickasaw Indians refused to abandon lands their leaders had obstensibly relinquished by treaty. This, too, would prove a source of future conflict.

In his "Farewell Address" (1796), Washington also expressed misgivings over the rise of political action. The "baneful effects of the spirit of party," he declared, were undermining the belief that government officials should "serve no interests save those of the people."

Washington knew that he was partly to blame. His two top advisers were the source of much of the partisan contention: Alexander Hamilton, secretary of the treasury, had become the chief proponent of Federalism, which sought to broaden the powers of the federal government; and Thomas Jefferson, secretary of state, of Republicanism, which sought to limit federal powers by enhancing those of individual citizens and the separate states.

The election of 1796 pitted Jefferson not against Hamilton, whose strident partisanship diminished his electoral appeal, but against Vice President John Adams. Adams, a Federalist, won by a narrow margin. He, too, soon became mired in partisan politics, and partisan politics inevitably turned on the great issue of the day: the French Revolution and the wars it precipitated between France and much of the rest of Europe. Adams and the Federalists generally supported Great Britain, while Jefferson and the Republicans were initially sympathetic to France, though their enthusiasm subsided as the toll from the guillotine mounted. Conspiracies (and conspiracy theories) abounded and for a time poisoned political affairs.

In 1800 Jefferson again ran against Adams. As in 1796, Jefferson prevailed in the South, and Adams, in New England. But this time Jefferson took all twelve electors in New York, giving him more electors than Adams. However, the Electoral College gave Jefferson and Aaron Burr, his presumptive vice president, the same number of votes; this "tie"—a consequence of ambiguous wording in the Constitution—threw the election into the House. It eventually decided for Jefferson.

Jefferson believed that the strength of American democracy was derived from the free farmers who worked the land. Perhaps for that reason he kept an eye on the West and its seemingly inexhaustible supply of land. When France offered to sell Louisiana for $15 million, then a region stretching from the Mississippi River to the Rocky Mountains, Jefferson grabbed it with both hands. In 1804, hoping to find an all-water route to the Pacific, he dispatched Meriwether Lewis and William Clark, army officers, to explore the entire region. They failed to find the all-water route, but their accounts stimulated interest in the West.

Jefferson had hoped to evade the consequences of the titanic struggle across the Atlantic as Napoleon, the French military genius, destroyed the armies of one European monarch after another and took control of much of the continent. Britain, saved from invasion by its invincible navy, then employed its best weapon by imposing a blockade of Europe and harassing American shipping destined for the continent; French ships retaliated by seizing American vessels en route to British ports. Jefferson's protests to the governments of both nations had little effect. His final response—the Embargo Act of 1807—prohibited all exports, which devastated the American economy.

In 1811, when President James Madison demanded that both nations abandon their restrictive policies and Napoleon offered his apparent assent, American enmity focused on Great Britain. Exacerbating relations with Great Britain was a resurgence of Indian militancy throughout the Midwest. Tecumseh, a brilliant Shawnee, had for several years succeeded in enlisting scores of tribes in a campaign to drive the whites "back whence they came, upon a trail of blood." General William Henry Harrison, governor of the Indiana Territory, went in pursuit of Tecumseh. On 7 November 1811, he crushed Tecumseh's army at the Battle of Tippecanoe. Settlers in the Indiana Territory denounced Tecumseh's uprising as "a British plot."

For these reasons, as well as the tempting lure of sparsely settled Canadian land, the United States declared war on Britain in June 1812. The next month American generals launched a complicated three-pronged assault on Canada. One army, led by General William Hull, advanced against Canadian forces threatening Fort Detroit. When Indians under Tecumseh threatened his flanks, Hull retreated to the fort and promptly surrendered it. A second army at Fort Niagara moved into Canada and was immediately defeated. A third army, ordered to take Montreal, refused to cross into Canada. In 1813 the British went

MAPS

on the offensive in the Great Lakes region, but Captain Oliver Hazard Perry threw together a navy that stabilized the American positions.

In 1814 the British mounted three major campaigns to break the stalemate. An army from Montreal was to follow Burgoyne's ill-fated route down Lake Champlain to New York; another, ferried by the Royal Navy, was to harass Washington or Baltimore; and the last was to land at the mouth of the Mississippi and take New Orleans. Although the invasion force from Canada made no progress whatsoever, the attack on Washington succeeded. British regulars burned the capital; but when they moved up the Chesapeake to Baltimore, they encountered stiff resistance and withdrew.

On 24 December 1814 British negotiators yielded to nearly all of the American claims, ending hostilities. Before word of the armistice was received in the Americas, however, the British attack on New Orleans had commenced. As the statesmen were celebrating the treaty, the British general Edward Pakenham had landed his 11,000-man force near New Orleans. Andrew Jackson, the American commander, chose a strong position behind a canal and fortified it. Two weeks later Pakenham attacked the fortifications, and the Americans held, inflicting heavy punishment. Jackson became "the hero of New Orleans." The Americans had vanquished the army that had defeated Napoleon. Although the battle had no effect on the treaty, it provided confirmation that the American nation was coming of age.

Tripoli, one of the Barbary States of the North African coast, had developed a trade in seizing ships that passed its shores. Between 1790 and 1800 the State Department sent over $2 million to buy off these pirates.

The ruler of Tripoli, dissatisfied with the payments, declared war on the United States. President Jefferson responded by sending a squadron of warships to the Mediterranean. Over a period of four years the navy struggled to control the Barbary coast. In 1805 Tripoli surrendered to U.S. pressure, though some payments continued to be made until 1816.

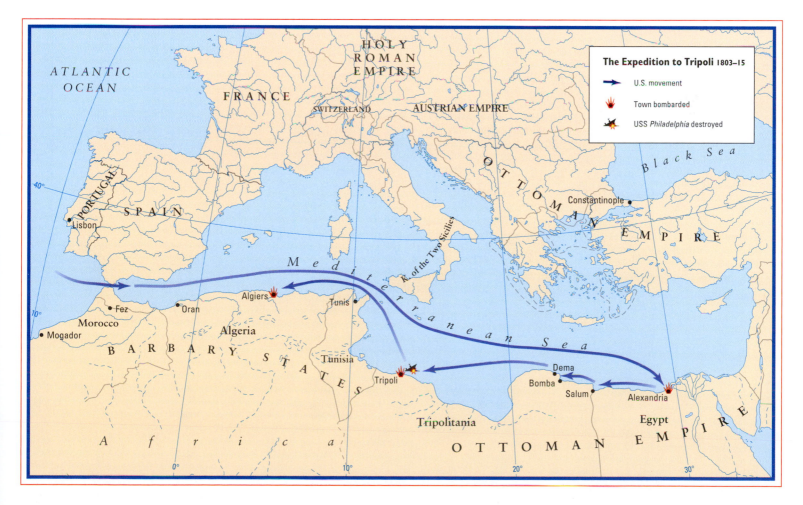

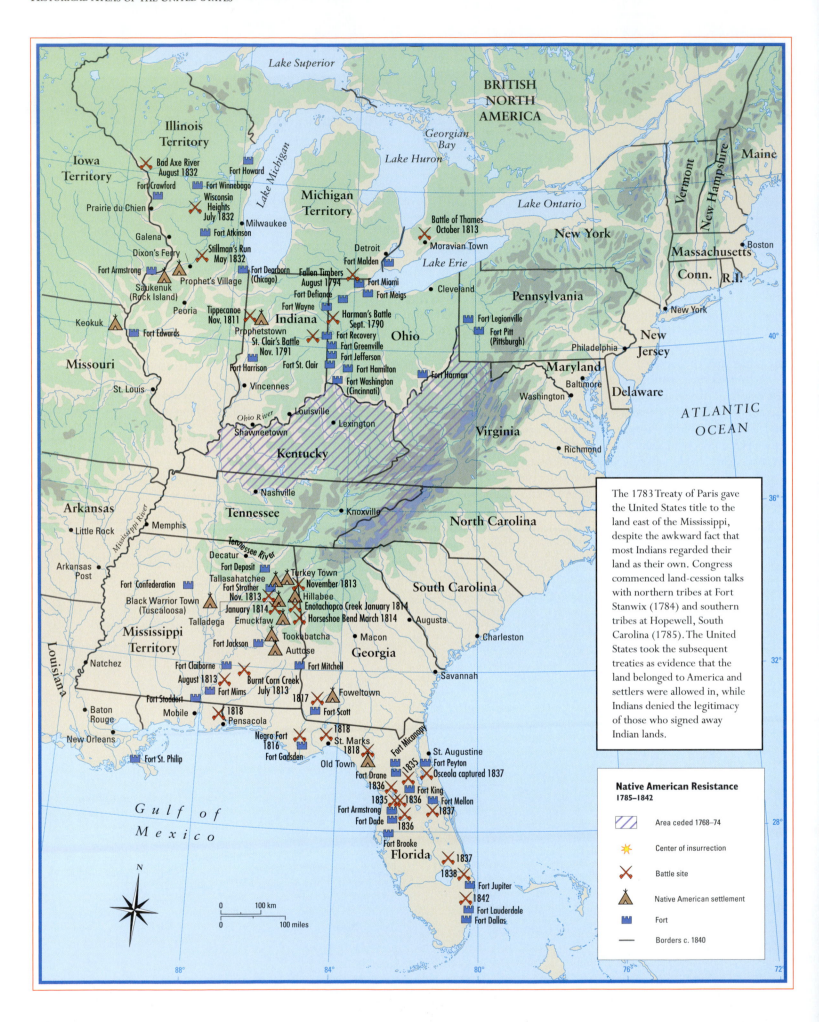

BRITISH NORTH AMERICA

Lake Superior

Georgian Bay

Lake Huron

Lake Ontario

Illinois Territory

Iowa Territory

Michigan Territory

New York

Vermont

New Hampshire

Maine

Massachusetts

Conn. R.I.

Bad Axe River August 1832

Fort Crawford

Fort Howard

Fort Winnebago

Wisconsin Heights July 1832

Fort Atkinson

Prairie du Chien

Milwaukee

Galena

Dixon's Ferry

Stillman's Run May 1832

Fort Armstrong

Saukenuk (Rock Island)

Prophet's Village

Keokuk

Fort Edwards

Peoria

Tippecanoe Nov. 1811

Indiana

Prophetstown

St. Clair's Battle Nov. 1791

Fort Harrison

Vincennes

Fort St. Clair

Missouri

St. Louis

Fort Dearborn (Chicago)

Fallen Timbers August 1794

Fort Defiance

Fort Wayne

Harman's Battle Sept. 1790

Fort Recovery

Fort Greenville

Fort Jefferson

Fort Hamilton

Fort Washington (Cincinnati)

Ohio

Detroit

Fort Malden

Battle of Thames October 1813

Moravian Town

Lake Erie

Fort Miami

Fort Meigs

Cleveland

Fort Legionville

Fort Pitt (Pittsburgh)

Pennsylvania

Philadelphia

New Jersey

New York

Maryland

Baltimore

Washington

Delaware

ATLANTIC OCEAN

Fort Harman

Ohio River

Louisville

Lexington

Shawneetown

Kentucky

Virginia

Richmond

Nashville

Arkansas

Little Rock

Memphis

Tennessee

Knoxville

North Carolina

Tennessee River

Decatur

Fort Deposit

Turkey Town November 1813

Arkansas Post

Fort Confederation

Tallasahatchee

Fort Strother Nov. 1813

Black Warrior Town (Tuscaloosa)

January 1814

Talladega

Emuckfaw

Hillabee

Enotachopco Creek January 1814

Horseshoe Bend March 1814

South Carolina

Augusta

Charleston

Mississippi Territory

Fort Jackson

Tookabatcha

Auttose

Macon

Georgia

Savannah

Fort Claiborne

August 1813

Fort Mims

Burnt Corn Creek July 1813

Fort Mitchell

1817

Foweltown

Louisiana

Natchez

Fort Stoddert

Mobile

1818

Pensacola

Fort Scott

1818

Negro Fort 1816

Fort Gadsden

St. Marks 1818

Fort Micanopy

St. Augustine

Baton Rouge

New Orleans

Fort St. Philip

Old Town

Fort Drane

1835

1836

1835

Fort Armstrong

Fort Dade

Fort Peyton

Osceola captured 1837

Fort King

1836

Fort Mellon

1837

1836

Gulf of Mexico

Fort Brooke

Florida

1837

1838

Fort Jupiter

1842

Fort Lauderdale

Fort Dallas

N

0   100 km

0   100 miles

The 1783 Treaty of Paris gave the United States title to the land east of the Mississippi, despite the awkward fact that most Indians regarded their land as their own. Congress commenced land-cession talks with northern tribes at Fort Stanwix (1784) and southern tribes at Hopewell, South Carolina (1785). The United States took the subsequent treaties as evidence that the land belonged to America and settlers were allowed in, while Indians denied the legitimacy of those who signed away Indian lands.

Native American Resistance
1785–1842

Area ceded 1768–74

Center of insurrection

Battle site

Native American settlement

Fort

Borders c. 1840

BRITISH NORTH AMERICA

Lower Canada

Upper Canada

Lake Superior

Lake Michigan

Lake Huron

Lake Ontario

Lake Erie

St. Lawrence River

Montreal

Mississippi River

N o r t h w e s t
Ceded by Virginia 1784

Ceded by Massachusetts 1785

Ceded by Connecticut 1786

T e r r i t o r y

Ceded by Conn.
1800

Ohio River

Ceded by Virginia 1789
(Kentucky)

Missouri River

L o u i s i a n a
Ceded by Spain to France 1800

Arkansas River

Ceded by North Carolina 1790
(Tennessee)

Tennessee River

Ceded by South Carolina to Georgia 1787

Ceded by Georgia 1802

Mississippi River

Ceded by Spain 1795

Spanish Florida

Gulf of Mexico

St. Augustine

Maine
(to Mass.)

Disputed with Britain

Vt.

N.H.

Mass.

Boston

Conn.

R.I.

New York

Pennsylvania

New Jersey

Philadelphia

New York

Baltimore

Md.

Delaware

Washington

Virginia

Williamsburg

North Carolina

South Carolina

Charleston

Georgia

Savannah

ATLANTIC
OCEAN

N

Western Land Cessions
1782–1802

— Boundary of territory ceded by New York 1782

— Boundary of territory ceded by Virginia 1784

▮ Original thirteen states by 1782

▮ Lands ceded by individual states to the federal government with date

▮ Spanish possessions

▮ British possessions

0   100 km

0   100 miles

The English monarchy took possession of all the lands immediately after the settlers reached this new land. Many kings gave areas of land to their friends and rewarded people with vast portions. This inevitably led to overlapping, which at the time did not matter, since the new land was not even mapped or surveyed. Explorers were also claiming lands when they reached them during their expeditions.

In 1629 Charles I granted the founders of Massachusetts Bay a defined area of land by saying, "in Length and Longitude … from the Atlantik on the east parte to the South Sea [Pacific] on the west parte."

Charles II presented William Penn with Pennsylvania in lieu of a debt of £16,000 that he had owed Penn's late father. There were boundary disputes as a result of these grants and favors, but at the time they did not amount to any significant fighting.

In 1775 Daniel Boone was employed by a group of North Carolina speculators to lead a party of settlers into eastern Kentucky and Tennessee, which they wanted known as Transylvania. The following year another group wanted to create a state called Westsylvania in the same area.

During the American Revolution all lands west of the Appalachian Mountains were ceded to Congress, hoping this would somehow ease the situation of state making.

STATES THAT NEVER WERE

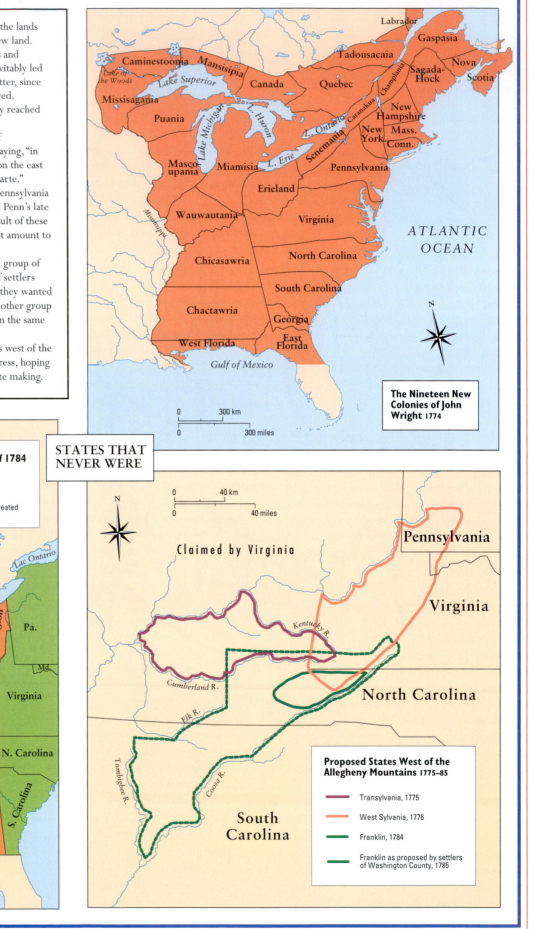

The Nineteen New Colonies of John Wright 1774

Jefferson's Proposal of 1784

- Existing states
- New states to be created

Proposed States West of the Allegheny Mountains 1775–85

- Transylvania, 1775
- West Sylvania, 1776
- Franklin, 1784
- Franklin as proposed by settlers of Washington County, 1785

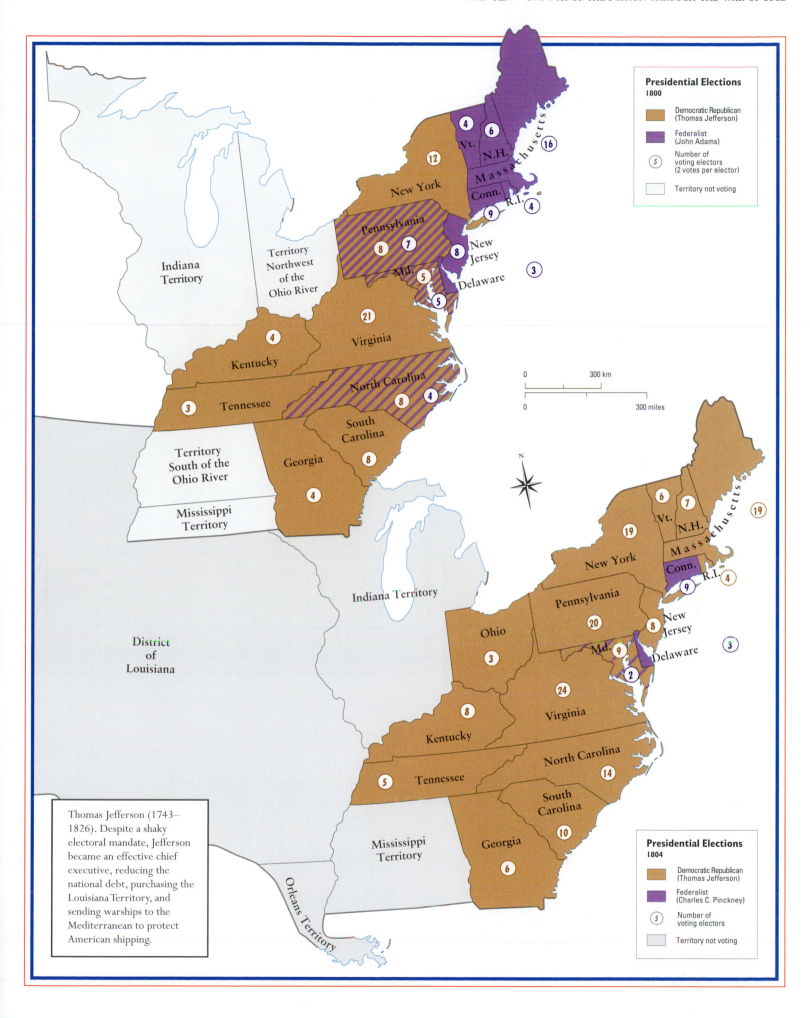

Presidential Elections
1800

Democratic Republican
(Thomas Jefferson)

Federalist
(John Adams)

⑤ Number of
voting electors
(2 votes per elector)

Territory not voting

Indiana Territory

Territory Northwest of the Ohio River

④ Vt.

⑥ N.H.

⑯ Massachusetts

⑫ New York

Conn. ⑨

R.I. ④

Pennsylvania ⑧ ⑦

New Jersey ⑧

Md. ⑤

Delaware ⑤

③

㉑ Virginia

④ Kentucky

③ Tennessee

North Carolina ⑧ ④

South Carolina ⑧

Territory South of the Ohio River

Georgia ④

Mississippi Territory

0   300 km

0   300 miles

District of Louisiana

Indiana Territory

⑥ Vt.

⑦ N.H.

⑲ Massachusetts

⑲ New York

Conn. ⑨

R.I. ④

Pennsylvania ⑳

New Jersey ⑧

Md. ⑨

Delaware ②

③

Ohio ③

㉔ Virginia

⑧ Kentucky

⑤ Tennessee

North Carolina ⑭

South Carolina ⑩

Georgia ⑥

Mississippi Territory

Orleans Territory

Thomas Jefferson (1743–1826). Despite a shaky electoral mandate, Jefferson became an effective chief executive, reducing the national debt, purchasing the Louisiana Territory, and sending warships to the Mediterranean to protect American shipping.

Presidential Elections
1804

Democratic Republican
(Thomas Jefferson)

Federalist
(Charles C. Pinckney)

⑤ Number of
voting electors

Territory not voting

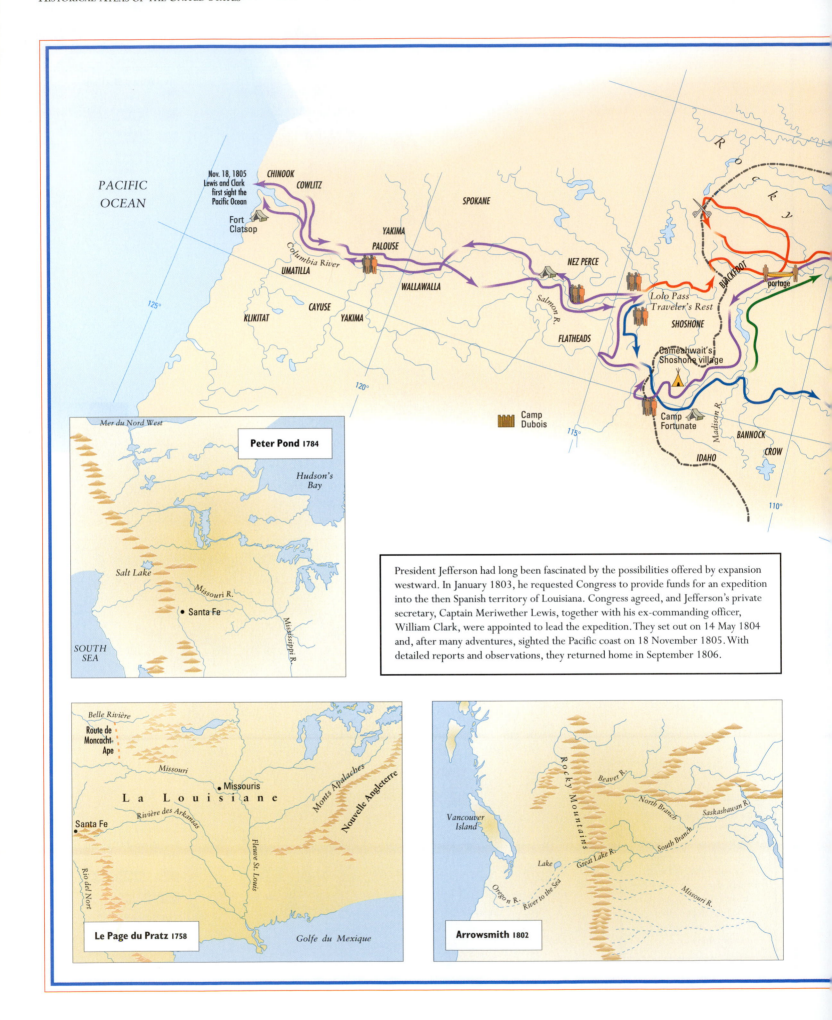

PACIFIC OCEAN

Nov. 18, 1805 Lewis and Clark first sight the Pacific Ocean

Fort Clatsop

CHINOOK
COWLITZ
SPOKANE
YAKIMA
PALOUSE
NEZ PERCE
Columbia River
UMATILLA
WALLAWALLA
Salmon R.
SHOSHONE
KLIKITAT
CAYUSE
YAKIMA
FLATHEADS
Lolo Pass
Traveler's Rest
BLACKFOOT
portage
Cameahwait's
Shoshone village
Camp
Fortunate
Madison R.
Camp
Dubois
BANNOCK
CROW
IDAHO

ROCKY

Peter Pond 1784

Mer du Nord West
Hudson's Bay
Salt Lake
Missouri R.
Santa Fe
SOUTH SEA
Mississippi R.

President Jefferson had long been fascinated by the possibilities offered by expansion westward. In January 1803, he requested Congress to provide funds for an expedition into the then Spanish territory of Louisiana. Congress agreed, and Jefferson's private secretary, Captain Meriwether Lewis, together with his ex-commanding officer, William Clark, were appointed to lead the expedition. They set out on 14 May 1804 and, after many adventures, sighted the Pacific coast on 18 November 1805. With detailed reports and observations, they returned home in September 1806.

Le Page du Pratz 1758

Belle Rivière
Route de Moncacht-Ape
Missouri
Missouris
La Louisiane
Monts Apalaches
Nouvelle Angleterre
Santa Fe
Rivière des Arkansas
Fleuve St. Louis
Rio del Nort
Golfe du Mexique

Arrowsmith 1802

Vancouver Island
Rocky Mountains
Beaver R.
North Branch
Saskashawan R.
South Branch
Lake
Great Lake R.
Oregon R.
River to the Sea
Missouri R.

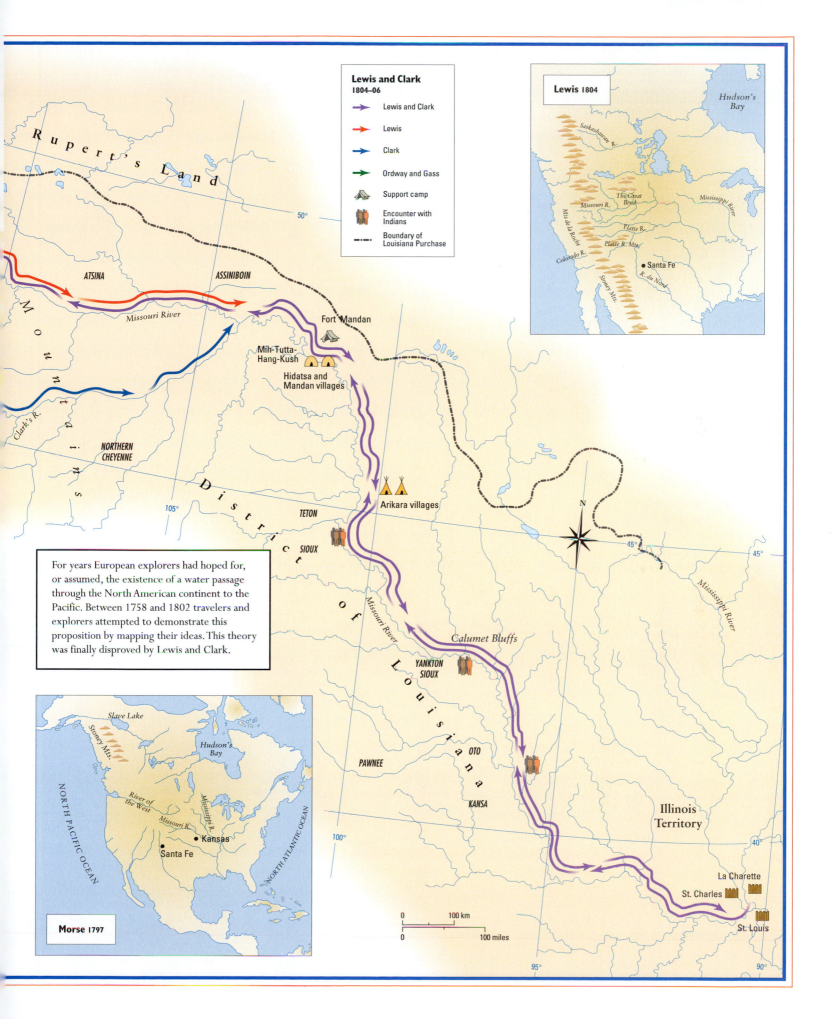

Lewis and Clark
1804–06

→ Lewis and Clark
→ Lewis
→ Clark
→ Ordway and Gass
Support camp
Encounter with Indians
Boundary of Louisiana Purchase

Lewis 1804

Hudson's Bay
Saskatchewan R.
Mts de la Roche
Missouri R.
The Great Bend
Mississippi River
Platte R.
Platte R. Mts
Colorado R.
Stoney Mts.
R. du Nord
Santa Fe

Rupert's Land

ATSINA
ASSINIBOIN
Missouri River
Fort Mandan
Mih-Tutta-Hang-Kush
Hidatsa and Mandan villages

Mountains

Clark's R.

NORTHERN CHEYENNE

District

TETON

SIOUX

Arikara villages

50°

105°

45°

N

45°

Mississippi River

For years European explorers had hoped for, or assumed, the existence of a water passage through the North American continent to the Pacific. Between 1758 and 1802 travelers and explorers attempted to demonstrate this proposition by mapping their ideas. This theory was finally disproved by Lewis and Clark.

of

Louisiana

Missouri River

Calumet Bluffs

YANKTON SIOUX

PAWNEE

OTO

KANSA

Illinois Territory

40°

La Charette
St. Charles

St. Louis

Morse 1797

Slave Lake
Stoney Mts.
Hudson's Bay
NORTH PACIFIC OCEAN
River of the West
Missouri R.
Mississippi R.
Kansas
Santa Fe
NORTH ATLANTIC OCEAN

0   100 km
0   100 miles

100°

95°

90°

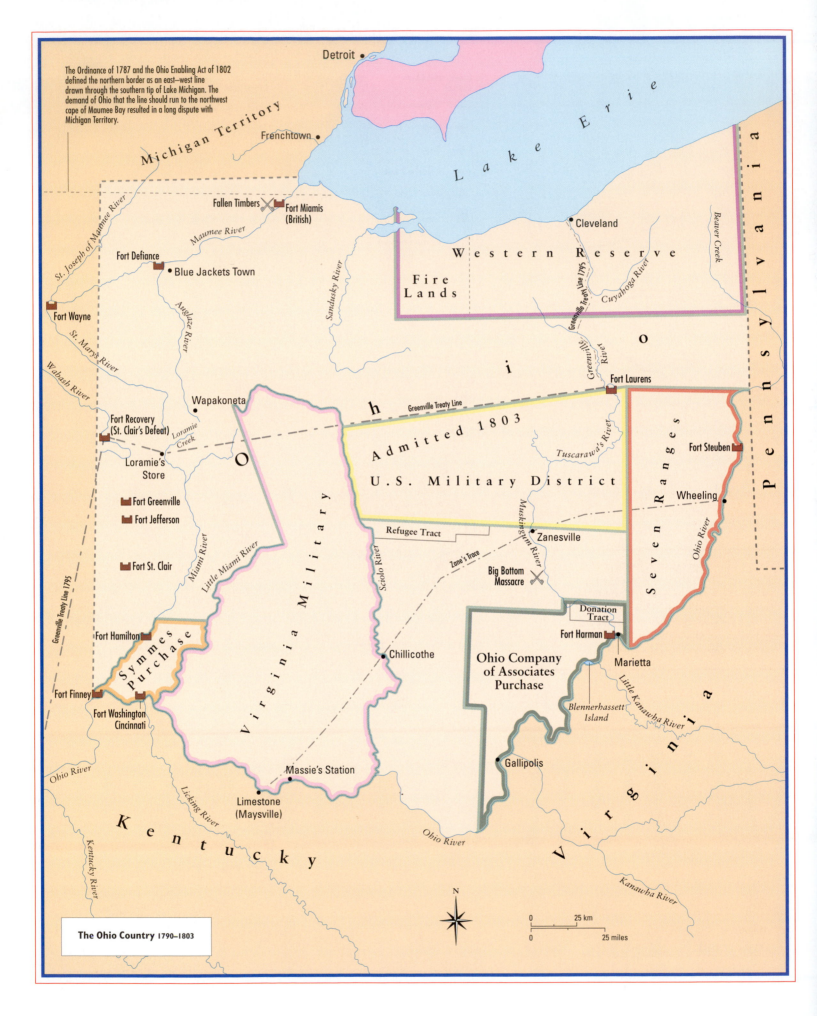

The Ordinance of 1787 and the Ohio Enabling Act of 1802 defined the northern border as an east–west line drawn through the southern tip of Lake Michigan. The demand of Ohio that the line should run to the northwest cape of Maumee Bay resulted in a long dispute with Michigan Territory.

Detroit

Lake Erie

Michigan Territory

Frenchtown

Fallen Timbers   Fort Miamis (British)

Maumee River

Fort Defiance   Blue Jackets Town

Cleveland

Western Reserve

Fire Lands

Sandusky River

Greenville Treaty Line 1795

Cuyahoga River

Auglaze River

St. Joseph of Maumee River

Fort Wayne

St. Mary's River

Wabash River

Wapakoneta

o

h

i

o

Fort Laurens

Fort Recovery (St. Clair's Defeat)

Loramie Creek

Greenville Treaty Line

Tuscarawa's River

Greenville River

Seven Ranges

Fort Steuben

Loramie's Store

O

Admitted 1803
U.S. Military District

Fort Greenville

Fort Jefferson

Fort St. Clair

Virginia Military

Refugee Tract

Zanesville

Wheeling

Ohio River

Muskingum River

Zane's Trace

Big Bottom Massacre

Miami River

Little Miami River

Fort Hamilton

Symmes Purchase

Donation Tract

Fort Harman

Marietta

Fort Finney

Fort Washington
Cincinnati

Sciolo River

Chillicothe

Ohio Company of Associates Purchase

Blennerhassett Island

Little Kanawha River

Ohio River

Licking River

Kentucky River

Massie's Station

Limestone (Maysville)

Gallipolis

Ohio River

Kentucky

Pennsylvania

Virginia

Kanawha River

Beaver Creek

N

0   25 km
0   25 miles

The Ohio Country 1790–1803

The Frontier in 1800

Area of settlement

Fort

BRITISH NORTH AMERICA

Disputed with Britain

To Mass.

Lake Superior

Lake Huron

Lake Michigan

Lake Ontario

Lake Erie

Portland

Vermont

N.H.

Salem
Boston

New York

Albany
Worcester
Mass.

Providence
New Bedford

Conn.
R.I.

Fort Detroit

Territory
Northwest
of Ohio River

Pennsylvania

New York
Brooklyn

Lancaster

New Jersey

Philadelphia

Wilmington

Indiana
Territory

Cumberland
Baltimore
Maryland
Delaware

Washington

Chillicothe

Cincinnati

Staunton

Fort Orleans

St. Louis

Louisville
Lexington

Virginia

Richmond

Williamsburg

Kentucky

Louisiana

Ceded by Spain to France in secret treaty, 1800
Possession not taken by France until 1803

North
Carolina

Raleigh

Tennessee

Charlotte

Memphis

South
Carlonia

Augusta

Charleston

Arkansas Post

Territory
South of
Ohio River

Georgia

Savannah

Mississippi Territory

Natchitoches
Natchez

Nacogdoches

West Florida

Pensacola

St. Augustine

New Orleans

East
Florida

ATLANTIC OCEAN

N

Gulf of Mexico

Bahamas

0   400 km
0   400 miles

BRITISH
NORTH
AMERICA

MICHIGAN TERRITORY
Created from Indiana Territory in 1805

Added to Indiana
Territory, 1802

Detroit

ILLINOIS TERRITORY

Fort Michilimackinac

Fort Howard

Prairie du Chien
Fort Crawford

Sauk Fox
Fort Armstrong

Fort Dearborn
(Chicago)

Fort Industry

Fort Clark
(Peoria)

Fort Edwards

Fort Wayne

Miami

Tippecanoe
Ouiatenon
Prophet's Town

Mississinewa
Fort Recovery

MILITARY BOUNTY TRACT

Illinois
Admitted as a state 1818

Indiana
Admitted as a state 1816

Ohio
Admitted as a state 1803

Fort Harrison
Spencer

Brookville

Lawrenceburg

St. Louis
Edwardsville
Cahokia

English Settlement

Vincennes

White Oak
Springs

Madison
Lexington
Jefferson
New Albany
Corydon
Clarksville

Vevay

Prairie du Rocher
Kaskaskia

Evansville

Kentucky

Shawneetown

Colconda

Northwest Territories 1800–18

- Indiana Territory 1800
- Added to Indiana Territory 1802
- Area added to Indiana Territory in 1802
- Michigan Territory created from Indiana Territory in 1805
- Illinois Territory 1809
- Modern borders

0   100 km
0   100 miles

In the fall of 1800 Napoleon Bonaparte prevailed on the king of Spain to cede Louisiana back to France in a secret treaty. The French were back in North America and in a position to block the westward expansion of the United States. Jefferson instructed Robert Livingston, the U.S. minister to France, to inform the French government that if France took possession of Louisiana, the friendship between the two countries would be destroyed. After intense political discussions between Washington and Paris, threats of a possibility of war and anti-French alliances with Britain, Napoleon abruptly offered the whole of Louisiana for $15 million. An astonished Monroe, realizing a bargain, accepted on behalf of the U.S. government.

Louisiana Purchase and Border Settlements 1803–1819

- Louisiana Purchase 1803, natural border of Louisiana, drainage of the Mississippi
- Territory of Louisiana from 1805–12, then Missouri Territory
- U.S.–British Treaty line of 1818, the 49th Parallel
- Adams–Onis Treaty line of 1819
- Red River Basin ceded by Great Britain to U.S. in 1818
- Area ceded by U.S. to Great Britain 1818
- Spanish territory

Rupert's Land (Hudson's Bay Company)

BRITISH NORTH AMERICA

Oregon Country
Jointly administered by Great Britain and the United States; also claimed by Spain

Lake of the Woods

Lake Superior

Illinois Territory

Lake Michigan

Manuel's Fort

Fort Mandan

Fort Manuel

Fort Snelling (St. Anthony)

Fort Howard

Fort aux Cedres (Loisels Post)

Fort Dearborn (Chicago)

District of Louisiana

Fort Lisa

Fort Armstrong

Fort Clark (Peoria)

Ohio

Fort Madison

UNITED STATES

Fort Osage (Clark)

Fort Bellefontaine

St. Louis

Kaskaskia

Louisville

Potosi

Kentucky

New Madrid

Tennessee

Nashville

MEXICO

Santa Fe

Colorado River

Fort Smith

Fort Pickering

Red River

Mississippi Territory

Mississippi

Nacogdoches

Sabine River

Florida

Pensacola

San Antonio

Fort Adams

New Orleans

Gulf of Mexico

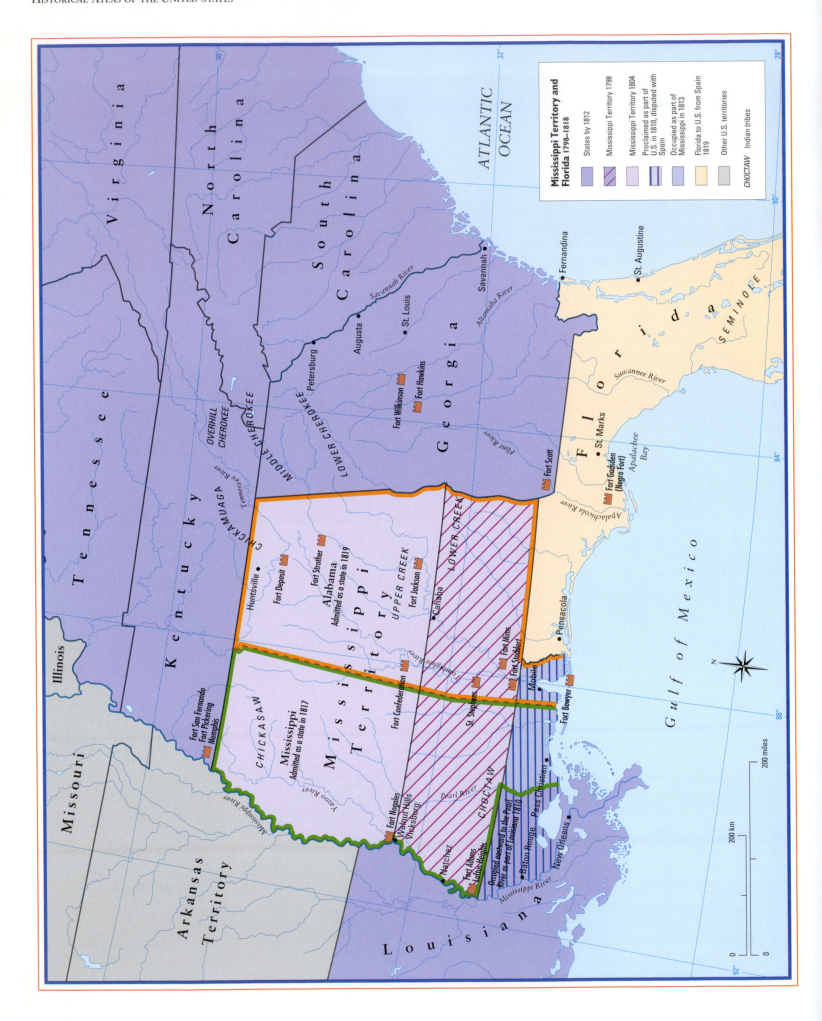

Mississippi Territory and Florida 1798–1818

States by 1812

Mississippi Territory 1798

Mississippi Territory 1804

Proclaimed as part of U.S. in 1810, disputed with Spain

Occupied as part of Mississippi in 1813

Florida to U.S. from Spain 1819

Other U.S. territories

CHOCTAW   Indian tribes

ATLANTIC OCEAN

Gulf of Mexico

F l o r i d a

SEMINOLE

Fernandina

St. Augustine

St. Marks

Fort Gadsden (Negro Fort)

Apalachee Bay

Apalachicola River

Suwannee River

Fort Scott

Pensacola

Flint River

Altamaha River

Savannah

Savannah River

St. Louis

Augusta

Petersburg

Fort Wilkinson

Fort Hawkins

G e o r g i a

S o u t h   C a r o l i n a

N o r t h   C a r o l i n a

V i r g i n i a

T e n n e s s e e

K e n t u c k y

OVERHILL CHEROKEE

MIDDLE CHEROKEE

LOWER CHEROKEE

CHICKAMAUGA

Tennessee River

LOWER CREEK

UPPER CREEK

Huntsville

Fort Deposit

Fort Strother

Fort Jackson

Cahaba

Alabama
Admitted as a state in 1819

M i s s i s s i p p i   T e r r i t o r y

Fort Confederation

Tombigbee River

Fort Mims

Fort Stoddert

St. Stephens

Mobile

Fort Bowyer

Fort Mitchell

Illinois

Missouri

Arkansas Territory

Fort San Fernando
Fort Pickering
Memphis

CHICKASAW

Mississippi
Admitted as a state in 1817

Yazoo River

Mississippi River

Fort Nogales
Walnut Hills
Vicksburg

M i s s i s s i p p i   T e r r i t o r y

Pearl River

Natchez

Fort Adams
Loftus Heights

Occupied eastward to the Pearl River as part of Louisiana 1810

CHOCTAW

Baton Rouge

Pass Christian

New Orleans

Mississippi River

L o u i s i a n a

N

200 miles

200 km

Native American Land Cessions
1783–1814

1800	Land cessions 1783–1804
1806	Land cessions 1805–1808
1810	Land cessions 1809–1814
⛺	Native American settlement
🏰	Fort
—	Borders c. 1840

The War of 1812

	U.S. and British movement, 1812
	U.S. and British movement, 1813
	U.S. and British movement, 1814–15
	British blockade
✕	Battle
	British occupied U.S. territory
	British territory
	Spanish territory

The War of 1812 was essentially a by-product of the rivalry between Britain and France. The United States traded with both sides of the conflict. Each was eager to obtain American goods and also determined to prevent the U.S. from trading with its rival. The United States declared war on Britain for various reasons: the British navy did more damage to American commerce; Anti-British sentiment was strong in the years after the Revolution; and Canada, controlled by the British, was an easy target for American expansion. The war raged from June 1812 to December 1814 and had largely gone in favor of the British until the battle of New Orleans, where the British were repulsed with heavy losses.

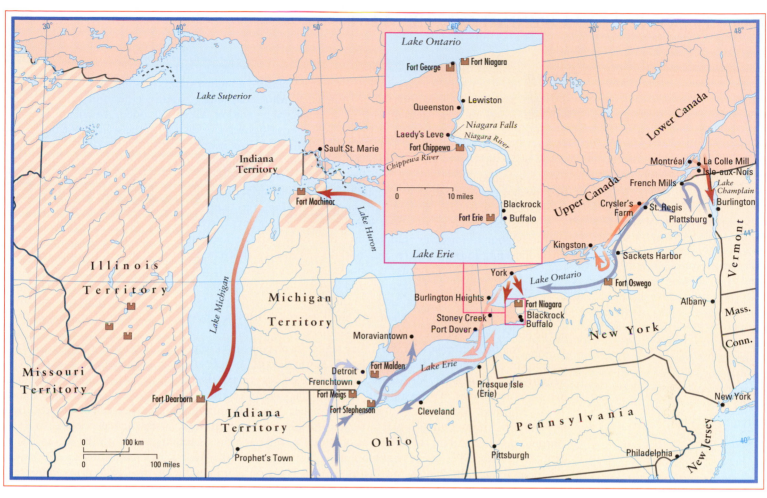

British New Orleans Campaign
22 November 1814–11 February 1815

→ British advance

→ Jackson's night attack

⇢ British withdrawal

▬ Fort

〜 Fortification

The Lakes Campaign
July 1812–November 1814

→ British advance

→ U.S. movements

▬ Major fort

▬ Fort

British occupied U.S. territory

British occupied U.S. territory

Operations around Washington and Baltimore
19 August–September 1814

→ British attack

⇢ British withdrawal

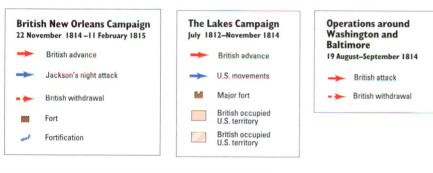

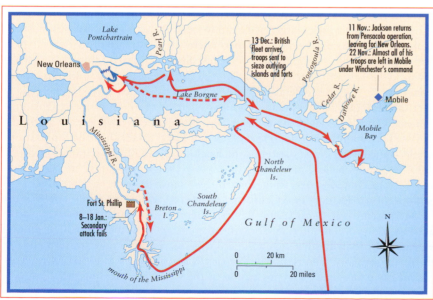

PART ELEVEN

OPENING OF THE WEST

THE WEST has figured prominently in the American imagination. Its pristine landscape and "savage" inhabitants appealed to Americans who increasingly lived in cities and worked inside stores, factories, and offices. Yet therein lay the paradox. Much as modern Americans pile into gas-guzzling campers and SUVs and speed along superhighways to delight in the solitude of unspoiled nature, Americans in the 1830s and 1840s longed to experience (if only vicariously) the rugged challenges of the West, but in doing so they transformed it into something else. John O'Sullivan, a New York journalist, explained that it was the "fulfillment of our manifest destiny to overspread the continent allotted by Providence for the free development of our yearly multiplying millions." Those millions called themselves settlers, a self-description that connoted their intent to "settle"—to tame the Wild West.

Yet the settlement of the West was accomplished in part through violence. As each new wave of explorers, soon followed by trappers, and then by settlers, flooded onto the western plains, they forced the Indians first into the deserts and foothills and then to different regions altogether. During the 1830s tens of thousands of Chickasaw, Chocktaw, Cherokee, and Creek Indians were driven or forcibly removed from Mississippi, Alabama, and Georgia to the region west of the Arkansas Territory. The Fox, Miami, and Shawnee Indians, among others, were removed from Ohio, Illinois, and parts of the Iowa Territory farther west to the Nebraska and Kansas Territories. Those who chose to fight instead, such as the Sauk, were crushed by American soldiers.

The American conquest of the Texas region involved usurpation of a different character. In 1821 a contingent of Americans led by Stephen F. Austin flocked into Texas, then a province of Mexico. The fledgling government of Mexico found it impossible to throw them out, and so granted them some autonomous powers. Within a decade, some 20,000 white Americans and 2,000 slaves had poured into Texas. Alarmed, Mexico in 1830 outlawed further American immigration to Texas. The law deterred few potential immigrants, but it provoked Austin and his followers to seek independence. In 1835 Antonio de Santa Anna, the president of Mexico, embarked on a campaign to crush the Texan insurgents. Santa Anna's large army annihilated a tiny garrison at the Alamo, near San Antonio. They then advanced toward the San Jacinto River. Samuel Houston, commander of the Texan army, retreated. Finally he attacked, suddenly and with force, routing Santa Anna's army and sending it fleeing across the Rio Grande. The people of Texas then voted to be annexed by the United States. The chief complication, which cast a long shadow over antebellum politics, was the fact that Texas endorsed slavery.

Looming sectional tensions were one reason why President James K. Polk favored war with Mexico. The war might help unify the nation and thereby obscure the impending division over slavery. The ostensible issues were unpaid Mexican debts and the boundary of Texas—Mexico claimed the region to the Nueces River, 150 miles north of the Rio Grande. In 1846 a 4,000-man army commanded by General Zachery Taylor marched to the Rio Grande, near the Mexican town of Matamoros. Mexico crossed the river and invested Fort Texas. Taylor's army defeated the Mexicans at Palo Alto, raised the siege of Fort Texas, and drove the Mexicans back across the border. The United States had decisively won the first battles of the Mexican–American War; the others would follow suit.

Taylor made preparations for a full-scale invasion of Mexico. In September, he attacked Monterey and, after five days of fighting, forced it to surrender. In February 1847, joined by another American army from San Antonio, Taylor defeated a much larger Mexican force at Buena Vista. Meanwhile, small contingents of American soldiers in California, backed by American settlers, overthrew the Mexican government there and proclaimed the Republic of California. The final blow to Mexico came in 1847 when an American army under Winfield Scott landed at Vera Cruz, on the Gulf of Mexico, and fought its way through large, but wholly ineffective, Mexican defenses. On 14 September, Mexico City surrendered.

The Mormon settlement of Utah during this decade was less coercive than the other expansionist actions. Partly this was because the Mormons chose as their new home a desert wilderness along the shores of the Great Salt Lake. They built elaborate irrigation systems and established the foundations of what they imagined would someday be a vast nation in the Rockies. By 1850, the population of the Utah Territory was 11,000. Mormon beliefs, in certain ways (especially polygamy) at odds with Christian practices elsewhere in the United States, strengthened their sense of community.

Less peaceable was the flood of prospectors into California after gold was discovered in 1848 in the foothills to the east of the Sacramento and San Joaquin Rivers. The next year some 55,000 Americans crossed the Rockies to get to California; another 25,000 booked passage on ships that sailed around South America to San Francisco. In 1859 another rich gold site was discovered on the western edge of the Utah Territory, north of Carson City. Thousands of Mexicans set out for California as well. By 1860, some 200,000 whites, mostly males, had taken possession of the state. The previous inhabitants—some 150,000 Indians—were virtually wiped out.

MAPS

As the United States grew in size and wealth, settlers flowed into the new territories. Some came directly from Europe, most from the eastern part of the United States. Between 1820 and 1850 the population expanded from 9.6 million to 23.2 million, including 2.4 million immigrants largely from Europe.

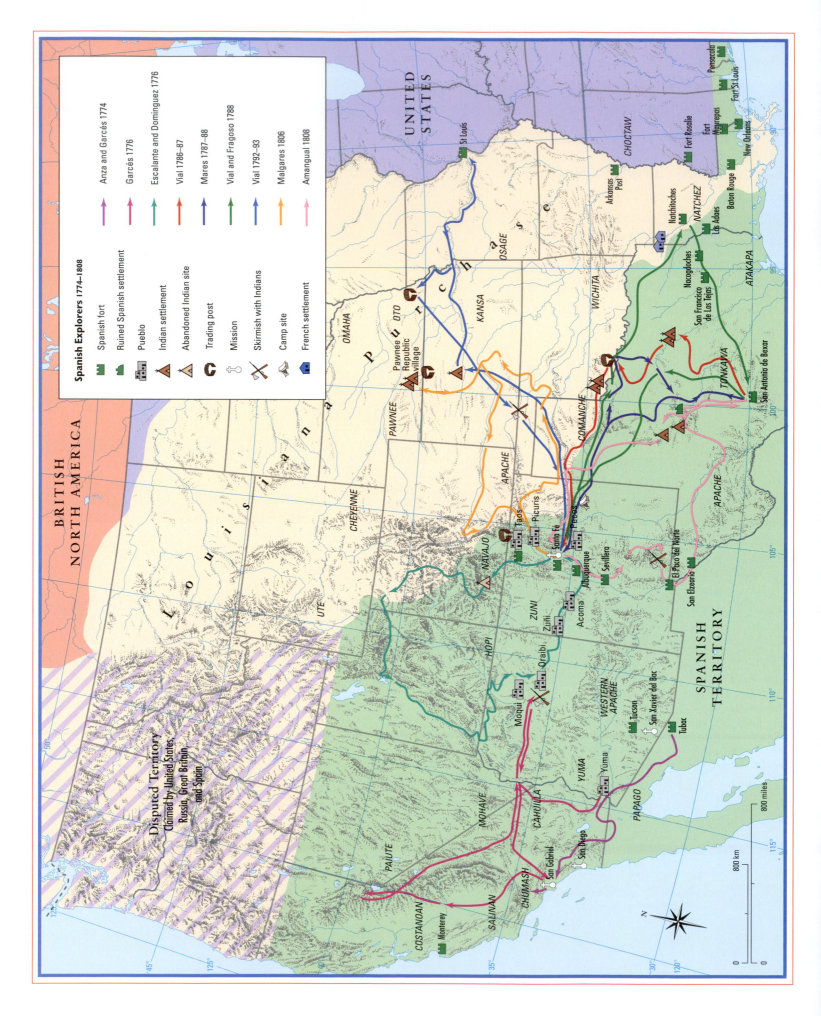

Spanish Explorers 1774–1808

Anza and Garcés 1774
Garcés 1776
Escalante and Dominguez 1776
Vial 1786–87
Mares 1787–88
Vial and Fragoso 1788
Vial 1792–93
Malgares 1806
Amangual 1808

Spanish fort
Ruined Spanish settlement
Pueblo
Indian settlement
Abandoned Indian site
Trading post
Mission
Skirmish with Indians
Camp site
French settlement

Disputed Territory
Claimed by United States,
Russia, Great Britain,
and Spain

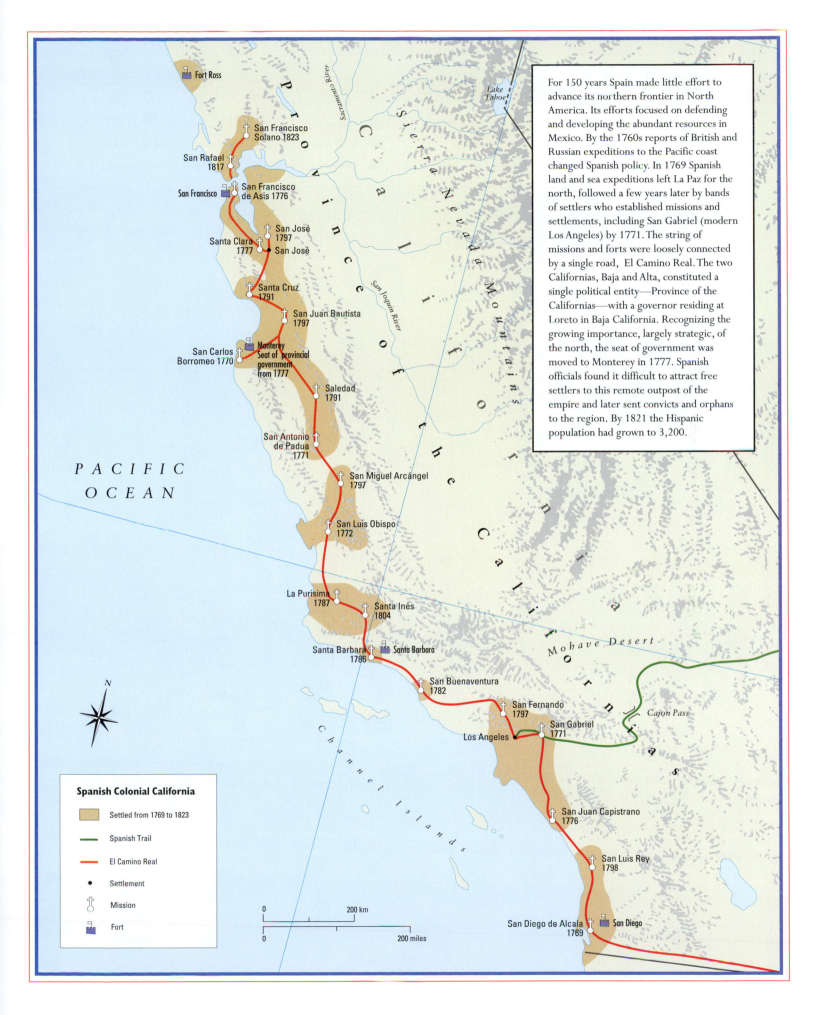

PACIFIC OCEAN

Fort Ross

San Francisco Solano 1823

San Rafael 1817

San Francisco

San Francisco de Asis 1776

San José 1797

Santa Clara 1777

San José

Santa Cruz 1791

San Juan Bautista 1797

San Carlos Borromeo 1770

Monterey Seat of provincial government from 1777

Saledad 1791

San Antonio de Padua 1771

San Miguel Arcángel 1797

San Luis Obispo 1772

La Purisima 1787

Santa Inés 1804

Santa Barbara

Santa Barbara 1786

San Buenaventura 1782

San Fernando 1797

San Gabriel 1771

Los Angeles

San Juan Capistrano 1776

San Luis Rey 1798

San Diego de Alcala 1769

San Diego

Cajon Pass

Mohave Desert

Province of the Californias

Sierra Nevada Mountains

Lake Tahoe

San Joaquin River

Sacramento River

Channel Islands

For 150 years Spain made little effort to advance its northern frontier in North America. Its efforts focused on defending and developing the abundant resources in Mexico. By the 1760s reports of British and Russian expeditions to the Pacific coast changed Spanish policy. In 1769 Spanish land and sea expeditions left La Paz for the north, followed a few years later by bands of settlers who established missions and settlements, including San Gabriel (modern Los Angeles) by 1771. The string of missions and forts were loosely connected by a single road, El Camino Real. The two Californias, Baja and Alta, constituted a single political entity—Province of the Californias—with a governor residing at Loreto in Baja California. Recognizing the growing importance, largely strategic, of the north, the seat of government was moved to Monterey in 1777. Spanish officials found it difficult to attract free settlers to this remote outpost of the empire and later sent convicts and orphans to the region. By 1821 the Hispanic population had grown to 3,200.

Spanish Colonial California

Settled from 1769 to 1823

Spanish Trail

El Camino Real

Settlement

Mission

Fort

0   200 km

0   200 miles

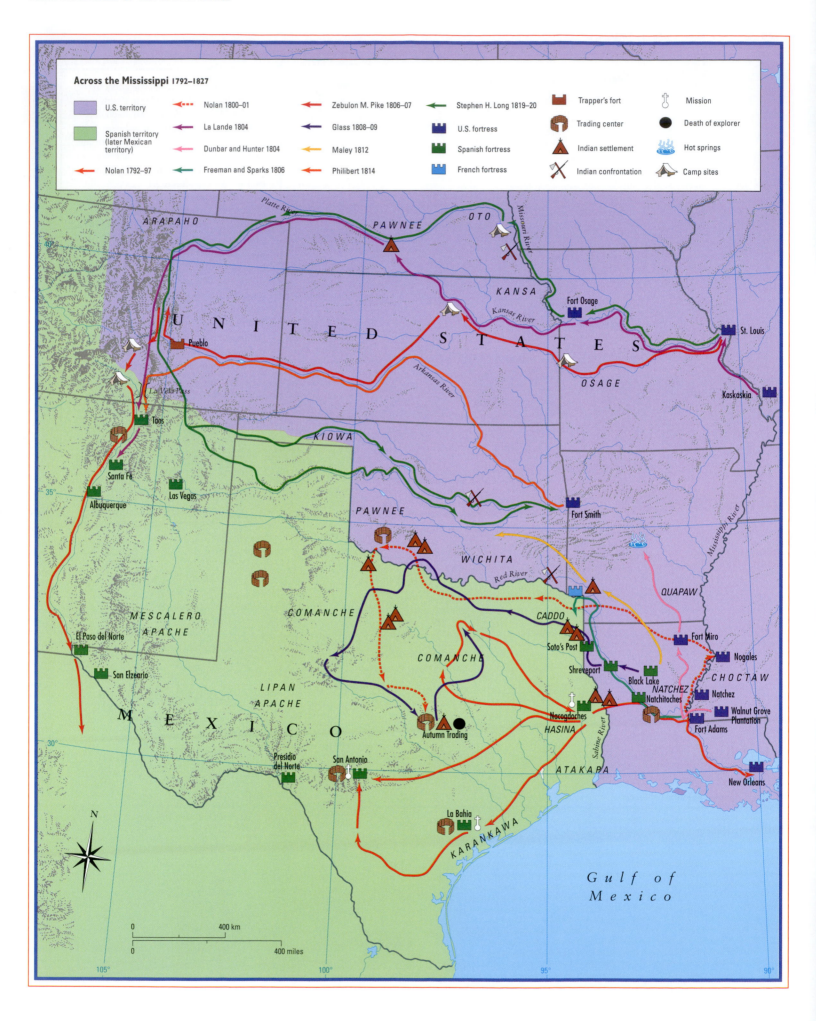

Across the Mississippi 1792–1827

- U.S. territory
- Spanish territory (later Mexican territory)
- Nolan 1792–97
- Nolan 1800–01
- La Lande 1804
- Dunbar and Hunter 1804
- Freeman and Sparks 1806
- Zebulon M. Pike 1806–07
- Glass 1808–09
- Maley 1812
- Philibert 1814
- Stephen H. Long 1819–20
- U.S. fortress
- Spanish fortress
- French fortress
- Trapper's fort
- Trading center
- Indian settlement
- Indian confrontation
- Mission
- Death of explorer
- Hot springs
- Camp sites

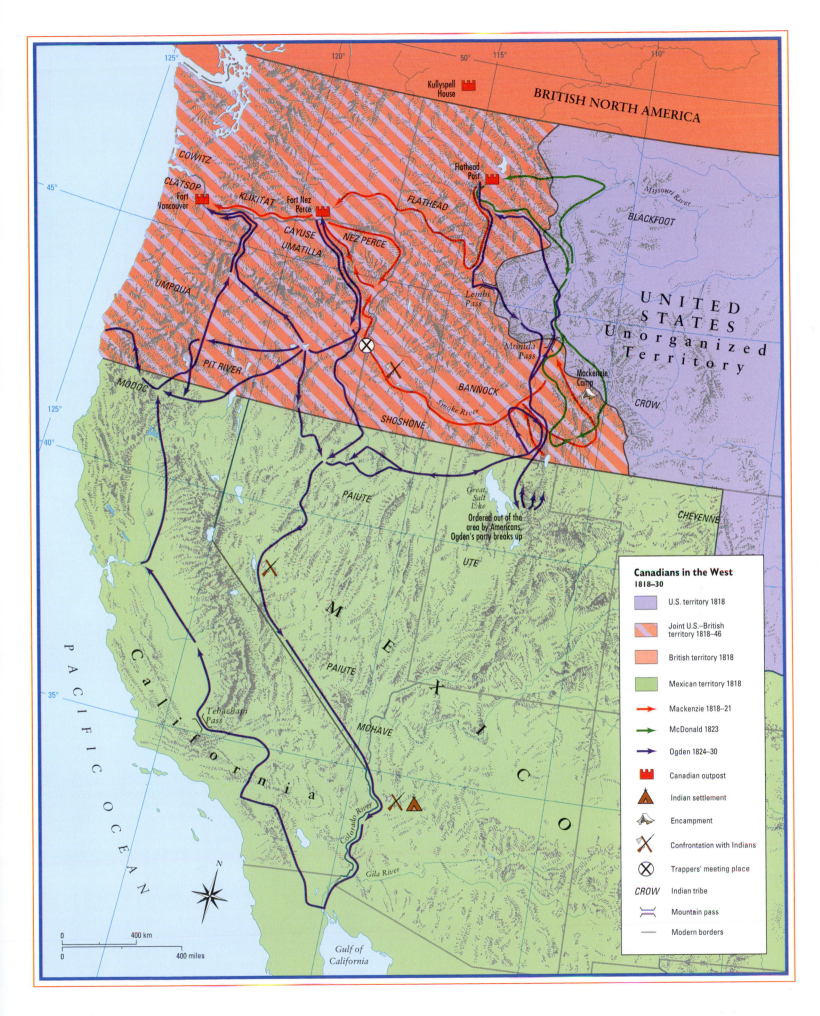

Canadians in the West
1818–30

- U.S. territory 1818
- Joint U.S.–British territory 1818–46
- British territory 1818
- Mexican territory 1818
- Mackenzie 1818–21
- McDonald 1823
- Ogden 1824–30
- Canadian outpost
- Indian settlement
- Encampment
- Confrontation with Indians
- Trappers' meeting place
- *CROW* Indian tribe
- Mountain pass
- Modern borders

BRITISH NORTH AMERICA

Kullyspell House

Flathead Post

Missouri River

BLACKFOOT

UNITED STATES Unorganized Territory

CROW

COWITZ

CLATSOP Fort Vancouver

KLIKITAT

Fort Nez Perce

CAYUSE

UMATILLA

NEZ PERCE

FLATHEAD

Lemhi Pass

Monida Pass

Mackenzie Camp

UMPQUA

PIT RIVER

MODOC

BANNOCK

Smoke River

SHOSHONE

Great Salt Lake

Ordered out of the area by Americans, Ogden's party breaks up

PAIUTE

UTE

CHEYENNE

M E X I C O

PAIUTE

Tehachapi Pass

MOHAVE

Colorado River

Gila River

C a l i f o r n i a

P A C I F I C   O C E A N

N

Gulf of California

0   400 km
0   400 miles

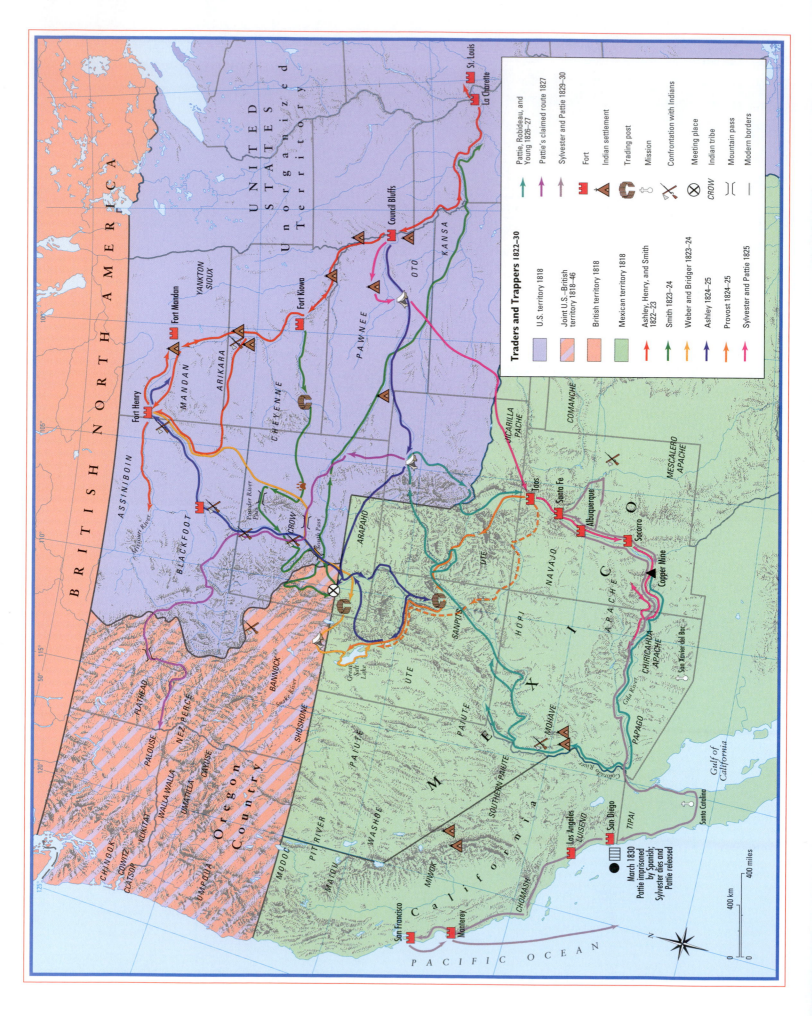

Traders and Trappers 1822–30

Pattie, Robideau, and Young 1826–27
Pattie's claimed route 1827
Sylvester and Pattie 1829–30

Fort
Indian settlement
Trading post
Mission
Confrontation with Indians
Meeting place
CROW Indian tribe
Mountain pass
Modern borders

U.S. territory 1818
Joint U.S.–British territory 1818–46
British territory 1818
Mexican territory 1818

Ashley, Henry, and Smith 1822–23
Smith 1823–24
Weber and Bridger 1823–24
Ashley 1824–25
Provost 1824–25
Sylvester and Pattie 1825

March 1830 Pattie imprisoned by Spanish; Sylvester dies and Pattie released

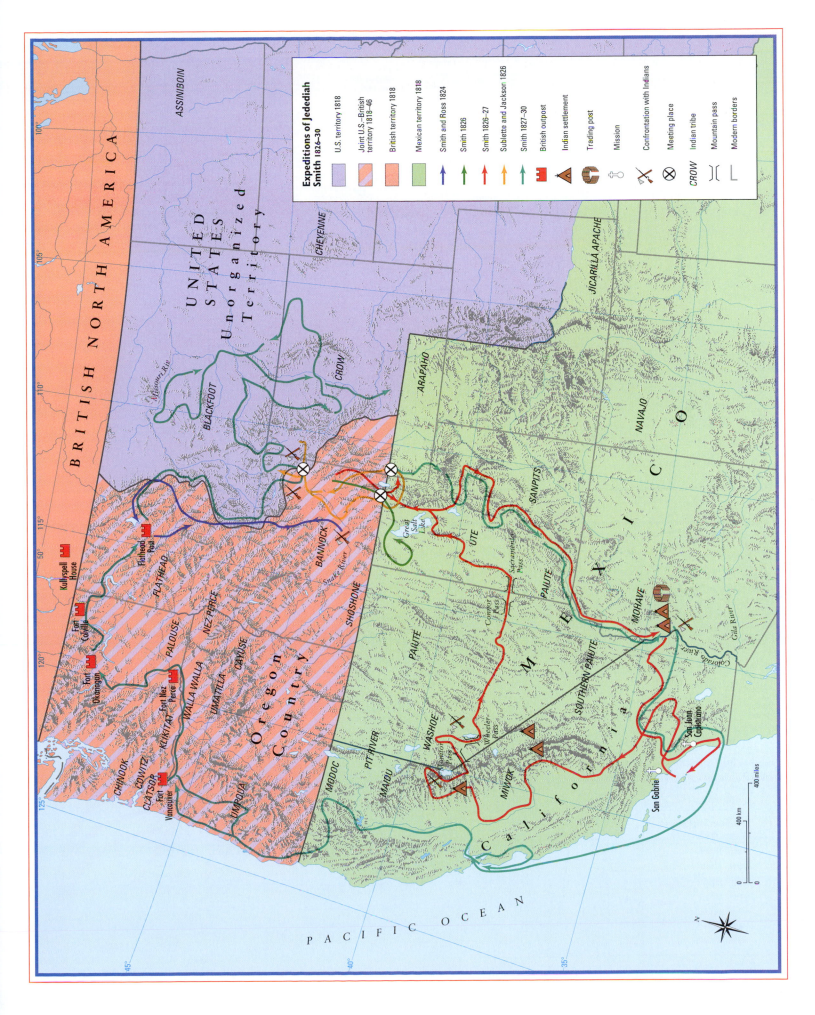

Expeditions of Jedediah Smith 1826–30

U.S. territory 1818	
Joint U.S.–British territory 1818–46	
British territory 1818	
Mexican territory 1818	
Smith and Ross 1824	
Smith 1826	
Smith 1826–27	
Sublette and Jackson 1826	
Smith 1827–30	
British outpost	
Indian settlement	
Trading post	
Mission	
Confrontation with Indians	
Meeting place	
CROW Indian tribe	
Mountain pass	
Modern borders	

0 50 km
0 50 miles

New York

Home of young
Joseph Smith
Palmyra
Manchester
Site of Hill Cumorah,
locale of golden plates

Fayette
First Mormon church
founded, 1830

Mormonism, founded in New York State in 1830, claimed that the Americans had witnessed a historical development in ancient times similar to that in the Bible. The Mormons began a series of westward treks, finally concentrating in the Salt Lake City area in 1847. With the immigration of converts from northwest Europe, the population of the theocratic state of Deseret had risen by 1880 to some 68,000. Ninety-five percent of them were Mormon.

Washington

Montana

North Dakota

Minnesota

Oregon

Idaho

Wyoming

South Dakota

Wisconsin

"City of James"

Beaver Island

Michigan

Maine

New York

Vt. N.H.

Mass.

Conn. R.I.

Palmyra
Manchester
Fayette

Salt Lake City
Mormon settlement, 1847
Permanent Mormon
headquarters

Yerba Buena

New Hope

from New York
via Hawaii

California

San Bernadino
1851–57

Utah

Nevada

Colorado

Kansas

Winter Quarters
1846–48

Nebraska

Iowa
Clay County
1833–36

Missouri

Independence
1831–33

Far West
1836–39

Illinois

Nauvoo
1839–44

Indiana

Ohio

Kirtland
1831–38

Pennsylvania

New York

N.J.

Del.

Md.

West Virginia

Virginia

Kentucky

North Carolina

Tennessee

Arizona

New Mexico

Oklahoma

Arkansas

Zodiac
Hill
Country

Texas

Lyman Wight

Mississippi

Alabama

Georgia

South Carolina

Louisiana

Florida

from England,
Scandinavia,
and Germany

Sam Branman

to California
via Hawaii

James Jesse Strank

Hawaii
Lanai
●
1854–58
Mormon colony

0 300 km
0 300 miles

N

Mormonism 1830–58

● Important Mormon locale

→ Mormon exodus

▭ Proposed Mormon state of Deseret, 1849

✳ Violence against Mormons

→ Immigration of European converts

▲ Mormon splinter group

→ Mormon splinter spread

● New York's "burned-over district"

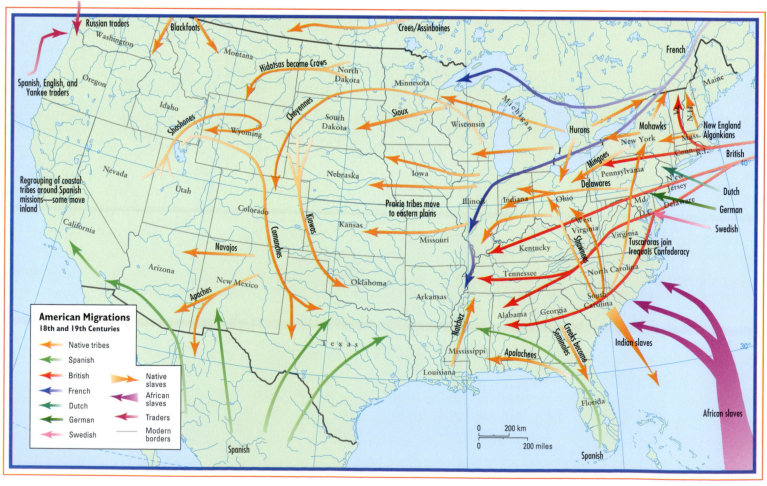

Russian traders

Blackfoots

Crees/Assinboines

French

Washington

Montana

Spanish, English, and
Yankee traders

Hidatsas become Crows

North Dakota

Minnesota

Maine

Oregon

Idaho

Shoshones

Wyoming

Cheyennes

South Dakota

Sioux

Wisconsin

Michigan

Hurons

Mohawks

New York

New England Algonkians

British

Regrouping of coastal
tribes around Spanish
missions—some move
inland

Nevada

Utah

Colorado

Kiowas

Nebraska

Iowa

Mingoes

Delawares

Pennsylvania

New Jersey

Dutch

German

Swedish

California

Comanches

Kansas

Missouri

Prairie tribes move
to eastern plains

Illinois

Indiana

Ohio

West Virginia

Virginia

D.C.

Md.

Del.

Shawnees

Tuscaroras join
Iroquois Confederacy

Navajos

Arizona

New Mexico

Apaches

Oklahoma

Arkansas

Tennessee

Kentucky

North Carolina

Texas

Natchez

Mississippi

Louisiana

Alabama

Georgia

South Carolina

Creeks become Seminoles

Apalachees

Indian slaves

Florida

African slaves

Spanish

Spanish

American Migrations
18th and 19th Centuries

→ Native tribes
→ Spanish
→ British
→ French
→ Dutch
→ German
→ Swedish
→ Native slaves
→ African slaves
→ Traders
— Modern borders

144

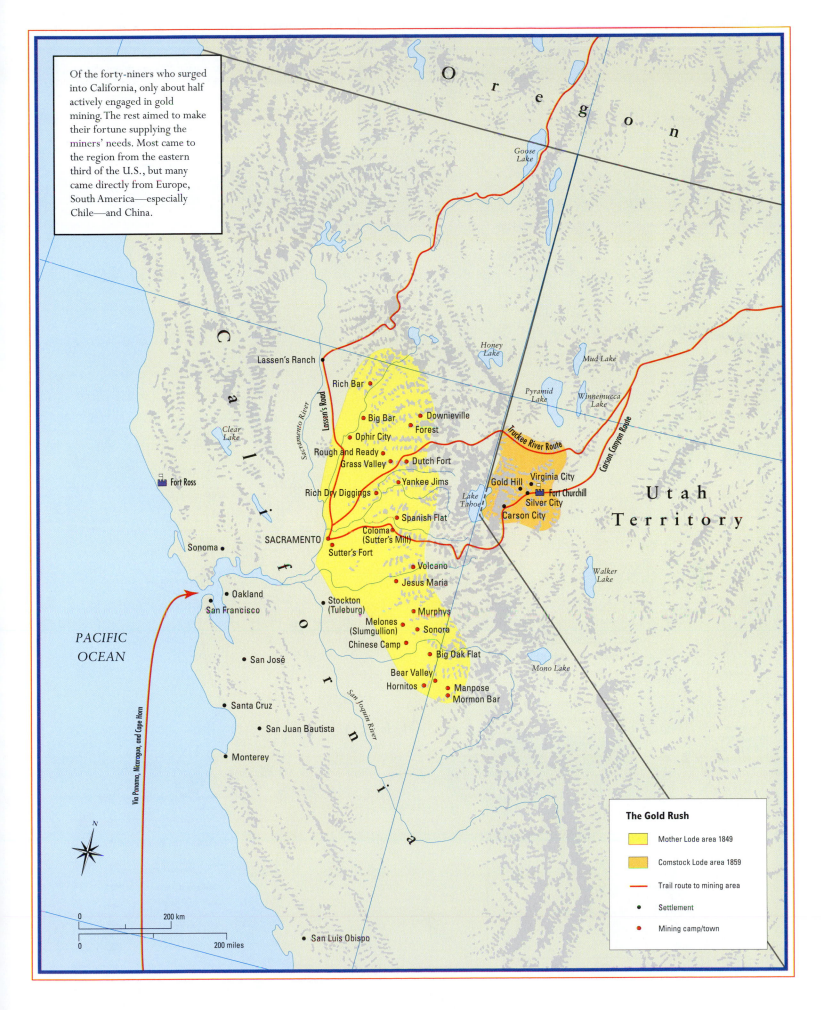

Of the forty-niners who surged into California, only about half actively engaged in gold mining. The rest aimed to make their fortune supplying the miners' needs. Most came to the region from the eastern third of the U.S., but many came directly from Europe, South America—especially Chile—and China.

O r e g o n

Goose Lake

C a l i f o r n i a

Lassen's Ranch

Rich Bar

Big Bar · · Downieville
Ophir City · Forest
Rough and Ready
Grass Valley · · Dutch Fort
Yankee Jims
Rich Dry Diggings
Spanish Flat
Coloma (Sutter's Mill)
SACRAMENTO
Sutter's Fort
Volcano
Jesus Maria
Stockton (Tuleburg)
Murphys
Melones (Slumgullion) · Sonora
Chinese Camp
Big Oak Flat
Bear Valley
Hornitos · Manpose
Mormon Bar

Sonoma ·

Fort Ross

Clear Lake

Sacramento River

Lassen's Road

Honey Lake

Mud Lake

Pyramid Lake

Winnemucca Lake

Truckee River Route

Carson Canyon Route

Virginia City
Gold Hill
Silver City
Carson City
Fort Churchill

Lake Tahoe

U t a h
T e r r i t o r y

Walker Lake

Mono Lake

· Oakland
San Francisco

· San José

· Santa Cruz

· San Juan Bautista

· Monterey

San Joaquin River

PACIFIC
OCEAN

Via Panama, Nicaragua, and Cape Horn

N

0   200 km
0   200 miles

· San Luis Obispo

The Gold Rush

Mother Lode area 1849

Comstock Lode area 1859

Trail route to mining area

· Settlement

· Mining camp/town

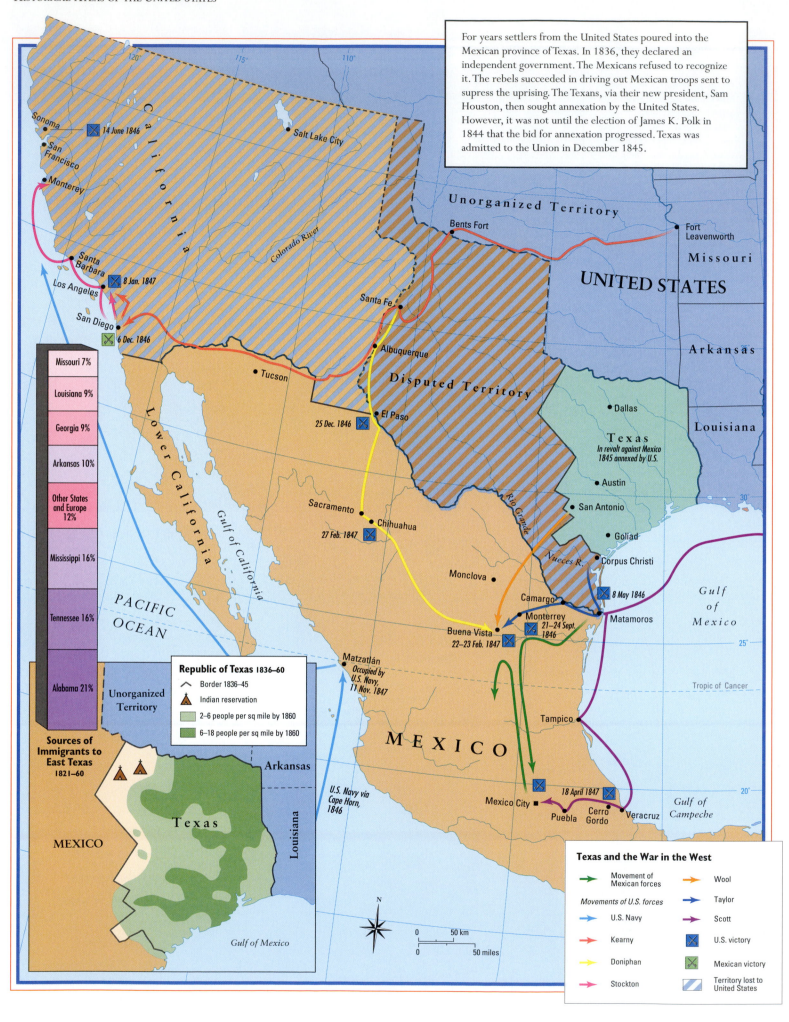

For years settlers from the United States poured into the Mexican province of Texas. In 1836, they declared an independent government. The Mexicans refused to recognize it. The rebels succeeded in driving out Mexican troops sent to supress the uprising. The Texans, via their new president, Sam Houston, then sought annexation by the United States. However, it was not until the election of James K. Polk in 1844 that the bid for annexation progressed. Texas was admitted to the Union in December 1845.

Sources of Immigrants to East Texas 1821–60

Missouri 7%
Louisiana 9%
Georgia 9%
Arkansas 10%
Other States and Europe 12%
Mississippi 16%
Tennessee 16%
Alabama 21%

Republic of Texas 1836–60

Border 1836–45
Indian reservation
2–6 people per sq mile by 1860
6–18 people per sq mile by 1860

Texas and the War in the West

Movement of Mexican forces
Wool
Movements of U.S. forces
U.S. Navy
Taylor
Kearny
Scott
Doniphan
U.S. victory
Stockton
Mexican victory
Territory lost to United States

Matzatlán
Occupied by U.S. Navy 11 Nov. 1847

U.S. Navy via Cape Horn, 1846

14 June 1846
8 Jan. 1847
6 Dec. 1846
25 Dec. 1846
27 Feb. 1847
8 May 1846
21–24 Sept. 1846
22–23 Feb. 1847
18 April 1847

Sonoma
San Francisco
Monterey
Santa Barbara
Los Angeles
San Diego
Salt Lake City
Bents Fort
Fort Leavenworth
Santa Fe
Albuquerque
Tucson
El Paso
Sacramento
Chihuahua
Monclova
Dallas
Austin
San Antonio
Goliad
Corpus Christi
Camargo
Monterrey
Matamoros
Buena Vista
Tampico
Mexico City
Puebla
Cerro Gordo
Veracruz

CALIFORNIA
UNITED STATES
Unorganized Territory
Missouri
Arkansas
Louisiana
Disputed Territory
Texas
In revolt against Mexico 1845 annexed by U.S.
Lower California
Gulf of California
PACIFIC OCEAN
MEXICO
Colorado River
Rio Grande
Nueces R.
Gulf of Mexico
Gulf of Campeche
Tropic of Cancer

Unorganized Territory
Arkansas
Louisiana
Texas
MEXICO
Gulf of Mexico

146

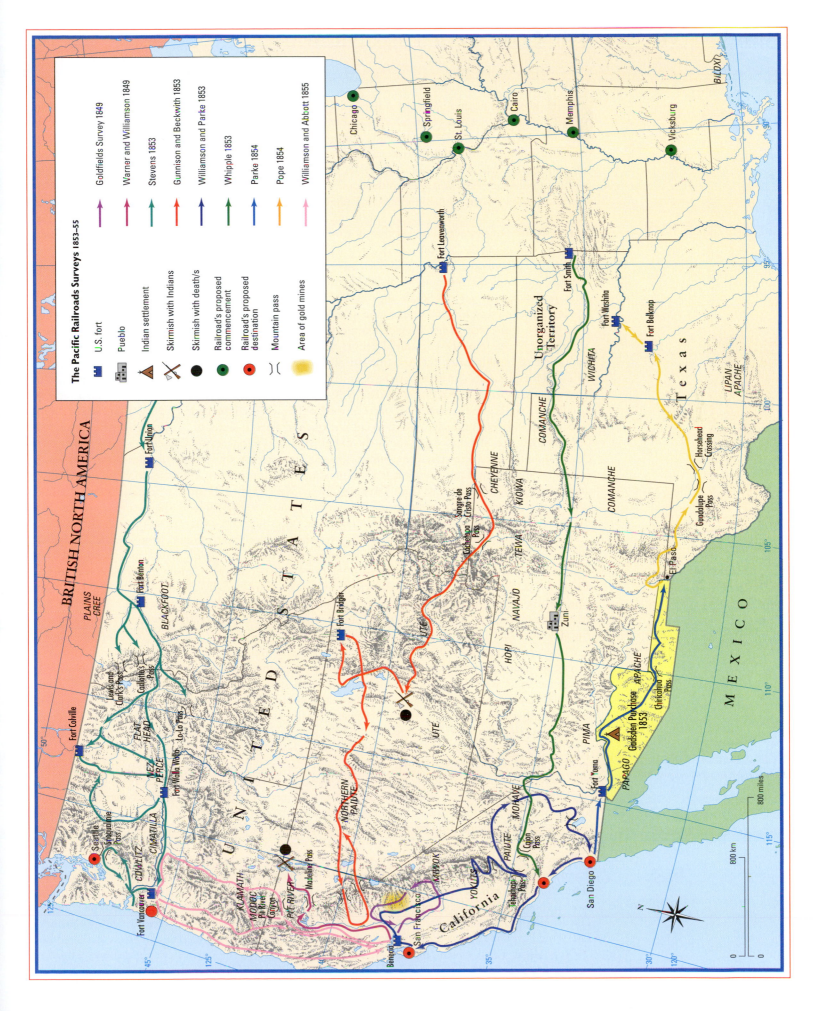

The Pacific Railroads Surveys 1853–55

U.S. fort	Goldfields Survey 1849
Pueblo	Warner and Williamson 1849
Indian settlement	Stevens 1853
Skirmish with Indians	Gunnison and Beckwith 1853
Skirmish with death/s	Williamson and Parke 1853
Railroad's proposed commencement	Whipple 1853
Railroad's proposed destination	Parke 1854
Mountain pass	Pope 1854
Area of gold mines	Williamson and Abbott 1855

PART TWELVE   THE COMING OF THE CIVIL WAR

FROM THE beginning of the American nation, the differing social systems in the North and the South generated political opposition: the Federalists drew their support chiefly from the North, and the Democratic Republicans, from the South. By 1820, the South and the North remained substantially in opposition, and thereafter abolitionist agitation over slavery hardened positions on both sides. To this point, however, the political geography, though oppositional, remained mostly in balance. What destabilized the equilibrium was the flood of settlers into the western territories, which then sought admission into the United States. This threatened to tip the balance in Congress between the slave (and chiefly rural) South and the non-slave (and increasingly urban and industrial) North. White Southerners worried that if Congress acquired antislavery majorities, it would find a means of outlawing the institution.

The 1828 presidential election reflected the new political realities. While Federalist John Quincy Adams carried New England, much as his father, John Adams, had done in 1796, his Democratic opponent, Andrew Jackson, swept the South and the West, which now had more electoral votes than all New England. In Congress, too, the votes of the western representatives were proving decisive in setting policy.

In 1820 a westerner, Henry Clay of Kentucky, had brokered a compromise over slavery. The state of Missouri, carved out of the Missouri Territory, sought admission to the United States. Much to the consternation of abolitionists, the constitution of the proposed state of Missouri allowed slavery. Clay arranged for Missouri's admission to be balanced by the admission of Maine as a free state. (Maine had been separated from Massachusetts.) The Missouri Compromise, as it became known, also "forever prohibited" slavery in the remaining parts of the Louisiana Purchase north of 36° 30' latitude, a region that few considered conducive to cotton cultivation, and thus to slavery.

For a time, the Missouri Compromise held; but when additional western lands were brought into the Union and organized into states, the political balance in Congress was again endangered. In 1850 another congressional compromise resulted in the admission of California as a free state, with the remainder of the land ceded by Mexico—the Utah Territory and the New Mexico Territory—to be admitted "with or without slavery as [its] constitution may prescribe." Another provision of the Compromise of 1850 strengthened the Fugitive Slave Act of 1793, making it easier for slave owners to seize escaped slaves.

This compromise was undone when Senator Stephen A. Douglas of Illinois proposed organizing the Nebraska Territory. His initiative resulted in the Kansas-Nebraska Act of 1854, which divided the territory into Kansas Territory and Nebraska Territory and allowed the legislature of each territory to decide for itself whether to allow slavery. Abolitionists were enraged by the settlement, because it repealed the provision of the Missouri Compromise prohibiting slavery north of 36° 30'. Their fury intensified each time plantation owners came north to recapture runaway slaves, in accord with the Fugitive Slave Act.

Moreover, politicians in the Kansas Territory wrangled over whether their constitution would allow slavery. Abolitionist societies in New England endorsed the migration of antislavery settlers to Kansas to ensure an antislavery constitution, while on election days pro-slavery sympathizers from Missouri streamed across the border to vote in Kansas. The collision of irreconcilable groups on the Kansas frontier, possessing only the rudiments of government, led to bloodshed and more recriminations in Congress.

Complicating matters further was the 1857 Dred Scott decision of the Supreme Court. Scott, a slave who lived in Missouri, had earlier been brought by his owner to the Wisconsin Territory. Scott reasoned that by the provisions of the Missouri Compromise, which prohibited slavery in that territory, he should have then been set free. However, the Court ruled that Scott was not entitled to his freedom because the Missouri Compromise itself was unconstitutional and deprived slave owners of their constitutional right to "property" as guaranteed by the Fifth Amendment, or so some of the justices held. The Dred Scott decision further provoked abolitionists, who now regarded the Supreme Court as being in league with southern politicians. They looked to the presidential election of 1860 to remedy the situation.

The election was complicated by historical, geographical, and political factors—all of them overshadowed by the issue of slavery. The Democrats were hopelessly split between northern and southern branches. The northern faction, which wanted each territory to decide for itself whether to countenance slavery, chose as its candidate Stephen A. Douglas, champion of "popular sovereignty" on the question. The southern Democrats, who endorsed a pro-slavery plank, named John Breckinridge of Kentucky. The Whig Party had nearly disintegrated during the 1850s, and some of its remnants were gathered into the Republican Party, which opposed the extension of slavery to the territories (but did not call for its eradication elsewhere). The Republicans chose Abraham Lincoln, a lawyer from rural Illinois. A fourth party, the Constitutional Union Party, ignored the slavery question altogether and merely pledged its support to the Union and the Constitution. It selected John Bell of Tennessee.

The outcome was never in doubt. With the Democratic Party deeply fractured, Lincoln swept the North, the upper Midwest, and California and Oregon; Breckinridge carried the Deep South, and Bell took the border states of Tennessee, Kentucky, and Virginia. Though Lincoln won only 40 percent of the popular vote, he took 60 percent of the tally in the Electoral College.

Many in the South regarded the election of Lincoln as tantamount to a declaration of war against slavery. They were wrong in that Lincoln's main goal was to preserve the Union. But southern radicals, who regarded war as inevitable, ensured the accuracy of the prediction by their reactions to it.

MAPS

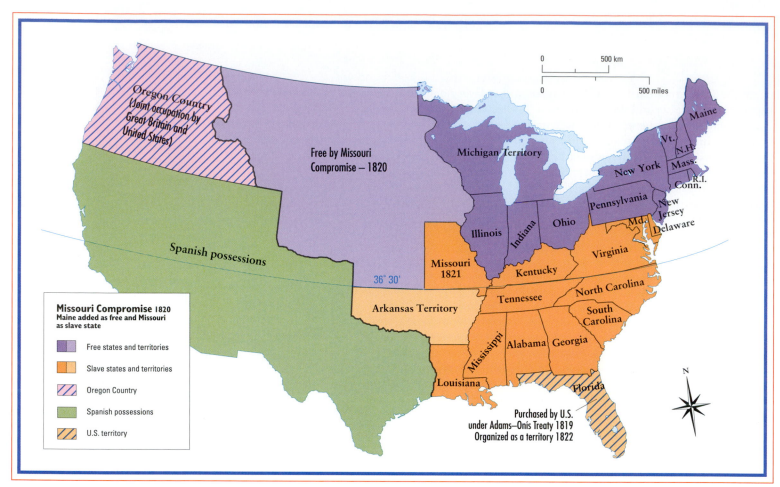

Missouri Compromise 1820
Maine added as free and Missouri as slave state

- Free states and territories
- Slave states and territories
- Oregon Country
- Spanish possessions
- U.S. territory

Oregon Country
(Joint occupation by Great Britain and United States)

Free by Missouri Compromise – 1820

Michigan Territory

Maine
Vt.
N.H.
New York
Mass.
R.I.
Conn.
Pennsylvania
New Jersey
Delaware
Md.

Illinois
Indiana
Ohio

Spanish possessions

Virginia

Missouri
1821

Kentucky

36° 30'

Arkansas Territory

Tennessee

North Carolina

South Carolina

Mississippi
Alabama
Georgia

Louisiana

Florida

Purchased by U.S.
under Adams–Onís Treaty 1819
Organized as a territory 1822

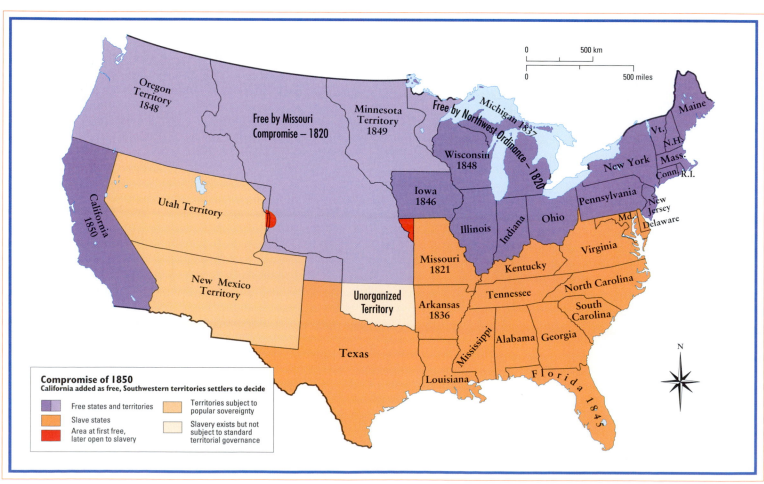

Compromise of 1850
California added as free, Southwestern territories settlers to decide

- Free states and territories
- Slave states
- Area at first free, later open to slavery
- Territories subject to popular sovereignty
- Slavery exists but not subject to standard territorial governance

Oregon Territory
1848

Free by Missouri Compromise – 1820

Minnesota Territory 1849

Free by Northwest Ordinance – 1820

Michigan 1837

Maine
Vt.
N.H.
New York
Mass.
Conn.
R.I.

Wisconsin 1848

California 1850

Utah Territory

Iowa 1846

Illinois
Indiana
Ohio

Pennsylvania

New Jersey
Delaware
Md.

Missouri 1821

Kentucky

Virginia

New Mexico Territory

Unorganized Territory

Arkansas 1836

Tennessee

North Carolina

South Carolina

Texas

Mississippi
Alabama
Georgia

Louisiana

Florida 1845

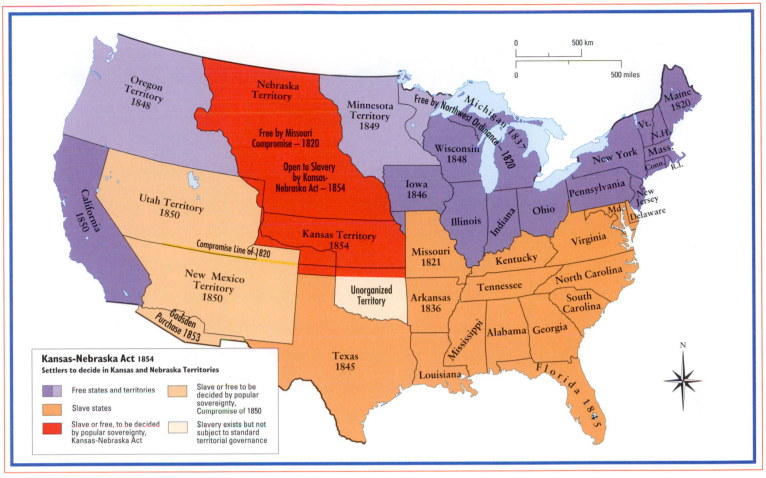

Kansas-Nebraska Act 1854
Settlers to decide in Kansas and Nebraska Territories

- Free states and territories
- Slave states
- Slave or free, to be decided by popular sovereignty, Kansas-Nebraska Act
- Slave or free to be decided by popular sovereignty, Compromise of 1850
- Slavery exists but not subject to standard territorial governance

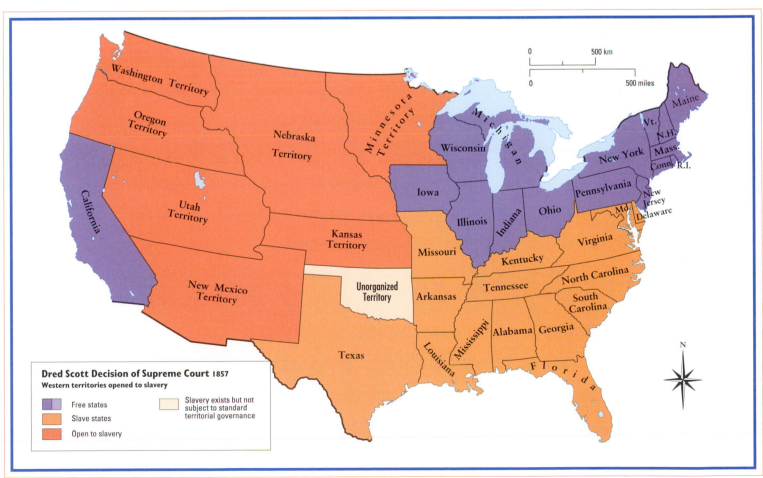

Dred Scott Decision of Supreme Court 1857
Western territories opened to slavery

- Free states
- Slave states
- Open to slavery
- Slavery exists but not subject to standard territorial governance

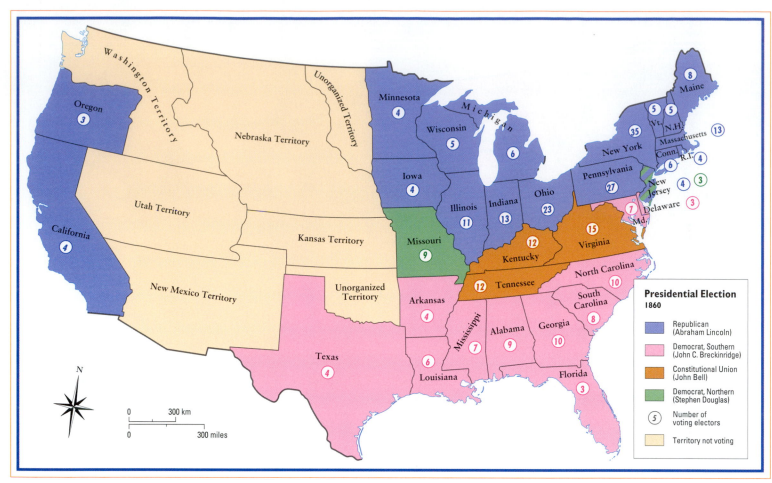

Presidential Election
1860

- Republican (Abraham Lincoln)
- Democrat, Southern (John C. Breckinridge)
- Constitutional Union (John Bell)
- Democrat, Northern (Stephen Douglas)
- ⑤ Number of voting electors
- Territory not voting

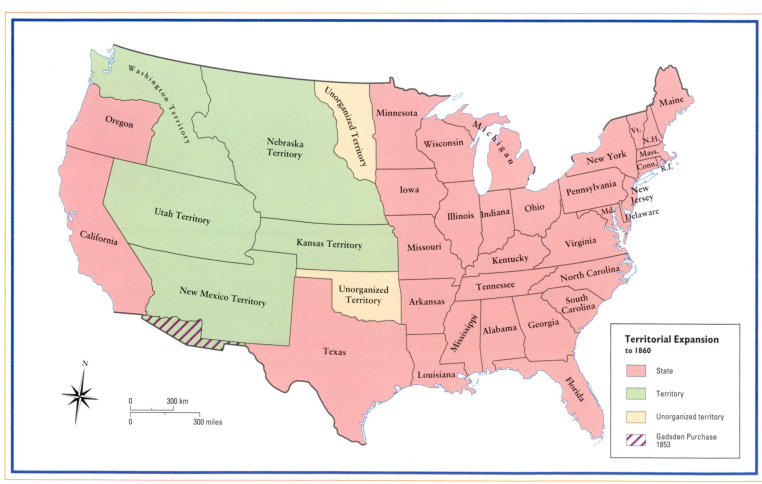

Territorial Expansion
to 1860

- State
- Territory
- Unorganized territory
- Gadsden Purchase 1853

In May 1856, 800 proslavery volunteers sacked the antislavery town of Lawrence in the Kansas Territory. Antislavery crusader John Brown, an extremist, decided to retaliate. In the dead of night, Brown and six companions crept into the township of Pottawatomie Creek and murdered five unsuspecting citizens. Enraged by this slaughter, men on both sides formed armed bands, prowling and looting the property of their enemies. By October around 200 people had been killed and "bleeding Kansas" took up the pages of northern newspapers.

John Brown's Raid 1858

✕ Battle or skirmish

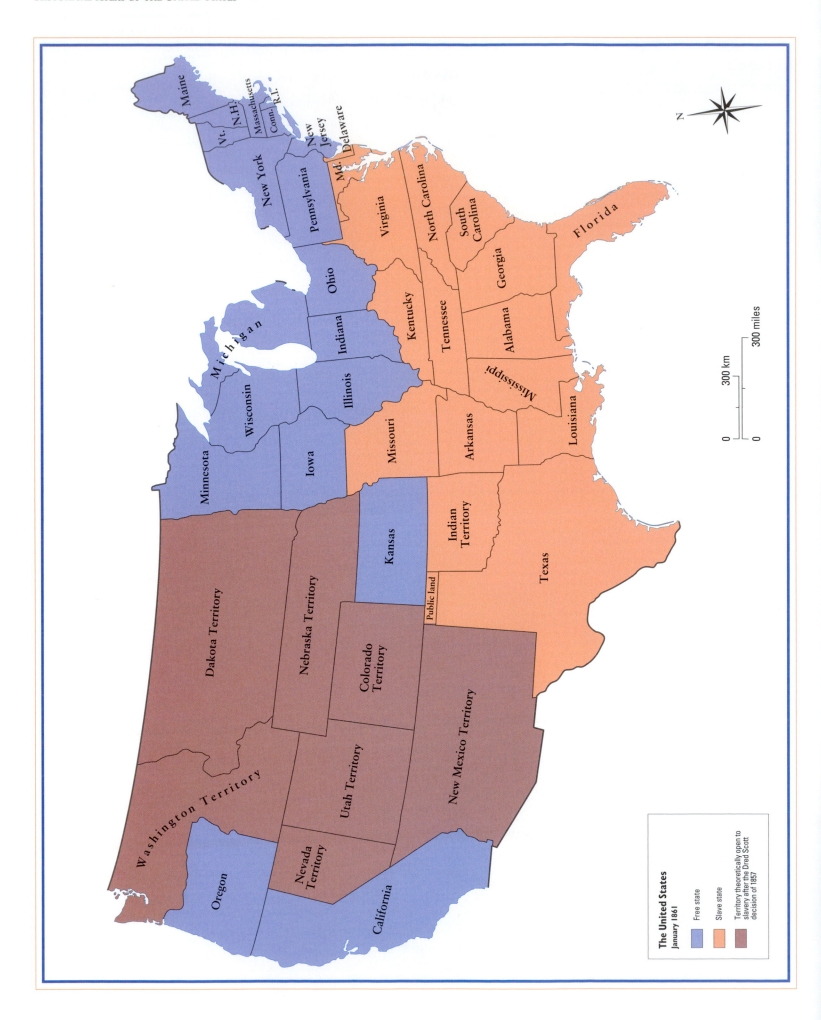

N

300 km

300 miles

The United States
January 1861

Free state

Slave state

Territory theoretically open to slavery after the Dred Scott decision of 1857

Maine

N.H.

Vt.

Massachusetts

R.I.

Conn.

New York

New Jersey

Md.

Delaware

Pennsylvania

Ohio

Michigan

Indiana

Illinois

Wisconsin

Minnesota

Iowa

Missouri

Kansas

Virginia

North Carolina

South Carolina

Florida

Georgia

Kentucky

Tennessee

Alabama

Mississippi

Louisiana

Arkansas

Indian Territory

Texas

Public land

Dakota Territory

Nebraska Territory

Colorado Territory

New Mexico Territory

Washington Territory

Utah Territory

Nevada Territory

Oregon

California

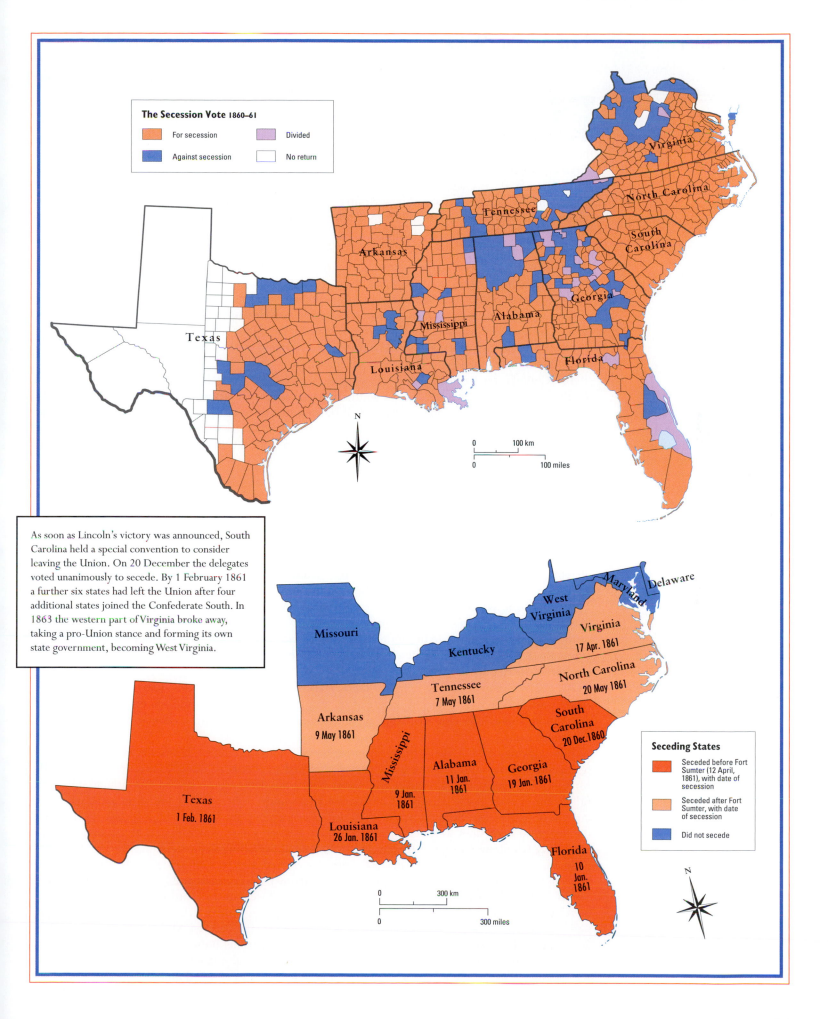

The Secession Vote 1860–61

- For secession
- Against secession
- Divided
- No return

Virginia

North Carolina

Tennessee

South Carolina

Arkansas

Georgia

Mississippi

Alabama

Texas

Louisiana

Florida

N

| 0 | 100 km |
| 0 | 100 miles |

As soon as Lincoln's victory was announced, South Carolina held a special convention to consider leaving the Union. On 20 December the delegates voted unanimously to secede. By 1 February 1861 a further six states had left the Union after four additional states joined the Confederate South. In 1863 the western part of Virginia broke away, taking a pro-Union stance and forming its own state government, becoming West Virginia.

Maryland

Delaware

Missouri

West Virginia

Virginia
17 Apr. 1861

Kentucky

North Carolina
20 May 1861

Tennessee
7 May 1861

Arkansas
9 May 1861

South Carolina
20 Dec.1860

Mississippi
9 Jan. 1861

Alabama
11 Jan. 1861

Georgia
19 Jan. 1861

Texas
1 Feb. 1861

Louisiana
26 Jan. 1861

Florida
10 Jan. 1861

Seceding States

- Seceded before Fort Sumter (12 April, 1861), with date of secession
- Seceded after Fort Sumter, with date of secession
- Did not secede

N

| 0 | 300 km |
| 0 | 300 miles |

155

PART THIRTEEN   THE CIVIL WAR

JUST WEEKS after the election of Lincoln, the South Carolina legislature, declaring its intention to resume its position "among the nations of the world," voted unanimously to secede from the United States. Within six weeks, Mississippi, Florida, Alabama, Georgia, Louisiana, and Texas also seceded. On 1 February 1861 they combined to form the Confederate States of America. Virginia, North Carolina, Tennessee, and Arkansas refrained from seceding, but threatened to do so if Lincoln attacked the Confederacy.

Like many other northerners, Lincoln initially regarded these actions as political posturing, a means of pressuring him on slavery. In his inaugural, he denounced secession but offered conciliation. "We are not enemies," he declared, "but friends."

Confederate officials, meanwhile, had taken possession of most federal facilities in the Deep South. In the spring they demanded the surrender of Fort Sumter in Charleston harbor. This presented Lincoln with a dilemma. To yield to this demand would validate secession, but to defend the fort would mean war. He chose a middle course, refraining from reinforcing the garrison yet sending ships to provision it. On 12 April, before the supply ships could arrive, Confederate artillery fired on the fort. Two days later, it surrendered. Lincoln, his hand forced, issued a call for 75,000 volunteers for the Union Army. The four other southern states, regarding this pronouncement as tantamount to an attack on the South, seceded and joined the Confederacy. War was inevitable.

The Confederacy had little chance of winning the war. The North had twice as many people as the South; worse, more than a third of the southern population were slaves, who could hardly be expected to defend the institution. Northern factories produced nine times more goods than their southern counterparts, and thirty times more firearms. The nation's railroad network had evolved chiefly to transport western grain to urban markets in the Northeast; this meant that Union armies and supplies could be rapidly shuttled from one front to another, another tremendous advantage. Yet the Confederacy fought for its survival and on its own soil, and it recruited a group of extraordinarily able military leaders. This became immediately apparent.

In July, a 30,000-man Union army commanded by Irvin McDowell lumbered across the Potomac and confronted a smaller Confederate force commanded by Pierre G.T. Beauregard. McDowell nearly swept away Beauregard's left flank, but the timely arrival of Thomas J. Jackson's brigade saved the position. Now reinforced, Beauregard ordered a counterattack, and as his troops surged forward they unloosed piercing screams all along the line. The green Union troops fled in panic, a complete rout. The Confederacy won the first Battle of Bull Run (Manassas).

Realizing the war would be a long one, Lincoln devised a three-pronged campaign to crush the Confederacy: the Union navy would impose a blockade to cripple the economy of the South; a Union army in the west would seize the entire Mississippi River, severing the Confederacy and disrupting its communications; and another, much larger army—the Army of the Potomac—would deliver a hammer-like blow against Virginia.

For nearly a year, both sides prepared for war; there were no major battles. The Union blockade was established, however, and over the course of the war it captured or destroyed some 1,500 ships, though many more slipped through. The blockade did not strangle the southern economy, but it did render it far less efficient.

In the spring of 1862, the fighting resumed, now in earnest. In April, Ulysses S. Grant commenced operations in the west, making good use of armored gunboats to seize Confederate forts on the Mississippi, Tennessee, and Cumberland Rivers. When his armies converged on Corinth, an important rail center in northern Mississippi, Confederate forces under Albert Sidney Johnston attacked, catching Grant by surprise. Both commanders hurled more men into the Battle of Shiloh, as it is called, and the losses on both sides were staggering. Johnston, himself killed, was replaced by Beauregard, who eventually withdrew. Grant was removed from command for failing to pursue him.

In the east, Lincoln's great army was being assembled and trained—slowly, all too slowly—by General George McClellan. At long last it was ferried down the Potomac and gradually disembarked at the edge of the Yorktown peninsula. It proceeded to crawl westward toward Richmond. But throughout the summer of 1862 McClellan made little progress against Robert E. Lee, a brilliant tactician who now commanded the Confederate army. When Lincoln finally ordered McClellan's troops back to Washington, Lee drove north, scattering a handful of Union armies until, on 17 September, McClellan stood his ground along the Antietam Creek in Maryland. The fighting was intense. In what was one of the bloodiest days in the annals of American war, 6,000 men were killed and 17,000 wounded. Lee's invasion of Maryland had been stopped, but McClellan, with more and fresher troops, failed to press the attack a second day, and Lee's army escaped to Virginia.

After Antietam, Lincoln issued the Emancipation Proclamation, which declared that, beginning 1 January 1863, slaves in rebellious states were "forever free." The Union also began to tap the manpower pool of African Americans, both free blacks and former slaves. Eventually 178,000 blacks served in the Union army.

In the summer of 1863 Lee, recognizing that the weight of northern resources would eventually crush the South, sought to demoralize the North with a dramatic victory. He again headed north. Instead of striking the Union defenses around Washington, D.C., he skirted the city, went to the west, and then invaded Pennsylvania. The Union army, now commanded by George G. Meade, moved north as well.

The two armies collided at Gettysburg. In the first day of fighting, Confederate forces swept through the town. Union armies, arriving en masse, took up positions on a hook-shaped cluster of hills along Cemetery Ridge to the south and east of the town. The next day, after a fierce artillery barrage, the Confederates repeatedly attacked the Union flanks. Then in the afternoon General George E. Pickett's brigade, 15,000 men in all, marched across a wheat field into the teeth of the Union center. His brigades were decimated, and fell back. Lee retreated to Virginia, his hopes of a decisive victory abandoned. The Union was saved.

Meanwhile, Grant, back in command in the west, sneaked around Confederate fortifications at Vicksburg, defeated the armies defending it, and forced it to surrender. Soon, the entire Mississippi was controlled by Union gunboats. Grant then took command of Union forces in Tennessee and turned back a Confederate advance at Chickamauga, near Chattanooga. He was then named commander of all Union forces and given the job of crushing what remained of Lee's army.

This proved no simple matter. In the spring and summer of 1864, Grant attacked repeatedly, trying to turn Lee's right flank. Lee gave ground, but his army did not collapse; when little more ground was left to yield, his men dug deep trenches, foreshadowing the trench warfare of the Great War. Grant's losses were appalling, but so were Lee's, and he had fewer men to lose.

In September, another Union army commanded by General George Sherman struck at the center of the Confederacy, seizing Atlanta. The Confederate armies in the region headed north, toward Tennessee, but Sherman ignored them and drove his 100,000 men, virtually unopposed, through Georgia to the Atlantic seaboard. He took Savannah in December, and in February 1865 he entered Columbia, South Carolina. Then he moved north through North Carolina and into Virginia.

Richmond fell to Grant's army on 3 April 1865. Lee surrendered a week later.

MAPS

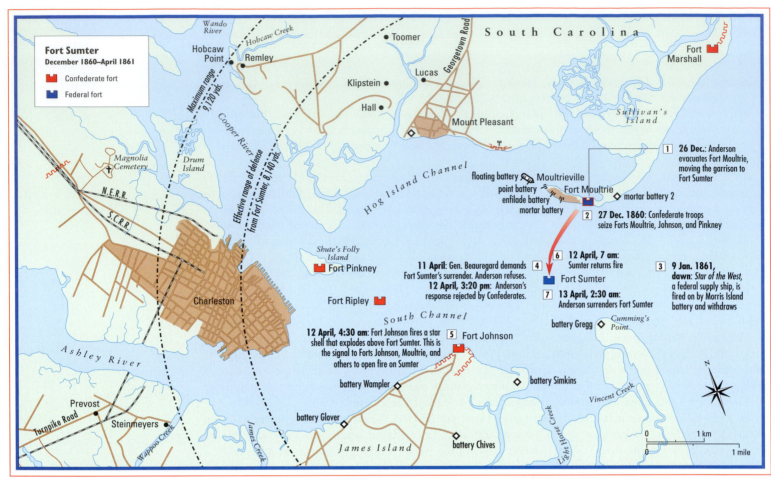

Fort Sumter
December 1860–April 1861

- Confederate fort
- Federal fort

Maximum range 9,120 yds.

Effective range of defense from Fort Sumter, 8,140 yds.

South Carolina

Wando River

Hobcaw Creek

Hobcaw Point   Remley   Toomer

Klipstein   Lucas

Hall   Mount Pleasant

Georgetown Road

Fort Marshall

Sullivan's Island

Magnolia Cemetery

Drum Island

N.E.R.R.

S.C.R.R.

Cooper River

Hog Island Channel

floating battery   Moultrieville
point battery   Fort Moultrie
enfilade battery   mortar battery 2
mortar battery

1 26 Dec.: Anderson evacuates Fort Moultrie, moving the garrison to Fort Sumter

2 27 Dec. 1860: Confederate troops seize Forts Moultrie, Johnson, and Pinkney

Shute's Folly Island
Fort Pinkney

Fort Ripley

11 April: Gen. Beauregard demands Fort Sumter's surrender. Anderson refuses.
12 April, 3:20 pm: Anderson's response rejected by Confederates.

4

6 **12 April, 7 am:** Sumter returns fire
Fort Sumter

3 9 Jan. 1861, dawn: *Star of the West*, a federal supply ship, is fired on by Morris Island battery and withdraws

7 **13 April, 2:30 am:** Anderson surrenders Fort Sumter

battery Gregg   Cumming's Point

Charleston

South Channel

12 April, 4:30 am: Fort Johnson fires a star shell that explodes above Fort Sumter. This is the signal to Forts Johnson, Moultrie, and others to open fire on Sumter

5 Fort Johnson

Ashley River

battery Wampler   battery Simkins

Prevost

Turnpike Road   Steinmeyers

battery Glover

James Creek

Wappoo Creek

James Island

battery Chives

Vincent Creek

Light Horse Creek

0   1 km
0   1 mile

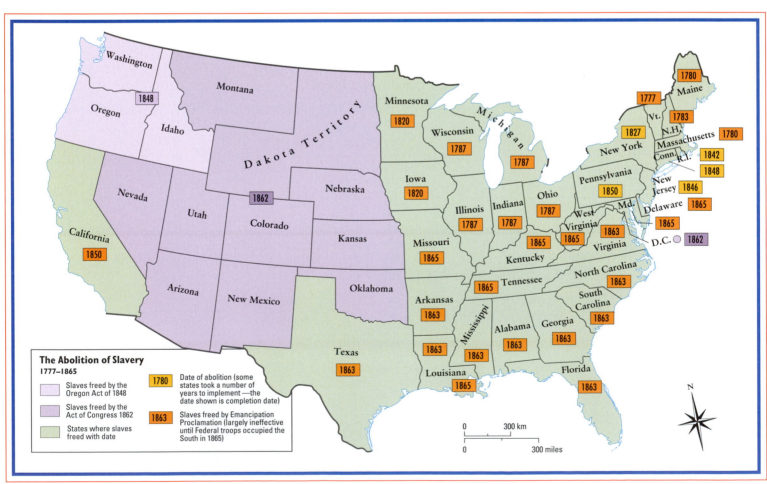

The Abolition of Slavery
1777–1865

- Slaves freed by the Oregon Act of 1848
- Slaves freed by the Act of Congress 1862
- States where slaves freed with date

1780 Date of abolition (some states took a number of years to implement —the date shown is completion date)

1863 Slaves freed by Emancipation Proclamation (largely ineffective until Federal troops occupied the South in 1865)

Washington **1848**

Oregon

Idaho

Montana

Dakota Territory

Minnesota **1820**

Wisconsin **1787**

Michigan

Maine **1780**

1777

Vt. **1783**

N.H. **1780**

New York **1827**

Massachusetts **1780**

Conn. **1842**

R.I. **1848**

Nevada

Utah

Colorado **1862**

Nebraska

Iowa **1820**

Illinois **1787**

Indiana **1787**

Ohio **1787**

Pennsylvania **1780**

New Jersey **1846**

California **1850**

Kansas

Missouri **1865**

West Virginia **1863**

Md. **1865**

Delaware **1865**

D.C. **1862**

Arizona

New Mexico

Oklahoma

Kentucky

Virginia **1865**

North Carolina **1863**

Arkansas **1863**

Tennessee **1865**

South Carolina **1863**

Texas **1863**

Mississippi **1863**

Alabama **1863**

Georgia **1863**

Louisiana **1865**

Florida **1863**

0   300 km
0   300 miles

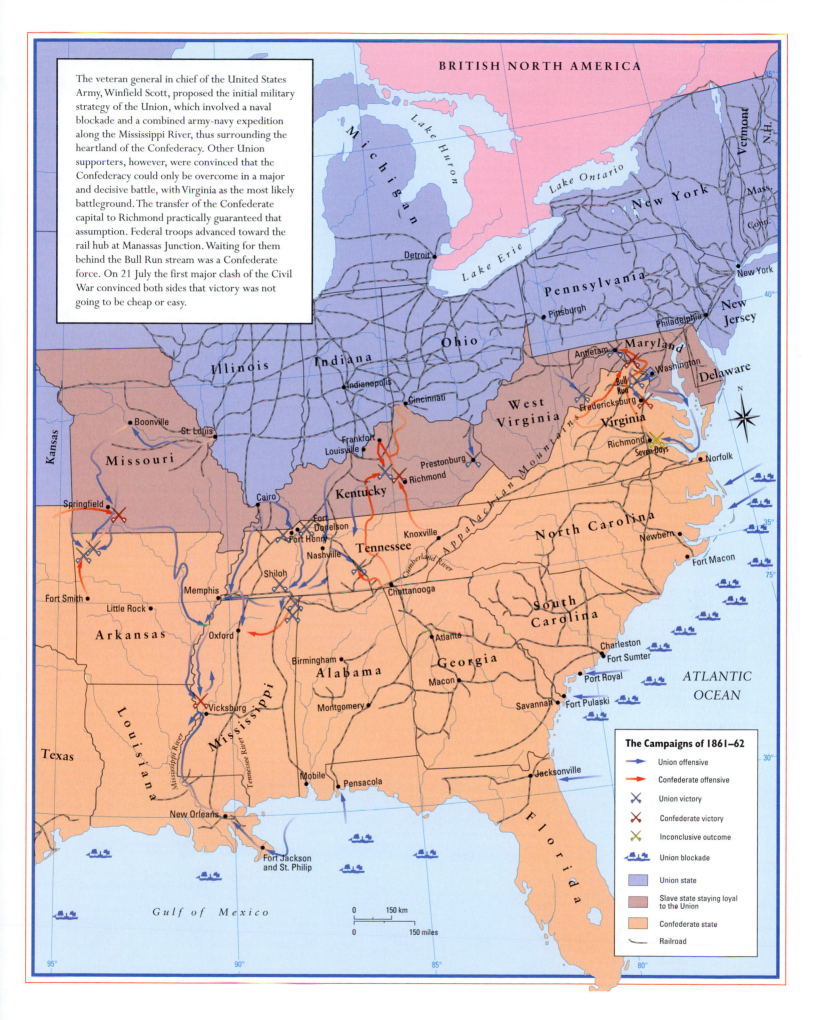

The veteran general in chief of the United States Army, Winfield Scott, proposed the initial military strategy of the Union, which involved a naval blockade and a combined army-navy expedition along the Mississippi River, thus surrounding the heartland of the Confederacy. Other Union supporters, however, were convinced that the Confederacy could only be overcome in a major and decisive battle, with Virginia as the most likely battleground. The transfer of the Confederate capital to Richmond practically guaranteed that assumption. Federal troops advanced toward the rail hub at Manassas Junction. Waiting for them behind the Bull Run stream was a Confederate force. On 21 July the first major clash of the Civil War convinced both sides that victory was not going to be cheap or easy.

BRITISH NORTH AMERICA

Lake Huron

Lake Ontario

Lake Erie

Michigan

Vermont

N.H.

New York

Mass.

Conn.

Pennsylvania

New Jersey

Detroit

New York

Pittsburgh

Philadelphia

Ohio

Delaware

Indiana

Illinois

Indianapolis

Cincinnati

West Virginia

Antietam

Maryland

Washington

Bull Run

Fredericksburg

Virginia

Boonville

St. Louis

Frankfort

Louisville

Prestonburg

Richmond

Richmond

Seven Days

Norfolk

Missouri

Kentucky

Kansas

Springfield

Cairo

Fort Donelson

Fort Henry

Knoxville

North Carolina

Newbern

Nashville

Tennessee

Appalachian Mountains

Cumberland River

Fort Macon

Fort Smith

Memphis

Shiloh

Chattanooga

South Carolina

Little Rock

Oxford

Arkansas

Atlanta

Charleston

Fort Sumter

Birmingham

Georgia

Alabama

Macon

Port Royal

ATLANTIC OCEAN

Texas

Louisiana

Vicksburg

Mississippi

Montgomery

Savannah

Fort Pulaski

Mississippi River

Tennessee River

Mobile

Pensacola

Jacksonville

Florida

New Orleans

Fort Jackson and St. Philip

Gulf of Mexico

The Campaigns of 1861–62

→	Union offensive
→	Confederate offensive
✕	Union victory
✕	Confederate victory
✕	Inconclusive outcome
⚓	Union blockade
	Union state
	Slave state staying loyal to the Union
	Confederate state
⌇	Railroad

0 150 km

0 150 miles

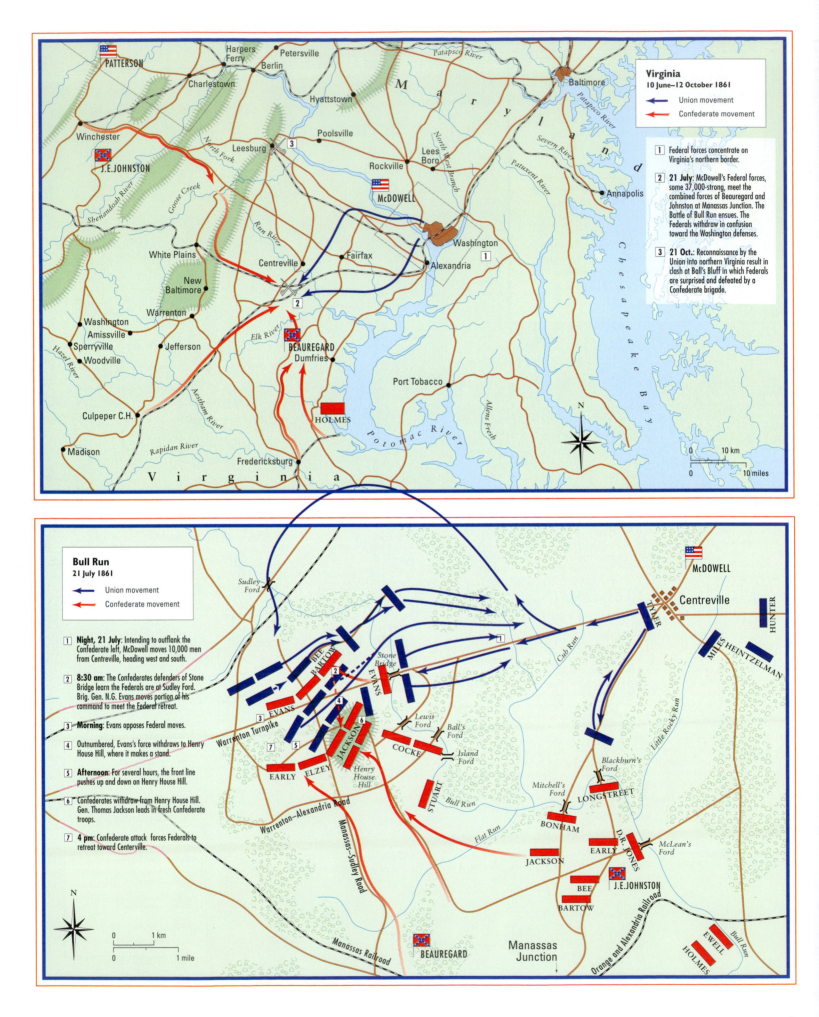

Virginia
10 June–12 October 1861

→ Union movement
→ Confederate movement

1 Federal forces concentrate on Virginia's northern border.

2 **21 July:** McDowell's Federal forces, some 37,000-strong, meet the combined forces of Beauregard and Johnston at Manassas Junction. The Battle of Bull Run ensues. The Federals withdraw in confusion toward the Washington defenses.

3 **21 Oct.:** Reconnaissance by the Union into northern Virginia result in clash at Ball's Bluff in which Federals are surprised and defeated by a Confederate brigade.

PATTERSON
Harpers Ferry · Petersville
Charlestown · Berlin
Winchester
J.E. JOHNSTON
Hyattstown
Poolsville
Leesburg
Rockville
Lees Boro
McDOWELL
Annapolis
Baltimore
White Plains
Centreville · Fairfax
Washington · Alexandria
New Baltimore
Warrenton
Washington
Amissville
Sperryville
Jefferson
Woodville
BEAUREGARD
Dumfries
Culpeper C.H.
HOLMES
Port Tobacco
Allens Fresh
Madison
Fredericksburg
Virginia
Chesapeake Bay
Potomac River
0 ___ 10 km
0 ___ 10 miles

Bull Run
21 July 1861

→ Union movement
→ Confederate movement

1 **Night, 21 July:** Intending to outflank the Confederate left, McDowell moves 10,000 men from Centreville, heading west and south.

2 **8:30 am:** The Confederates defenders of Stone Bridge learn the Federals are at Sudley Ford. Brig. Gen. N.G. Evans moves portion of his command to meet the Federal retreat.

3 **Morning:** Evans opposes Federal moves.

4 Outnumbered, Evans's force withdraws to Henry House Hill, where it makes a stand.

5 **Afternoon:** For several hours, the front line pushes up and down on Henry House Hill.

6 Confederates withdraw from Henry House Hill. Gen. Thomas Jackson leads in fresh Confederate troops.

7 **4 pm:** Confederate attack forces Federals to retreat toward Centreville.

McDOWELL
Centreville
HUNTER
Sudley Ford
MILES
HEINTZELMAN
BEE BARTOW
Stone Bridge
EVANS
EVANS
Lewis Ford
Ball's Ford
JACKSON
COCKE
Island Ford
Blackburn's Ford
EARLY ELZEY
Henry House Hill
STUART
Mitchell's Ford
LONGSTREET
Warrenton Turnpike
Warrenton–Alexandria Road
Manassas–Sudley Road
Bull Run
BONHAM
D.R. JONES
McLean's Ford
JACKSON
EARLY
BEE
J.E. JOHNSTON
BARTOW
Manassas Railroad
BEAUREGARD
Manassas Junction
Orange and Alexandria Railroad
EWELL
HOLMES
0 ___ 1 km
0 ___ 1 mile

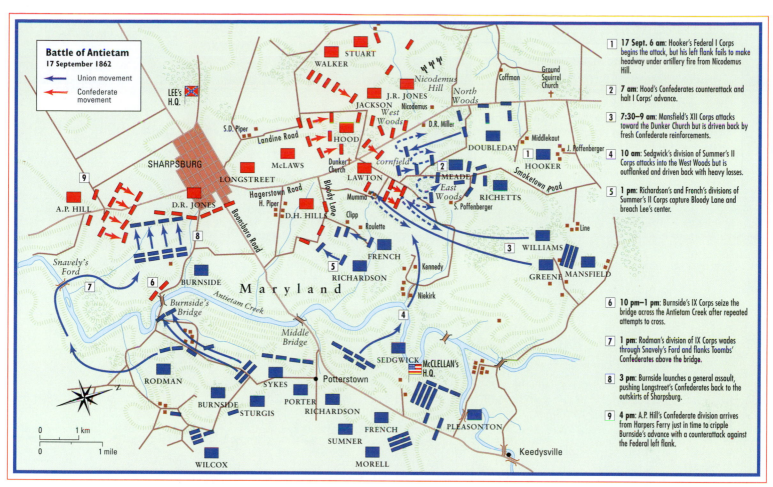

Battle of Antietam
17 September 1862

- → Union movement
- → Confederate movement

LEE'S H.Q.

STUART
WALKER
Nicodemus Hill
J.R. JONES
Coffman
Ground Squirrel Church
North Woods
JACKSON
West Woods
Nicodemus
S.D. Piper
Landine Road
HOOD
D.R. Miller
DOUBLEDAY
Middlekaut
J. Poffenberger
SHARPSBURG
McLAWS
Dunker Church
cornfield
LAWTON
MEADE
East Woods
HOOKER
LONGSTREET
Hagerstown Road
H. Piper
Mumma
S. Poffenberger
RICHETTS
Smoketown Road
A.P. HILL
D.R. JONES
D.H. HILLS
Bloody Lane
Clipp
Line
Boonsboro Road
Roulette
FRENCH
WILLIAMS
Snavely's Ford
RICHARDSON
Kennedy
GREENE MANSFIELD
BURNSIDE
Burnside's Bridge
Antietam Creek
M a r y l a n d
Niekirk
Middle Bridge
RODMAN
SYKES
PORTER
SEDGWICK
McCLELLAN'S H.Q.
BURNSIDE
STURGIS
RICHARDSON
Potterstown
WILCOX
SUMNER
FRENCH
PLEASONTON
MORELL
Keedysville

0   1 km
0   1 mile

1. **17 Sept. 6 am:** Hooker's Federal I Corps begins the attack, but his left flank fails to make headway under artillery fire from Nicodemus Hill.

2. **7 am:** Hood's Confederates counterattack and halt I Corps' advance.

3. **7:30–9 am:** Mansfield's XII Corps attacks toward the Dunker Church but is driven back by fresh Confederate reinforcements.

4. **10 am:** Sedgwick's division of Summer's II Corps attacks into the West Woods but is outflanked and driven back with heavy losses.

5. **1 pm:** Richardson's and French's divisions of Summer's II Corps capture Bloody Lane and breach Lee's center.

6. **10 pm–1 pm:** Burnside's IX Corps seize the bridge across the Antietam Creek after repeated attempts to cross.

7. **1 pm:** Rodman's division of IX Corps wades through Snavely's Ford and flanks Toombs' Confederates above the bridge.

8. **3 pm:** Burnside launches a general assault, pushing Longstreet's Confederates back to the outskirts of Sharpsburg.

9. **4 pm:** A.P. Hill's Confederate division arrives from Harpers Ferry just in time to cripple Burnside's advance with a counterattack against the Federal left flank.

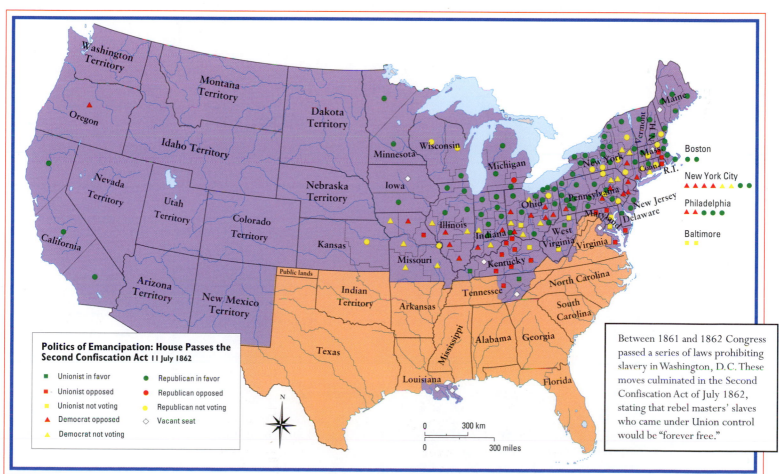

Politics of Emancipation: House Passes the Second Confiscation Act 11 July 1862

- ■ Unionist in favor
- ■ Unionist opposed
- ■ Unionist not voting
- ▲ Democrat opposed
- ▲ Democrat not voting
- ● Republican in favor
- ● Republican opposed
- ● Republican not voting
- ◇ Vacant seat

Washington Territory
Montana Territory
Oregon
Idaho Territory
Dakota Territory
Minnesota
Wisconsin
Maine
Michigan
New York
Vermont
N.H.
Mass.
Boston
Nevada Territory
Utah Territory
Nebraska Territory
Iowa
New York City
Conn.
R.I.
Pennsylvania
Philadelphia
California
Colorado Territory
Kansas
Illinois
Indiana
Ohio
New Jersey
Maryland
Delaware
Baltimore
Missouri
West Virginia
Virginia
Arizona Territory
New Mexico Territory
Public lands
Indian Territory
Kentucky
Tennessee
North Carolina
Arkansas
South Carolina
Mississippi
Alabama
Georgia
Louisiana
Texas
Florida

N

0   300 km
0   300 miles

Between 1861 and 1862 Congress passed a series of laws prohibiting slavery in Washington, D.C. These moves culminated in the Second Confiscation Act of July 1862, stating that rebel masters' slaves who came under Union control would be "forever free."

161

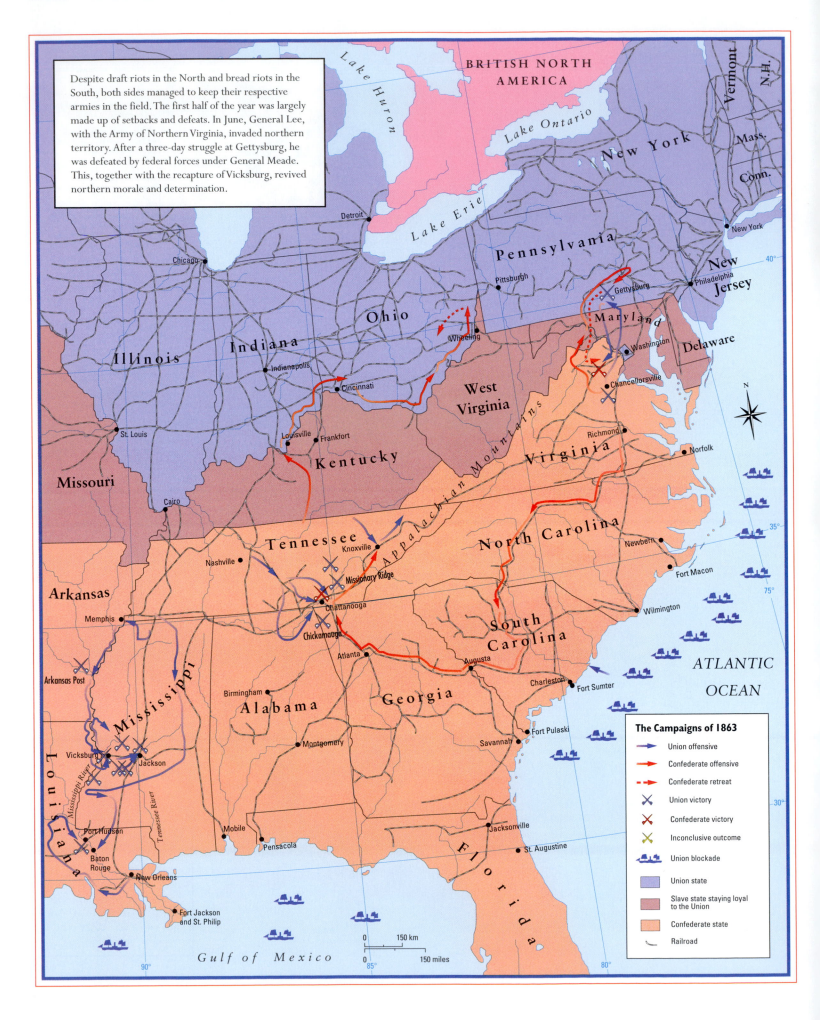

Despite draft riots in the North and bread riots in the South, both sides managed to keep their respective armies in the field. The first half of the year was largely made up of setbacks and defeats. In June, General Lee, with the Army of Northern Virginia, invaded northern territory. After a three-day struggle at Gettysburg, he was defeated by federal forces under General Meade. This, together with the recapture of Vicksburg, revived northern morale and determination.

The Campaigns of 1863

- → Union offensive
- → Confederate offensive
- ⇢ Confederate retreat
- ✕ Union victory
- ✕ Confederate victory
- ✕ Inconclusive outcome
- ⛴ Union blockade
- Union state
- Slave state staying loyal to the Union
- Confederate state
- ⌒ Railroad

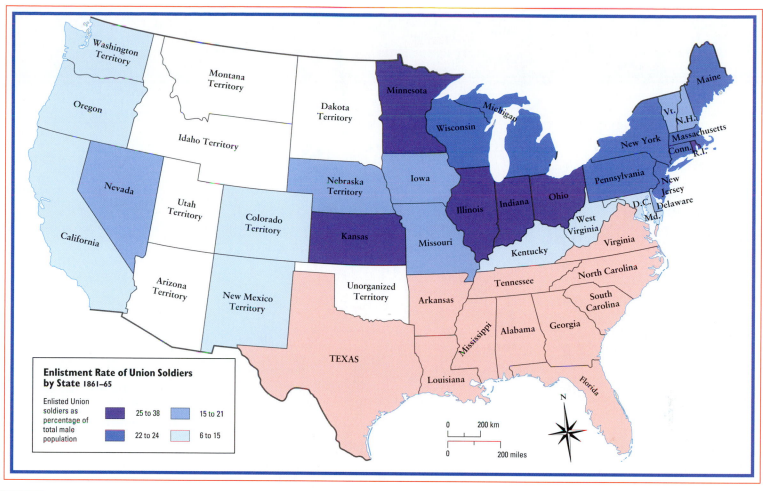

Enlistment Rate of Union Soldiers by State 1861–65

Enlisted Union soldiers as percentage of total male population

- 25 to 38
- 22 to 24
- 15 to 21
- 6 to 15

0   200 km

0   200 miles

N

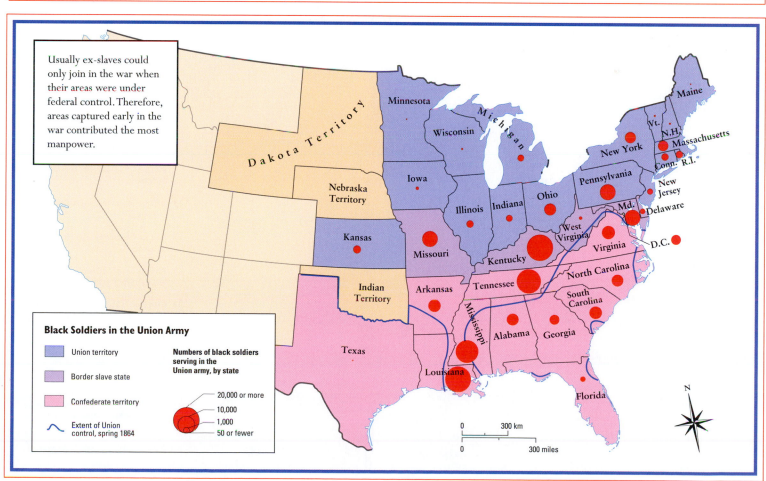

Usually ex-slaves could only join in the war when their areas were under federal control. Therefore, areas captured early in the war contributed the most manpower.

Black Soldiers in the Union Army

- Union territory
- Border slave state
- Confederate territory
- Extent of Union control, spring 1864

Numbers of black soldiers serving in the Union army, by state

- 20,000 or more
- 10,000
- 1,000
- 50 or fewer

0   300 km

0   300 miles

N

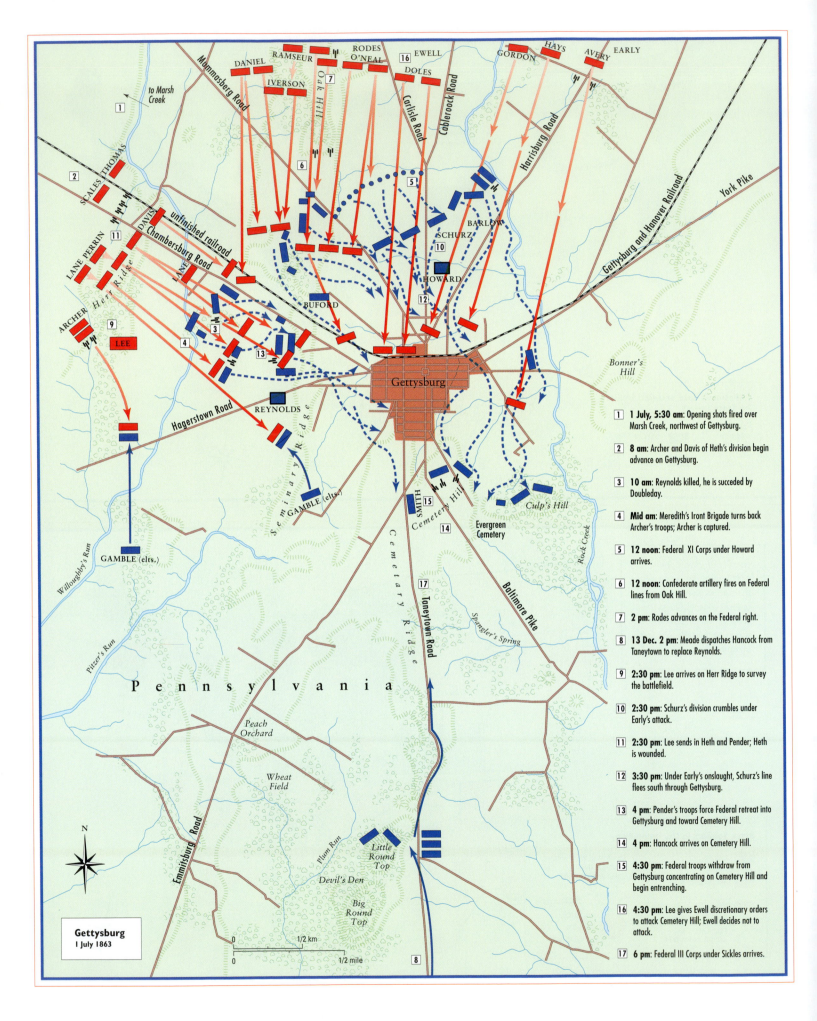

Gettysburg
1 July 1863

PENNSYLVANIA

to Marsh Creek

Mummasberg Road

DANIEL RAMSEUR RODES O'NEAL EWELL GORDON HAYS AVERY EARLY

IVERSON Oak Hill DOLES

Carlisle Road

Cashtown Road

Harrisburg Road

York Pike

Gettysburg and Hanover Railroad

SCALES THOMAS

unfinished railroad

Chambersburg Road

DAVIS

LANE PERRIN

Herr Ridge

LANE

ARCHER

LEE

BUFORD

BARLOW

SCHURZ

HOWARD

Bonner's Hill

Hagerstown Road

REYNOLDS

Seminary Ridge

GAMBLE (elts.)

GAMBLE (elts.)

Willoughby's Run

Pitzer's Run

Gettysburg

SMITH

Evergreen Cemetery

Cemetery Hill

Culp's Hill

Rock Creek

Cemetery Ridge

Spangler's Spring

Baltimore Pike

Taneytown Road

Emmitsburg Road

Peach Orchard

Wheat Field

Plum Run

Little Round Top

Devil's Den

Big Round Top

N

1 **1 July, 5:30 am**: Opening shots fired over Marsh Creek, northwest of Gettysburg.

2 **8 am**: Archer and Davis of Heth's division begin advance on Gettysburg.

3 **10 am**: Reynolds killed, he is succeded by Doubleday.

4 **Mid am**: Meredith's Iron Brigade turns back Archer's troops; Archer is captured.

5 **12 noon**: Federal XI Corps under Howard arrives.

6 **12 noon**: Confederate artillery fires on Federal lines from Oak Hill.

7 **2 pm**: Rodes advances on the Federal right.

8 **13 Dec. 2 pm**: Meade dispatches Hancock from Taneytown to replace Reynolds.

9 **2:30 pm**: Lee arrives on Herr Ridge to survey the battlefield.

10 **2:30 pm**: Schurz's division crumbles under Early's attack.

11 **2:30 pm**: Lee sends in Heth and Pender; Heth is wounded.

12 **3:30 pm**: Under Early's onslaught, Schurz's line flees south through Gettysburg.

13 **4 pm**: Pender's troops force Federal retreat into Gettysburg and toward Cemetery Hill.

14 **4 pm**: Hancock arrives on Cemetery Hill.

15 **4:30 pm**: Federal troops withdraw from Gettysburg concentrating on Cemetery Hill and begin entrenching.

16 **4:30 pm**: Lee gives Ewell discretionary orders to attack Cemetery Hill; Ewell decides not to attack.

17 **6 pm**: Federal III Corps under Sickles arrives.

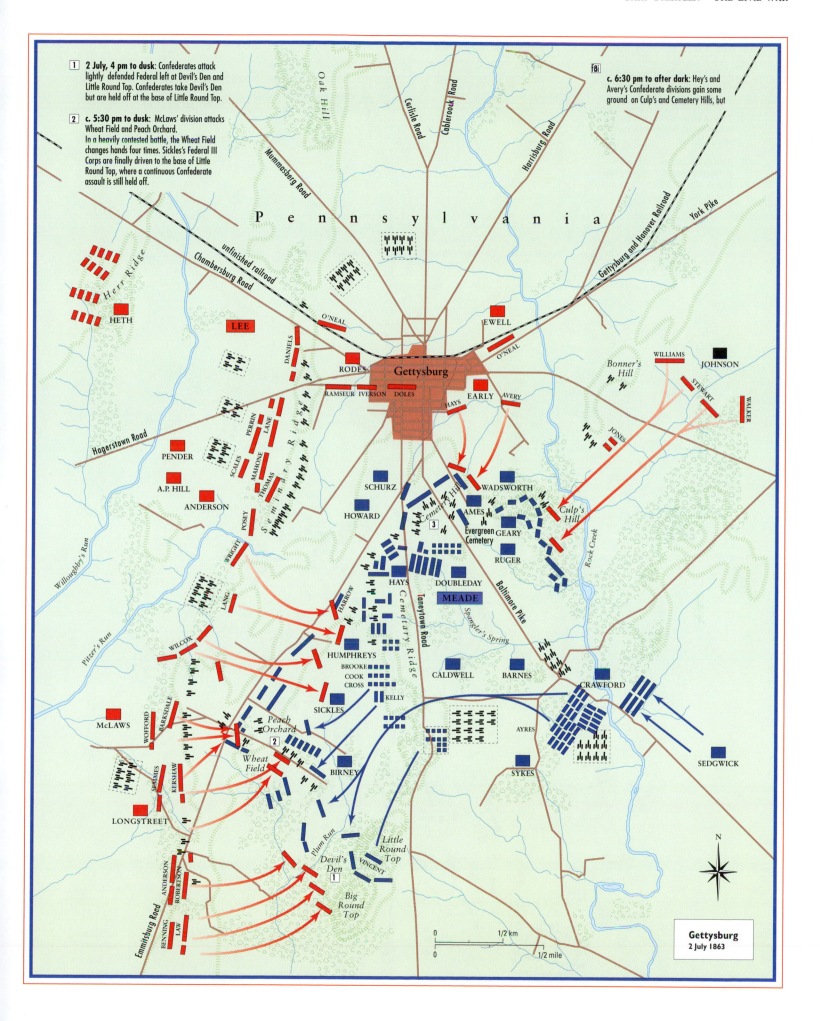

1 **2 July, 4 pm to dusk:** Confederates attack lightly defended Federal left at Devil's Den and Little Round Top. Confederates take Devil's Den but are held off at the base of Little Round Top.

2 **c. 5:30 pm to dusk:** McLaws' division attacks Wheat Field and Peach Orchard. In a heavily contested battle, the Wheat Field changes hands four times. Sickles's Federal III Corps are finally driven to the base of Little Round Top, where a continuous Confederate assault is still held off.

8i **c. 6:30 pm to after dark:** Hey's and Avery's Confederate divisions gain some ground on Culp's and Cemetery Hills, but

P e n n s y l v a n i a

Oak Hill

Carlisle Road

Cashtown Road

Harrisburg Road

Gettysburg and Hanover Railroad

York Pike

unfinished railroad

Chambersburg Road

Herr Ridge

HETH

O'NEAL

LEE

DANIELS

RODES

RAMSEUR IVERSON DOLES

Gettysburg

EWELL

O'NEAL

Bonner's Hill

WILLIAMS

JOHNSON

STEWART

WALKER

HAYS

EARLY

AVERY

JONES

Hagerstown Road

PERRIN

LANE

MAHONE

THOMAS

SCALES

PENDER

A.P. HILL

ANDERSON

POSEY

WRIGHT

Willoughby's Run

Seminary Ridge

SCHURZ

HOWARD

Cemetery Hill

AMES

WADSWORTH

Evergreen Cemetery

GEARY

RUGER

Culp's Hill

Rock Creek

LANG

HARROW

HAYS

DOUBLEDAY

MEADE

Baltimore Pike

Spangler's Spring

Pitzer's Run

WILCOX

HUMPHREYS

BROOKE

COOK

CROSS

KELLY

Cemetery Ridge

Taneytown Road

CALDWELL

BARNES

CRAWFORD

McLAWS

BARKSDALE

WOFFFORD

SICKLES

2

Peach Orchard

Wheat Field

BIRNEY

AYRES

SYKES

SEMMES

KERSHAW

LONGSTREET

Plum Run

Devil's Den

1

VINCENT

Little Round Top

SEDGWICK

ANDERSON

ROBERTSON

BENNING

LAW

Emmitsburg Road

Big Round Top

N

0   1/2 km

0   1/2 mile

Gettysburg
2 July 1863

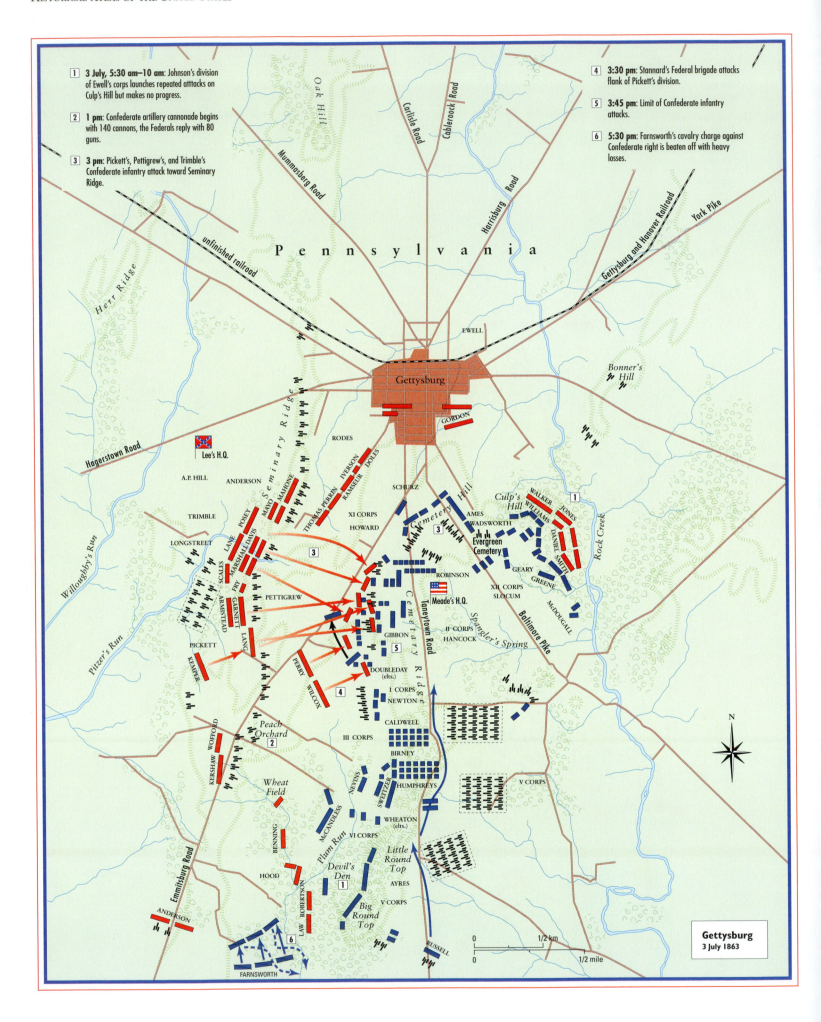

1. **3 July, 5:30 am–10 am:** Johnson's division of Ewell's corps launches repeated atttacks on Culp's Hill but makes no progress.

2. **1 pm:** Confederate artillery cannonade begins with 140 cannons, the Federals reply with 80 guns.

3. **3 pm:** Pickett's, Pettigrew's, and Trimble's Confederate infantry attack toward Seminary Ridge.

4. **3:30 pm:** Stannard's Federal brigade attacks flank of Pickett's division.

5. **3:45 pm:** Limit of Confederate infantry attacks.

6. **5:30 pm:** Farnsworth's cavalry charge against Confederate right is beaten off with heavy losses.

Gettysburg
3 July 1863

By 1864 defeat Was staring the Confederacy in the face. In the fall a Confederate War Department official wrote: "Steadfastness is yielding to a sense of hopelessness." However, some clung to the hope that by inflicting enough casualties on the Union armies they might weaken the northern resolve to continue the war and that voters might reject Lincoln and elect a peace candidate in the forthcoming election. Meanwhile on the battlefields, Grant launched his 1864 campaigns aimed at the two principal Confederate armies in Virginia and Georgia, while smaller Union forces engaged the enemy simultaneously on the periphery.

The Campaigns of 1864

- Union offensive
- Confederate offensive
- Union victory
- Confederate victory
- Inconclusive outcome
- Union blockade
- Union state
- Slave state staying loyal to the Union
- Confederate state
- Railroad

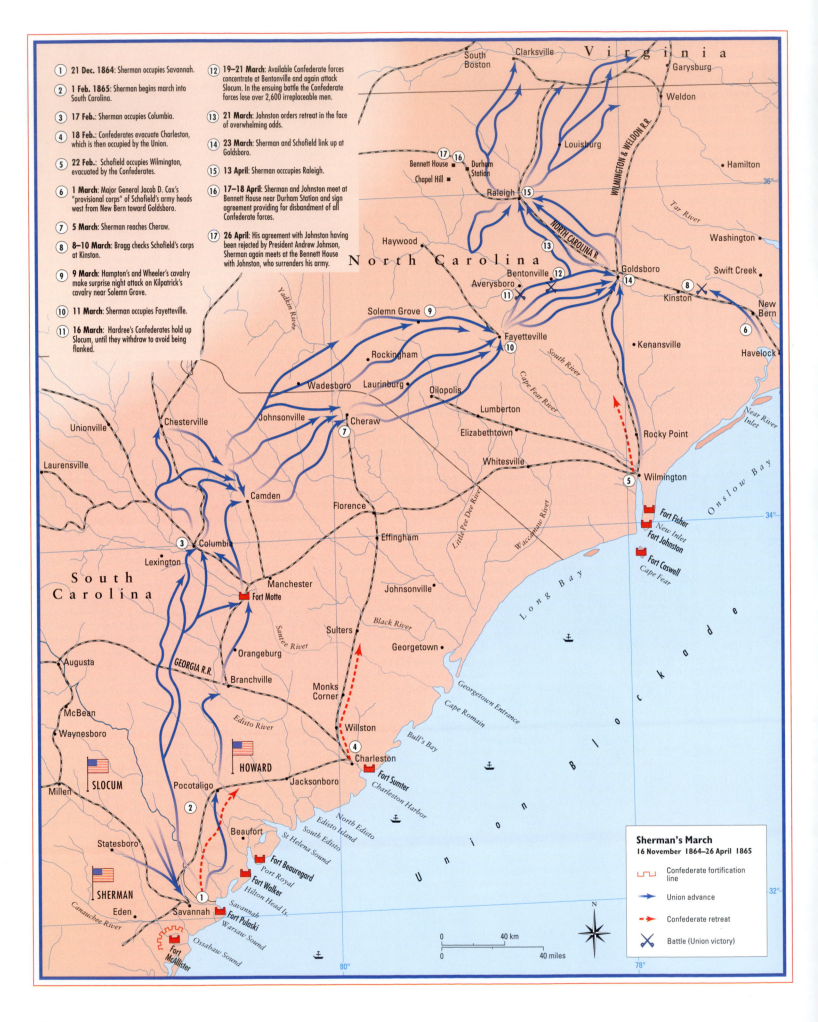

① **21 Dec. 1864:** Sherman occupies Savannah.

② **1 Feb. 1865:** Sherman begins march into South Carolina.

③ **17 Feb.:** Sherman occupies Columbia.

④ **18 Feb.:** Confederates evacuate Charleston, which is then occupied by the Union.

⑤ **22 Feb.:** Schofield occupies Wilmington, evacuated by the Confederates.

⑥ **1 March:** Major General Jacob D. Cox's "provisional corps" of Schofield's army heads west from New Bern toward Goldsboro.

⑦ **5 March:** Sherman reaches Cheraw.

⑧ **8–10 March:** Bragg checks Schofield's corps at Kinston.

⑨ **9 March:** Hampton's and Wheeler's cavalry make surprise night attack on Kilpatrick's cavalry near Solemn Grove.

⑩ **11 March:** Sherman occupies Fayetteville.

⑪ **16 March:** Hardree's Confederates hold up Slocum, until they withdraw to avoid being flanked.

⑫ **19–21 March:** Available Confederate forces concentrate at Bentonville and again attack Slocum. In the ensuing battle the Confederate forces lose over 2,600 irreplaceable men.

⑬ **21 March:** Johnston orders retreat in the face of overwhelming odds.

⑭ **23 March:** Sherman and Schofield link up at Goldsboro.

⑮ **13 April:** Sherman occcupies Raleigh.

⑯ **17–18 April:** Sherman and Johnston meet at Bennett House near Durham Station and sign agreement providing for disbandment of all Confederate forces.

⑰ **26 April:** His agreement with Johnston having been rejected by President Andrew Johnson, Sherman again meets at the Bennett House with Johnston, who surrenders his army.

Sherman's March
16 November 1864–26 April 1865

⊔ Confederate fortification line

→ Union advance

⇢ Confederate retreat

✕ Battle (Union victory)

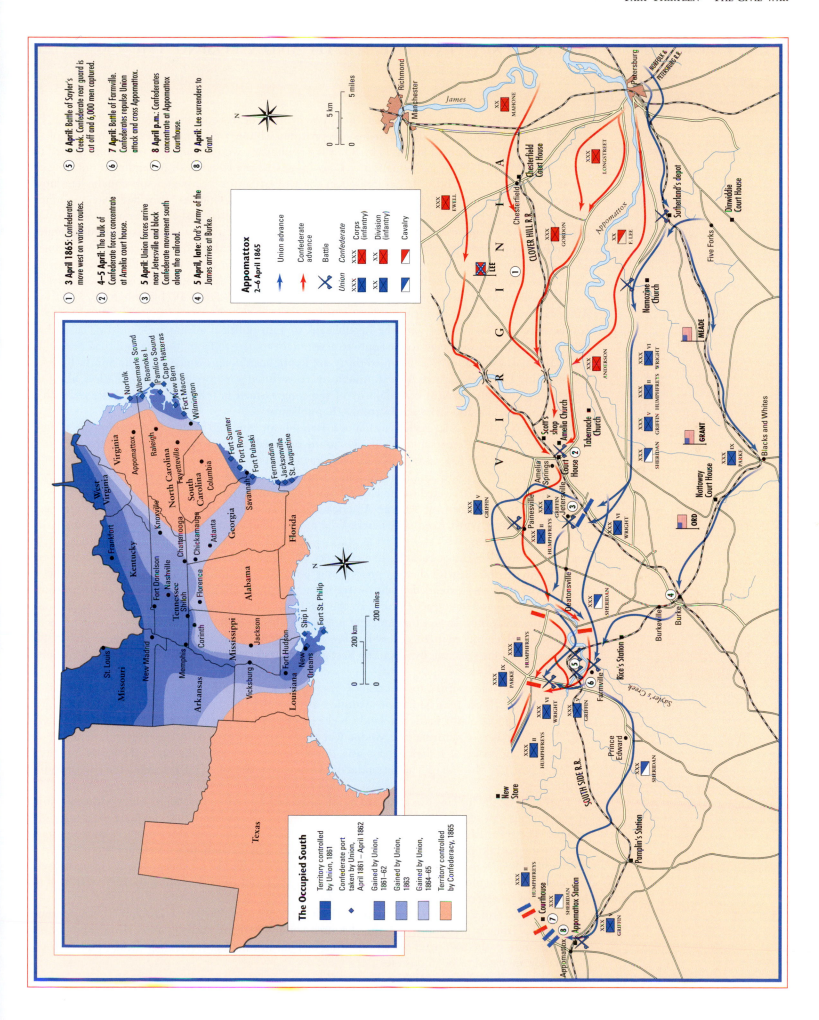

Appomattox
2–6 April 1865

① **3 April 1865:** Confederates move west on various routes.

② **4–5 April:** The bulk of Confederate forces concentrate at Amelia court house.

③ **5 April:** Union forces arrive near Jetersville and block Confederate movement south along the railroad.

④ **5 April, late:** Ord's Army of the James arrives at Burke.

⑤ **6 April:** Battle of Sayler's Creek. Confederate rear guard is cut off and 6,000 men captured.

⑥ **6 April:** The bulk of Confederate forces concentrate at Amelia court house.

⑦ **7 April:** Battle of Farmville. Confederates repulse Union attack and cross Appomattox.

⑧ **8 April p.m.:** Confederates concentrate at Appomattox Courthouse.

⑨ **9 April:** Lee surrenders to Grant.

Union advance
Confederate advance
Battle

	Confederate	
XXX	Corps (infantry)	
XX	Division (infantry)	
	Cavalry	

	Union	
XXX		
XX		

The Occupied South

- Territory controlled by Union, 1861
- Confederate port taken by Union, April 1861 – April 1862
- Gained by Union, 1861–62
- Gained by Union, 1863
- Gained by Union, 1864–65
- Territory controlled by Confederacy, 1865

PART FOURTEEN   RECONSTRUCTING THE SOUTH AND CLOSING THE FRONTIER

T HE SURRENDER of Lee's army left the Union army in nearly complete control of the South. For a time, Union generals and their staffs provided whatever government existed in much of the region. Congress, dominated by Radical Republicans whose vindictive intentions toward the South were inflamed by the assassination of Lincoln, passed the Fourteenth Amendment granting citizenship to "all persons born or naturalized in the United States." This and subsequent legislation sought to ensure that slaves had the right to vote and hold office. Congress provided that if southern states accepted the Fourteenth Amendment, they would be readmitted to the Union and freed of Union military control. Tennessee did so, and was readmitted in 1866; all of the others refused. Congress responded with more repressive measures. In June 1868, Arkansas adopted the Fourteenth Amendment and was readmitted to the Union. By July 1870, all of the southern states had done so as well. Former slaves were granted voting rights, and army officials ensured that they could exercise those rights.

The former slaves faithfully supported the party of Lincoln. From 1871 through 1875, African Americans precipitated a political revolution in the South. In this they were assisted by "scalawags"—Southerners who cooperated with the Republicans to gain political advantage—and by "carpetbaggers"—Northerners who went to the South to assist in, or to benefit from, the new political order. The 43rd Congress, elected in 1872, included thirty-six Republican congressmen from the South. In South Carolina and Louisiana, where African Americans constituted a majority of the population, all of the congressmen were Republicans. A majority of the congressmen in other largely black states, such as Mississippi, Florida, and Arkansas, were also Republicans.

But white Southerners struggled to eliminate Republican rule, and in the congressional elections of 1874, the Republican representation in the South declined by fourteen members in the House of Representatives. After federal troops were withdrawn from the South, and blacks were consequently disenfranchised, the South was again solidly Democratic. In the 1878 congressional elections, only three Republicans were elected to the House from the South. Soon, there would be none.

The disenfranchisement of African Americans was accompanied by the reassertion of their economic dependency. Most freed slaves lacked the money, land, and equipment to establish their own farms. Although some with skills such as blacksmithing or carpentry managed to go into business or trades for themselves, most became sharecroppers who farmed land owned by others. Former plantations were reorganized, with sharecroppers taking possession (but not ownership) of small patches of land. The landowners extended credit for seeds and supplies, often at inflated rates and prices, and received a portion of the crop in return. By the 1880s, although African Americans in the rural South were legally free, they lacked fundamental political rights and the economic wherewithal to secure them. The problem of legalized slavery had been solved, but a more subtle (and thus more intractable) racial problem long festered. By the 1890s Reconstruction in the South was, if not a failure, a woefully incomplete success.

By the end of the century, too, another region had become the focus of considerable speculation. The area in the West that had been identified as "frontier" had been shrinking for decades. The Indians, having lost major battles at Sand Creek (1864), the Red River (1874–75), Bear Paw Mountain (1877), and northern California (the Modoc War 1872–73), were forced into reservations. (The famous exception to the string of Indian defeats was, of course, Custer's annihilation by the Sioux Indians at Little Big Horn in Montana.) The surrender of Geronimo in Arizona (1886) marked the end of Indian resistance.

The defeat of the Indians was hastened by the destruction of tribal life. White buffalo hunters, some of them firing repeating rifles from moving trains, decimated the herds that provided food for Plains Indians. The railroads, by slashing across the Plains, disrupted the migratory patterns to fresh grasslands of the buffalo herds. By the 1870s, Texas ranchers were driving huge cattle herds northward to railroad heads in Kansas, Nebraska, and Colorado. Increasingly, the ranchers became entangled with farmers, who were plowing up grasslands. The Indians lost out to both groups. By 1890 nearly all the Indians lived on reservations.

By 1890, the frontier had nearly disappeared. In 1893 historian Frederick Jackson Turner contended that the frontier had imparted the distinctive individualism and vigorous democracy of the American nation; the waning of the frontier thus had unsettling implications for the nation. American democracy appeared to be in trouble.

MAPS

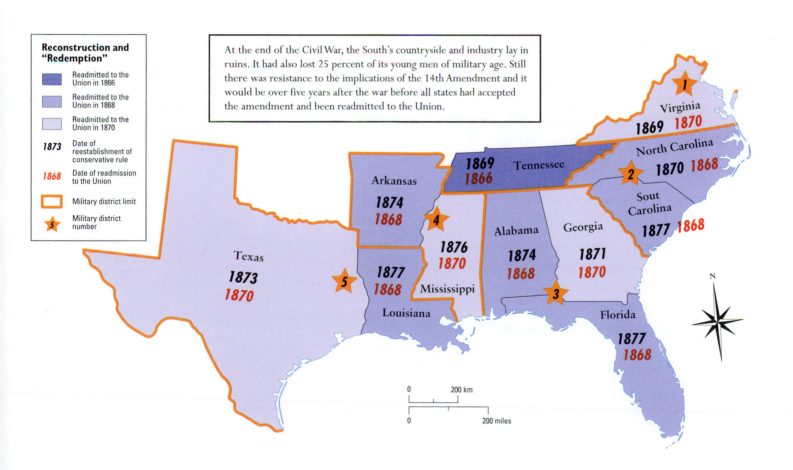

Reconstruction and "Redemption"

Readmitted to the Union in 1866

Readmitted to the Union in 1868

Readmitted to the Union in 1870

1873 Date of reestablishment of conservative rule

1868 Date of readmission to the Union

Military district limit

5 Military district number

At the end of the Civil War, the South's countryside and industry lay in ruins. It had also lost 25 percent of its young men of military age. Still there was resistance to the implications of the 14th Amendment and it would be over five years after the war before all states had accepted the amendment and been readmitted to the Union.

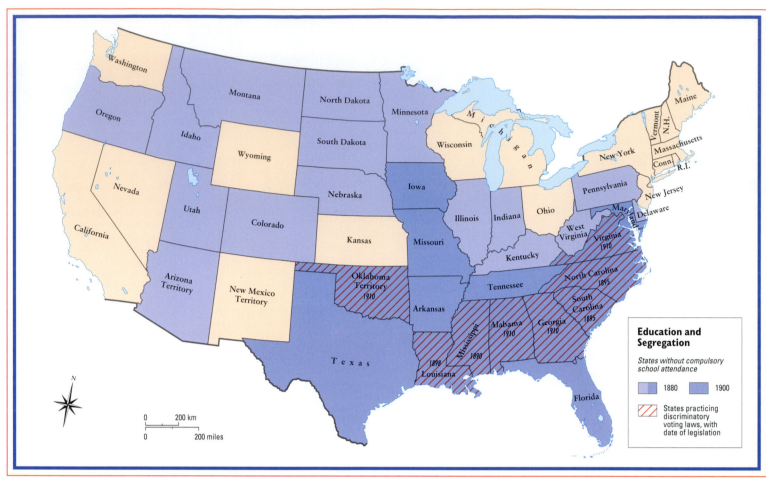

Education and Segregation

States without compulsory school attendance

1880

1900

States practicing discriminatory voting laws, with date of legislation

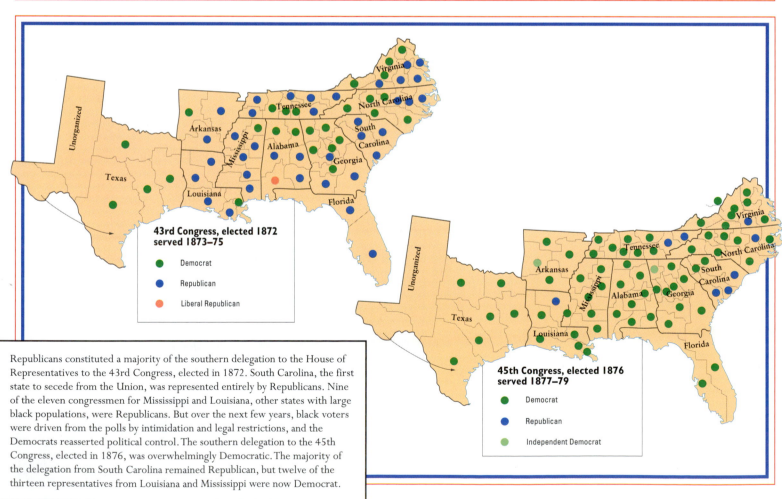

43rd Congress, elected 1872 served 1873–75

● Democrat
● Republican
● Liberal Republican

45th Congress, elected 1876 served 1877–79

● Democrat
● Republican
● Independent Democrat

Republicans constituted a majority of the southern delegation to the House of Representatives to the 43rd Congress, elected in 1872. South Carolina, the first state to secede from the Union, was represented entirely by Republicans. Nine of the eleven congressmen for Mississippi and Louisiana, other states with large black populations, were Republicans. But over the next few years, black voters were driven from the polls by intimidation and legal restrictions, and the Democrats reasserted political control. The southern delegation to the 45th Congress, elected in 1876, was overwhelmingly Democratic. The majority of the delegation from South Carolina remained Republican, but twelve of the thirteen representatives from Louisiana and Mississippi were now Democrat.

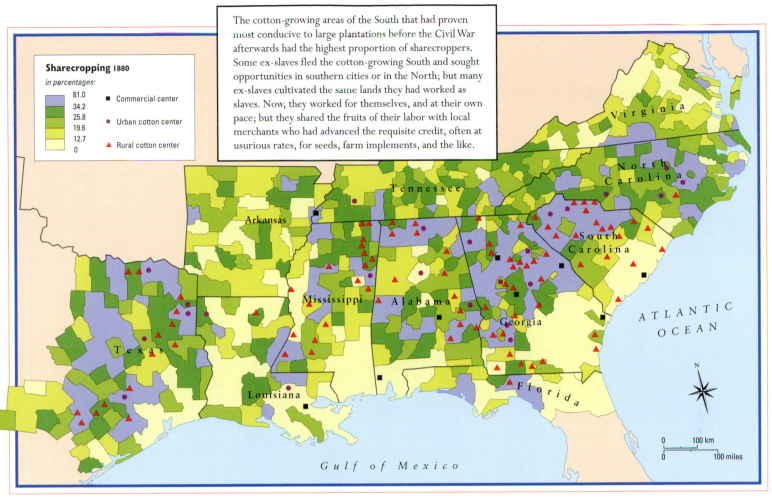

The cotton-growing areas of the South that had proven most conducive to large plantations before the Civil War afterwards had the highest proportion of sharecroppers. Some ex-slaves fled the cotton-growing South and sought opportunities in southern cities or in the North; but many ex-slaves cultivated the same lands they had worked as slaves. Now, they worked for themselves, and at their own pace; but they shared the fruits of their labor with local merchants who had advanced the requisite credit, often at usurious rates, for seeds, farm implements, and the like.

Sharecropping 1880

in percentages:

81.0	■ Commercial center
34.2	
25.8	● Urban cotton center
19.6	
12.7	▲ Rural cotton center
0	

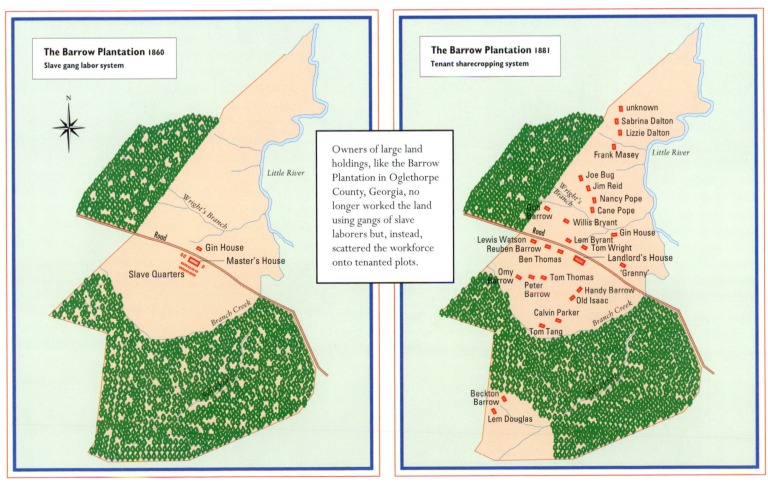

The Barrow Plantation 1860
Slave gang labor system

The Barrow Plantation 1881
Tenant sharecropping system

Owners of large land holdings, like the Barrow Plantation in Oglethorpe County, Georgia, no longer worked the land using gangs of slave laborers but, instead, scattered the workforce onto tenanted plots.

Washington

Oregon

Montana

North Dakota

Idaho

South Dakota

Wyoming

Nevada

Nebraska

Utah
Territory

Colorado

Kansas

California

Arizona
Territory

New Mexico
Territory

Greer
County

Oklahoma
Territory

T e x a s

Alaska
Unorganized
Territory

Not to scale

In 1845 a news editor called the westward movement, "our manifest destiny…" which, he wrote, "is to overspread the continent allotted by providence for the free development of our yearly multiplying millions." The overland settlers, largely family groups, would begin in late spring. Most left via Missouri, heading westward at fifteen miles per day, braving Indian attacks and contagious diseases. For those heading to the far west, the grueling 2000-mile journey would take some 6 months. By 1890 most suitable land had been settled, "Wild Indians" placed safely on reservations, and domesticated cattle and farmsteads had replaced the roaming herds of buffalo. The frontier was virtually at an end.

The Frontier 1890

Settled area

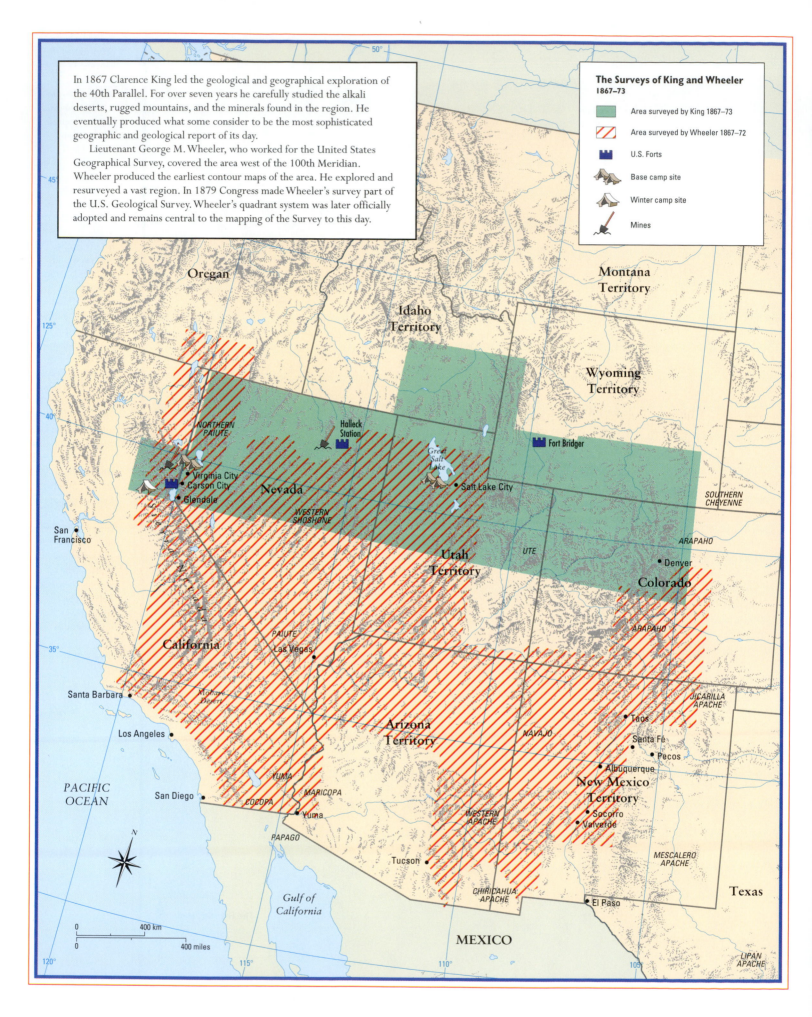

The Surveys of King and Wheeler
1867–73

- Area surveyed by King 1867–73
- Area surveyed by Wheeler 1867–72
- U.S. Forts
- Base camp site
- Winter camp site
- Mines

In 1867 Clarence King led the geological and geographical exploration of the 40th Parallel. For over seven years he carefully studied the alkali deserts, rugged mountains, and the minerals found in the region. He eventually produced what some consider to be the most sophisticated geographic and geological report of its day.

Lieutenant George M. Wheeler, who worked for the United States Geographical Survey, covered the area west of the 100th Meridian. Wheeler produced the earliest contour maps of the area. He explored and resurveyed a vast region. In 1879 Congress made Wheeler's survey part of the U.S. Geological Survey. Wheeler's quadrant system was later officially adopted and remains central to the mapping of the Survey to this day.

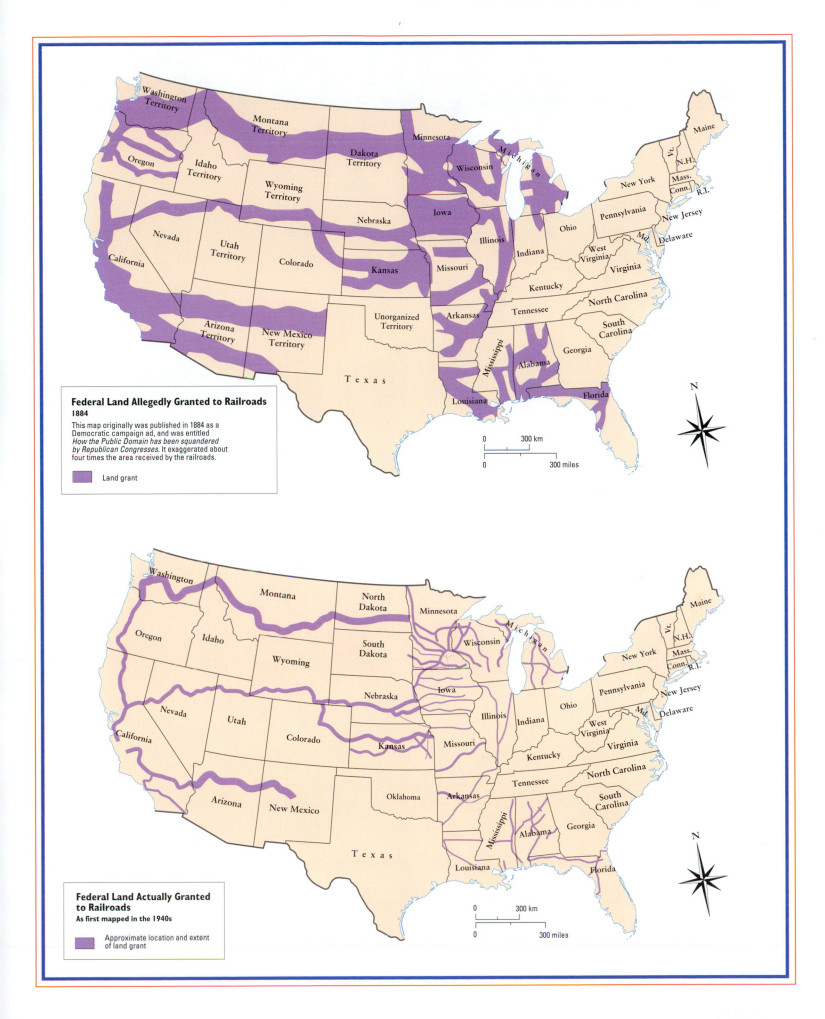

Federal Land Allegedly Granted to Railroads
1884

This map originally was published in 1884 as a Democratic campaign ad, and was entitled *How the Public Domain has been squandered by Republican Congresses.* It exaggerated about four times the area received by the railroads.

Land grant

Federal Land Actually Granted to Railroads
As first mapped in the 1940s

Approximate location and extent of land grant

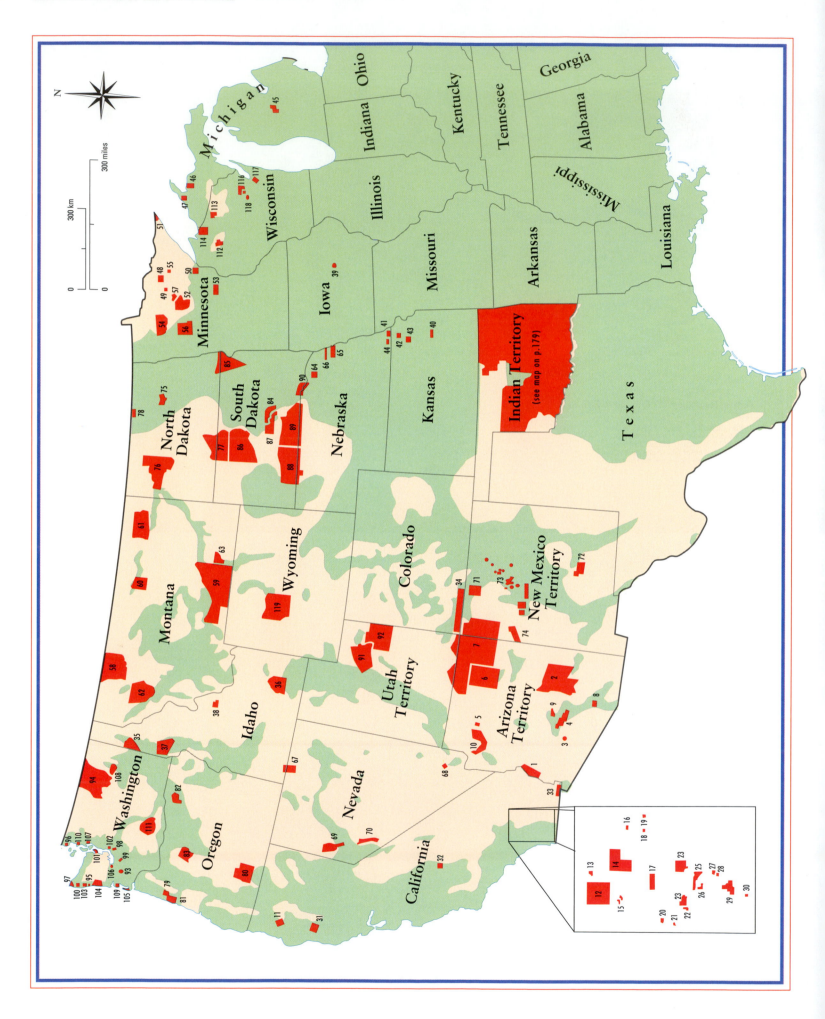

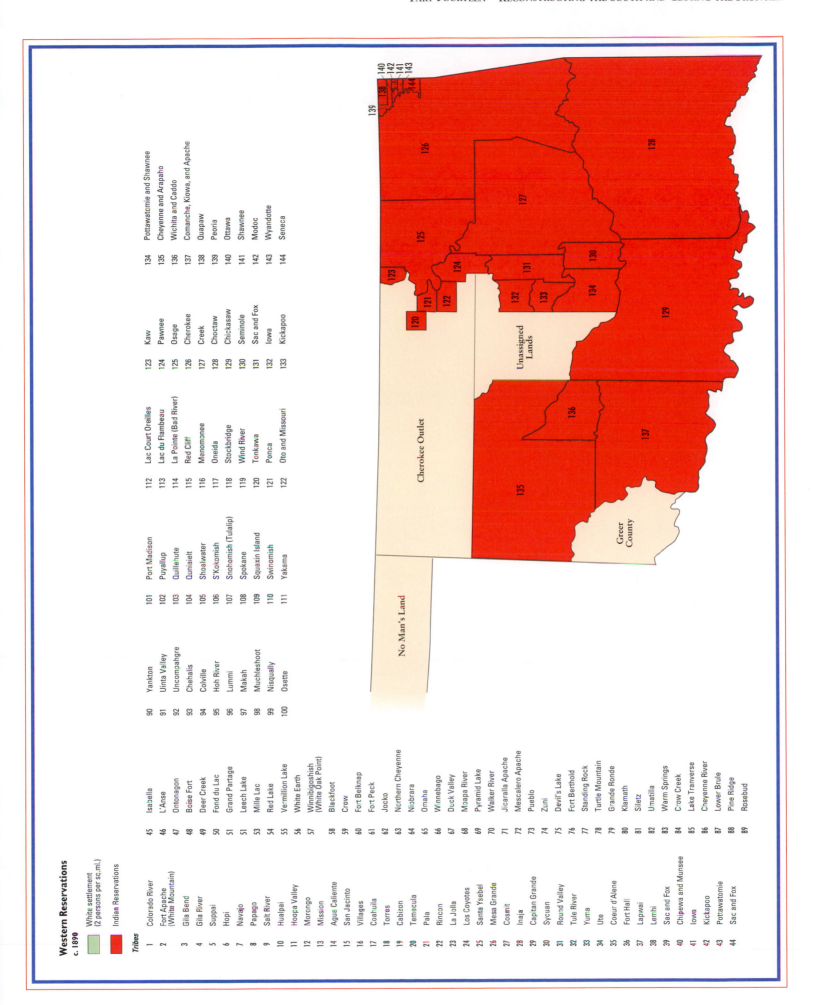

Western Reservations

c. 1890

White settlement
(2 persons per sq.ml.)

Indian Reservations

Tribes

1 Colorado River
2 Fort Apache (White Mountain)
3 Gila Bend
4 Gila River
5 Suppai
6 Hopi
7 Navajo
8 Papago
9 Salt River
10 Hualpai
11 Hoopa Valley
12 Morongo
13 Mission
14 Agua Caliente
15 San Jacinto
16 Villages
17 Coahuila
18 Torros
19 Cabizon
20 Temecula
21 Pala
22 Rincon
23 La Jolla
24 Los Coyotes
25 Santa Ysebel
26 Mesa Grande
27 Cosmit
28 Inaja
29 Capitan Grande
30 Sycuan
31 Round Valley
32 Tule River
33 Yuma
34 Ute
35 Coeur d'Alene
36 Fort Hall
37 Lapwai
38 Lemhi
39 Sac and Fox
40 Chipewa and Munsee
41 Iowa
42 Kickapoo
43 Pottawatomie
44 Sac and Fox

45 Isabella
46 L'Anse
47 Ontonagon
48 Boise Fort
49 Deer Creek
50 Fond du Lac
51 Grand Partage
51 Leech Lake
53 Mille Lac
54 Red Lake
55 Vermillion Lake
56 White Earth
57 Winnibigoshish (White Oak Point)
58 Blackfoot
59 Crow
60 Fort Belknap
61 Fort Peck
62 Jocko
63 Northern Cheyenne
64 Niobrara
65 Omaha
66 Winnebago
67 Duck Valley
68 Moapa River
69 Pyramid Lake
70 Walker River
71 Jicaralla Apache
72 Mescalero Apache
73 Pueblo
74 Zuni
75 Devil's Lake
76 Fort Berthold
77 Standing Rock
78 Turtle Mountain
79 Grande Ronde
80 Klamath
81 Siletz
82 Umatilla
83 Warm Springs
84 Crow Creek
85 Lake Tranverse
86 Cheyenne River
87 Lower Brule
88 Pine Ridge
89 Rosebud

90 Yankton
91 Uinta Valley
92 Uncompahgre
93 Chehalis
94 Colville
95 Hoh River
96 Lummi
97 Makah
98 Muchleshoot
99 Nisqually
100 Osette

101 Port Madison
102 Puyallup
103 Quillehute
104 Quniaielt
105 Shoalwater
106 S'Kokomish
107 Snohomish (Tulalip)
108 Spokane
109 Squaxin Island
110 Swinomish
111 Yakama
112 Lac Court Oreilles
113 Lac du Flambeau
114 La Pointe (Bad River)
115 Red Cliff
116 Menomonee
117 Oneida
118 Stockbridge
119 Wind River
120 Tonkawa
121 Ponca
122 Oto and Missouri

123 Kaw
124 Pawnee
125 Osage
126 Cherokee
127 Creek
128 Choctaw
129 Chickasaw
130 Seminole
131 Sac and Fox
132 Iowa
133 Kickapoo

134 Pottawatomie and Shawnee
135 Cheyenne and Arapaho
136 Wichita and Caddo
137 Comanche, Kiowa, and Apache
138 Quapaw
139 Peoria
140 Ottawa
141 Shawnee
142 Modoc
143 Wyandotte
144 Seneca

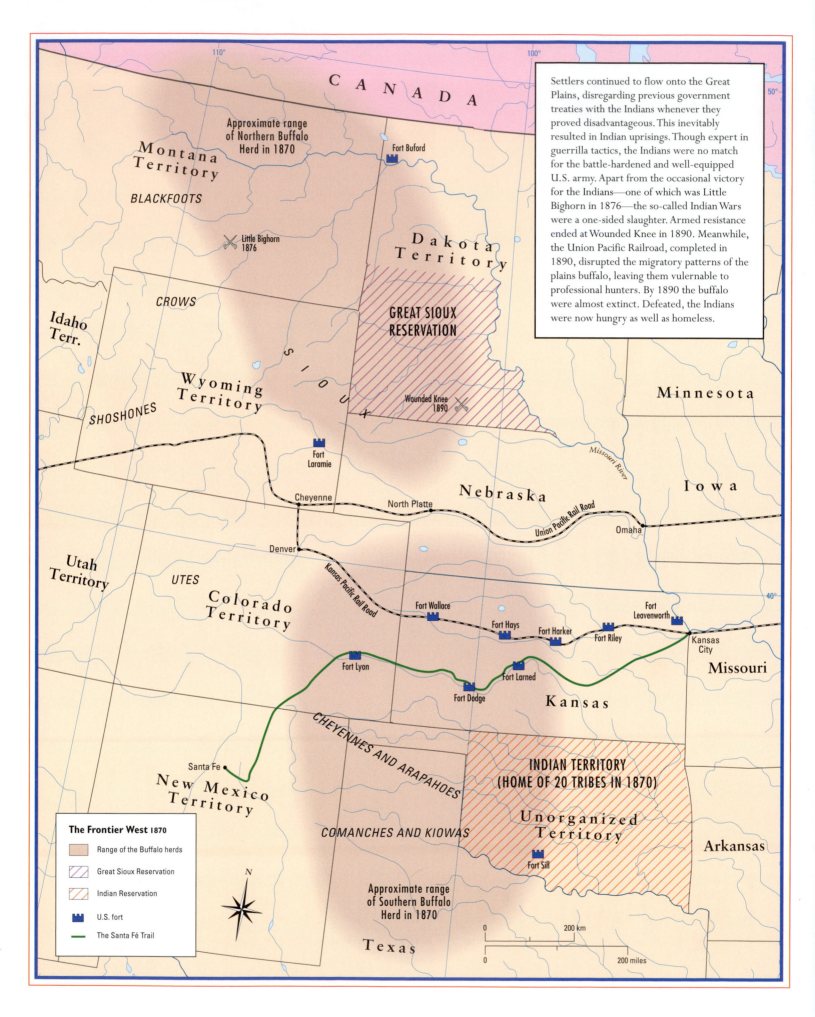

CANADA

Montana
Territory

BLACKFOOTS

Approximate range
of Northern Buffalo
Herd in 1870

Fort Buford

Little Bighorn
1876

CROWS

Dakota
Territory

Idaho
Terr.

GREAT SIOUX
RESERVATION

Wyoming
Territory

S I O U X

SHOSHONES

Wounded Knee
1890

Minnesota

Fort
Laramie

Utah
Territory

UTES

Cheyenne

North Platte

Nebraska

Missouri River

I o w a

Union Pacific Rail Road

Omaha

Denver

Colorado
Territory

Kansas Pacific Rail Road

Fort Wallace

40°

Fort
Leavenworth

Fort Hays

Fort Harker

Kansas
City

Fort Lyon

Fort Larned

Fort Riley

Missouri

Fort Dodge

Kansas

Santa Fe

New Mexico
Territory

CHEYENNES AND ARAPAHOES

INDIAN TERRITORY
(HOME OF 20 TRIBES IN 1870)

Unorganized
Territory

Arkansas

COMANCHES AND KIOWAS

Fort Sill

The Frontier West 1870

Range of the Buffalo herds

Great Sioux Reservation

Indian Reservation

U.S. fort

The Santa Fé Trail

N

Approximate range
of Southern Buffalo
Herd in 1870

Texas

0   200 km

0   200 miles

Settlers continued to flow onto the Great
Plains, disregarding previous government
treaties with the Indians whenever they
proved disadvantageous. This inevitably
resulted in Indian uprisings. Though expert in
guerrilla tactics, the Indians were no match
for the battle-hardened and well-equipped
U.S. army. Apart from the occasional victory
for the Indians—one of which was Little
Bighorn in 1876—the so-called Indian Wars
were a one-sided slaughter. Armed resistance
ended at Wounded Knee in 1890. Meanwhile,
the Union Pacific Railroad, completed in
1890, disrupted the migratory patterns of the
plains buffalo, leaving them vulnerable to
professional hunters. By 1890 the buffalo
were almost extinct. Defeated, the Indians
were now hungry as well as homeless.

110°   100°   50°

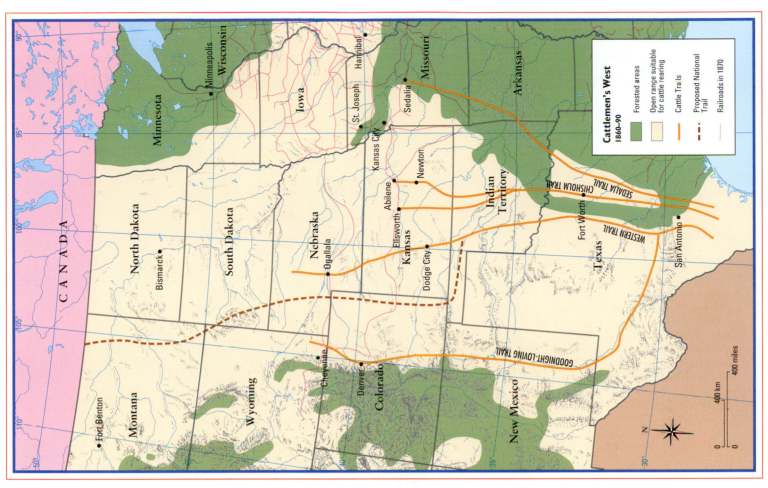

Cattlemen's West 1860–90

- Forested areas
- Open range suitable for cattle rearing
- Cattle Trails
- Proposed National Trail
- Railroads in 1870

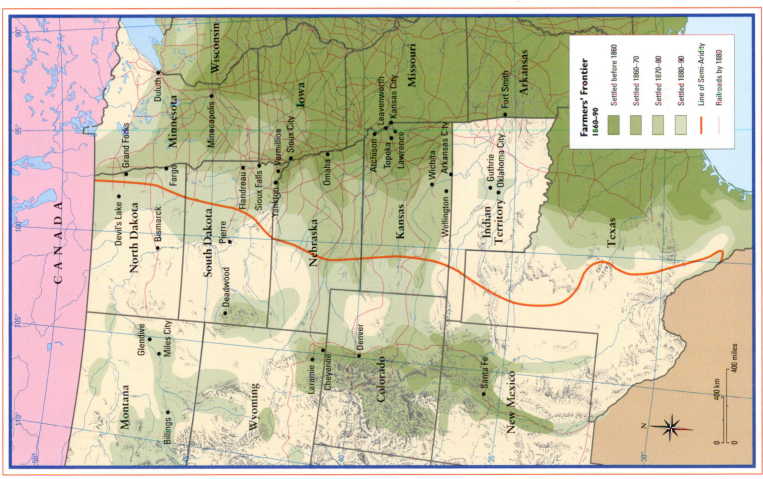

Farmers' Frontier 1860–90

- Settled before 1860
- Settled 1860–70
- Settled 1870–80
- Settled 1880–90
- Line of Semi-Aridity
- Railroads by 1880

Among the health hazards facing 19th-century Americans, cholera did not cause the greatest number of deaths, but it struck with so little warning and produced such terrible symptoms that the only course open to most was to flee from its path. An outbreak occurred in Montreal on 6 June 1832. It moved south arriving in New York on the 26th.

Between 1849 and 1870 the connection between infected water supplies and the spread of the disease had been established. Many cities such as New York constructed extensive aqueducts and pipelines to ensure clean water supplies. However, Nashville, Tennessee, lagged behind. As the city grew upriver from its water-pumphouse, sewage found its way into the water supply in several parts of the city. In the outbreak of 1873, 647 people died.

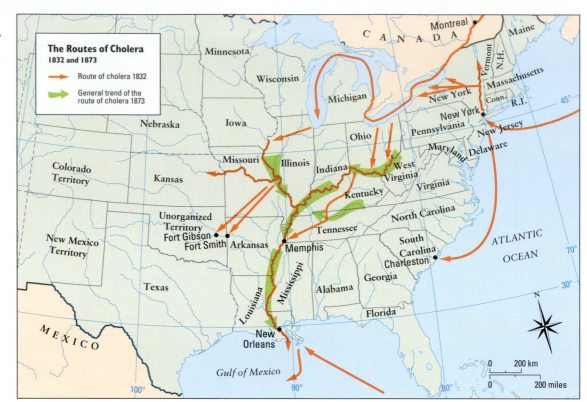

The Routes of Cholera
1832 and 1873

→ Route of cholera 1832

➤ General trend of the route of cholera 1873

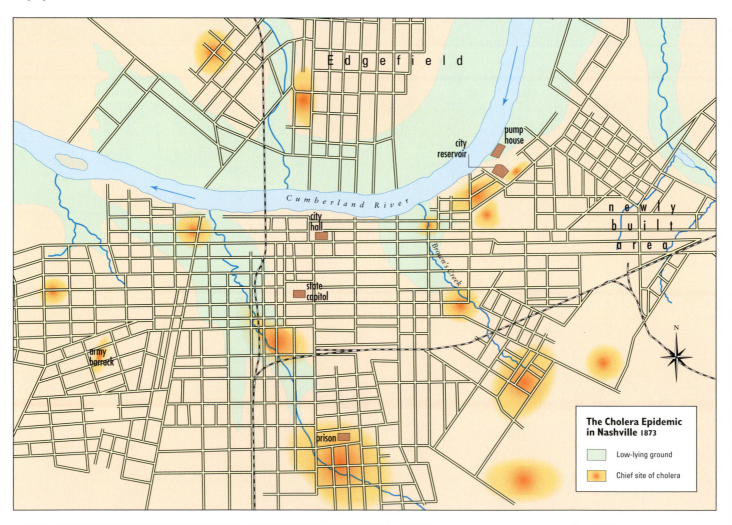

The Cholera Epidemic in Nashville 1873

Low-lying ground

Chief site of cholera

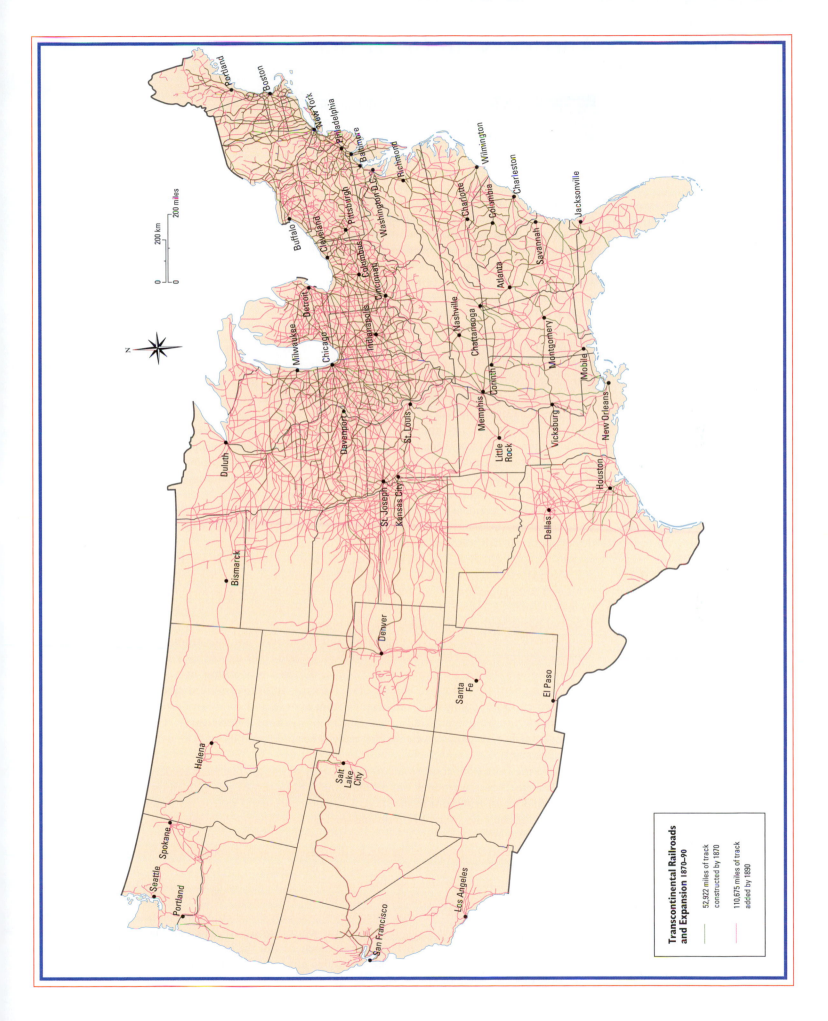

**Transcontinental Railroads
and Expansion 1870–90**

52,922 miles of track
constructed by 1870

110,675 miles of track
added by 1890

PART FIFTEEN   AMERICA IN THE GILDED AGE

I N 1877, federal troops were withdrawn from the South, part of the settlement that broke the deadlock 1876 election and gave the presidency to Rutherford B. Hayes, a Republican. This marked the formal end of the Civil War. But too many dinner tables still had vacant chairs, too many veterans bore battle scars, and too many Southerners, white and black alike, remained mired in poverty, to allow the legacy of the war to be entirely forgotten.

But many others were readily distracted by the rapid changes of the last quarter of the 19th century. The engine that drove these changes was the new industrial economy, a powerful force that transformed the environment, attracted millions of workers from rural areas and foreign lands, restructured political and financial institutions, and impelled statesmen to look abroad for new markets, raw materials, and workers. These changes altered the nation, and had repercussions throughout the world.

The federal government sought to promote an efficient transportation system, and to that end it stimulated railroad construction by offering grants of public land. Many congressmen learned, as if they needed an illustration, that it is better to give than to receive, in part because the former ensured the latter. The Pacific Railway Act of 1862 gave the Union Pacific and Central Pacific railroads five miles of public land for each mile of track laid.

The railroads, so central to the Union military effort, played an equally important role in the economic transformations decades afterwards. In 1865, the nation had some 35,000 miles of track. Five years later, it was at 53,000 miles. By 1890, the trackage had more than doubled, to 111,000 miles. By then, the nation's railroads took in over $1 billion in revenue, well over twice as much as the budget of the entire federal government.

As the railroads became knitted into an effective transportation grid, requiring standardized parts, accounting methods, and management systems, they also changed conceptions of how business corporations and the federal government should function. In 1883, to eliminate confusion over shipping schedules, the railroads imposed four separate time zones, still in use today; three years later, they standardized the gauge (axle width) of railroad track (4 feet 8 $1/2$ inches).

In addition to reducing transportation costs, the railroads were heavy users of steel, an industry that was central to the nation's industrial transformation. Blast furnaces and rolling mills were built throughout iron-rich western Pennsylvania and Ohio, but soon appeared in central Indiana and northeastern Illinois. Pittsburgh, Cleveland, and Chicago became major steel-producing cities. In 1901 J. P. Morgan merged nearly a dozen separate steel companies, including Andrew Carnegie's behemoth firm, into a single company, U.S. Steel, the world's first billion-dollar corporation. U.S. Steel, Inc. was the most visible of a wave of industrial mergers that swept over the nation. By 1904, over 300 industrial corporations held aggregate capital of $7.5 billion.

Industrialization gave rise to a population shift from rural areas to cities. This process had global overtones, begun decades earlier, as peasants from Ireland and England took passage on sailing vessels and steamships across the Atlantic and found themselves working in textile factories and iron foundries in New York, Boston, Philadelphia, Newark, and other eastern cities. By the late 19th century, however, more immigrants were coming from eastern and southern Europe, and they were finding work in the burgeoning industrial centers of western Pennsylvania, Ohio, Illinois, Indiana, Wisconsin, and Michigan. Cleveland, like many other industrial cities, had become a kaleidoscope of ethnic diversity.

By 1893 the shift from countryside to urban areas prompted historian Frederick Jackson Turner to declare that the western frontier was all but gone. This assertion, though an overstatement, reflected the profound transformations in the West. The transcontinental railroads further undermined Indian life, disrupting the migration of buffalo and leaving them vulnerable to hunters, and the railroads also accelerated the influx of miners, ranchers, and settlers. In 1874, the Sioux Indians, outraged by encroachment onto their lands in the Black Hills Reservation and unnerved by the laying of tracks for the Northern Pacific Railroad, mounted one final campaign.

In the summer of 1876, some 2500 Indian warriors, commanded by Rain-in-the-Face, Crazy Horse, and Sitting Bull, had encamped near the Bighorn Mountains. When Colonel George A. Custer attacked, his tiny troop of 264 cavalrymen was wiped out. But there would be no more Indian victories. Whatever fighting remained was between the whites, who fenced in water holes, fields, and grazing lands to the exclusion of other farmers and ranchers. But the heroic era of the gun-toting cowboy and homesteader was shortlived; by the late 1800s much of the valuable land in the West had been taken over by large companies.

MAPS

The election of 1896 represented more than just a choice between two men or two political parties. It involved two competing visions for America's future, rival sections of the country, and different interests. Bryan equated silver with the common people, and charged that the gold standard represented the priviledged interests of the Northeast, home of America's elite, whose interests were inimical to those of the average American. He stood as the defender of the farmer and of Amerians wracked by debt and economic hardship; he was the voice of the West and the South. Most important, Bryan looked to America's past as a blueprint for its future. Holding the interests of the farmer paramount, he extolled the ideals of rural America, representing an alternative to the crushing onslaught of industrialization and urbanization. McKinley and the Republicans, by contrast, stood for an American future that was oriented toward business, manufacturing, and commerce, and favored the Northeast over other sections of the country.

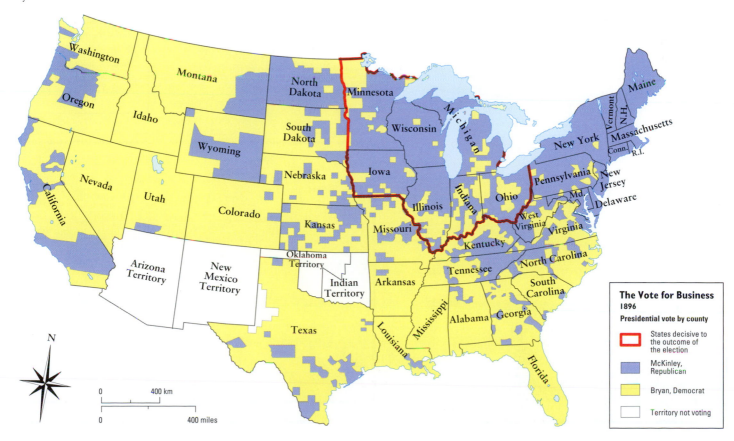

The Vote for Business
1896
Presidential vote by county

- States decisive to the outcome of the election
- McKinley, Republican
- Bryan, Democrat
- Territory not voting

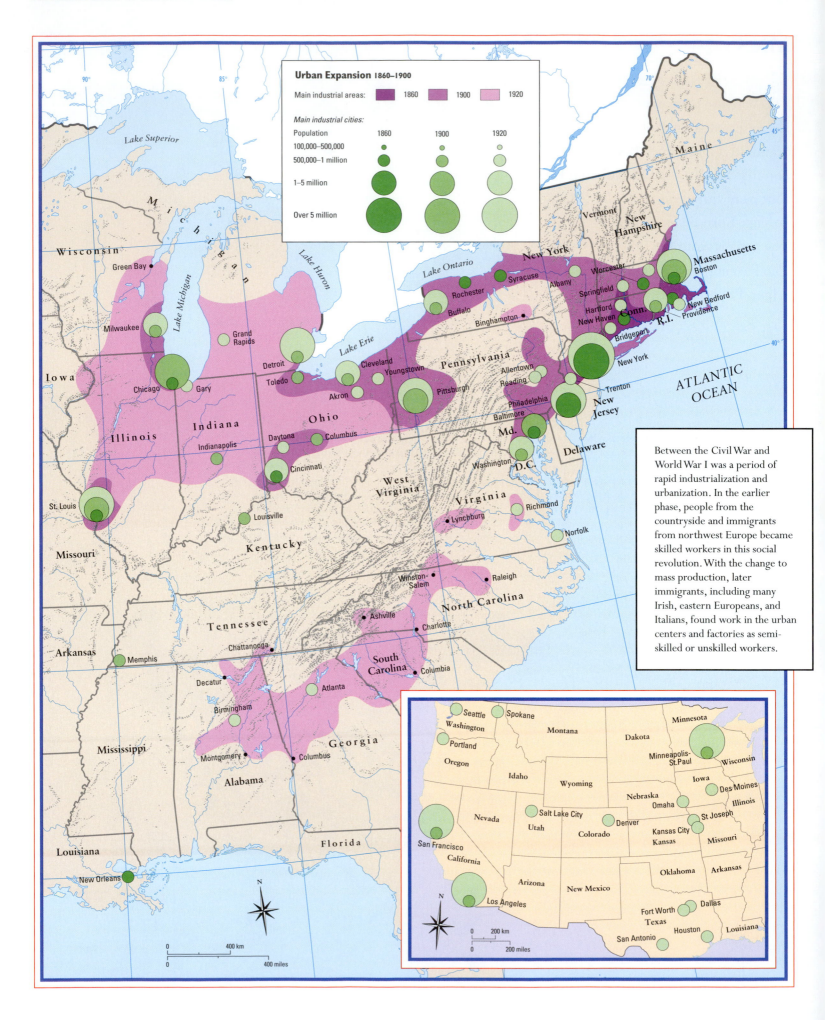

Urban Expansion 1860–1900

Main industrial areas: 1860 1900 1920

Main industrial cities:
Population 1860 1900 1920
100,000–500,000
500,000–1 million
1–5 million
Over 5 million

Between the Civil War and World War I was a period of rapid industrialization and urbanization. In the earlier phase, people from the countryside and immigrants from northwest Europe became skilled workers in this social revolution. With the change to mass production, later immigrants, including many Irish, eastern Europeans, and Italians, found work in the urban centers and factories as semi-skilled or unskilled workers.

Standard Time Zones 1883

- Pacific Time
- Mountain Time
- Central Time
- Eastern Time

0   300 km
0   300 miles

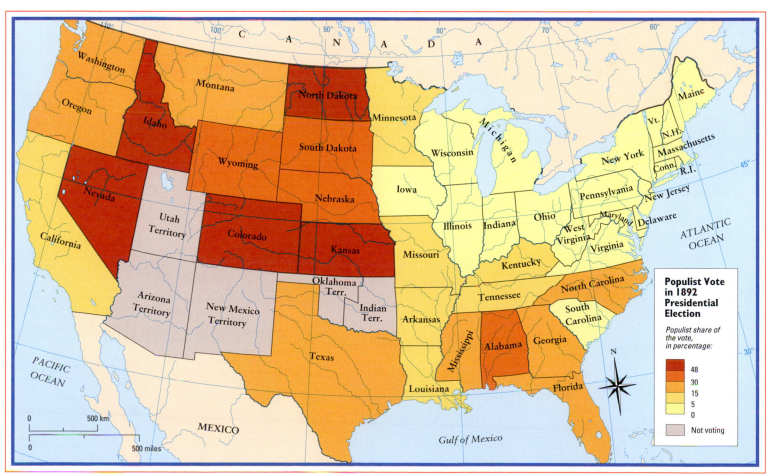

Populist Vote in 1892 Presidential Election

Populist share of the vote, in percentage:

- 48
- 30
- 15
- 5
- 0
- Not voting

0   500 km
0   500 miles

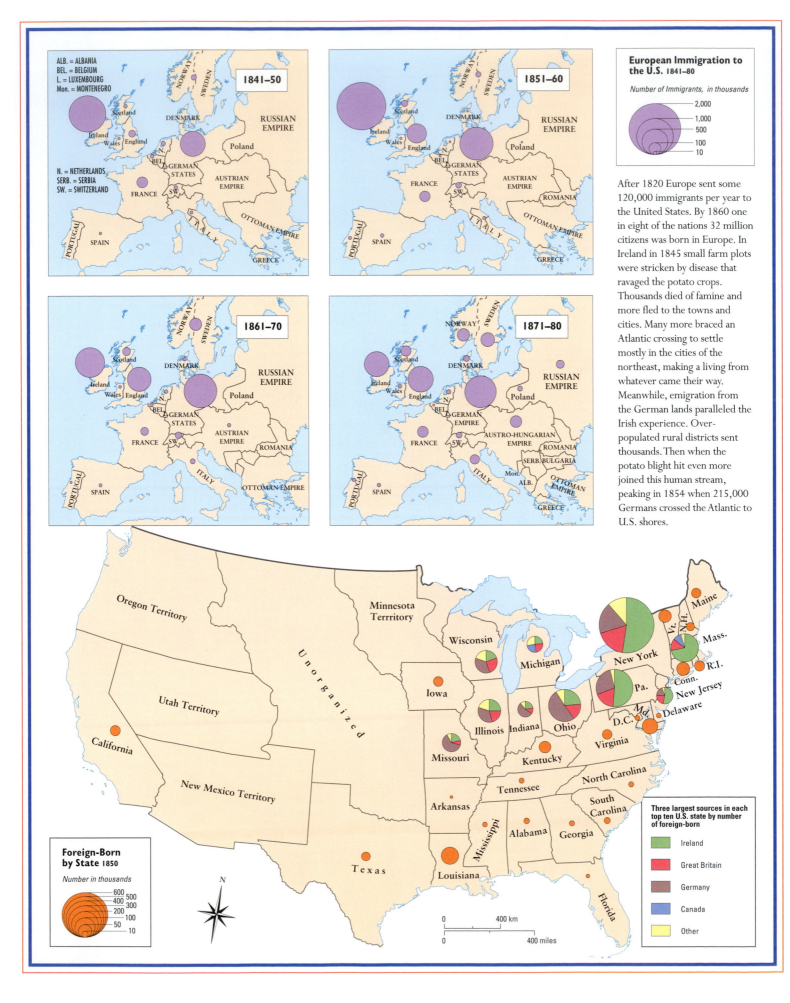

ALB. = ALBANIA
BEL. = BELGIUM
L. = LUXEMBOURG
Mon. = MONTENEGRO

N. = NETHERLANDS
SERB. = SERBIA
SW. = SWITZERLAND

1841–50

1851–60

1861–70

1871–80

European Immigration to the U.S. 1841–80

Number of Immigrants, in thousands

2,000
1,000
500
100
10

After 1820 Europe sent some 120,000 immigrants per year to the United States. By 1860 one in eight of the nations 32 million citizens was born in Europe. In Ireland in 1845 small farm plots were stricken by disease that ravaged the potato crops. Thousands died of famine and more fled to the towns and cities. Many more braced an Atlantic crossing to settle mostly in the cities of the northeast, making a living from whatever came their way. Meanwhile, emigration from the German lands paralleled the Irish experience. Over-populated rural districts sent thousands. Then when the potato blight hit even more joined this human stream, peaking in 1854 when 215,000 Germans crossed the Atlantic to U.S. shores.

Foreign-Born by State 1850

Number in thousands

600
500
400
300
200
100
50
10

Three largest sources in each top ten U.S. state by number of foreign-born

- Ireland
- Great Britain
- Germany
- Canada
- Other

Oregon Territory

Minnesota Territory

Utah Territory

Unorganized

New Mexico Territory

California

Wisconsin

Michigan

Iowa

Illinois

Indiana

Ohio

Missouri

Kentucky

Virginia

Arkansas

Tennessee

North Carolina

South Carolina

Mississippi

Alabama

Georgia

Texas

Louisiana

Florida

New York

Pa.

Maine

Vt.

N.H.

Mass.

R.I.

Conn.

New Jersey

Md.

Delaware

D.C.

N

0   400 km

0   400 miles

The Strikes from 1887 to 1984

Labor-related riots

Strike marked by extreme violence

1934 A bold date indicates a general strike

Industry or service disrupted by strike:

Steel

Textile

Mining

Electrical

Automobile

Trolly or subway

Trucking

Railroad or Pullman car

Shoes

Sanitation workers

Police

Farm workers

Construction workers

Sailors, Dock workers

Rubber workers

Maine

Vt.

N.H.

New York

Massachusetts

Conn.

R.I.

New Jersey

Delaware

Md.

D.C.

Michigan

Wisconsin

Minnesota

Iowa

Illinois

Indiana

Ohio

West Virginia

Virginia

Kentucky

Tennessee

North Carolina

South Carolina

Missouri

Arkansas

Mississippi

Alabama

Georgia

Louisiana

Florida

Pennsylvania

1934 Minneapolis

Flint 1936–37

Detroit 1941, 1945

Chicago: 1886 (at Pullman and nationwide) 1894 1919 1937 1972

Gary 1919

Des Moines 1934

Virden 1898

Pana 1898

Williamson County 1922

Cleveland 1937

Akron 1936

Toledo 1934

Massillon 1937

St.Clairsville 1931

Louisville 1984

Kanawha Valley 1931

Statewide 1921

Marlan County 1931–32

Pineville 1932

Lynch 1932

Elizabethtown 1929

Marion 1929

Gastonia 1929

Memphis 1968

Elaine 1984

Georgetown 1971

New York City: 1803, 1954 1919, 1973

1972

1926, 1966, 1980

Lawrence 1912

Lynn 1860

Boston 1919

Boston 1984

New Bedford 1934

Pawtucket 1824

Brooklyn 1895

Edison 1972

Paterson 1912–13

Paterson 1934

Passaic 1925–26

Wilmington 1984

1902

PA. 1865–75

Lattimer Mines 1897

Hazleton 1897

Homestead 1892

Allentown 1931

1902

1972

Pittsburgh: 1919 1877

1931 Washington County

Martinsburg 1887

Chesapeake & Ohio Canal 1834

Baltimore 1877

1972

1974

1984

N

0   200 km

0   200 miles

Washington

Oregon

Montana

North Dakota

South Dakota

Idaho

Nevada

Utah

Colorado

Nebraska

Kansas

California

Arizona

New Mexico

Texas

Oklahoma

Everett 1916

Centralia **1918–20**

Portland 1917

Northern California 1974

San Francisco **1934** 1972

1975

Delano 1965–70

Los Angeles 1910

Long Beach 1983

Lead **1972**

Leadville 1896

Telluride 1901

Lake City 1899

Cripple Creek 1884

Colorado City 1903

El Paso 1983

Tulsa **1984**

Texas & Pacific R.R. 1884–85

189

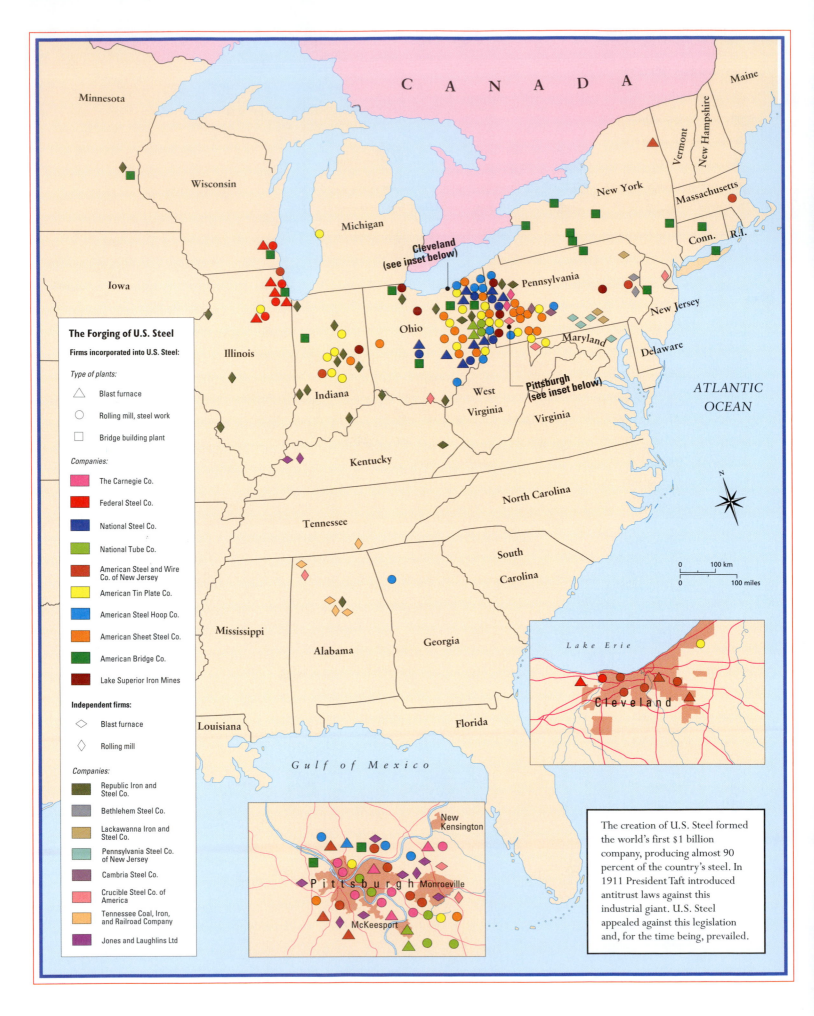

The Forging of U.S. Steel

Firms incorporated into U.S. Steel:

Type of plants:

△ Blast furnace

○ Rolling mill, steel work

□ Bridge building plant

Companies:

The Carnegie Co.

Federal Steel Co.

National Steel Co.

National Tube Co.

American Steel and Wire Co. of New Jersey

American Tin Plate Co.

American Steel Hoop Co.

American Sheet Steel Co.

American Bridge Co.

Lake Superior Iron Mines

Independent firms:

◇ Blast furnace

◇ Rolling mill

Companies:

Republic Iron and Steel Co.

Bethlehem Steel Co.

Lackawanna Iron and Steel Co.

Pennsylvania Steel Co. of New Jersey

Cambria Steel Co.

Crucible Steel Co. of America

Tennessee Coal, Iron, and Railroad Company

Jones and Laughlins Ltd

The creation of U.S. Steel formed the world's first $1 billion company, producing almost 90 percent of the country's steel. In 1911 President Taft introduced antitrust laws against this industrial giant. U.S. Steel appealed against this legislation and, for the time being, prevailed.

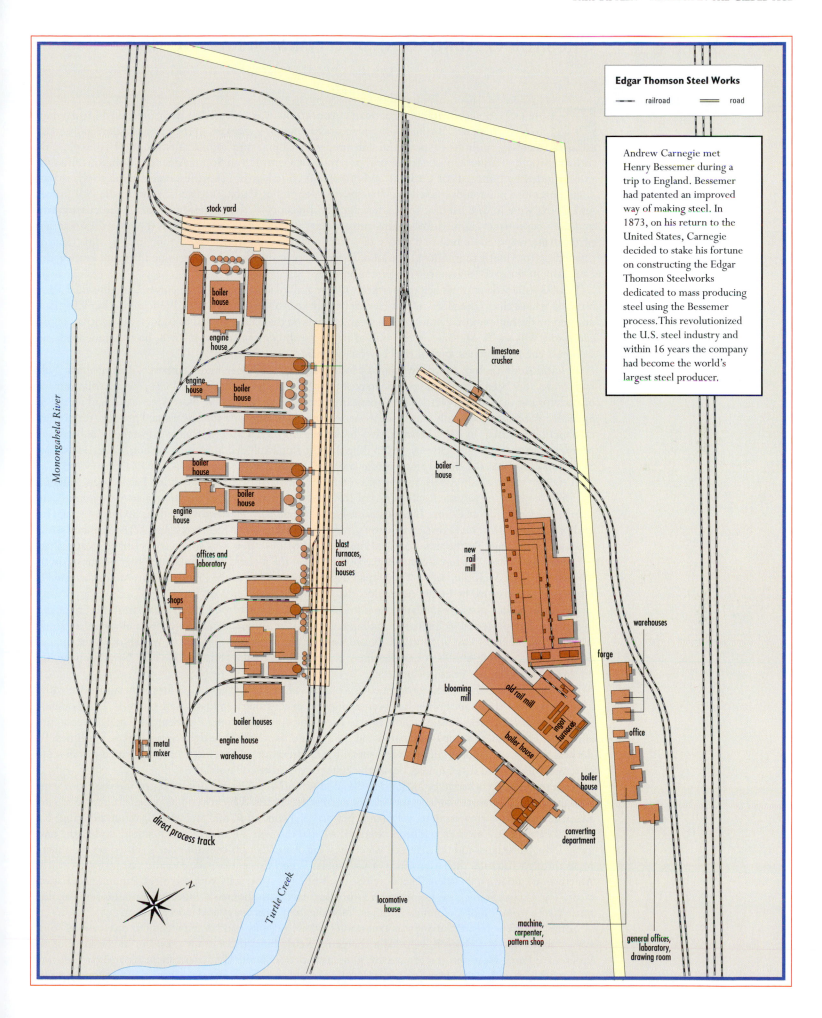

Edgar Thomson Steel Works

railroad   road

Andrew Carnegie met Henry Bessemer during a trip to England. Bessemer had patented an improved way of making steel. In 1873, on his return to the United States, Carnegie decided to stake his fortune on constructing the Edgar Thomson Steelworks dedicated to mass producing steel using the Bessemer process. This revolutionized the U.S. steel industry and within 16 years the company had become the world's largest steel producer.

Monongahela River

stock yard

boiler house

engine house

engine house

boiler house

boiler house

boiler house

engine house

offices and laboratory

shops

boiler houses

engine house

metal mixer

warehouse

direct process track

blast furnaces, cast houses

limestone crusher

boiler house

new rail mill

warehouses

forge

blooming mill

old rail mill

ingot furnaces

office

boiler house

boiler house

converting department

machine, carpenter, pattern shop

general offices, laboratory, drawing room

Turtle Creek

locomotive house

PART SIXTEEN   CRUSADERS ABROAD AND REFORMERS AT HOME

T HE LENTHENING reach of American corporations was reflected in their increased involvement in foreign affairs. Business sought access to emerging markets in the Far East, especially to the teeming millions of potential consumers in China; and industrialists sought to exploit the mostly untapped mineral and agricultural potential of Central and South America. Religious missionaries, funded by hundreds of Catholic and Protestant churches and charities, contributed to the expansionist pressure: the impoverished and "backward" peoples of Cuba, the Pacific islands, the Philippines, and China were in dire need of the knowledge and precepts of the proper faith, or so the missionaries and their supporters claimed. Politicians and scholars warned, furthermore, that the boundless energies of the American people required plenty of space; now that the frontier was gone, new realms must be opened up to American initiative. For all of these reasons, the United States joined Britain, France, and Germany in the race to acquire an overseas empire.

In 1893 American marines helped overthrow Queen Liliuokalana, the ruler of Hawaii, and installed a government whose chief objective was that Hawaii be annexed to the United States. President Grover Cleveland, angered by the highhanded actions of American officials on the scene, refused to endorse annexation, but his successor, William B. McKinley was troubled by few such compunctions. In 1898, he recommended, and Congress endorsed, annexation of the Hawaiian Islands.

In Latin America, too, Americans played a more conspicuous role in internal matters. Insurgents in Cuba had for decades been locked in a struggle to oust their Spanish overlords. By the 1890s, the guerrilla war had heated up, and the Cubans pleaded for American assistance. McKinley, like most Americans, had no use for Spanish colonialism, especially within the western hemisphere, but for a time he resisted pressure for outright intervention in Cuba. In 1898, however, riots broke out in Havana and McKinley dispatched the battleship *Maine* to protect American citizens. On 15 February, the ship exploded in Havana harbor, killing 260 sailors. Several months later, the United States was at war with Spain.

Although the Spanish–American war was ostensibly fought to free Cuba, the first battles were fought in the Philippines, in the western Pacific. In April 1898, shortly after the war declaration, a navy squadron, commanded by Commodore George Dewey, steamed into Manila harbor where it found the Spanish Pacific Fleet anchored in shallow water. Five times Dewey's ships, deployed in single file, took a pass at the Spaniards, each time at closer range. By the time they had finished, the Spanish fleet was smoking wreckage. Not a single American was killed. Because a Spanish garrison still held the fortress at Manila and other positions on the islands, President McKinley sent a 11,000-man expeditionary army to the Philippines. In August, assisted by Filipino nationalists led by Emilio Aquinaldo, the Americans captured Manila.

The fighting in Cuba was similarly one-sided. An American squadron located the Spanish fleet at anchor in Santiago Bay, protected by forts at the harbor entrance. The American navy imposed a blockade and landed a 17,000-man army east of Santiago. By late summer, the army had punched its way through the Spanish defenses along a string of hills at Las Gausimas, Kettle Hill, El Caney, and San Juan Hill. Now Santiago harbor lay within range of American artillery.

The Spanish Fleet, hopelessly outgunned and outclassed, made a valiant dash for the Atlantic. But within four hours, all of the Spanish ships had been sunk or disabled; American losses were minimal. Utterly defeated, Spain eventually relinquished Cuba, Puerto Rico, and the Philippines. President McKinley's decision to annex the Philippines stunned Aquinaldo and the Filipino nationalists, and precipitated new hostilities. For the next three years, Filipino guerrillas and some 70,000 American soldiers fought a full-throated war in scores of remote islands and dense jungles before the Filipino resistance collapsed.

That separate fleets had to be assigned to the Atlantic and to the Pacific demonstrated the need for a canal though Central America to connect the Atlantic and Pacific oceans. A French company had attempted to build a canal across the narrow isthmus at Panama, but malarial conditions and an imposing mountain range had foiled their efforts. American engineers pondered a canal through Nicaragua, which would exploit the navigable Lake Nicaragua and other inland waterways, but American officials ultimately settled on the shorter route through Panama, then a province of Colombia. When Colombia balked at the sale terms offered by American negotiators, President Theodore Roosevelt ordered American troops to assist Panamanian nationalists. The United States then negotiated a favorable treaty with the newly independent nation of Panama, much to the irritation of Colombia. Begun in 1904, the canal was completed a decade later.

Some historians regard the overseas expansion of these years as another expression of a reforming spirit. For example, Teddy Roosevelt, who led a charge up Kettle Hill, also ran for president at the head of the Progressive Party. However, the progressive movement defies simple characterization; its agenda—efficient government, an end to civic corruption by urban bosses and corporations, the weakening of monopoly power, prohibition, direct election of legislators, eugenics, wages and hours laws to protect women and children, woman suffrage—was so broad that some historicans contend that it lacked any coherence whatsoever.

The truth of this assertion is reflected by the maps in this section. The states that, by 1920, had passed laws restricting the daily working hours for women to less than ten hours, were mostly located in the Far West and the Northeast (New York, Massachusetts, Ohio, and Michigan); with the exception of Texas, none of the states in the South had placed such protections for working women. Similarly, the 1919 vote on the woman's suffrage amendment showed that very few members of the House of Representatives from the South supported the measure, with the exception of Arkansas, central Texas, and Florida.

On the other hand, prohibition, a measure to protect women and children from abusive husbands, had been adopted by many counties in the deep South by 1904. A decade later, prohibition spread nearly throughout the South, through much of the Midwest, and to Washington and Oregon. The regional support for prohibition partly reflects opposition to immigrants from Europe, for whom alcoholic consumption was a traditional part of life. The states with the largest immigrant populations—New York, Massachusetts, Pennsylvania, Illinois, and New Jersey—provided the least support for prohibition.

The crusading mindset of the age culminated in the agonizing decision to intervene in the Great War in Europe. President Woodrow Wilson, who campaigned as a type of progressive in 1912, ran for re-election in 1916 as a peace candidate. He won the election, but peace eluded the nation. The German government, desperate to break the British economy, resumed submarine operations against neutral shipping, including that of the United States. In April 1917, after a half dozen ships had been torpedoed, Congress declared war.

Mobilization was slow and disorganized. But in the spring of 1918 American troops began to arrive in France in force. With the arrival of every fresh American regiment, Germany's prospects declined. Germany immediately attacked toward the Somme and the Marne rivers; the Germans broke through the trench defenses, gained considerable territory, and for a time even threatened Paris. But American reinforcements helped firm up the line. In the early Fall, combined French and American forces attacked the weakened German positions north of Verdun. The Meuse–Argonne Offensive threw the Germans back toward the Rhine. The armistice was signed in November.

MAPS

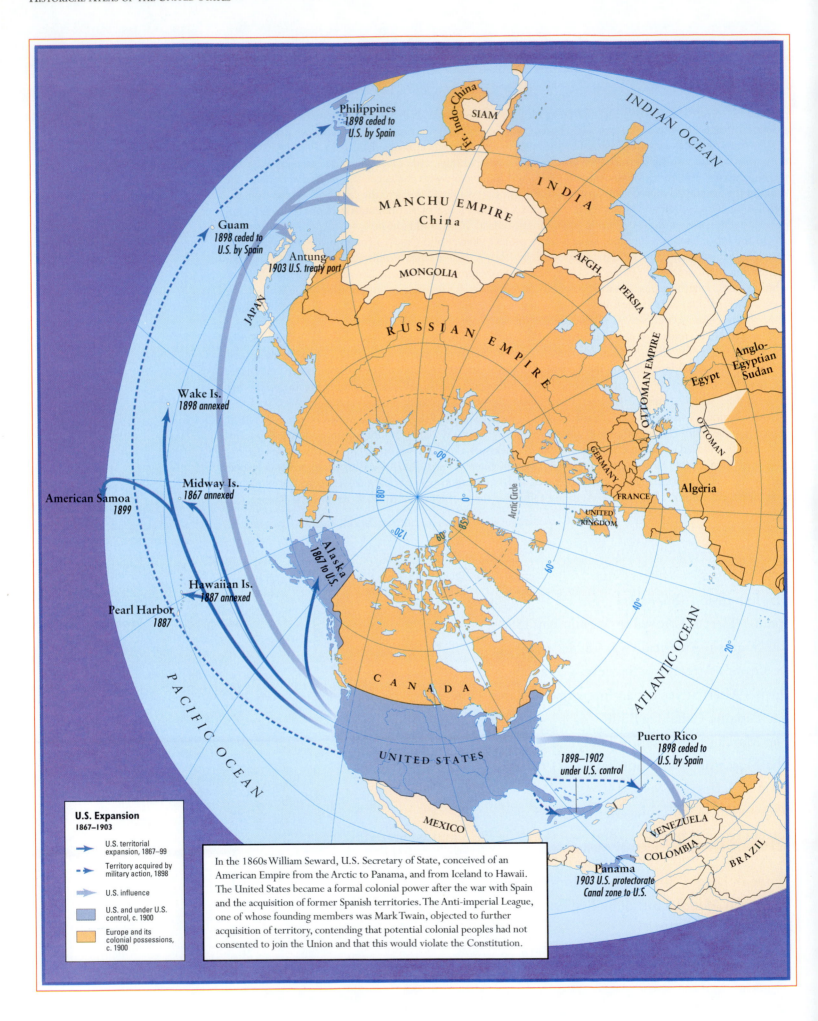

Philippines
*1898 ceded to
U.S. by Spain*

SIAM
Fr. Indo-China

INDIAN OCEAN

INDIA

MANCHU EMPIRE
China

Guam
*1898 ceded to
U.S. by Spain*

Antung
1903 U.S. treaty port

MONGOLIA

AFGH.

PERSIA

JAPAN

RUSSIAN EMPIRE

OTTOMAN EMPIRE

Anglo-
Egyptian
Sudan

Egypt

Wake Is.
1898 annexed

GERMANY

OTTOMAN

Algeria

FRANCE

American Samoa
1899

Midway Is.
1867 annexed

Arctic Circle

UNITED
KINGDOM

Alaska
1867 to U.S.

Hawaiian Is.
1887 annexed

Pearl Harbor
1887

CANADA

ATLANTIC OCEAN

PACIFIC OCEAN

Puerto Rico
*1898 ceded to
U.S. by Spain*

UNITED STATES

*1898–1902
under U.S. control*

MEXICO

VENEZUELA

COLOMBIA

BRAZIL

Panama
*1903 U.S. protectorate
Canal zone to U.S.*

U.S. Expansion
1867–1903

→ U.S. territorial
expansion, 1867–99

⇢ Territory acquired by
military action, 1898

⟶ U.S. influence

▨ U.S. and under U.S.
control, c. 1900

▨ Europe and its
colonial possessions,
c. 1900

In the 1860s William Seward, U.S. Secretary of State, conceived of an
American Empire from the Arctic to Panama, and from Iceland to Hawaii.
The United States became a formal colonial power after the war with Spain
and the acquisition of former Spanish territories. The Anti-imperial League,
one of whose founding members was Mark Twain, objected to further
acquisition of territory, contending that potential colonial peoples had not
consented to join the Union and that this would violate the Constitution.

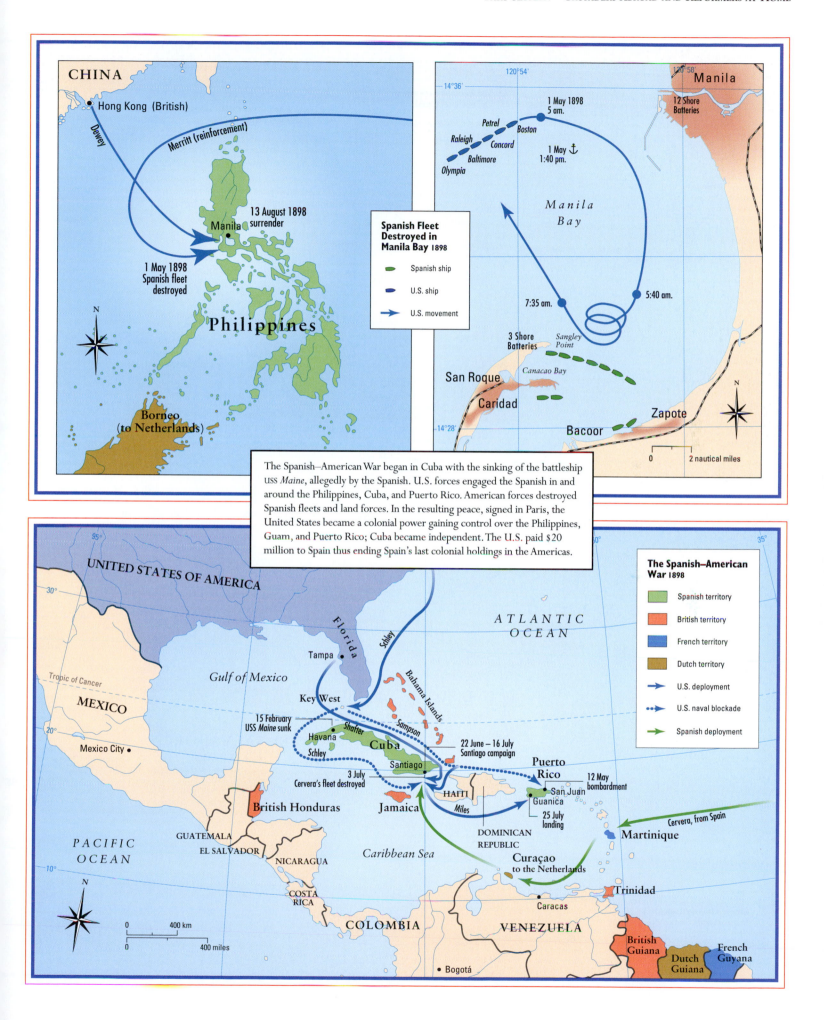

CHINA

Hong Kong (British)

Dewey

Merritt (reinforcement)

Manila

13 August 1898
surrender

1 May 1898
Spanish fleet
destroyed

Philippines

Borneo
(to Netherlands)

N

**Spanish Fleet
Destroyed in
Manila Bay** 1898

- 🟩 Spanish ship
- 🟦 U.S. ship
- → U.S. movement

120°54'   120°58'

14°36'   **Manila**

1 May 1898
5 am.   12 Shore
Batteries

Petrel
Raleigh   Boston
Concord
Baltimore   1 May ⚓
1:40 pm.

Olympia

*Manila
Bay*

7:35 am.   5:40 am.

3 Shore
Batteries   *Sangley
Point*

San Roque   *Canacao Bay*

Caridad   Zapote

Bacoor

14°28'

0   2 nautical miles

N

The Spanish–American War began in Cuba with the sinking of the battleship USS *Maine*, allegedly by the Spanish. U.S. forces engaged the Spanish in and around the Philippines, Cuba, and Puerto Rico. American forces destroyed Spanish fleets and land forces. In the resulting peace, signed in Paris, the United States became a colonial power gaining control over the Philippines, Guam, and Puerto Rico; Cuba became independent. The U.S. paid $20 million to Spain thus ending Spain's last colonial holdings in the Americas.

95°   90°   85°   80°   75°   70°   65°   35°

UNITED STATES OF AMERICA

30°

Tropic of Cancer

MEXICO

Mexico City

20°

Gulf of Mexico

Tampa

Key West

15 February
USS *Maine* sunk

Havana   Shaffer

Schley   **Cuba**

Santiago

3 July
Cervera's fleet destroyed

Schley

Miles

Jamaica

*ATLANTIC
OCEAN*

Bahama Islands

Sampson

22 June – 16 July
Santiago campaign

Florida

Schley

**Puerto
Rico**   12 May
bombardment

San Juan
Guanica

25 July
landing

HAITI

**DOMINICAN
REPUBLIC**

**The Spanish–American
War** 1898

- 🟩 Spanish territory
- 🟧 British territory
- 🟦 French territory
- 🟫 Dutch territory
- → U.S. deployment
- ▪▪▪ U.S. naval blockade
- → Spanish deployment

Cervera, from Spain

Martinique

British Honduras

*PACIFIC
OCEAN*

GUATEMALA
EL SALVADOR

NICARAGUA

COSTA
RICA

N

0   400 km
0   400 miles

Caribbean Sea

Curaçao
to the Netherlands

Trinidad

Caracas

COLOMBIA   **VENEZUELA**

Bogotá

**British
Guiana**
**Dutch
Guiana**   **French
Guiana**

10°

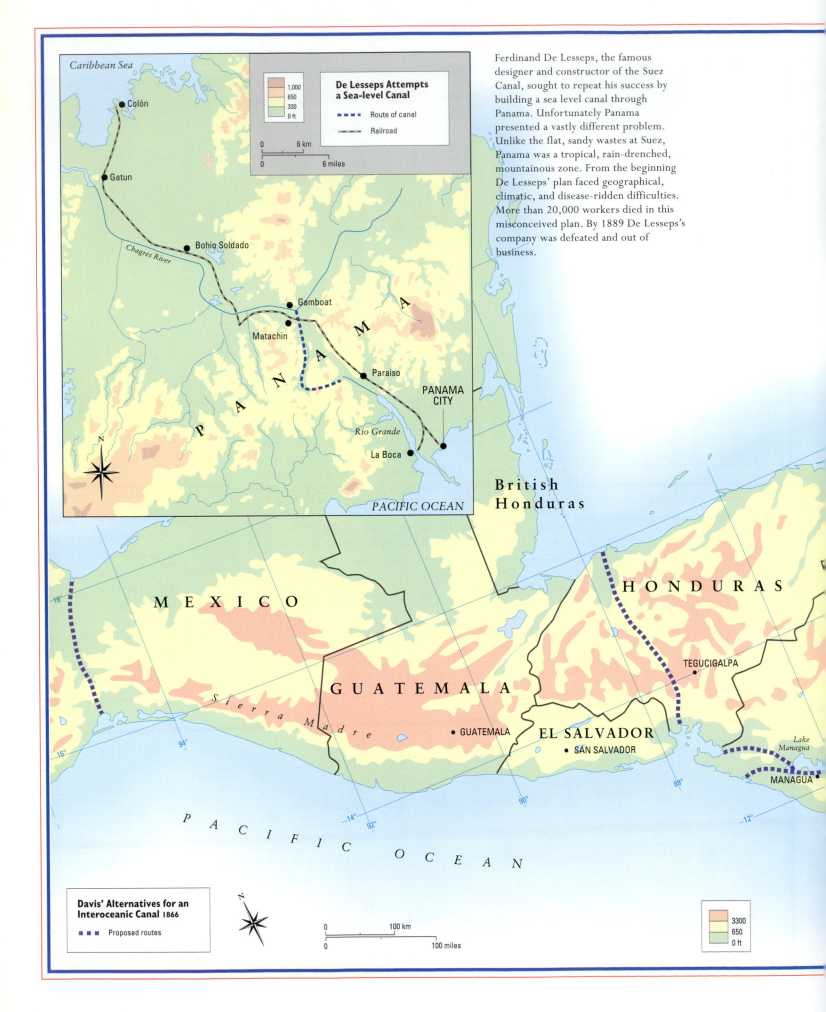

Caribbean Sea

Colón

De Lesseps Attempts a Sea-level Canal

1,000	
650	
330	
0 ft	

- - - Route of canal
Railroad

0   6 km

0   6 miles

Gatun

Chagres River

Bohio Soldado

Gamboat

Matachin

Paraiso

PANAMA

P A N A M A

Rio Grande

La Boca

PANAMA
CITY

PACIFIC OCEAN

Ferdinand De Lesseps, the famous designer and constructor of the Suez Canal, sought to repeat his success by building a sea level canal through Panama. Unfortunately Panama presented a vastly different problem. Unlike the flat, sandy wastes at Suez, Panama was a tropical, rain-drenched, mountainous zone. From the beginning De Lesseps' plan faced geographical, climatic, and disease-ridden difficulties. More than 20,000 workers died in this misconceived plan. By 1889 De Lesseps's company was defeated and out of business.

British
Honduras

HONDURAS

M E X I C O

TEGUCIGALPA

GUATEMALA

Sierra Madre

GUATEMALA

EL SALVADOR

SAN SALVADOR

Lake Managua

MANAGUA

P A C I F I C   O C E A N

Davis' Alternatives for an Interoceanic Canal 1866

- - - Proposed routes

0   100 km

0   100 miles

3300	
650	
0 ft	

In 1898 the United States Navy destroyed Spanish fleets in the Atlantic and the Pacific Oceans. Assistant Secretary of the Navy, Theodore Roosevelt, a proponent of naval power, had seen the need for a U.S. controlled canal. This would immediately double the effective strength of the U.S. Navy. After the assassination of President McKinley in 1901, the new President, Roosevelt, focused his efforts to build a canal under U.S. protection. When the French offered to sell their holdings in Panama at a bargain price of $40 million, President Roosevelt quickly accepted. Construction started in 1904 and was completed ten years later.

Caribbean Sea

• Colón

Gatun
Locks

Gatun

Gatun
Dam

Lake
Gatun

Canal Zone

Madden
Lake

Culebra
Cut

P A N A M A

Pedro Miguel Locks

Miraflores Lake

Miraflores

Miraflores Locks

PANAMA
CITY

Balboa

PACIFIC OCEAN

N

1,000	
650	
330	
0 ft	

U.S Panama Canal, as Built

━━━ Panama zone
┅┅┅ Route of canal

0   8 km
0   8 miles

N I C A R A G U A

Mosquito Coast

Lake de Nicaragua

San Juan River

C a r i b b e a n   S e a

Darien

Colón

PANAMA CITY

C O S T A   R I C A

• SAN JOSÉ

P A N A M A

86°   10°

84°

82°   8°

80°

78°

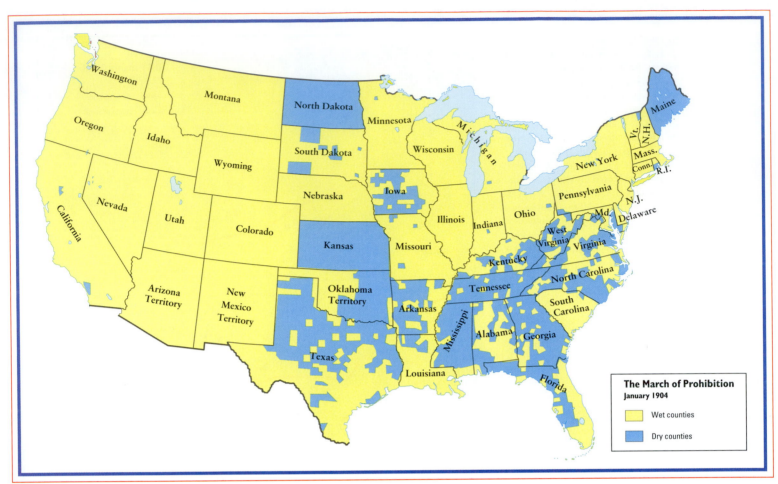

The March of Prohibition
January 1904

Wet counties

Dry counties

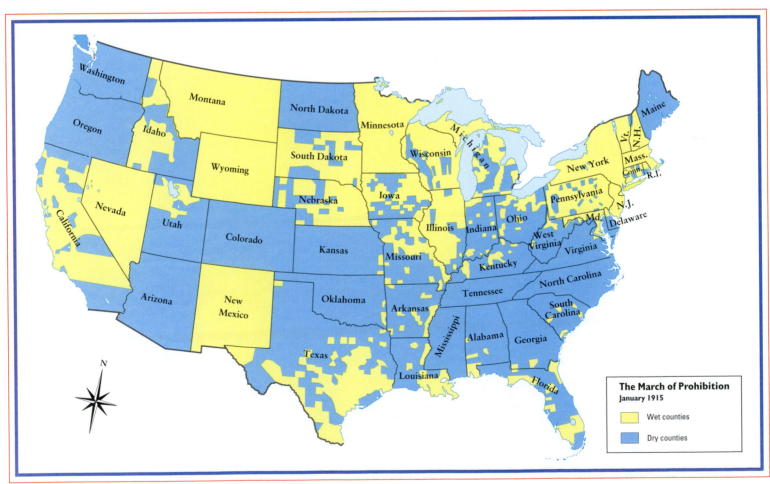

N

The March of Prohibition
January 1915

Wet counties

Dry counties

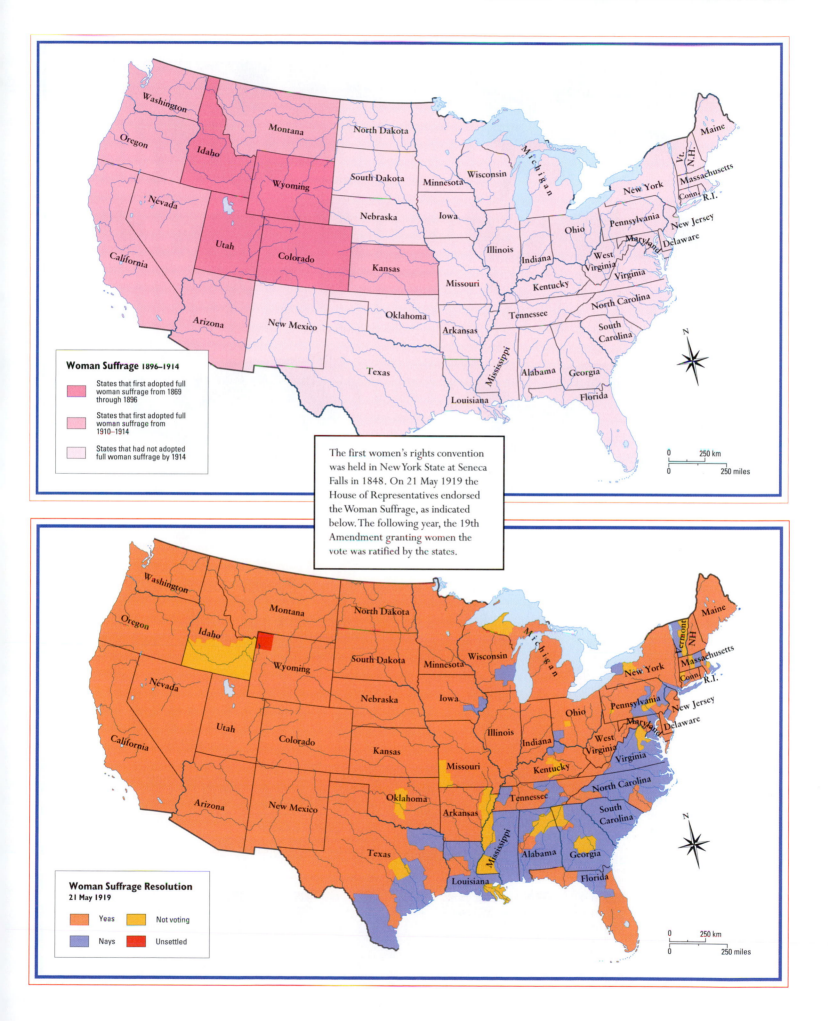

Woman Suffrage 1896–1914

- States that first adopted full woman suffrage from 1869 through 1896
- States that first adopted full woman suffrage from 1910–1914
- States that had not adopted full woman suffrage by 1914

0   250 km
0   250 miles

The first women's rights convention was held in New York State at Seneca Falls in 1848. On 21 May 1919 the House of Representatives endorsed the Woman Suffrage, as indicated below. The following year, the 19th Amendment granting women the vote was ratified by the states.

Woman Suffrage Resolution
21 May 1919

- Yeas
- Nays
- Not voting
- Unsettled

0   250 km
0   250 miles

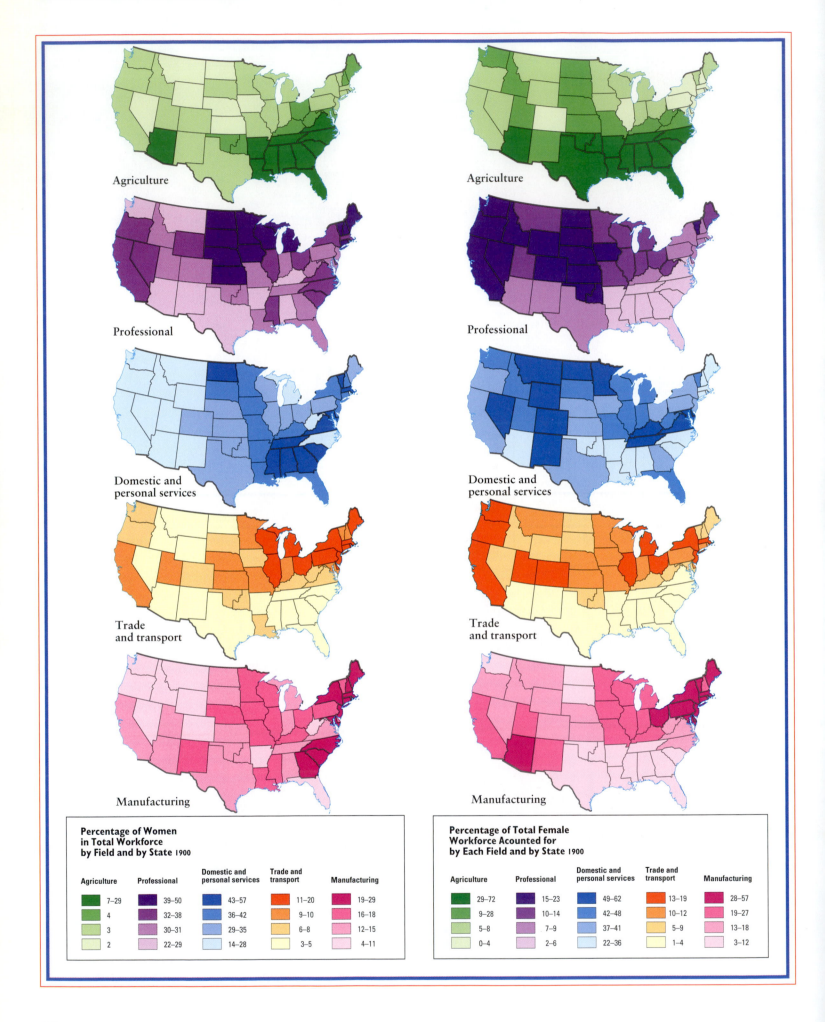

Agriculture

Professional

Domestic and
personal services

Trade
and transport

Manufacturing

Agriculture

Professional

Domestic and
personal services

Trade
and transport

Manufacturing

**Percentage of Women
in Total Workforce
by Field and by State** 1900

Agriculture	Professional	Domestic and personal services	Trade and transport	Manufacturing
7–29	39–50	43–57	11–20	19–29
4	32–38	36–42	9–10	16–18
3	30–31	29–35	6–8	12–15
2	22–29	14–28	3–5	4–11

**Percentage of Total Female
Workforce Acounted for
by Each Field and by State** 1900

Agriculture	Professional	Domestic and personal services	Trade and transport	Manufacturing
29–72	15–23	49–62	13–19	28–57
9–28	10–14	42–48	10–12	19–27
5–8	7–9	37–41	5–9	13–18
0–4	2–6	22–36	1–4	3–12

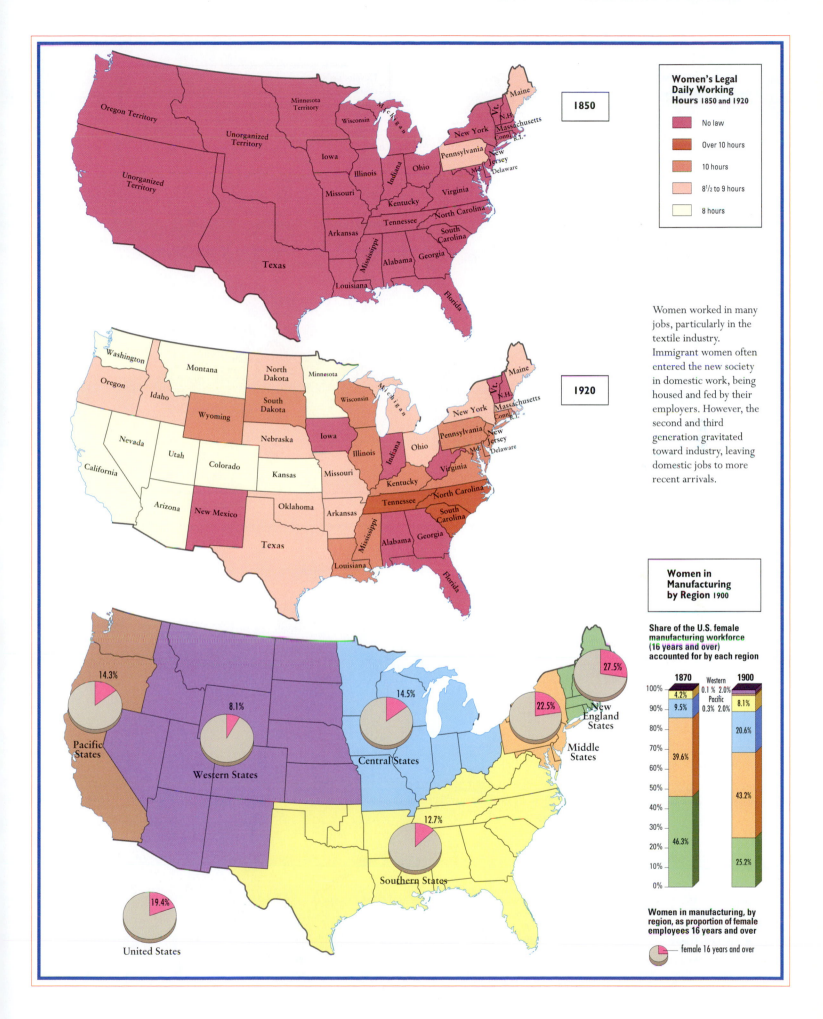

1850

1920

Women's Legal Daily Working Hours 1850 and 1920

- No law
- Over 10 hours
- 10 hours
- 8½ to 9 hours
- 8 hours

Women worked in many jobs, particularly in the textile industry. Immigrant women often entered the new society in domestic work, being housed and fed by their employers. However, the second and third generation gravitated toward industry, leaving domestic jobs to more recent arrivals.

Women in Manufacturing by Region 1900

Share of the U.S. female manufacturing workforce (16 years and over) accounted for by each region

	1870	1900
Western	0.1%	2.0%
Pacific	0.3%	2.0%
	4.2%	8.1%
	9.5%	20.6%
	39.6%	43.2%
	46.3%	25.2%

Pacific States 14.3%

Western States 8.1%

Central States 14.5%

New England States 27.5%

Middle States 22.5%

Southern States 12.7%

United States 19.4%

Women in manufacturing, by region, as proportion of female employees 16 years and over

- female 16 years and over

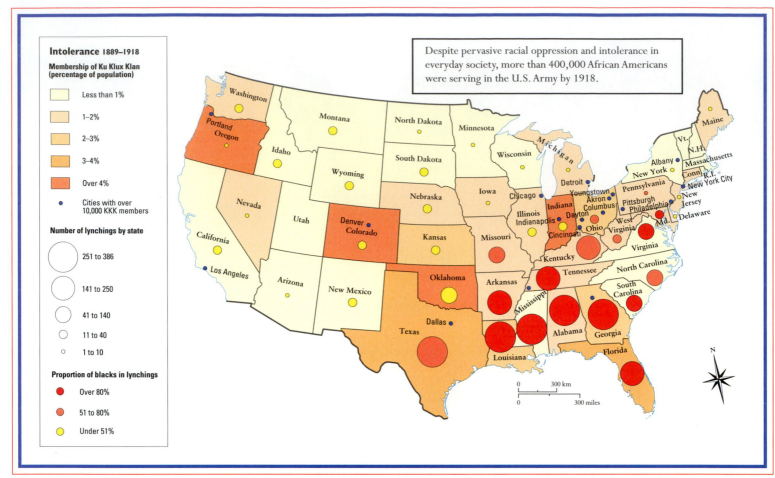

Intolerance 1889–1918

Membership of Ku Klux Klan (percentage of population)

- Less than 1%
- 1–2%
- 2–3%
- 3–4%
- Over 4%

• Cities with over 10,000 KKK members

Number of lynchings by state

- 251 to 386
- 141 to 250
- 41 to 140
- 11 to 40
- 1 to 10

Proportion of blacks in lynchings

- Over 80%
- 51 to 80%
- Under 51%

Despite pervasive racial oppression and intolerance in everyday society, more than 400,000 African Americans were serving in the U.S. Army by 1918.

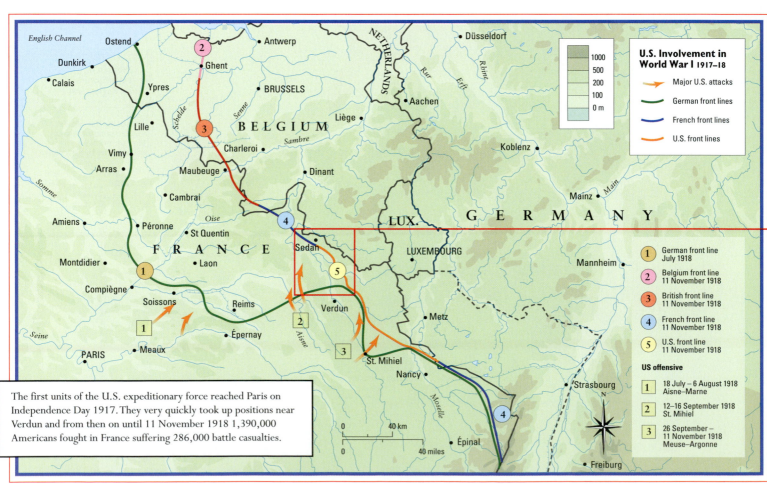

U.S. Involvement in World War I 1917–18

- Major U.S. attacks
- German front lines
- French front lines
- U.S. front lines

1. German front line July 1918
2. Belgium front line 11 November 1918
3. British front line 11 November 1918
4. French front line 11 November 1918
5. U.S. front line 11 November 1918

US offensive

1. 18 July – 6 August 1918 Aisne–Marne
2. 12–16 September 1918 St. Mihiel
3. 26 September – 11 November 1918 Meuse–Argonne

The first units of the U.S. expeditionary force reached Paris on Independence Day 1917. They very quickly took up positions near Verdun and from then on until 11 November 1918 1,390,000 Americans fought in France suffering 286,000 battle casualties.

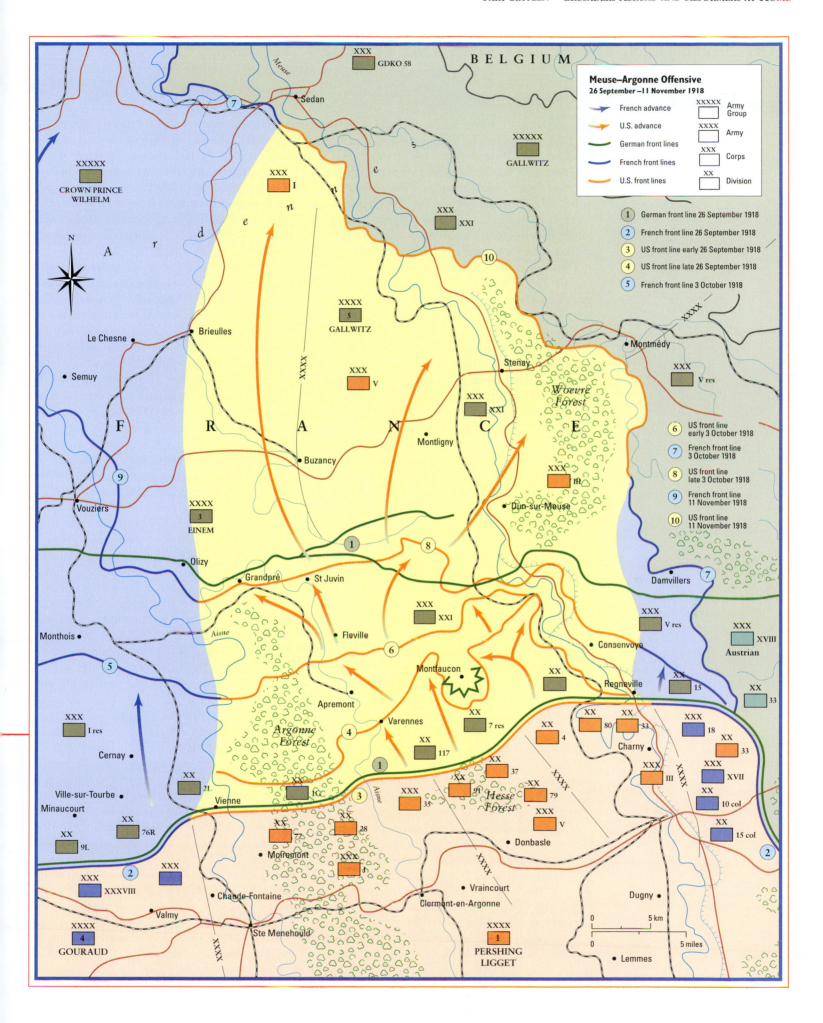

BELGIUM

XXX GDKO 58

Meuse

Sedan

Meuse–Argonne Offensive
26 September –11 November 1918

→ French advance
→ U.S. advance
— German front lines
— French front lines
— U.S. front lines

XXXXX Army Group
XXXX Army
XXX Corps
XX Division

7

XXXXX CROWN PRINCE WILHELM

XXX I

XXXXX GALLWITZ

XXX XXI

A r d e n n e

10

1 German front line 26 September 1918
2 French front line 26 September 1918
3 US front line early 26 September 1918
4 US front line late 26 September 1918
5 French front line 3 October 1918

Le Chesne
Brieulles

XXXX 5 GALLWITZ

Montmédy

Woevre Forest

XXX V res

Semuy

F R A N C E

Stenay

XXX XXI

Montligny

XXX V

Buzancy

6 US front line early 3 October 1918
7 French front line 3 October 1918
8 US front line late 3 October 1918
9 French front line 11 November 1918
10 US front line 11 November 1918

Vouziers

XXXX 3 EINEM

Dun-sur-Meuse

XXX III

9

Olizy

1 8

7

Damvillers

Grandpré St Juvin

XXX XXI

XXX V res

Monthois

Aisne

Fleville

Consenvoye

XXX XVIII Austrian

5

6

Montfaucon

XX

Regneville

XX 15

XX 33

XXX I res

Apremont

Argonne Forest

4

Varennes

XX 7 res

XX

XX 80 XX 33

XXX 18

Charny

Cernay

1

XX 117

XX 4

XXX III

XX 33

XXX XVII

Ville-sur-Tourbe

XX 2L

Vienne

FCC

3

Aisne

XX 37

Hesse Forest

XX 79

XX 10 col

Minaucourt

Aisne

XX 35

XX V

XX 15 col

XX 9L

XX 76R

XX 72

XX 28

Moiremont

XX 6

Donbasle

2

XXX XXXVIII

XXX

Chaude-Fontaine

Vraincourt

Clermont-en-Argonne

Dugny

Valmy

Ste Menehould

XXXX 4 GOURAUD

XXXX 1 PERSHING LIGGET

Lemmes

0   5 km
0   5 miles

PART SEVENTEEN   THE TWENTIES AND THIRTIES

ALTHOUGH THE fighting ceased on 11 November 1918, the negotiations to end the Great War dragged on for months. Britain, France, and Italy looked on the German Empire as so much meat to be divided up, though they disagreed as to who should get the largest share. President Wilson despaired over the short-sighted cupidity of his Allies. Their demands ensured that, at the heart of Europe, German enmity would smolder. Wilson relied on the creation of a League of Nations to promote world order and prevent future wars. The Allies regarded the notion with skepticism, but supported it in return for concessions on territorial matters. When Wilson presented the treaty to the United States Senate for ratification, however, Republicans, led by Henry Cabot Lodge, bitterly opposed the League of Nations as a threat to the nation's sovereignty. In 1919, the Senate voted it down.

Opposition to the League was symptomatic of a wider skepticism toward foreign affairs and domestic reform. People were eager to enjoy themselves. They spent more money on entertainment, especially movies, and on consumer goods, especially automobiles, than ever before. Although the first flickering images were first shown in nickelodeon arcades, by the 1920s full-length movies were distributed by Hollywood syndicates in theaters throughout the nation. Some 10 million people watched movies every day.

The automobile emerged as the most significant consumer good, and the automobile industry became a powerful engine of economic growth. Much as Andrew Carnegie and J.P. Morgan had taken the lead in rationalizing the nation's heavy industries in the late 19th century, Henry Ford devised the methods of mass production that transformed the manufacture of automobiles, and most other durable consumer goods. In 1916, the nation produced over a million automobiles; by 1929, largely in consequence of Ford's assembly line production techniques, some 23 million cars were on the highways. Nearly every family owned a car.

The automobile also generated a host of related changes: the construction of tens of thousands of local roads and, very shortly, of interstate highways. The perfection of gasoline engines accelerated the development of airplanes, and by the late 1920s the aviation industry was superceding railroads as the leading sector for collective transportation.

The net effect of this revolution in transportation was to help shake people loose from their home towns. One of the most consequential shifts was the great northward migration of blacks from the rural South—especially Louisiana, Mississippi, Alabama, Tennessee, and Kentucky. During the decade, nearly 400,000 African Americans moved to New York, Pennsylvania, and Illinois. The black population of New York City more than doubled.

Although sociologists have often contended that blacks from sharecropping southern farmsteads were unprepared for life in the teeming tenements of industrial cities in the North, many African Americans found the new lifestyle exhilarating. Harlem, a 60-block section of northern Manhattan, became the cultural hub for many, a center of the "Harlem Renaissance." Black churches, newspapers, community centers and theaters, and other institutions helped define this new culture. There Marcus Garvey, a black separatist leader, established his Universal Negro Improvement Association to promote black resettlement to Africa.

But the collapse of the stock market in 1929 smothered the exuberant economy. The Great Depression became the dominant fact of the next decade. It harmed people in nearly all parts of the nation, but it did so in different ways. Farmers in the "dust bowl" of the Texas panhandle, western Oklahoma, Kansas, and Nebraska, were driven off farms beset both by drought and low wheat and corn prices. Farmers in West Virginia, the northern plains, and the Southeast were devastated for similar reasons, and miners in Appalachia, especially West Virginia, and in Utah, Colorado and Idaho, suffered when factories closed. More than 15 percent of people in the Deep South received some form of public assistance.

The Great Depression had many consequences. One was political. Where Republican President Herbert Hoover had proposed few federal initiatives to jolt the nation out of the Depression, Democrat President Franklin D. Roosevelt implemented a host of federal work and agricultural relief programs. One of the most successful, in part because it applied advanced principles in engineering and planning, was the Tennessee Valley Authority. Authorized by Congress in 1933, the TVA built dams and power plants and stimulated the economic development of a large section of Tennessee and western North Carolina and northern Alabama.

Roosevelt's handling of the crisis of the Great Depression was vigorous and politically adroit—he won by a landslide in 1932, 1936, and 1940, taking nearly every section of the nation. But the decades of the 1920s and 1930s, inaugurated by one Great War, were followed by another.

MAPS

In Roosevelt's inaugural address, he asked for legislation to create the Tennessee Valley Authority, a government body, but with the flexibility of a private enterprise. The TVA, managed by three directors appointed by the President, enjoyed the right to produce, distribute, sell electric power; build dams, reservoirs, power lines; improve navigation, and control floods. It was also charged with promoting the social and economic welfare of the Tennessee basin, this included parts of Alabama, Georgia, Kentucky, Mississippi, North Carolina, Tennessee, and Virginia. The TVA provided 630 miles of navigable waterways and abundant electrical power which encouraged rapid industrial development in the region. During the next 15 years, per capita income in the TVA area increased by 500 percent.

The Tennessee Valley Authority

- Limit of the TVA
- Dam
- Dam operated by Corps of Engineers
- Dam operated by Aluminium Co. of America
- Steam plant

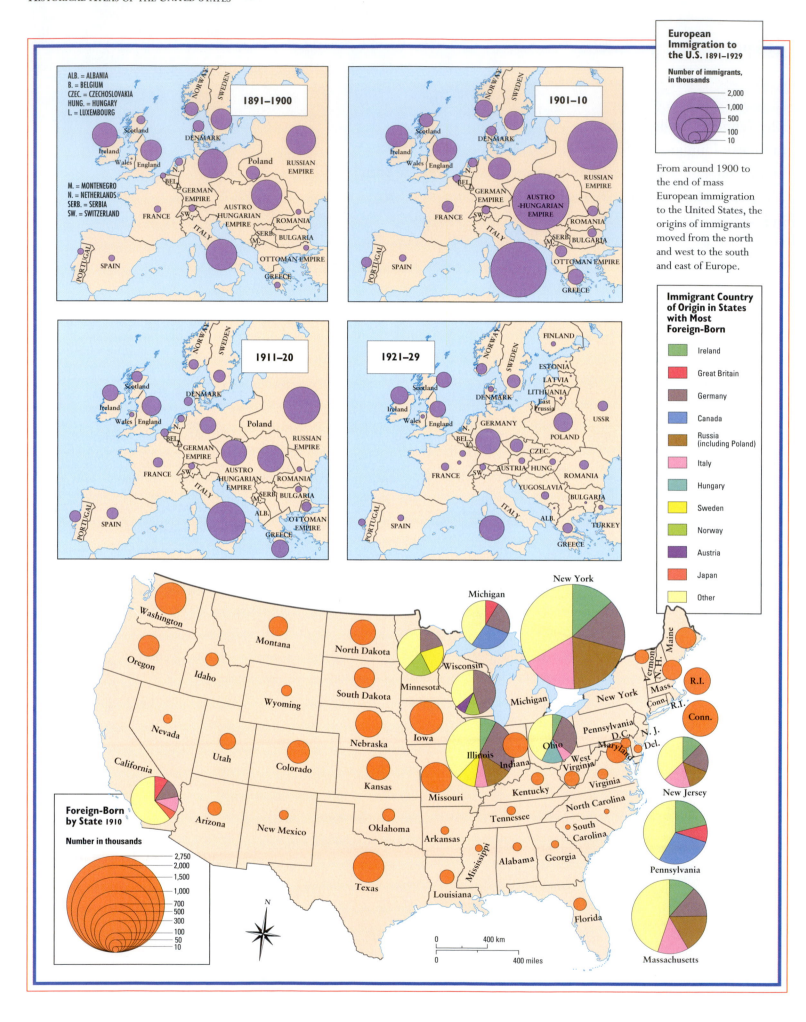

European Immigration to the U.S. 1891–1929

Number of immigrants, in thousands

2,000
1,000
500
100
10

From around 1900 to the end of mass European immigration to the United States, the origins of immigrants moved from the north and west to the south and east of Europe.

Immigrant Country of Origin in States with Most Foreign-Born

- Ireland
- Great Britain
- Germany
- Canada
- Russia (including Poland)
- Italy
- Hungary
- Sweden
- Norway
- Austria
- Japan
- Other

ALB. = ALBANIA
B. = BELGIUM
CZEC. = CZECHOSLOVAKIA
HUNG. = HUNGARY
L. = LUXEMBOURG

M. = MONTENEGRO
N. = NETHERLANDS
SERB. = SERBIA
SW. = SWITZERLAND

1891–1900

1901–10

1911–20

1921–29

Foreign-Born by State 1910

Number in thousands

2,750
2,000
1,500
1,000
700
500
300
100
50
10

Cleveland: Major Ethnic Groups by Ward c. 1930

- Non-immigrant white
- Czechoslovak
- Polish
- Italian
- Hungarian
- Yugoslav
- Russian
- Black
- No clear majority

Lake Erie

Cleveland

0   2 km
0   2 miles

N

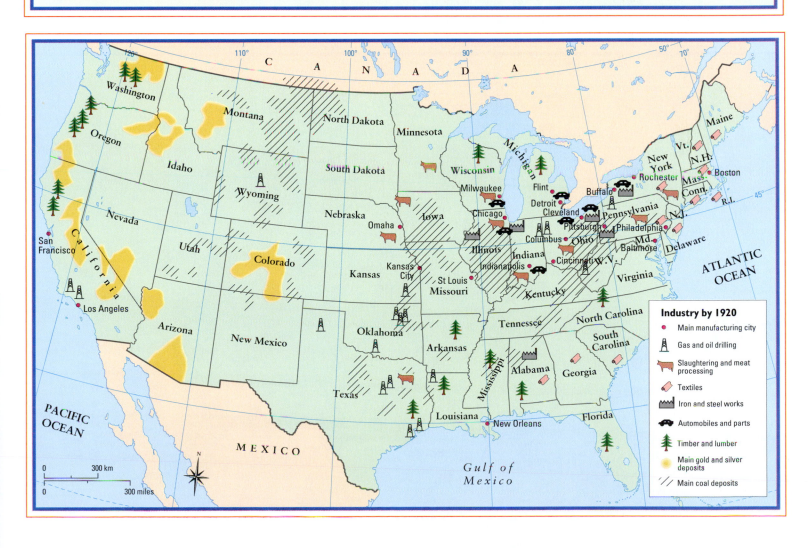

Industry by 1920

- ● Main manufacturing city
- Gas and oil drilling
- Slaughtering and meat processing
- Textiles
- Iron and steel works
- Automobiles and parts
- Timber and lumber
- Main gold and silver deposits
- Main coal deposits

CANADA

Washington
Montana
North Dakota
Minnesota
Oregon
Idaho
South Dakota
Wisconsin
Michigan
Maine
Milwaukee
Flint
Buffalo
Rochester
Vt.
N.H.
Boston
Detroit
New York
Mass.
Conn.
Wyoming
Nebraska
Iowa
Chicago
Cleveland
Pennsylvania
R.I.
N.J.
San Francisco
Nevada
Utah
Omaha
Illinois
Indiana
Columbus
Pittsburgh
Philadelphia
Ohio
Baltimore
Delaware
California
Colorado
Kansas
Kansas City
St Louis
Missouri
Indianapolis
Cincinnati
W.V.
Md.
ATLANTIC OCEAN
Los Angeles
Kentucky
Virginia
Arizona
New Mexico
Oklahoma
Arkansas
Tennessee
North Carolina
South Carolina
Texas
Mississippi
Alabama
Georgia
Louisiana
New Orleans
Florida

PACIFIC OCEAN

MEXICO

Gulf of Mexico

0   300 km
0   300 miles

N

Southern blacks, mired in a cylce of vicious racism and limited economic opportunities, took advantage of a severe labor shortage during World War I to commence a "Great Migration" to Northern and Midwestern cities. Between 1916 and 1920, some 500,000 African Americans left the rural South for the industrial centers of Chicago, New York, Detroit, Cleveland, Philadelphia, St. Louis, and Kansas City. The Great Migration remade the racial landscape of the entire nation.

The Great Migration of African Americans

→ Migration stream

Black population in selected cities, 1920

◯ More than 100,000

○ 50,000 to 100,000

∘ Fewer than 50,000

Changes in black population, in percent of increase, 1910–20

+70
+40
+10
0

Agriculture in 1920

● Main farming cities

🐷 Hog farming

🐂 Cattle ranching and Range

Wheat
Tobacco
Corn
Cotton
Dairy
Fruit and Vegetables

Important crops

🍎 Apples
🍇 Grapes
🍊 Oranges
🌾 Rice
🌱 Sugar beet

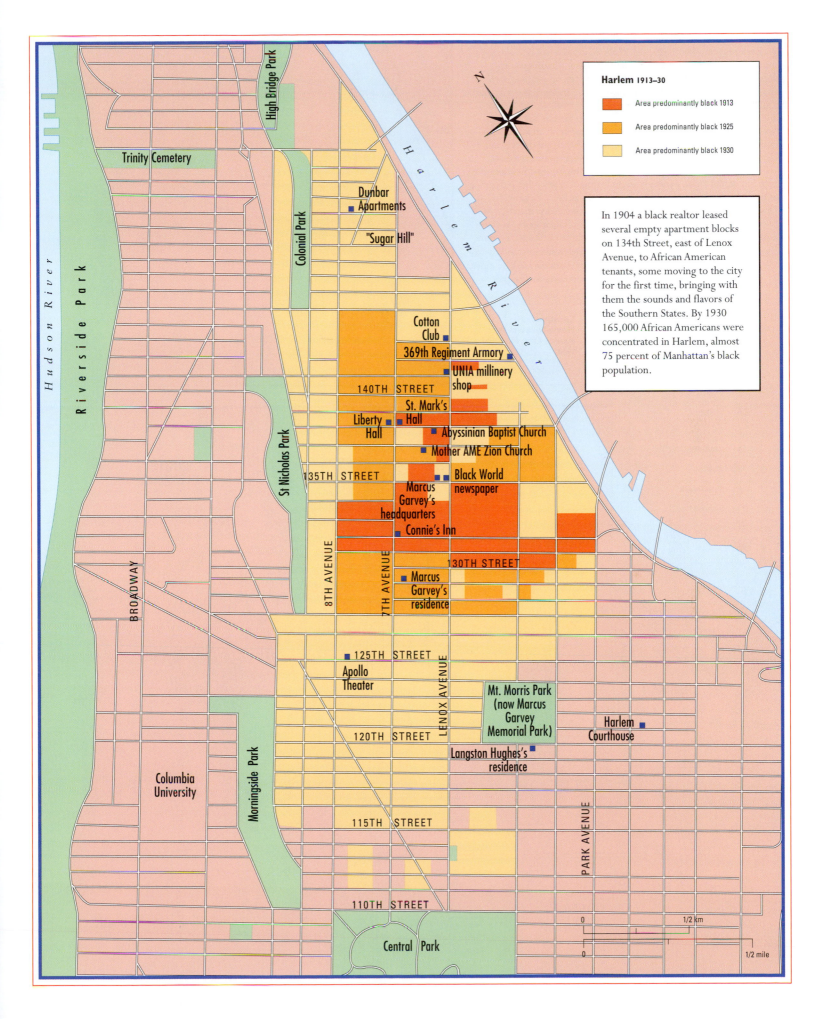

Harlem 1913–30

- Area predominantly black 1913
- Area predominantly black 1925
- Area predominantly black 1930

In 1904 a black realtor leased several empty apartment blocks on 134th Street, east of Lenox Avenue, to African American tenants, some moving to the city for the first time, bringing with them the sounds and flavors of the Southern States. By 1930 165,000 African Americans were concentrated in Harlem, almost 75 percent of Manhattan's black population.

Trinity Cemetery

Hudson River

Riverside Park

High Bridge Park

Colonial Park

Dunbar Apartments

"Sugar Hill"

Harlem River

Cotton Club

369th Regiment Armory

UNIA millinery shop

140TH STREET

St. Mark's Hall

Liberty Hall

Abyssinian Baptist Church

Mother AME Zion Church

135TH STREET

Black World newspaper

Marcus Garvey's headquarters

Connie's Inn

130TH STREET

8TH AVENUE

7TH AVENUE

Marcus Garvey's residence

St Nicholas Park

BROADWAY

125TH STREET

Apollo Theater

LENOX AVENUE

Mt. Morris Park (now Marcus Garvey Memorial Park)

Harlem Courthouse

120TH STREET

Langston Hughes's residence

Columbia University

Morningside Park

115TH STREET

PARK AVENUE

110TH STREET

Central Park

0   1/2 km

0   1/2 mile

The movies had begun as a somewhat disreputable amusement for work-ing-class immigrants but during the 1920s they developed into a major entertainment medium for Americans of all classes. Dazzling movie palaces drew huge audiences, particularly after "talking pictures" were introduced in 1927. By 1930, the average weekly audience hovered near 80 million. To understand the impact at the local level, see the accompa-nying map, which shows that in 1928 even a city such as Kansas City, Missouri, had more than 50 downtown movie theaters. Men held com-manding positions in the film industry as studio heads, producers, and directors, but in the one occupation where physical appearance mat-tered—performing—the top female stars not only equaled men's earning power but outdid them, a pattern not to be found in any other industry at that time. No one would suggest that stars such as Mary Pickford and Gloria Swanson achieved their fame on looks alone. Nevertheless, it is clear that their careers were built at least in part on their looks, as were the careers of many lesser female performers who embellished the come-dies, romances, and adven-ture stories that held movie audiences spellbound.

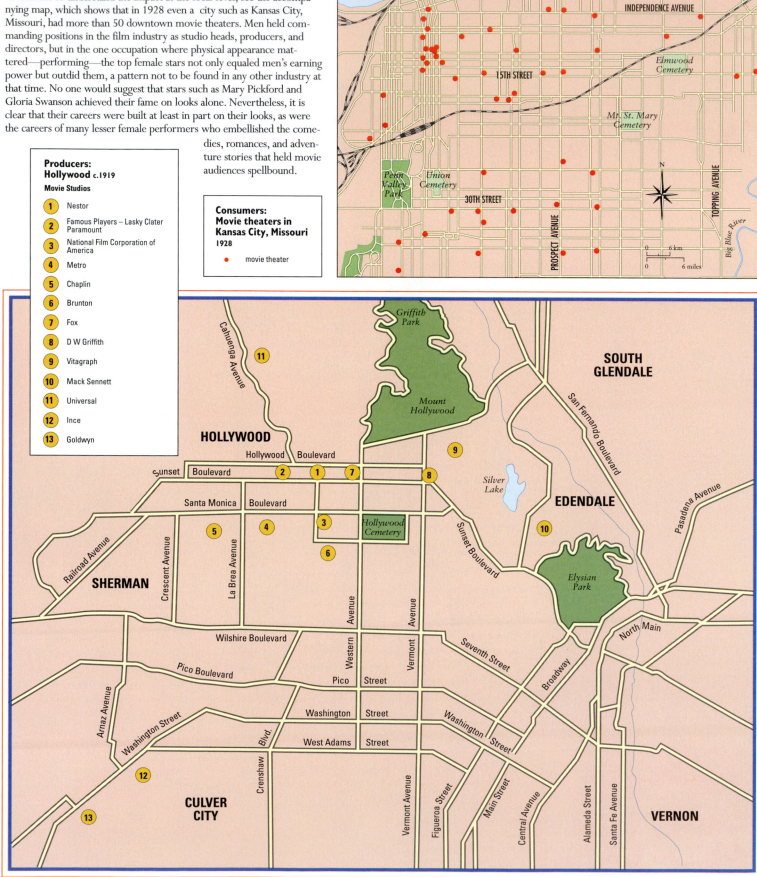

Producers:
Hollywood c.1919

Movie Studios

1. Nestor
2. Famous Players – Lasky Clater Paramount
3. National Film Corporation of America
4. Metro
5. Chaplin
6. Brunton
7. Fox
8. D W Griffith
9. Vitagraph
10. Mack Sennett
11. Universal
12. Ince
13. Goldwyn

Consumers:
Movie theaters in Kansas City, Missouri 1928

• movie theater

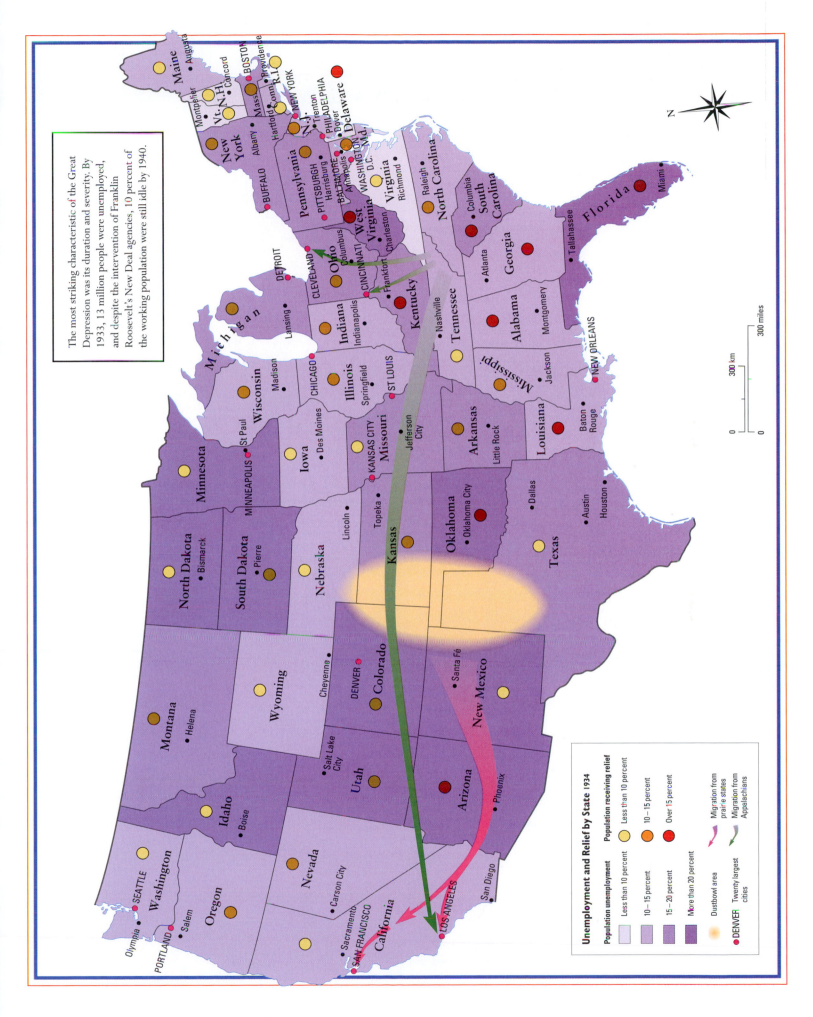

The most striking characteristic of the Great Depression was its duration and severity. By 1933, 13 million people were unemployed, and despite the intervention of Franklin Roosevelt's New Deal agencies, 10 percent of the working population were still idle by 1940.

Maine
Augusta •
Montpelier • Concord • BOSTON
Vt. N.H. Mass. R.I.
Hartford • Conn. Providence •
NEW YORK
Albany •
New York
N. J. Trenton
PHILADELPHIA
Dover
Delaware
Md.
BALTIMORE
Harrisburg • Annapolis •
WASHINGTON D.C.
BUFFALO •
Pennsylvania
PITTSBURGH •
Virginia
Richmond •
Raleigh •
North Carolina
Florida
Miami
Columbia •
South Carolina
West Virginia
Charleston •
Frankfort •
Georgia
Tallahassee •
CLEVELAND
Ohio
Columbus •
CINCINNATI
Kentucky
Atlanta •
DETROIT
Nashville •
Tennessee
Alabama
Montgomery •
Michigan
Lansing •
Indiana
Indianapolis •
Illinois
Springfield •
ST LOUIS
Madison •
Wisconsin
CHICAGO
Mississippi
Jackson •
NEW ORLEANS
St Paul •
Jefferson City •
Arkansas
Little Rock •
Louisiana
Baton Rouge •
Des Moines •
Iowa
MINNEAPOLIS
Minnesota
KANSAS CITY
Missouri
Topeka •
Lincoln •
Kansas
Oklahoma
Oklahoma City •
Dallas •
Austin •
Houston •
Texas
North Dakota
Bismarck •
South Dakota
Pierre •
Nebraska
Cheyenne •
DENVER
Colorado
Santa Fé •
New Mexico
Wyoming
Montana
Helena •
Salt Lake City •
Utah
Arizona
Phoenix •
Idaho
Boise •
Nevada
Carson City •
SEATTLE •
Olympia •
Washington
Oregon
Salem •
PORTLAND
Sacramento •
SAN FRANCISCO
California
LOS ANGELES
San Diego •

300 miles
300 km

Unemployment and Relief by State 1934

Population unemployment · Population receiving relief

Less than 10 percent · ○ Less than 10 percent
10 – 15 percent · ○ 10 – 15 percent
15 – 20 percent · ● Over 15 percent
More than 20 percent

↗ Migration from prairie states
↗ Migration from Appalachians

Dustbowl area

● DENVER Twenty largest cities

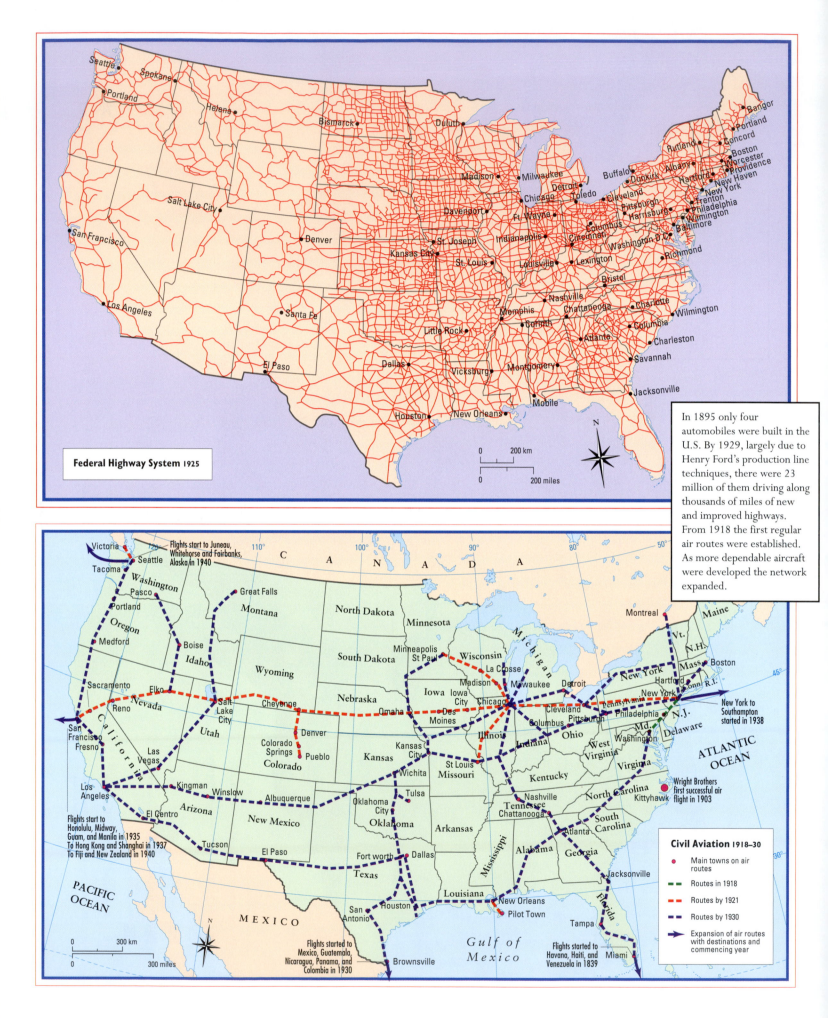

Federal Highway System 1925

In 1895 only four automobiles were built in the U.S. By 1929, largely due to Henry Ford's production line techniques, there were 23 million of them driving along thousands of miles of new and improved highways. From 1918 the first regular air routes were established. As more dependable aircraft were developed the network expanded.

Flights start to Juneau, Whitehorse and Fairbanks, Alaska in 1940

New York to Southampton started in 1938

Wright Brothers first successful air flight in 1903

Flights start to Honolulu, Midway, Guam, and Manila in 1935
To Hong Kong and Shanghai in 1937
To Fiji and New Zealand in 1940

Flights started to Mexico, Guatemala, Nicaragua, Panama, and Colombia in 1930

Flights started to Havana, Haiti, and Venezuela in 1839

Civil Aviation 1918–30
- ● Main towns on air routes
- — — Routes in 1918
- — — Routes by 1921
- — — Routes by 1930
- → Expansion of air routes with destinations and commencing year

Republican to Democrat 1928–36

Vote in 1928

- Hoover (Republican)
- Smith (Democrat)

Vote in 1932

- Roosevelt (Democrat)
- Hoover (Republican)

Vote in 1936

- Roosevelt (Democrat)
- Landon (Republican)

0   500 km

0   500 miles

PART EIGHTEEN   WORLD WAR II

THE GREAT Depression loomed large over Roosevelt's first two terms. He and Congress were preoccupied with ameliorating its effects and stimulating the economy. But the Depression was a worldwide phenomenon, and it further destabilized the fragile postwar European polity. Adolf Hitler, leader of the National Socialist (Nazi) Party, successfully pandered to German voters for revenge against France, Britain, and Jews, among others. His main goal was to remilitarize Germany. Meanwhile, Japan was bent on creating an economic empire under its aegis throughout the Far East. It seized Manchuria and, by the mid-1930s, had begun its conquest of China. By the late 1930s, many statesmen regarded a second world war as inevitable.

President Roosevelt was among those who expected war. While he assumed that the United States would again side with France and Britain against Germany, Congress was more isolationist. In 1938 it nearly passed the Ludlow Amendment, which would have required that any war declaration await a national referendum. As indicated by the vote in the House of Representatives for the Ludlow Amendment, isolationist sentiment was strongest in the South and Far West, and in some large northern cities, like New York, St. Louis, and Chicago, with high concentrations of Italians and Germans.

Less than three years after the defeat of the Ludlow Amendment, however, the United States was at war, and no referendum was necessary to determine national sentiment. Without warning, on 7 December 1941, several hundred bombers from Japanese aircraft carriers attacked the American base at Pearl Harbor, Hawaii. The American Pacific fleet was caught by surprise. In two hours, the Japanese air force sank two battleships and battered six others, most anchored around Ford Island. It also destroyed 174 planes. Over 2,300 American servicemen were killed. The next day, at Roosevelt's request, Congress declared war on Japan. Germany, bound to Japan by treaty, entered the war, too.

Although most Americans sought revenge against Japan, Roosevelt chose to concentrate on weakening Germany, which seemed on the verge of defeating the Soviet Union. Mobilization, however, took considerable time, and the United States could not mount an invasion of Europe for well over a year. In early June 1942, the American Pacific Fleet won a decisive engagement. A Japanese flotilla, supported by a half dozen aircraft carriers, attempted to seize Midway Island, an essential stepping stone for an invasion of Hawaii. But fighter bombers from naval task forces, commanded by admirals Frank Fletcher and Raymond Spruance, and from Midway Island itself, caught the Japanese by surprise. The *Yorktown* was lost to the Americans, but four Japanese carriers—*Kaga, Soryu, Akagi,* and *Hiryu*—were destroyed. Deprived of air cover, the Japanese invasion was called off. Midway was saved.

The Allied attack on western Europe was slow in coming and indirect in manner of approach. In November 1942, British and American troops launched an invasion of North Africa. German armored divisions offered stiff resistance, but by the summer of 1943 the Germans retreated to Italy. In July, Allied forces invaded Sicily then moved up the boot of Italy, taking Rome in June 1944.

That month an enormous Allied invasion force was ferried across the English Channel and struck elaborate German defenses on the beaches of Normandy, in France. The D-Day invasion was initially in doubt; American troops at code-named Omaha Beach were deposited at the wrong place and in water that was too deep. Many became entangled in obstacles and were decimated by German troops hiding in concrete bunkers in the cliffs above. By the end of the first day, 2000 Americans were dead or wounded. But within a week, the beachhead was secure, and Allied troops began to fight their way through northern France. In August, General George S. Patron, a recklessly aggressive tank commander, broke through the German lines and raced toward Paris. The German position in France crumbled. By mid-September, Allied forces approached the German border. Soviet troops, advancing from the east, had crossed the Polish frontier. On 16 December, Hitler ordered a desperate counterattack against the British and American troops in the Ardennes Forest. The Germans initially sliced through Allied lines; American losses were heavy in what became known as the Battle of the Bulge. But the German army exhausted its reserves and now was vulnerable to repeated Allied counterattacks. In March 1945, American troops crossed the Rhine. In May, Germany surrendered.

After Midway, Japan was thrown on the defensive. The American navy and marines conducted amphibious operations in seizing one Japanese-held island after another: the Marshalls, Solomons, Marianas, Philippines, Okinawa. The Japanese resisted heroically, and military planners estimated huge losses in any invasion of Japan itself.

But there was no invasion. Since 1942, American and some British scientists had been working on the secret Manhattan Project to design and build nuclear weapons. The $2 billion project included bomb development laboratories at Los Alamos, and also huge industrial facilities at Oak Ridge, Tennessee, and Hanford, Washington, to create the fissionable nuclear materials. Hundreds of other mining, industrial, and university facilities were involved in the project.

In the summer of 1945, President Truman ordered use of these new weapons against Japan. On 6 August, an atomic bomb was dropped on Hiroshima, killing nearly 80,000 people and wounding many more; two days later a second bomb was dropped on Nagasaki, where the torpedoes used at Pearl Harbor had been manufactured. Ground zero was near the Nagasaki Medical College and Hospital, the Chinzoo High School, and the Yamazato Elementary School. Although the blast was more powerful than that which destroyed Hiroshima, this one was contained by steep hills on both sides of the Urakami River. About 75,000 died. Japan surrendered on 15 August.

MAPS

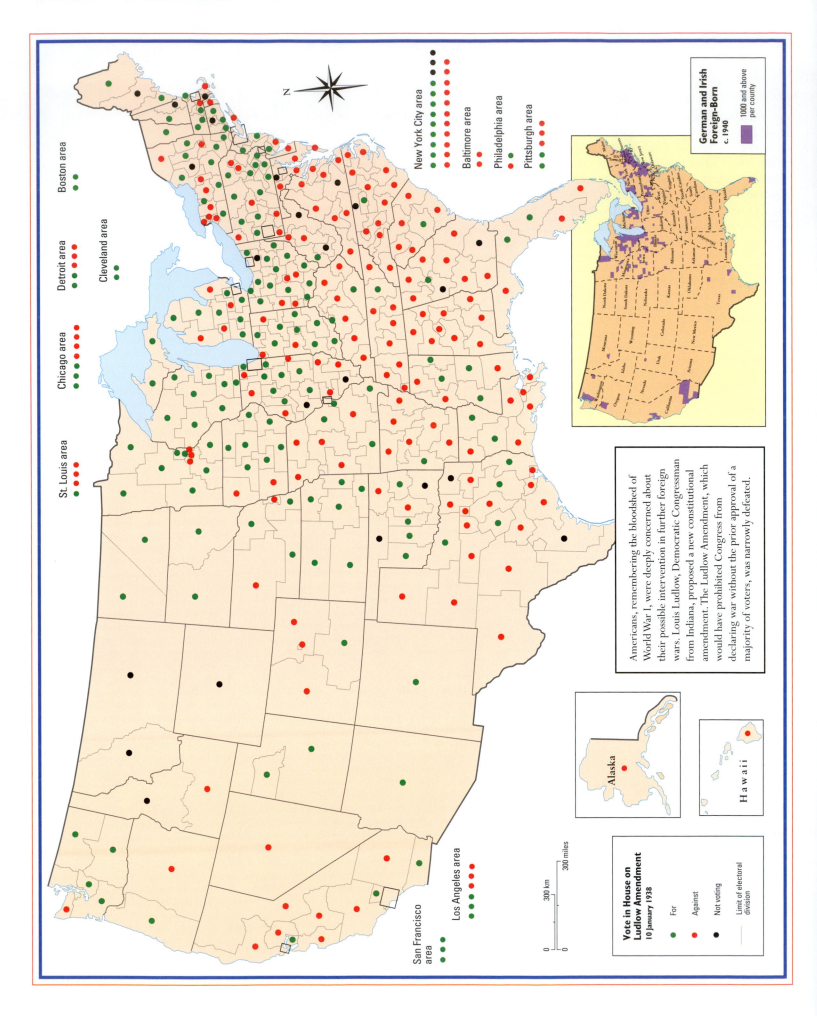

Boston area

Detroit area   Cleveland area

Chicago area

St. Louis area

San Francisco area   Los Angeles area

New York City area   Baltimore area   Philadelphia area   Pittsburgh area

German and Irish Foreign-Born
c. 1940

1000 and above per county

Americans, remembering the bloodshed of World War I, were deeply concerned about their possible intervention in further foreign wars. Louis Ludlow, Democratic Congressman from Indiana, proposed a new constitutional amendment. The Ludlow Amendment, which would have prohibited Congress from declaring war without the prior approval of a majority of voters, was narrowly defeated.

Alaska   Hawaii

Vote in House on Ludlow Amendment
10 January 1938

● For
● Against
● Not voting
— Limit of electoral division

300 km   300 miles

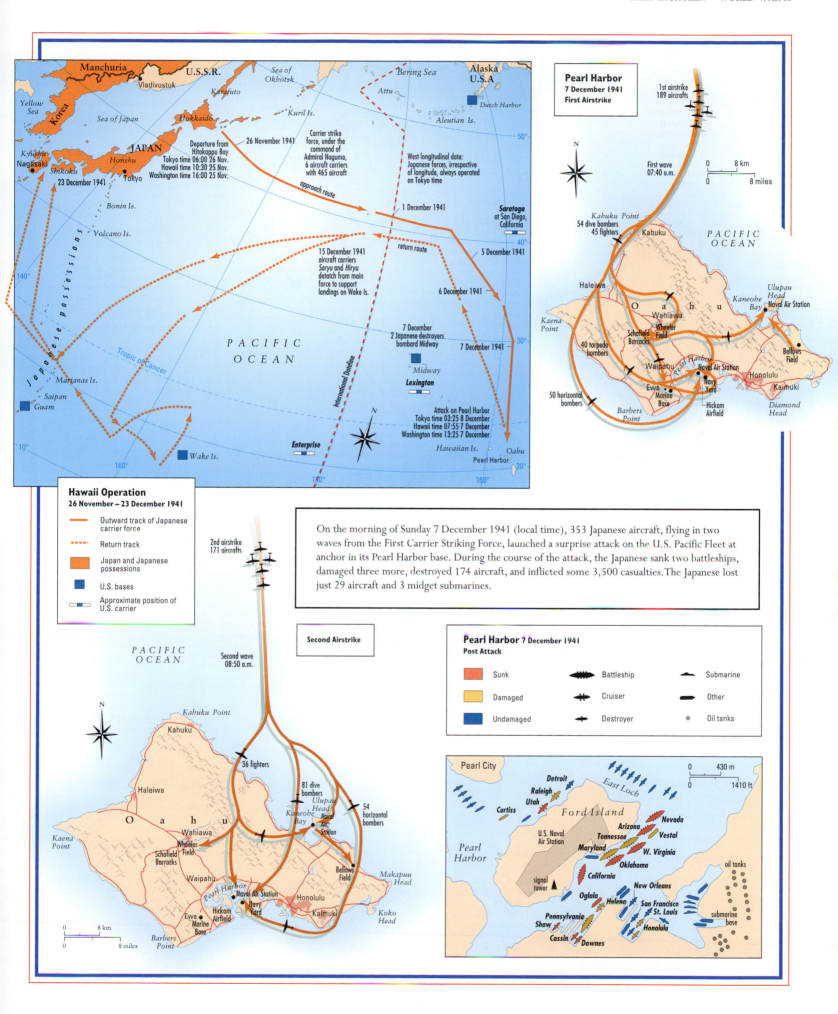

Pearl Harbor
7 December 1941
First Airstrike

1st airstrike
189 aircrafts

First wave
07:40 a.m.

0   8 km
0   8 miles

Manchuria
U.S.S.R.
Vladivostok
Yellow Sea
Korea
Sea of Japan
Karafuto
Sea of Okhotsk
Kuril Is.
Hokkaido
Bering Sea
Attu
Aleutian Is.
Alaska U.S.A
Dutch Harbor

Kyushu
Nagasaki
23 December 1941
JAPAN
Honshu
Tokyo
Shikoku
Bonin Is.

Departure from
Hitokappu Bay
Tokyo time 06:00 26 Nov.
Hawaii time 10:30 25 Nov.
Washington time 16:00 25 Nov.

26 November 1941

Carrier strike
force, under the
command of
Admiral Nagumo,
6 aircraft carriers
with 465 aircraft

approach route

West longitudinal date:
Japanese forces, irrespective
of longitude, always operated
on Tokyo time

1 December 1941

Saratoga
at San Diego,
California

5 December 1941

15 December 1941
aircraft carriers
Soryu and *Hiryu*
detach from main
force to support
landings on Wake Is.

return route

6 December 1941

7 December
2 Japanese destroyers
bombard Midway

7 December 1941

Japanese possessions

Volcano Is.

PACIFIC
OCEAN

Tropic of Cancer

Marianas Is.
Saipan
Guam

Midway

Lexington

Attack on Pearl Harbor
Tokyo time 03:25 8 December
Hawaii time 07:55 7 December
Washington time 13:25 7 December

International Dateline

N

Enterprise

Wake Is.

Hawaiian Is.
Oahu
Pearl Harbor

PACIFIC
OCEAN

Kahuku Point
54 dive bombers
45 fighters
Kahuku

Haleiwa

Kaena
Point

O a h u

Wahiawa
Schofield
Barracks
Wheeler
Field

Waipahu

40 torpedo
bombers

50 horizontal
bombers

Ewa
Marine
Base

Barbers
Point

Pearl Harbor
Naval Air Station
Navy
Yard

Hickam
Airfield

Ulupau
Head
Kaneohe
Bay
Naval Air Station

Bellows
Field

Honolulu
Kaimuki

Diamond
Head

Hawaii Operation
26 November – 23 December 1941

Outward track of Japanese
carrier force

Return track

Japan and Japanese
possessions

U.S. bases

Approximate position of
U.S. carrier

On the morning of Sunday 7 December 1941 (local time), 353 Japanese aircraft, flying in two waves from the First Carrier Striking Force, launched a surprise attack on the U.S. Pacific Fleet at anchor in its Pearl Harbor base. During the course of the attack, the Japanese sank two battleships, damaged three more, destroyed 174 aircraft, and inflicted some 3,500 casualties. The Japanese lost just 29 aircraft and 3 midget submarines.

2nd airstrike
171 aircrafts

Second Airstrike

Second wave
08:50 a.m.

PACIFIC
OCEAN

N

Kahuku Point
Kahuku

Haleiwa

36 fighters

81 dive
bombers

Ulupau
Head
Kaneohe
Bay
Naval
Air
Station

54
horizontal
bombers

O a h u

Wahiawa
Wheeler
Field

Kaena
Point

Schofield
Barracks

Waipahu

Bellows
Field

Makapuu
Head

Pearl Harbor
Naval Air Station
Navy
Yard

Ewa
Marine
Base

Hickam
Airfield

Honolulu
Kaimuki

Koko
Head

Barbers
Point

0   8 km
0   8 miles

Pearl Harbor 7 December 1941
Post Attack

Sunk   Battleship   Submarine
Damaged   Cruiser   Other
Undamaged   Destroyer   Oil tanks

Pearl City

East Loch

Detroit
Raleigh
Utah
Curtiss

Ford Island

U.S. Naval
Air Station

Pearl
Harbor

signal
tower

Arizona   Nevada
Tennessee   Vestal
Maryland   W. Virginia
                 Oklahoma
California   New Orleans

Oglala
Helena   San Francisco
Pennsylvania   St. Louis
Shaw   Honolulu
Cassin Downes

oil tanks

submarine
base

0   430 m
0   1410 ft

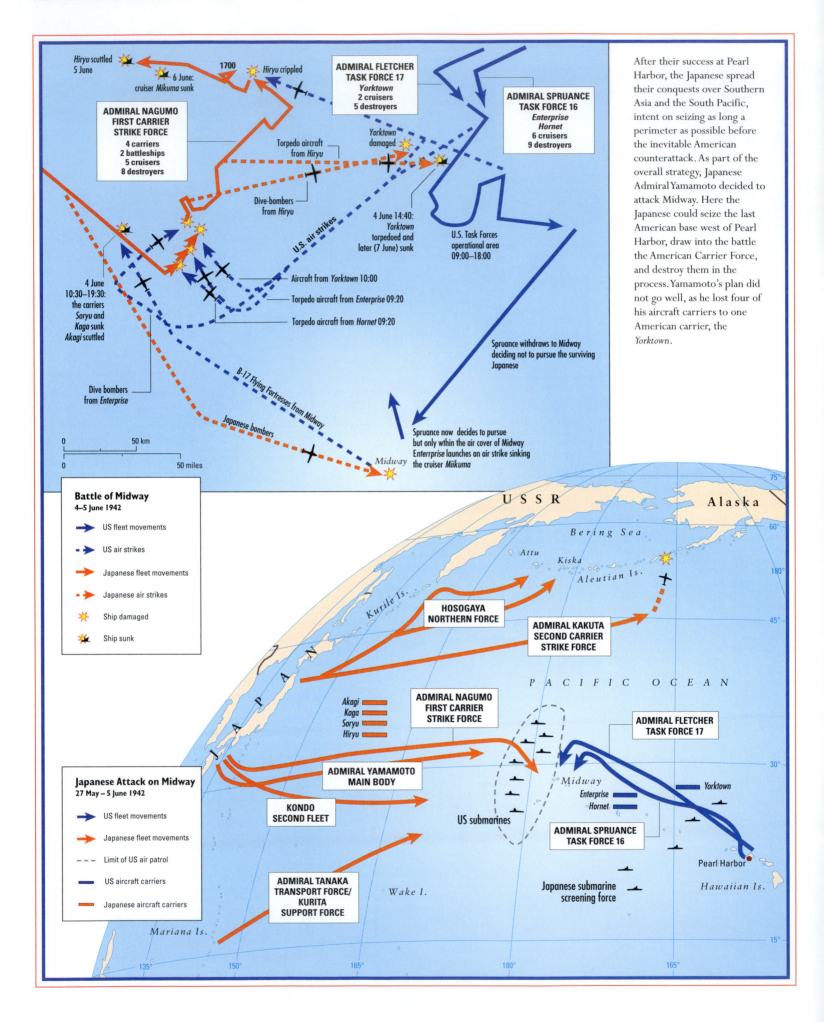

Hiryu scuttled 5 June

6 June: cruiser **Mikuma** sunk

1700   **Hiryu** crippled

ADMIRAL FLETCHER TASK FORCE 17
Yorktown
2 cruisers
5 destroyers

ADMIRAL SPRUANCE TASK FORCE 16
Enterprise
Hornet
6 cruisers
9 destroyers

ADMIRAL NAGUMO FIRST CARRIER STRIKE FORCE
4 carriers
2 battleships
5 cruisers
8 destroyers

Torpedo aircraft from **Hiryu**

Yorktown damaged

Dive-bombers from **Hiryu**

4 June 14:40: **Yorktown** torpedoed and later (7 June) sunk

U.S. air strikes

U.S. Task Forces operational area 09:00–18:00

4 June 10:30–19:30: the carriers **Soryu** and **Kaga** sunk **Akagi** scuttled

Aircraft from **Yorktown** 10:00

Torpedo aircraft from **Enterprise** 09:20

Torpedo aircraft from **Hornet** 09:20

Spruance withdraws to Midway deciding not to pursue the surviving Japanese

Dive bombers from **Enterprise**

B-17 Flying Fortresses from Midway

Japanese bombers

Spruance now decides to pursue but only within the air cover of Midway Enterrprise launches an air strike sinking the cruiser Miikuma

Midway

0   50 km
0   50 miles

Battle of Midway
4–5 June 1942

→ US fleet movements
--→ US air strikes
→ Japanese fleet movements
--→ Japanese air strikes
✦ Ship damaged
✦ Ship sunk

After their success at Pearl Harbor, the Japanese spread their conquests over Southern Asia and the South Pacific, intent on seizing as long a perimeter as possible before the inevitable American counterattack. As part of the overall strategy, Japanese Admiral Yamamoto decided to attack Midway. Here the Japanese could seize the last American base west of Pearl Harbor, draw into the battle the American Carrier Force, and destroy them in the process. Yamamoto's plan did not go well, as he lost four of his aircraft carriers to one American carrier, the **Yorktown**.

U S S R   Alaska

Bering Sea

Attu   Kiska
Aleutian Is.

HOSOGAYA NORTHERN FORCE

ADMIRAL KAKUTA SECOND CARRIER STRIKE FORCE

Kurile Is.

PACIFIC OCEAN

Akagi
Kaga
Soryu
Hiryu

ADMIRAL NAGUMO FIRST CARRIER STRIKE FORCE

ADMIRAL FLETCHER TASK FORCE 17

J A P A N

ADMIRAL YAMAMOTO MAIN BODY

Midway

Japanese Attack on Midway
27 May – 5 June 1942

→ US fleet movements
→ Japanese fleet movements
--- Limit of US air patrol
▬ US aircraft carriers
▬ Japanese aircraft carriers

KONDO SECOND FLEET

Enterprise
Hornet

Yorktown

US submarines

ADMIRAL SPRUANCE TASK FORCE 16

ADMIRAL TANAKA TRANSPORT FORCE/ KURITA SUPPORT FORCE

Wake I.

Japanese submarine screening force

Pearl Harbor

Hawaiian Is.

Mariana Is.

135°   150°   165°   180°   165°

75°
60°
180°
45°
30°
15°

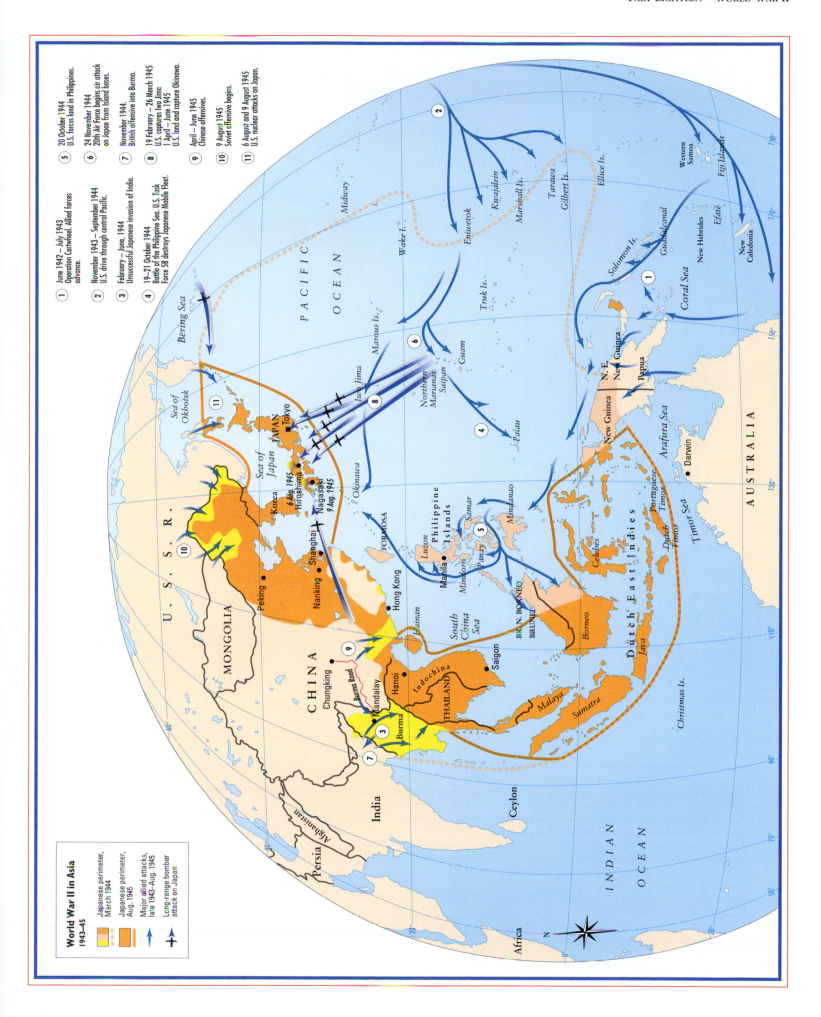

World War II in Asia
1943–45

Japanese perimeter, March 1944

Japanese perimeter, Aug. 1945

Major allied attacks, late 1943–Aug. 1945

Long-range bomber attack on Japan

1. June 1942 – July 1943
Operation Cartwheel. Allied forces advance.

2. November 1943 – September 1944
U.S. drive through central Pacific.

3. February – June, 1944
Unsuccessful Japanese invasion of India.

4. 19–21 October 1944
Battle of the Philippine Sea. U.S. Task Force 58 destroys Japanese Mobile Fleet.

5. 20 October 1944
U.S. forces land in Philippines.

6. 24 November 1944
20th Air Force begins air attack on Japan from island bases.

7. November 1944.
British offensive into Burma.

8. 19 February – 26 March 1945
U.S. captures Iwo Jima.
1 April – June 1945
U.S. land and capture Okinawa.

9. April – June 1945
Chinese offensives.

10. 9 August 1945
Soviet offensive begins.

11. 6 August and 9 August 1945
U.S. nuclear attacks on Japan.

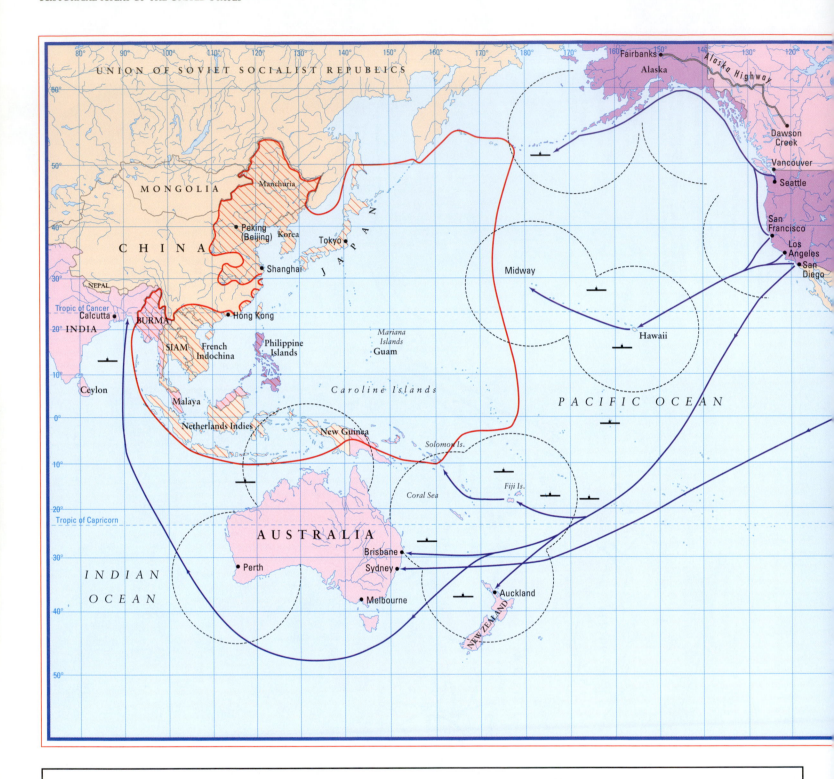

More so than any previous war, the Second World War was a contest between industrial systems. Blitzkrieg—lightning warfare, as the Germans termed it—depended on huge numbers of machines: bombers, artillery, tanks. The task of building these heavy weapons, moving them around the world, and supplying them with millions of tons of ammunition, required enormous industrial capacity as well as a vast transportation system.

Immediately after Pearl Harbor, American industry was confronted not only with the problem of war production but also of shipping war materiel to the Allies. On declaring war on the United States, Germany ordered its U-boat commanders to range throughout the Atlantic Ocean, even to the shores of the United States, and destroy shipping destined for Britain and the Soviet Union. U-boat commanders dubbed these early months the "American Turkey-shoot," as hundreds of American ships went to the bottom of the Atlantic. By June 1942, nearly 5 million tons of Allied shipping had been sunk. The British and Soviet allies, desperate for foodstuffs and war materiel, were in grave danger.

Later that year enough American destroyers became available to shepherd merchant ships across the Atlantic and Pacific, though U-boats still took a fearful toll. But German submarines, which could not long remain underwater, were vulnerable to bombers while cruising on the surface. By late 1942, some sections of the major convoy routes close to allied air bases had been nearly cleared of U-boats. In March 1943, the deployment of scores of B24 Very Long Range Liberator Bombers protected convoys in the mid-Atlantic. During the next four months, not one of the 3,456 U.S. merchant ships that attempted an Atlantic crossing was sunk.

By the end of the war, American factories had built nearly 300,000 airplanes, 700,000 jeeps, 90,000 tanks, and 7,500 ships—a vast arsenal that ensured victory.

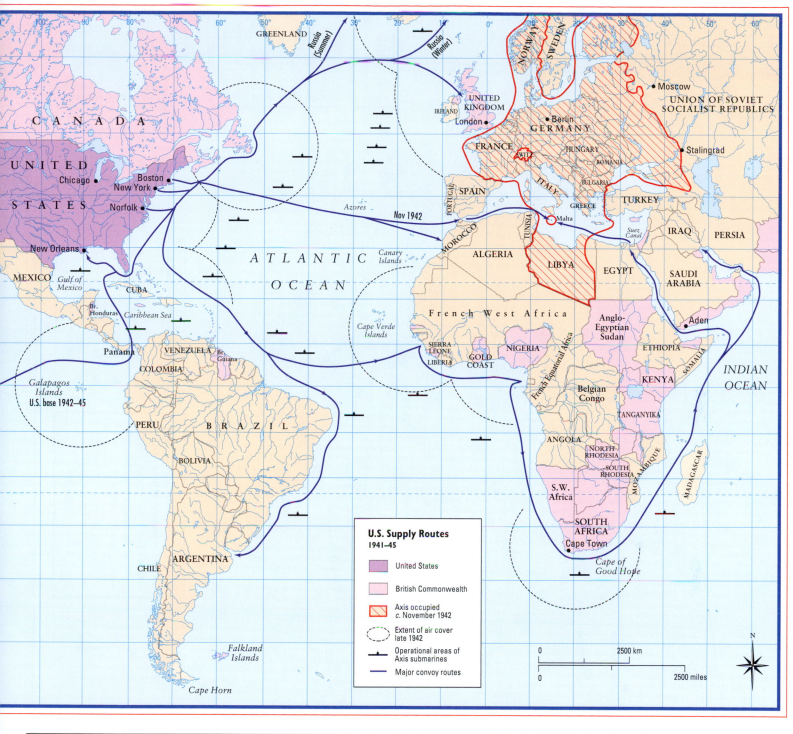

U.S. Supply Routes
1941–45

United States

British Commonwealth

Axis occupied
c. November 1942

Extent of air cover
late 1942

Operational areas of
Axis submarines

Major convoy routes

**Allied and Neutral
Mercantile Losses**
**December 1941–
August 1945**

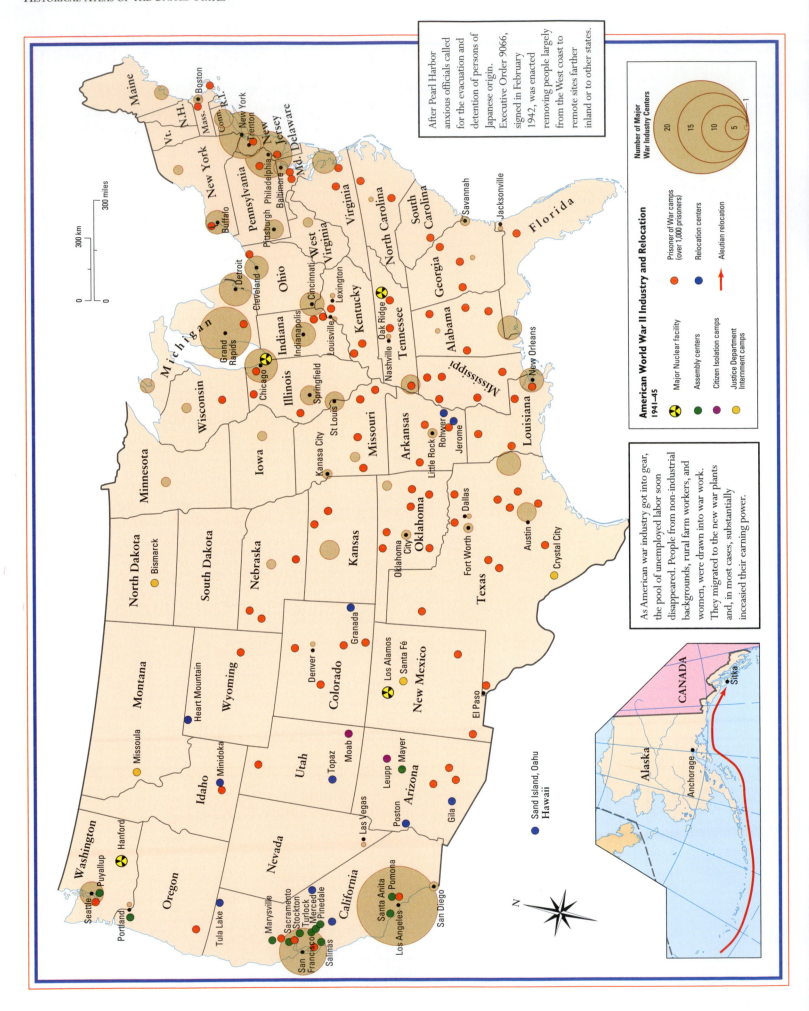

After Pearl Harbor anxious officials called for the evacuation and detention of persons of Japanese origin. Executive Order 9066, signed in February 1942, was enacted removing people largely from the West coast to remote sites farther inland or to other states.

Number of Major War Industry Centers

20
15
10
5

American World War II Industry and Relocation 1941–45

● Prisoner of War camps (over 1,000 prisoners)
● Relocation centers
↑ Aleutian relocation

☢ Major Nuclear facility
● Assembly centers
● Citizen Isolation camps
● Justice Department Internment camps

As American war industry got into gear, the pool of unemployed labor soon disappeared. People from non-industrial backgrounds, rural farm workers, and women, were drawn into war work. They migrated to the new war plants and, in most cases, substantially increased their earning power.

Maine
N.H.
Vt.
Mass.
Conn. R.I.
New York
New Jersey
Delaware
Md.
Pennsylvania
Philadelphia
Baltimore
Trenton
New York
Boston
Buffalo
Pittsburgh
Cincinnati
West Virginia
Virginia
North Carolina
South Carolina
Jacksonville
Florida
Savannah
Georgia
Alabama
New Orleans
Mississippi
Louisiana
Detroit
Cleveland
Ohio
Michigan
Indiana
Indianapolis
Louisville
Kentucky
Lexington
Oak Ridge
Nashville
Tennessee
Grand Rapids
Chicago
Illinois
Springfield
St Louis
Wisconsin
Iowa
Kanasa City
Missouri
Arkansas
Little Rock
Rohwer
Jerome
Minnesota
North Dakota
Bismarck
South Dakota
Nebraska
Kansas
Oklahoma
Oklahoma City
Dallas
Fort Worth
Austin
Crystal City
Texas
El Paso
Montana
Wyoming
Heart Mountain
Denver
Colorado
Granada
Los Alamos
Santa Fé
New Mexico
Missoula
Idaho
Minidoka
Utah
Topaz
Moab
Leupp
Mayer
Arizona
Poston
Gila
Nevada
Las Vegas
Washington
Hanford
Puyallup
Seattle
Portland
Oregon
Tula Lake
Marysville
Sacramento
Stockton
Turlock
Merced
Pinedale
San Francisco
Salinas
California
Santa Anita
Pomona
Los Angeles
San Diego

Sand Island, Oahu
Hawaii

CANADA
Sitka
Alaska
Anchorage

N

300 miles
300 km

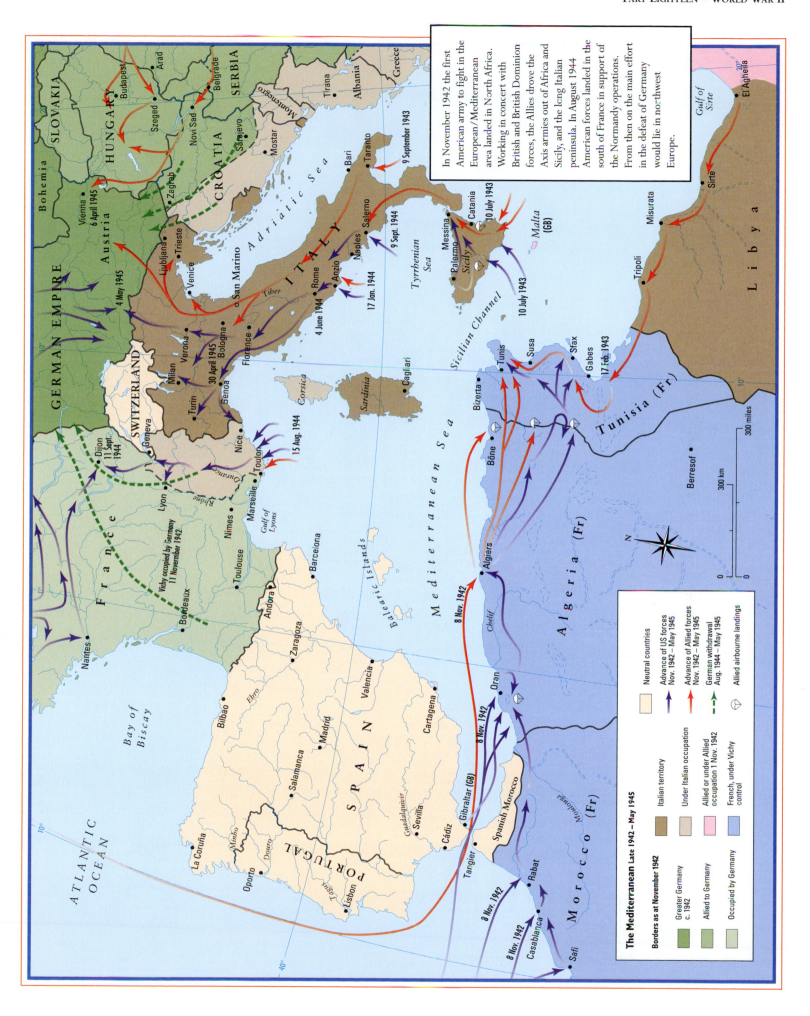

In November 1942 the first American army to fight in the European/Mediterranean area landed in North Africa. Working in concert with British and British Dominion forces, the Allies drove the Axis armies out of Africa and Sicily, and the long Italian peninsula. In August 1944 American forces landed in the south of France in support of the Normandy operations. From then on the main effort in the defeat of Germany would lie in north-west Europe.

The Mediterranean Late 1942 – May 1945

Borders as at November 1942

- Greater Germany c. 1942
- Allied to Germany
- Occupied by Germany

- Italian territory
- Under Italian occupation
- Allied or under Allied occupation 1 Nov. 1942
- French, under Vichy control

- Neutral countries
- Advance of US forces Nov. 1942 – May 1945
- Advance of Allied forces Nov. 1942 – May 1945
- German withdrawal Aug. 1944 – May 1945
- Allied airbourne landings

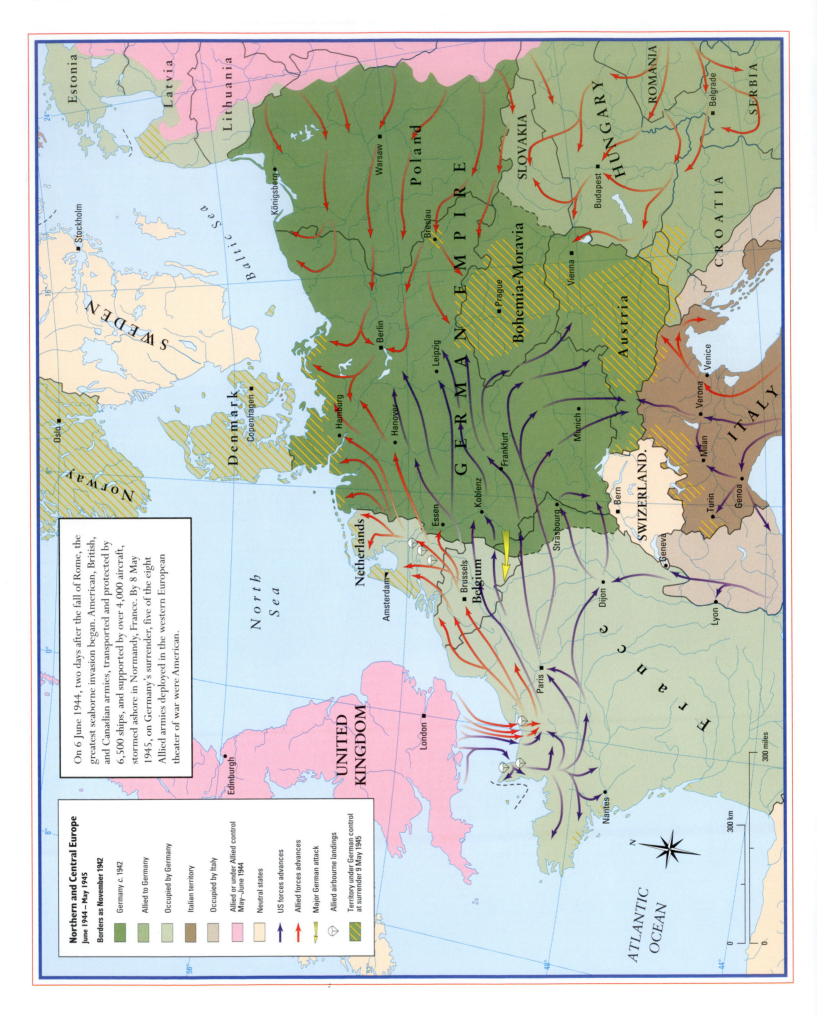

On 6 June 1944, two days after the fall of Rome, the greatest seaborne invasion began. American, British, and Canadian armies, transported and protected by 6,500 ships, and supported by over 4,000 aircraft, stormed ashore in Normandy, France. By 8 May 1945, on Germany's surrender, five of the eight Allied armies deployed in the western European theater of war were American.

Northern and Central Europe
June 1944 – May 1945
Borders as November 1942

Germany c. 1942
Allied to Germany
Occupied by Germany
Italian territory
Occupied by Italy
Allied or under Allied control May–June 1944
Neutral states
US forces advances
Allied forces advances
Major German attack
Allied airbourne landings
Territory under German control at surrender 9 May 1945

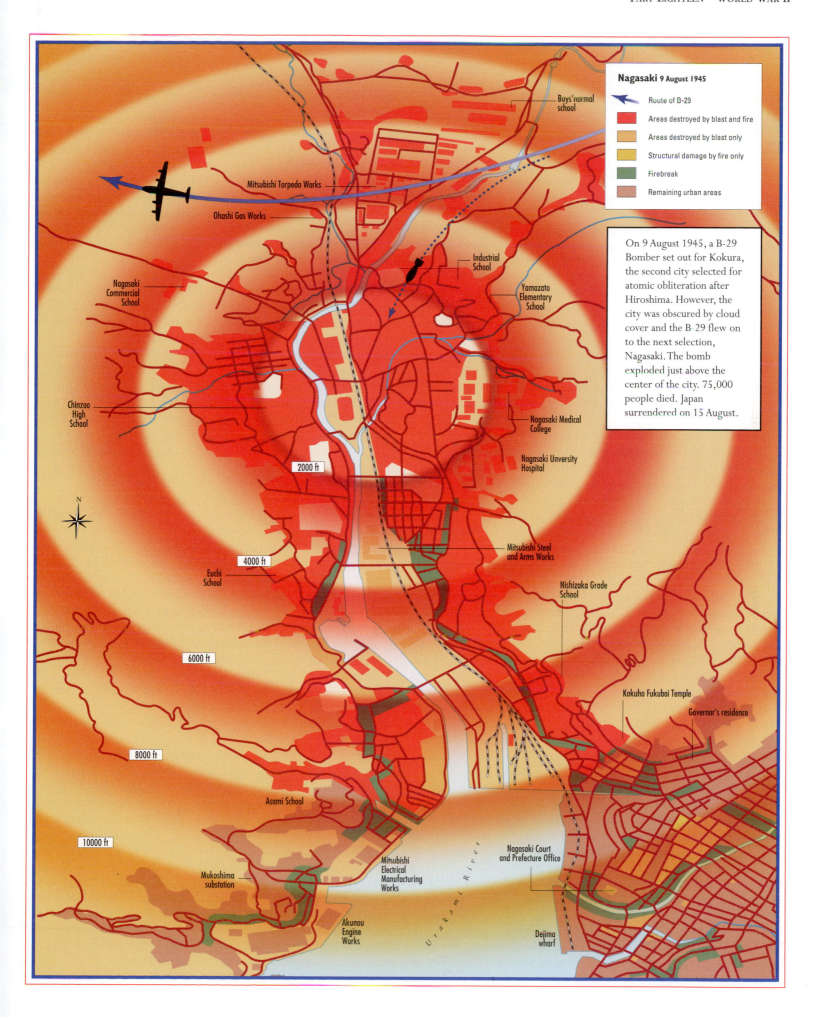

Nagasaki 9 August 1945

Route of B-29

Areas destroyed by blast and fire

Areas destroyed by blast only

Structural damage by fire only

Firebreak

Remaining urban areas

On 9 August 1945, a B-29 Bomber set out for Kokura, the second city selected for atomic obliteration after Hiroshima. However, the city was obscured by cloud cover and the B-29 flew on to the next selection, Nagasaki. The bomb exploded just above the center of the city. 75,000 people died. Japan surrendered on 15 August.

Boys' normal school

Mitsubishi Torpedo Works

Ohashi Gas Works

Nagasaki Commercial School

Industrial School

Yamazato Elementary School

Chinzoo High School

Nagasaki Medical College

Nagasaki Unversity Hospital

2000 ft

4000 ft

Euchi School

Mitsubishi Steel and Arms Works

Nishizaka Grade School

6000 ft

8000 ft

Kokuho Fukubai Temple

Governor's residence

Asami School

10000 ft

Mukoshima substation

Mitsubishi Electrical Manufacturing Works

Nagasaki Court and Prefecture Office

Urakami River

Akunou Engine Works

Dejima wharf

N

PART NINETEEN   THE COLD WAR

IN THE Fall of 1945, the United States was the most powerful nation in the world. It alone possessed nuclear bombs, the most destructive weapon ever devised. Its forces were formidable, and their might was projected throughout the world by a vast network of bases. The American economy, when geared up for war, had proven to be a dynamo. And its enemies had been crushed.

Although Americans exulted over the surrender of Germany and Japan, victory brought with it one intractable problem. After years of sacrifice, Americans wanted to get on with their lives, and no politician could resist the pressure to "bring the boys home." Rapid American demobilization left the Soviet Union as the dominant power in eastern Europe, at least with respect to ground forces. The power of its army allowed the Soviet Union to install Communist client states throughout eastern Europe: Bulgaria, Romania, Poland, Yugoslavia, East Germany, Czechoslovakia, Albania, Hungary. In 1947, after Communists attempted to overthrow the monarchy in Greece, President Harry S. Truman sent military assistance "to support free peoples who are resisting attempted subjugation by armed minorities or by outside pressures." With American help, the Communists in Greece were defeated.

The next year, after the Czechoslovakian government was ousted by Soviet-backed Communists, Truman called for massive economic assistance to prevent the Communist contagion from spreading throughout the weakened postwar economies of Europe. The Marshall Plan, as it came to be known, injected some $13 billion into the region. When the United States proposed the North Atlantic Treaty Organization (NATO), a military alliance, most of the nations of western Europe agreed to join it. The Soviet Union's satellites excepting Yugoslavia, followed suit by joining the Warsaw Treaty Organization, an alliance also known as the Warsaw Pact.

Truman refused to initiate all-out war to crush Soviet Communism and liberate eastern Europe, nor would he allow the Soviets to increase the region under their domination. Truman's policy was known as containment.

The greatest test of the concept came not in Europe, where the United States had strong economic and cultural ties, but in Korea. In June 1950, communist North Korea, backed by the Soviet Union and Communist China, attacked the non-Communist government of South Korea. Seoul, the South Korean capital, fell within days; within weeks the North Koreans had taken all of South Korea except an enclave around Pusan, a port on the southeast tip of the Korean peninsula. Truman dispatched tens of thousands of soldiers to reinforce the line around Pusan. On 15 September, in one of the boldest moves in the history of warfare, General Douglas MacArthur landed an invasion force at low tide along a beach at Inchon, a port deep in South Korean territory held by North Korea. The attackers caught the North Koreans by surprise and raced to Seoul, cutting off the North Koreans fighting at Pusan. The North Korean army was routed.

Virtually unopposed, MacArthur crossed into North Korea and divided his army into two main forces, one proceeding up the west coast and the other landing on the east coast and moving toward the Yalu River (the boundary with communist China). MacArthur predicted that all of North Korea would fall by Christmas. MacArthur's boldness had made possible the spectacular victory at Inchon; it also contributed to the debacle two months later. Unbeknown to MacArthur, some 300,000 Communist Chinese troops had crossed the Yalu River and hidden themselves in mountain fastnesses along the central spine of North Korea. On 26 November, they struck, shattering both of MacArthur's armies. American troops fled southward; within several weeks, Communist Chinese troops had re-entered Seoul. The Americans then rallied, and the front stabilized along the 38th parallel, nearly the original boundary between the Koreas. But by then, the United States had lost tens of thousands of men and had committed much of its enormous military to the Far East. Worldwide containment would prove costly.

President Dwight D. Eisenhower preferred to use the threat of nuclear weapons to prevent communist advances, a strategy that made some sense so long as the Soviets lacked an air force capable of eluding American bomber defenses. But in 1957 the Soviets launched the first man-made satellite, Sputnik; Soviet nuclear weapons would soon be placed on intercontinental missiles. The Cold War had entered a new and unimaginably more dangerous stage.

In October 1962, this became painfully clear to President John F. Kennedy, Eisenhower's successor. American reconnaissance aircraft had determined that the Soviet Union had for some time been sneaking scores of medium-range nuclear missiles into Cuba. These missiles were capable of hitting most American cities. While the American armed forces prepared to bomb the missiles and invade Cuba, Kennedy conducted tense negotiations with Soviet Premier Nikita Khrushchev. Kennedy finally imposed an embargo, threatening to stop and search any Soviet ships bound for Cuba. As the Soviet ships approached the embargo line, tension mounted. Finally, Kennedy and Khrushchev made a deal. In return for a (public) promise not to invade Cuba and a (secret) promise to withdraw American nuclear missiles from Turkey, Khrushchev pulled the missiles out of Cuba.

Kennedy was widely praised for his statesmanship, but the Cuban missile crisis in one way intensified the Cold War. Hardliners in Moscow ousted Khrushchev; his successors resolved never to back down in a nuclear confrontation with the United States. They pursued a crash-program in construction and deployment of nuclear weapons. By 1970, both nations had thousands of nuclear missiles, many of them tipped with unimaginably destructive hydrogen bombs.

The United States fell behind in the arms race because it was preoccupied with a Communist threat in Vietnam. In 1954 Ho Chi Minh, a Vietnamese nationalist and also a Communist, had defeated the French, who had dominated Indochina for nearly a century. He proclaimed Vietnam's independence. Eisenhower, unwilling to allow southeast Asia to slip into the Communist camp, resolved instead to create a democratic non-Communist state called South Vietnam. In 1956 Ngo Dinh Diem, sustained by a massive infusion of American aid, built up the South Vietnamese army. In the early 1960s, Ho's forces in the north, supported by Communist cadres in the South, began a guerrilla war that Diem could not contain. In 1962, Kennedy sent thousands of military advisers to guide Diem's forces. By the summer of 1963, Diem's government was tottering; soon he fell victim to a military coup. The war continued. In November, Kennedy was assassinated.

MAPS

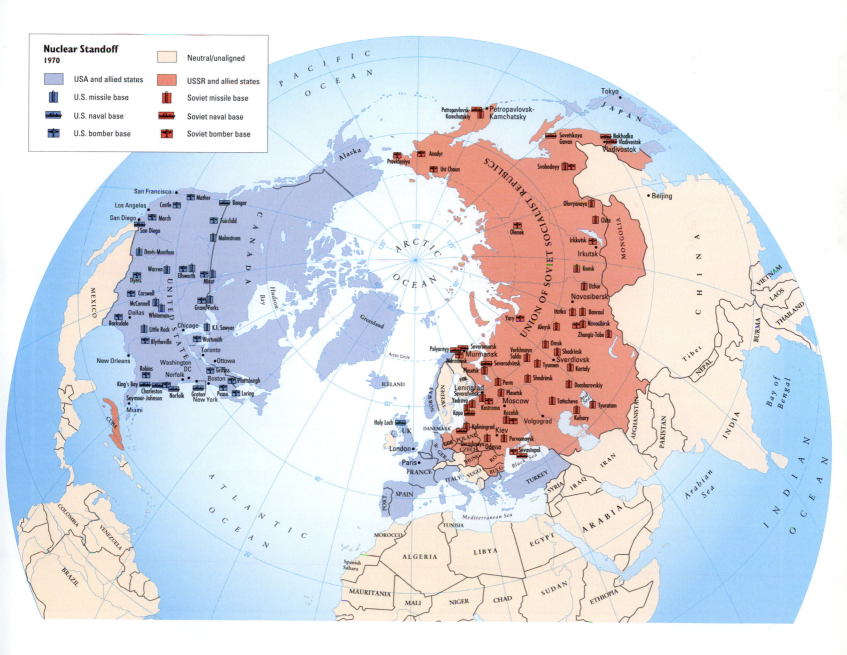

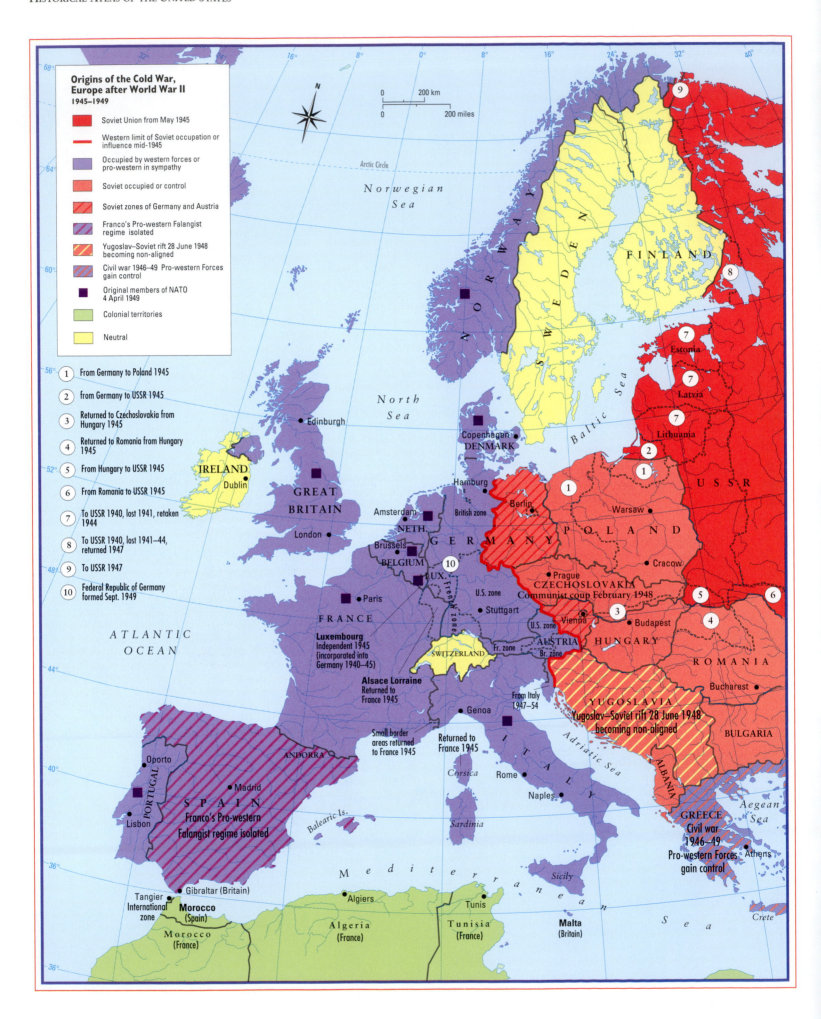

**Origins of the Cold War,
Europe after World War II**
1945–1949

- Soviet Union from May 1945
- Western limit of Soviet occupation or influence mid-1945
- Occupied by western forces or pro-western in sympathy
- Soviet occupied or control
- Soviet zones of Germany and Austria
- Franco's Pro-western Falangist regime isolated
- Yugoslav–Soviet rift 28 June 1948 becoming non-aligned
- Civil war 1946–49 Pro-western Forces gain control
- Original members of NATO 4 April 1949
- Colonial territories
- Neutral

1 From Germany to Poland 1945

2 from Germany to USSR 1945

3 Returned to Czechoslovakia from Hungary 1945

4 Returned to Romania from Hungary 1945

5 From Hungary to USSR 1945

6 From Romania to USSR 1945

7 To USSR 1940, lost 1941, retaken 1944

8 To USSR 1940, lost 1941–44, returned 1947

9 To USSR 1947

10 Federal Republic of Germany formed Sept. 1949

Luxembourg Independent 1945 (incorporated into Germany 1940–45)

Alsace Lorraine Returned to France 1945

Small border areas returned to France 1945

Returned to France 1945

SPAIN Franco's Pro-western Falangist regime isolated

Tangier International zone Morocco (Spain)

Morocco (France)

Algeria (France)

Tunisia (France)

Malta (Britain)

CZECHOSLOVAKIA Communist coup February 1948

YUGOSLAVIA Yugoslav–Soviet rift 28 June 1948 becoming non-aligned

GREECE Civil war 1946–49 Pro-western Forces gain control

From Italy 1947–54

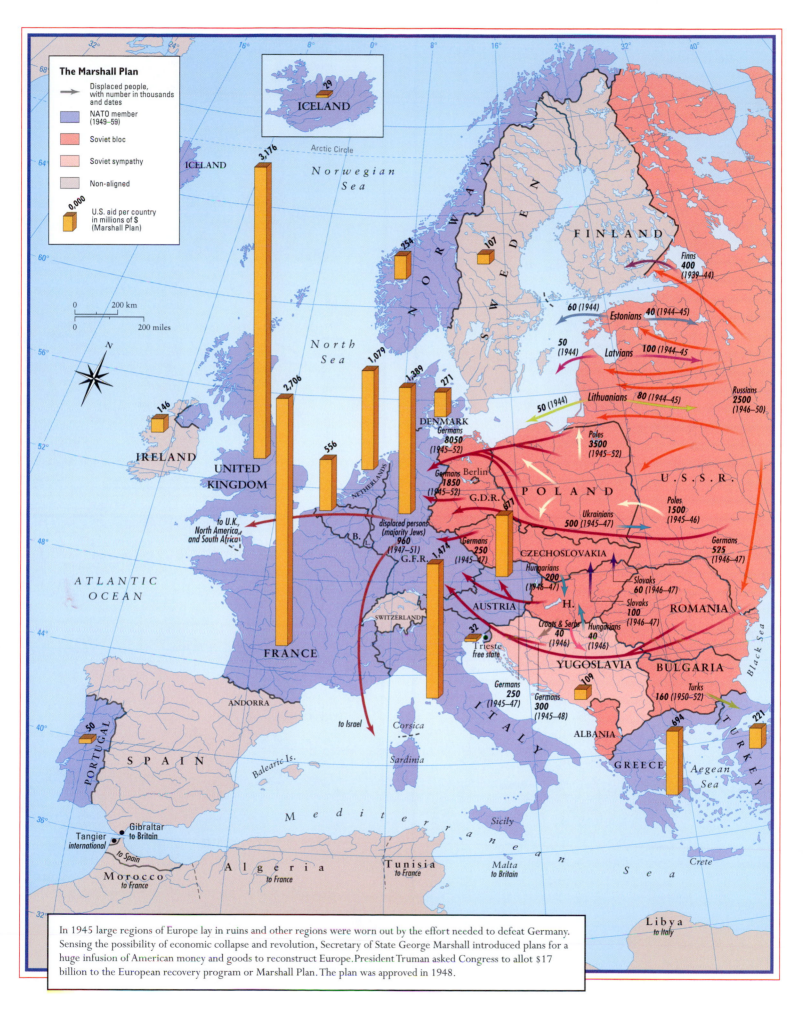

The Marshall Plan

Displaced people, with number in thousands and dates

NATO member (1949–59)

Soviet bloc

Soviet sympathy

Non-aligned

0,000 U.S. aid per country in millions of $ (Marshall Plan)

ICELAND 29

ICELAND 3,176

Norwegian Sea

Arctic Circle

FINLAND

Finns 400 (1939–44)

60 (1944) Estonians 40 (1944–45)

50 (1944) Latvians 100 (1944–45)

Russians 2500 (1946–50)

North Sea

254 NORWAY 107 SWEDEN

Lithuanians 80 (1944–45)

50 (1944) Poles 3500 (1945–52)

146 IRELAND

2,706 UNITED KINGDOM

200 km

200 miles

N

1,079 556 1,389 271

DENMARK Germans 8050 (1945–52)

NETHERLANDS

Germans 1850 (1945–52) Berlin

G.D.R. 677 POLAND U.S.S.R.

Poles 1500 (1945–46)

Ukrainians 500 (1945–47)

Germans 525 (1946–47)

to U.K., North America, and South Africa

B. L.

displaced persons (majority Jews) 960 (1947–51)

Germans 250 (1945–47)

G.F.R. 1,474

CZECHOSLOVAKIA

Hungarians 200 (1946–47)

Slovaks 60 (1946–47) Slovaks 100 (1946–47)

ROMANIA

ATLANTIC OCEAN

AUSTRIA

SWITZERLAND

H.

Croats & Serbs 40 (1946) Hungarians 40 (1946)

FRANCE

32 Trieste free state

Germans 250 (1945–47)

Germans 300 (1945–48)

YUGOSLAVIA BULGARIA

Black Sea

ANDORRA

109

Turks 160 (1950–52)

50 PORTUGAL

SPAIN

Balearic Is.

Corsica

Sardinia

ITALY

ALBANIA GREECE 694 TURKEY 221

to Israel

Mediterranean

Sicily

Aegean Sea

Gibraltar to Britain

Tangier international

to Spain

Morocco to France

Algeria to France

Tunisia to France

Malta to Britain

Crete

Sea

Libya to Italy

In 1945 large regions of Europe lay in ruins and other regions were worn out by the effort needed to defeat Germany. Sensing the possibility of economic collapse and revolution, Secretary of State George Marshall introduced plans for a huge infusion of American money and goods to reconstruct Europe. President Truman asked Congress to allot $17 billion to the European recovery program or Marshall Plan. The plan was approved in 1948.

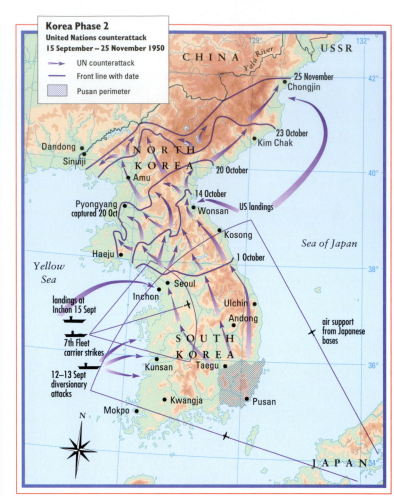

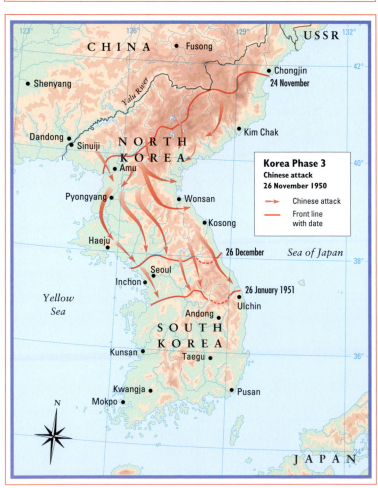

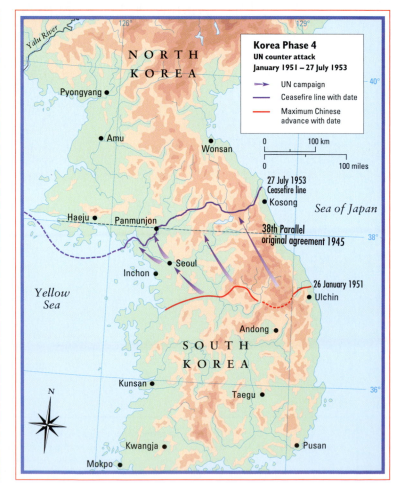

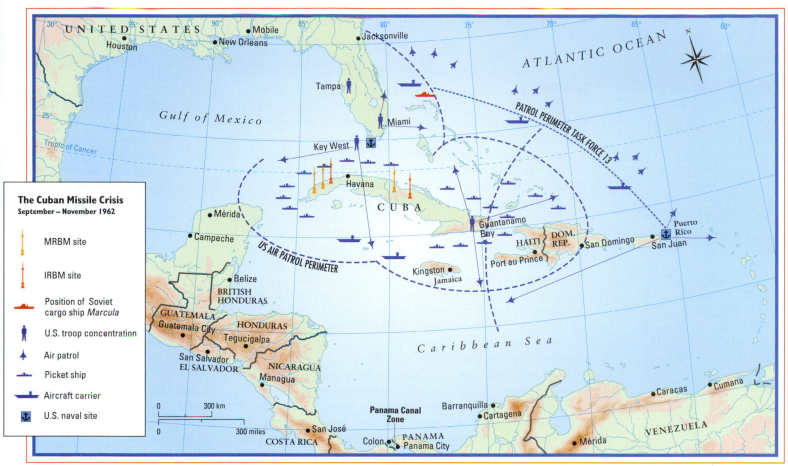

The Cuban Missile Crisis
September – November 1962

- MRBM site
- IRBM site
- Position of Soviet cargo ship *Marcula*
- U.S. troop concentration
- Air patrol
- Picket ship
- Aircraft carrier
- U.S. naval site

Missiles to Cuba 1962

- Supply route from Soviet ports
- US and NATO allies
- USSR and Warsaw Pact allies

PART TWENTY

AMERICA IN THE FIFTIES AND SIXTIES

I T IS customary to think of the 1950s as a period of social consolidation and of political consensus. Dwight D. Eisenhower, the President and a duffer at golf, is the symbol of the times: contented, even complacent; amiable, perhaps to a fault; and devoid of deep thoughts. The great questions that confronted the preceding generation—could the nation climb out of the Great Depression and survive the cataclysm of war?—had been emphatically answered in the affirmative. The United States had emerged from the Second World War as the undisputed victor, and its economy was perhaps stronger than ever before. The postwar economic boom lasted into the early 1970s, with a consistently high rate of growth and low unemployment.

The war had done much to knit the nation closer together. As young men (and some women) left their farms, small towns, and urban neighborhoods to serve in the military, or perhaps in the burgeoning defense plants in the Far West, local and regional differences became less pronounced. The 1950s accelerated this consolidation. The most obvious manifestation of this trend was the development of the interstate highway system, begun under Eisenhower in 1956. Even more people than before hit the road. In 1950, Americans consumed 35 billion gallons of gasoline; in 1970, 92 billion.

This exuberant consumerism caused many to indict the 1950s as an era of shallow materialism, yet the decade also witnessed an extraordinary expansion of institutionalized religion. The Catholic Church built more than a thousand new schools and hundreds of hospitals. Nearly all denominations attracted more adherents and built many more churches. "In God We Trust" was added to the nation's currency.

But if economic growth, the triumph of the automobile, and a general mood of postwar optimism promoted cohesion, these same developments placed new stresses and caused new fractures in American Society. The increasing number of African Americans who now could afford to stay in motels and eat at restaurants chafed at laws that obliged them to patronize segregated facilities; and the automobile, which promoted the development of far-flung suburbs, allowed for the deterioration of the mass transit systems on which inner city residents depended.

In the 1950s the civil rights movement entered a new phase as leaders called on African Americans to act in concert to protest segregation. In 1954 Martin Luther King, Jr., a Baptist minister, led a successful boycott against segregated seating on the public buses of Montgomery, Alabama. This action, which unified the black community and drew considerable media attention, was followed by hundreds of civil rights boycotts, protest marches, voter registration drives, and other activities.

These initiatives sent a shock wave through political life. Since World War II, most scholars championed (or sometimes derided) the American party system as devoid of the collision of philosophies and social classes that characterized European political life. In the United States, Democrats and Republicans stood for much the same thing. But the civil rights protests proved that the American consensus was less deep than many had imagined.

The 1960 election pointed up the emerging dilemma for Democrats in particular. John F. Kennedy won the 1960 election by carrying the white South, which had voted for Democratic candidates for nearly a century, and by taking several states, including Michigan, Illinois, and Pennsylvania, where black support had proven critical. But as the civil rights movement drew media attention, Kennedy confronted a dilemma: if he endorsed King and the protesters, he would alienate white voters in the Deep South (where, at this time, few blacks were allowed to register to vote); but if he failed to support the civil rights movement, he might lose the crucial black vote in the big cities of the Midwest and Northeast.

Kennedy's assassination in 1963, and the ascension of Vice President Lyndon Johnson, a Texan, changed these dynamics. Johnson, rightly confident that southern voters would endorse one of their own, was able to support civil rights measures. The Civil Rights Acts of 1964 and 1965 were signal events in American race relations. The Voting Rights Act of 1965, for example, provided for the assignment of federal officials to register prospective voters in the South.

Another example of the profound social effects of economic growth and the automobile was seen in the transformation of urban areas. The new cities of the South and West, such as Los Angeles, Phoenix, and Dallas, spread out over vast areas; middle-class people lived in the suburbs, and commuted to work downtown by automobile. But as Los Angeles spread out over hundreds of square miles, connected by a bewildering web of concrete roadways, inner city residents were nearly imprisoned in ghettos such as Watts. The cleavage between middle-class suburbs and lower and working-class inner cities contributed to the race riots of the mid-1960s.

The Civil Rights movement inspired and provided the tactics for other social movements during the 1960s. Feminists, Native Americans, environmentalists, and others became increasingly visible. The largest and most heated protest movement, however, was directed against the Vietnam War.

In August 1964, after an incident involving American destroyers and North Vietnamese surface craft in the Gulf of Tonkin, President Lyndon B. Johnson ordered the bombing of coastal facilities in North Vietnam. The bombing campaign intensified. Despite the bombing, however, Ho Chi Minh's forces gained in the South. In the summer of 1965, Johnson decided to send hundreds of thousands of American soldiers to crush the insurgents. By 1968, a half a million Americans, backed by flotillas of helicopters and hundreds of bombers, undertook "search and destroy" missions throughout the jungles of South Vietnam to inflict punishing losses on the Communists.

But in late January 1968, during the Tet holidays, Ho unleashed a wild assault, attacking six major cities, 34 provincial capitals, 64 district capitals, hundreds of hamlets, and countless other targets. By exposing themselves directly to the awesome firepower of American bombers, helicopters, and armored vehicles, the North Vietnamese sustained tremendous losses; but the ferocity of Ho's fighters showed that the United States had little chance of winning the war in Vietnam. Johnson chose not to run for re-election and his successor, Richard M. Nixon, spent much of his time in office trying to find an honorable way to extricate the nation from the war.

MAPS

In the years following World War II Americas's appetite for energy outstriped traditional sources of supply, oil and coal. To reduce reliance on imported oil, a civil nuclear energy program was instigated. In the fifties nuclear power was seen as a clean and almost limitless source of energy. However, during the late sixties, there emerged concerns over its radioactive by-products which required secure storage for hundreds, perhaps thousands, of years. In March 1979 the nuclear reactor at the Three-Mile Island power plant went out of control, forcing the evacuation of 150,000 people. This and other nuclear accidents abroad have left a legacy of anxiety about nuclear energy.

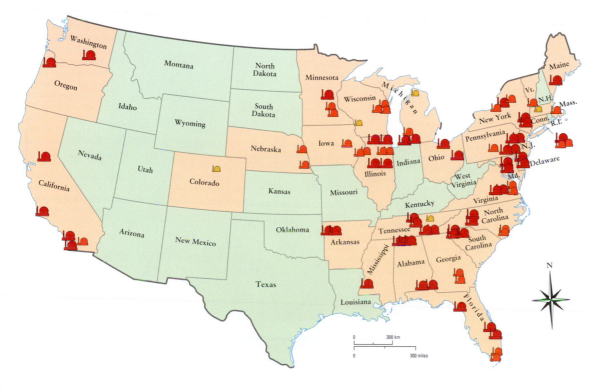

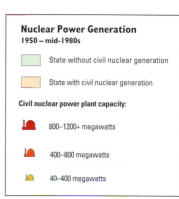

Nuclear Power Generation
1950 – mid-1980s

State without civil nuclear generation

State with civil nuclear generation

Civil nuclear power plant capacity:

800–1200+ megawatts

400–800 megawatts

40–400 megawatts

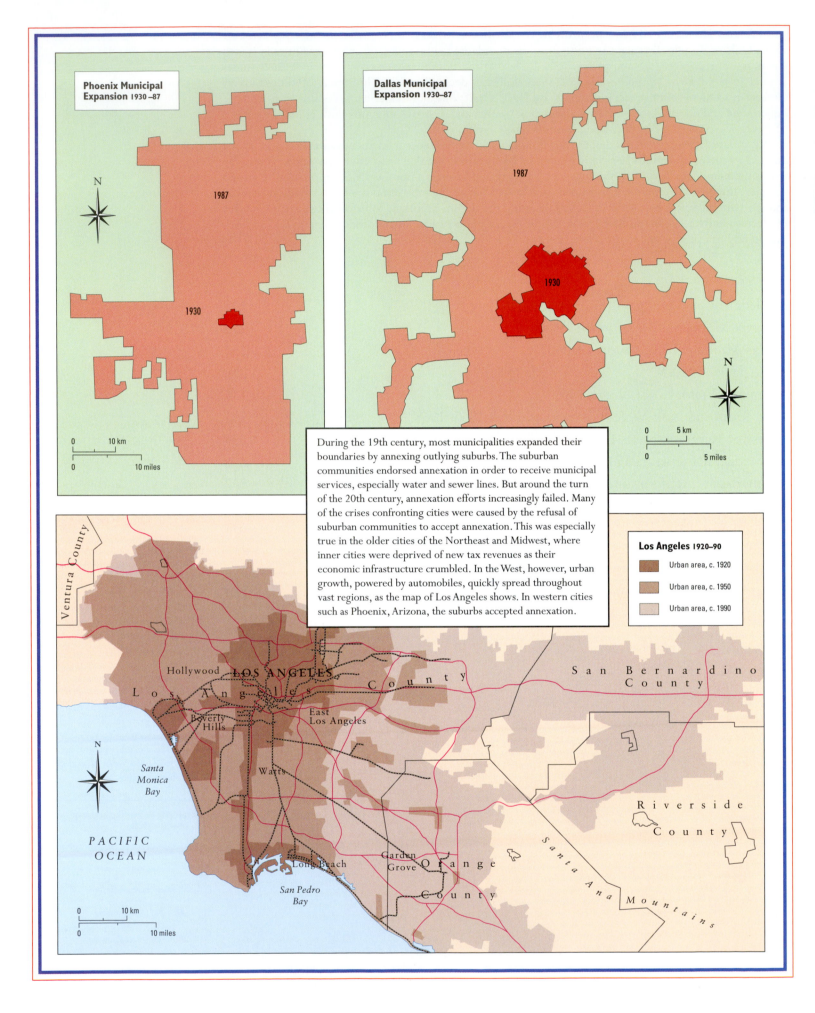

Phoenix Municipal Expansion 1930–87

1987

1930

0   10 km

0   10 miles

Dallas Municipal Expansion 1930–87

1987

1930

0   5 km

0   5 miles

During the 19th century, most municipalities expanded their boundaries by annexing outlying suburbs. The suburban communities endorsed annexation in order to receive municipal services, especially water and sewer lines. But around the turn of the 20th century, annexation efforts increasingly failed. Many of the crises confronting cities were caused by the refusal of suburban communities to accept annexation. This was especially true in the older cities of the Northeast and Midwest, where inner cities were deprived of new tax revenues as their economic infrastructure crumbled. In the West, however, urban growth, powered by automobiles, quickly spread throughout vast regions, as the map of Los Angeles shows. In western cities such as Phoenix, Arizona, the suburbs accepted annexation.

Los Angeles 1920–90

Urban area, c. 1920
Urban area, c. 1950
Urban area, c. 1990

Ventura County

Hollywood   LOS ANGELES

Los Angeles   County

Beverly Hills

East Los Angeles

San Bernardino County

Santa Monica Bay

Watts

PACIFIC OCEAN

Long Beach

Garden Grove   Orange County

San Pedro Bay

Santa Ana Mountains

Riverside County

0   10 km

0   10 miles

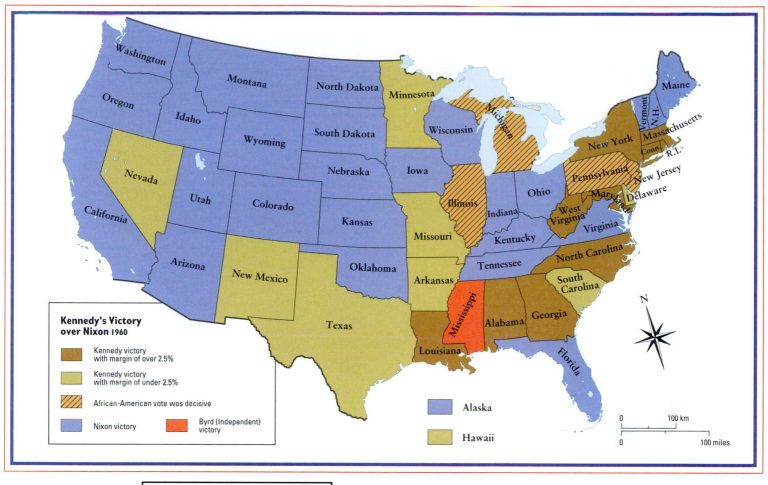

Kennedy's Victory over Nixon 1960

- Kennedy victory with margin of over 2.5%
- Kennedy victory with margin of under 2.5%
- African-American vote was decisive
- Nixon victory
- Byrd (Independent) victory

- Alaska
- Hawaii

0 — 100 km
0 — 100 miles

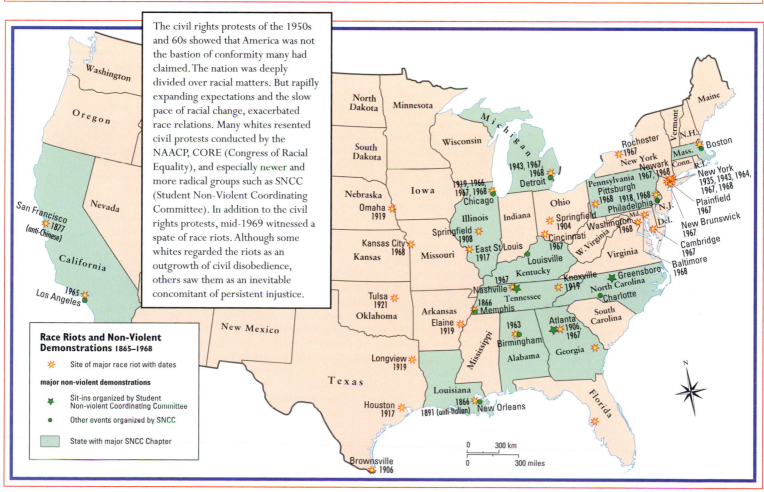

The civil rights protests of the 1950s and 60s showed that America was not the bastion of conformity many had claimed. The nation was deeply divided over racial matters. But rapidly expanding expectations and the slow pace of racial change, exacerbated race relations. Many whites resented civil protests conducted by the NAACP, CORE (Congress of Racial Equality), and especially newer and more radical groups such as SNCC (Student Non-Violent Coordinating Committee). In addition to the civil rights protests, mid-1969 witnessed a spate of race riots. Although some whites regarded the riots as an outgrowth of civil disobedience, others saw them as an inevitable concomitant of persistent injustice.

Race Riots and Non-Violent Demonstrations 1865–1968

- ☀ Site of major race riot with dates

major non-violent demonstrations

- ★ Sit-ins organized by Student Non-violent Coordinating Committee
- ● Other events organized by SNCC
- State with major SNCC Chapter

0 — 300 km
0 — 300 miles

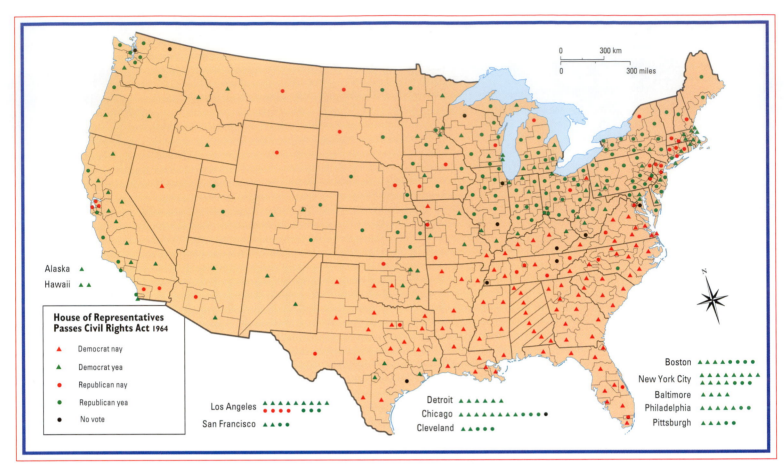

House of Representatives Passes Civil Rights Act 1964

Alaska ▲

Hawaii ▲ ▲

▲ Democrat nay

▲ Democrat yea

● Republican nay

● Republican yea

● No vote

Los Angeles ▲ ▲ ▲ ▲ ● ● ● ●

San Francisco ▲ ▲ ● ● ●

Detroit ▲ ▲ ▲ ▲ ▲ ▲

Chicago ▲ ▲ ▲ ▲ ▲ ▲ ▲ ● ● ●

Cleveland ▲ ▲ ▲ ● ● ●

Boston ▲ ▲ ▲ ▲ ● ● ● ●

New York City ▲ ▲ ▲ ▲ ▲ ▲ ▲ ▲ ●

Baltimore ▲ ▲ ▲ ▲ ●

Philadelphia ▲ ▲ ▲ ▲ ▲ ●

Pittsburgh ▲ ▲ ▲ ▲ ● ●

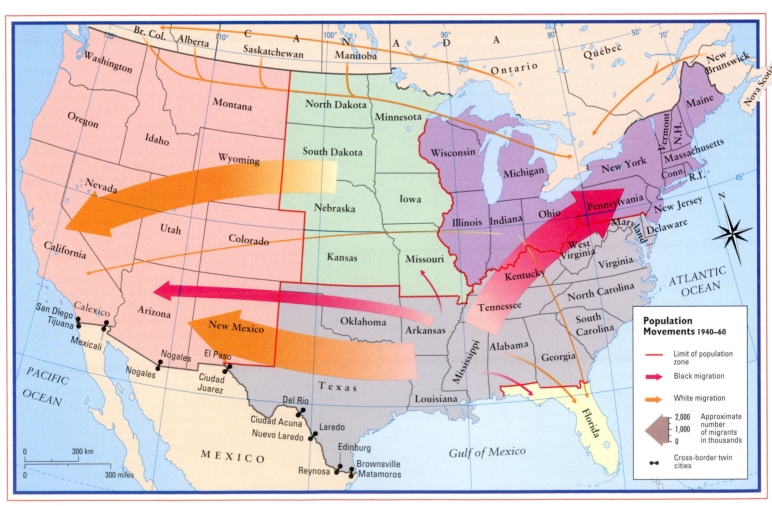

Population Movements 1940–60

— Limit of population zone

➡ Black migration

➡ White migration

Approximate number of migrants in thousands — 2,000 / 1,000 / 0

●—● Cross-border twin cities

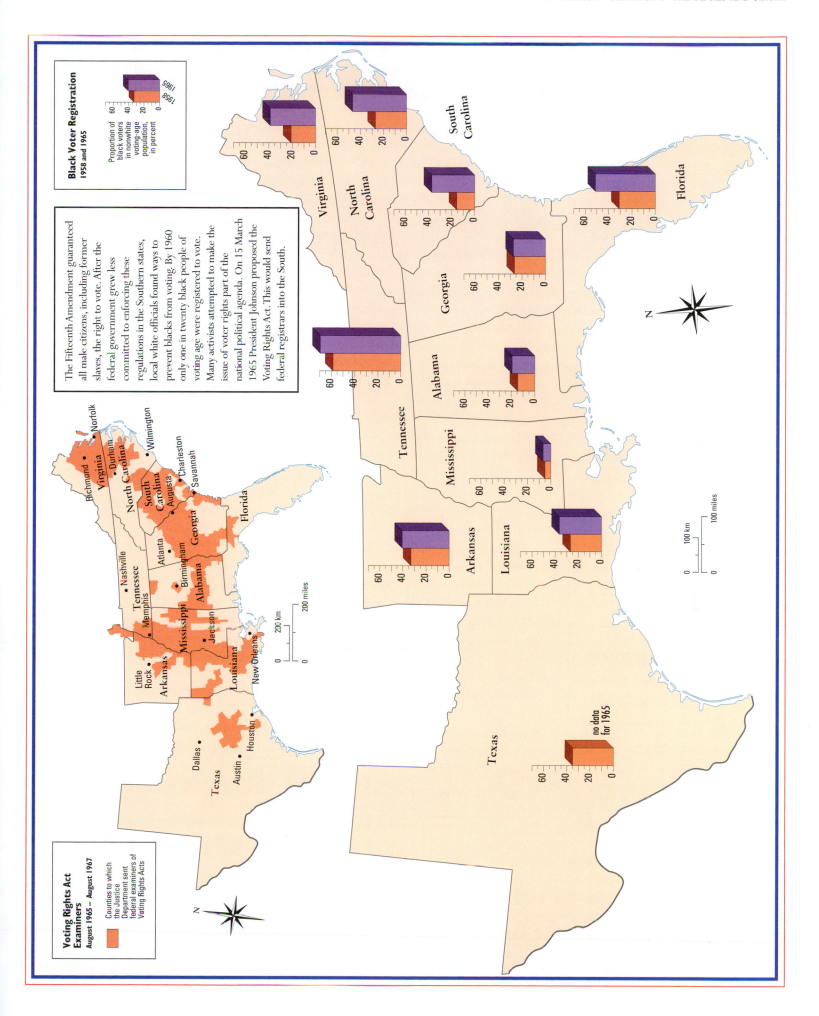

Black Voter Registration
1958 and 1965

Proportion of black voters in nonwhite voting-age population, in percent

1965
1958

The Fifteenth Amendment guaranteed all male citizens, including former slaves, the right to vote. After the federal government grew less committed to enforcing these regulations in the Southern states, local white officials found ways to prevent blacks from voting. By 1960 only one in twenty black people of voting age were registered to vote. Many activists attempted to make the issue of voter rights part of the national political agenda. On 15 March 1965 President Johnson proposed the Voting Rights Act. This would send federal registrars into the South.

no data for 1965

Voting Rights Act Examiners
August 1965 – August 1967

Counties to which the Justice Department sent federal examiners of Voting Rights Acts

Vietnam War
1959–75

- Communist-held area January 1973 "ceasefire"
- U.S. corps command area
- North Vietnam subject to air attack
- Communist-controlled area in Laos and Cambodia 1950–75
- Controlled by Khmer Rouge c. 1975
- Controlled by Pathet Lao c. 1975
- Area of Communist guerrilla activity c. 1975

Communist Supply Routes

- Ho Chi Minh Trail
- Sihanouk Trail
- Sea supply routes
- Communist-held area 1959–60

In October 1954, after the departure of the French from Indochina, Eisenhower backed President Diem's regime and offered military support. Between January 1955 and December 1963 the steady growth in U.S. commitment had raised troop levels to 389,000.

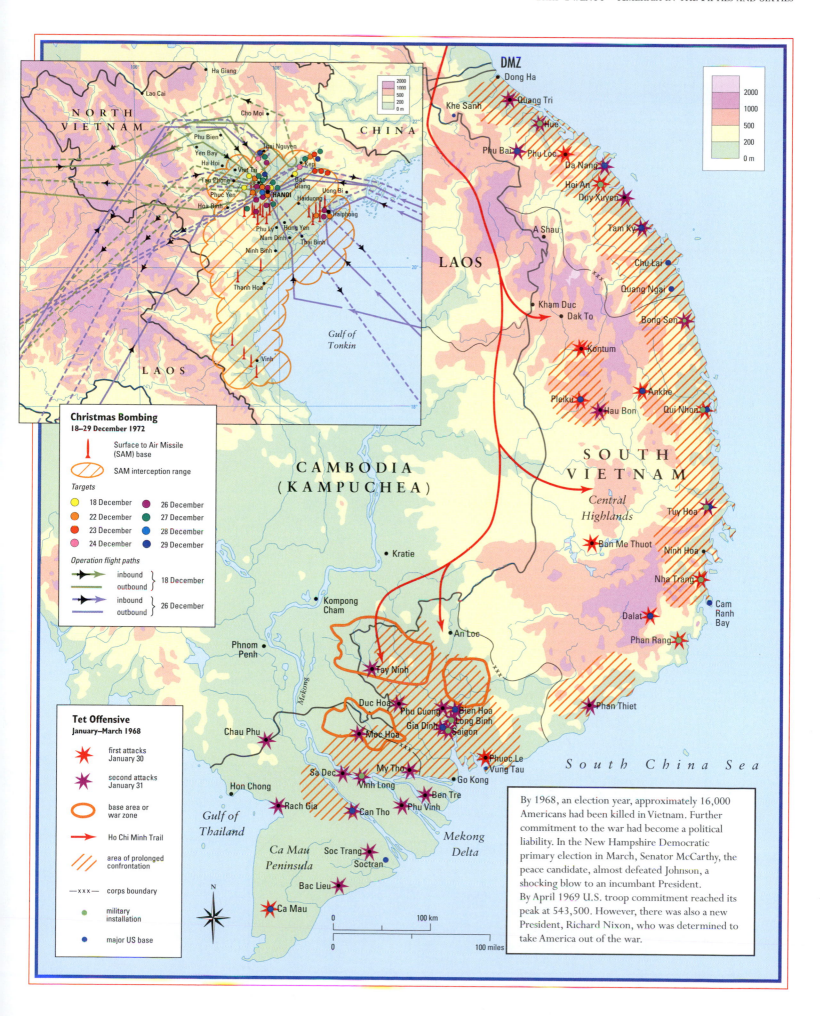

Christmas Bombing
18–29 December 1972

- ▮ Surface to Air Missile (SAM) base
- ⬭ SAM interception range

Targets
- ● 18 December
- ● 22 December
- ● 23 December
- ● 24 December
- ● 26 December
- ● 27 December
- ● 28 December
- ● 29 December

Operation flight paths
- ➤ inbound
- ─ outbound } 18 December
- ➤ inbound
- ─ outbound } 26 December

Tet Offensive
January–March 1968

- ✴ first attacks January 30
- ✴ second attacks January 31
- ⬭ base area or war zone
- ➤ Ho Chi Minh Trail
- ⫽ area of prolonged confrontation
- —x x x— corps boundary
- ● military installation
- ● major US base

By 1968, an election year, approximately 16,000 Americans had been killed in Vietnam. Further commitment to the war had become a political liability. In the New Hampshire Democratic primary election in March, Senator McCarthy, the peace candidate, almost defeated Johnson, a shocking blow to an incumbent President.
By April 1969 U.S. troop commitment reached its peak at 543,500. However, there was also a new President, Richard Nixon, who was determined to take America out of the war.

Olympic 1938

North Cascades 1968

Washington

Glacier 1910

Mount Rainier 1899

Montana

North Dakota

Minnesota

Oregon

Crater Lake 1902

Idaho

Yellowstone
1872

Grand Teton
1929

Wyoming

South Dakota

Redwood 1928

Lassen Volcanic 1916

Wind Cave
1903

Nebraska

Yosemite
1890

Nevada

Great Basin
1986

Utah

Arches
1971

Rocky Mountain
1915

King's Canyon
1940

Sequoia
1890

Death Valley

Capitol Reef
1971

Canyonlands
1964

Colorado

Kansas

California

Zion 1919

Bryce Canyon
1924

Mesa Verde
1906

Grand Canyon
1919

Joshua Tree

Petrified Forest
1962

Arizona

New Mexico

Oklahoma

Carlsbad Caverns
1923

Guadalupe Mountains
1966

Texas

Platt
1906

Kobuk Valley
1980

Gates of the Arctic
1980

Big Bend
1935

Alaska

Not to scale

Denali
1917

Lake Clark
1980

Wrangell-
St Elias
1980

Katmai
1918

Kenai Fjords
1980

Glacier Bay
1925

Admiralty I.

The national forest reserves were created in 1891; in 1896 President Cleveland greatly expanded them. In 1905, the forest reserves were transformed to what became the Forest Service, directed by conservationist Gifford Pinchot. President Theodore Roosevelt supported Pinchot's efforts to expand the forest reserves and supervise utilization of the nation's river systems. During the presidency of William Howard Taft, however, Pinchot ran afoul of business and mining interests that sought to exploit mineral and timber resources on public lands, typical of a recurrent dispute between developers and conservationists throughout the 20th century.

National Parks and Forests 1872–1986

National Forests

National Parks with date of foundation

PART TWENTY-ONE   CONTEMPORARY CHALLENGES AT HOME AND ABROAD

I N 1973, the last American soldiers returned from Vietnam. President Richard M. Nixon claimed that the long awaited "peace with honor" had finally been attained. Two years later, North Vietnam resumed its offensive against South Vietnam. Although South Vietnam's army and air force were, on paper, among the strongest in the world, they crumpled before the Communist onslaught. For the United States, the Vietnam War had been a failure. America's armed forces no longer seemed invincible. Moreover, the American economy, the backbone of the nation's military might for a quarter of a century, was also in trouble.

The first blow was struck in the Mideast. On 6 October 1973, Egypt and Syria attacked Israel. Six years earlier Israel had easily repulsed an Egyptian attack, but this time Egyptian tanks slashed through the Sinai and threatened to slice Israel in two. Israeli forces, helped by an infusion of American fighter bombers, went on the offensive, crossing the Suez Canal into Egypt, severing the invading army's supply lines and forcing it to surrender. Israel won the war, but the Arab world retaliated by cutting off the flow of Middle Eastern oil to the United States.

Oil prices skyrocketed, and long lines at gas stations were but the most irritating manifestation of a body blow to the oil-hungry American economy. By the mid-1970s the nation had been plunged into a severe recession. Real incomes declined. Higher oil prices drove up the cost of nearly everything else, this at a time when more people were out of work.

If prosperity had helped fuel the reforms of the 1960s, allowing voters and the government to distribute resources more generously, the weakening economy inaugurated a period of political retrenchment. In 1972, for example, Congress approved the Equal Rights Amendment, which would ensure that legal rights not be abridged "on account of sex." Women were to be ensured the same rights as men. Before the end of the year, 22 states had ratified the measure, ranging from Hawaii to New Hampshire, from Texas to Wisconsin. Eight more states ratified the following year. But that year Phyllis Schlafly, publisher of a conservative newsletter, initiated a "Stop ERA" campaign. Her strongest argument was that when the economy was bad, "equal rights" left women vulnerable and unprotected in the event of divorce or domestic abuse. As a result of her campaign, only five more states ratified the ERA, three short of the total necessary for ratification. (Four states also rescinded their pro-ratification votes, a measure of uncertain legality.) Opposition to the ERA was strongest in the South.

The 1960s had also spawned an exuberant iconoclasm, sometimes creative and subversive, but often mindless and materialistic. Marijuana and psychedelic drugs, which pervaded college campuses in the 1960s, were replaced by more powerful drugs, especially cocaine, during the 1970s and 1980s. These drugs harmed the fabric of most communities, but they especially ravaged the nation's ghettos. Crime rates soared, and this provoked a severe crackdown by police and state and federal legislators. "Law and order" became the mantra, repeated in each election, of most candidates.

But the chief problem remained the economy. From 1976 to 1980 President Jimmy Carter proved powerless to loosen the grip of "stagflation"—a combination of stagnation and inflation. When Islamic radicals toppled an American-backed regime in Iran and took American embassy employees hostage, Carter's reputation declined further. In 1980 he was defeated for re-election by Republican Ronald Reagan, a former movie star.

Reagan advanced a simple agenda. He sought to resist the "evil empire" of Soviet Communism by building up the armed forces and to strengthen the economy by "getting government off peoples' backs." Reagan's most startling military gambit was the Strategic Defense Initiative (or "Star Wars," at it was called), a space-based network of nuclear and laser weapons whose purpose was to destroy Soviet intercontinental ballistic missiles after they had been launched. By the early 1980s, the nuclear arsenals of both nations were unimaginably large, with a destructive capability far out of proportion to meaningful military targets. The Soviet Union, whose economy was weaker than western observers thought, was overburdened by the strain of the escalating arms race with the United States, and it began to falter. In 1985, Soviet-initiated internal reforms outpaced the objectives of those who initiated them, and soon the Communist government collapsed. The Soviet Union crumbled. Soviet Communism had lost the Cold War.

Yet this did not bring the "peace dividend" many had hoped. In 1990, Saddam Hussein, leader of Iraq, invaded and quickly occupied Kuwait, an oil-rich (and small) Arab neighbor. His goal was oil. The United Nations demanded an Iraqi withdrawal. When he refused, Saudi Arabia and other Arab states joined the United States, Britain, and France to drive Iraq from Kuwait. On 17 January 1991, President George Bush ordered the bombing of Iraqi front lines, air defenses, and nuclear and poison gas facilities. Though powerless against the American-led air armada, Saddam felt confident that his army, which had fought millions of Iranian troops to a standstill in the 1980s, could survive the impending ground attacks. When the air campaign was nearly completed, U.S. General H. Norman Schwarzkopf positioned his army directly opposite the strongest Iraqi concentrations, as if he intended to storm the Iraqi defenses head-on. Instead, he secretly shifted his fastest armor hundreds of miles to the northwest. On the morning of 24 February, they slashed through the thin Iraqi desert defenses, penetrated deep into Iraq, and then wheeled to the east, threatening to capture the entire Iraqi army in Kuwait. When the Iraqis abandoned their positions, they were shredded by fighter bombers and heavily-armed helicopters. The Iraqi military was crushed, and Bush called off the campaign. He assumed that, deprived of much of his army, Saddam's regime would fall. It did not. In the late 1990s, when Saddam refused to allow UN weapons inspectors access to suspicious facilities, many assumed that he was developing biological and nuclear weapons.

The military success of the Gulf War was thus tempered by its political failure. A generation of military leaders and statesmen, sobered by the American defeat in Vietnam and the elusive victory against Iraq, grew wary of future military crusades whose objectives had not been precisely set out in advance. The matter came to a head when General Slobodan Milosevic, a Serb and former Communist official, resorted to genocide ("ethnic cleansing") to prevent Muslims in Bosnia and Kosovo from seceding from Yugoslavia. In 1999, after years of debate, President William Clinton persuaded NATO to bomb Serbia to force Milosevic to withdraw from Kosovo. Shortly afterwards, his own people drove Milosevic from office.

Throughout the postwar years—indeed, throughout the 20th century—America's military might defended the nation by fighting abroad. With the exception of the bombing of Pearl Harbor, and the vague if unimaginably ominous threat of Soviet nuclear missiles, American citizens were not at risk of foreign attack while on the soil of the United States.

That changed on 11 September 2001. That morning, nineteen Arab men hijacked four American airliners. Two of the planes, having departed from Boston, were diverted south. As they neared New York harbor, they revved the engines to full throttle and slammed into the 110-story twin towers of the World Trade Center. Both towers were immediately engulfed in flames. Within several hours, they collapsed, choking much of lower Manhattan with dust. Another jetliner, which had taken off from Washington D.C., plunged into the Pentagon. The fourth plane, from Newark, crashed in a field in central Pennsylvania. Nearly 3,000 perished in the attacks.

Osama bin Laden, an Islamic radical who had inherited a fortune, was blamed for the attacks. (Bin Laden had been indicted—but not apprehended—for earlier terrorist attacks.) Bin Laden was being protected by the Taliban, an extremist Islamic group that ruled Afghanistan. President George W. Bush (not to be confused with his president-father, George Bush) funneled weapons and money to form a coalition hostile to the Taliban in Afghanistan. While coalition forces attacked the Taliban army on the ground, laser-wielding American spotters marked Taliban positions, which were obliterated by bombers dropping precision-guided bombs. The Taliban surrendered, though some fled to remote Pakistan. The fate of bin Laden was unknown. But the war on terrorism was far from over.

MAPS

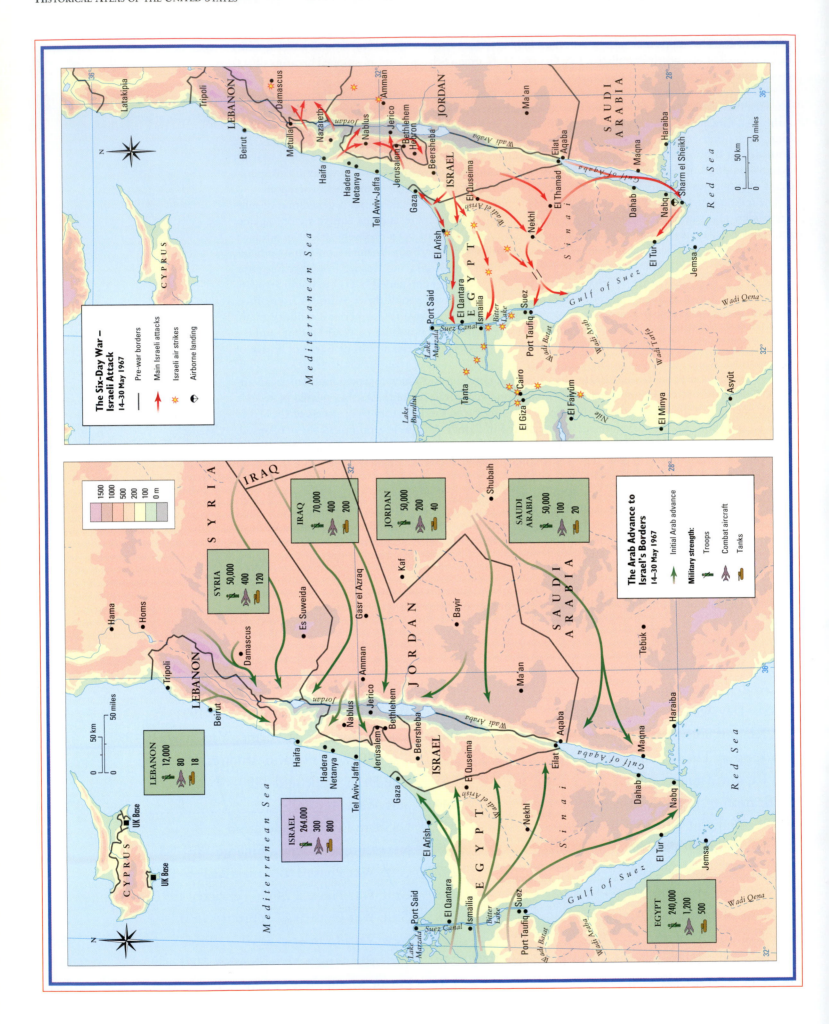

The Six-Day War –
Israeli Attack
14–30 May 1967

Pre-war borders
Main Israeli attacks
Israeli air strikes
Airborne landing

The Arab Advance to
Israel's Borders
14–30 May 1967

Initial Arab advance
Military strength:
Troops
Combat aircraft
Tanks

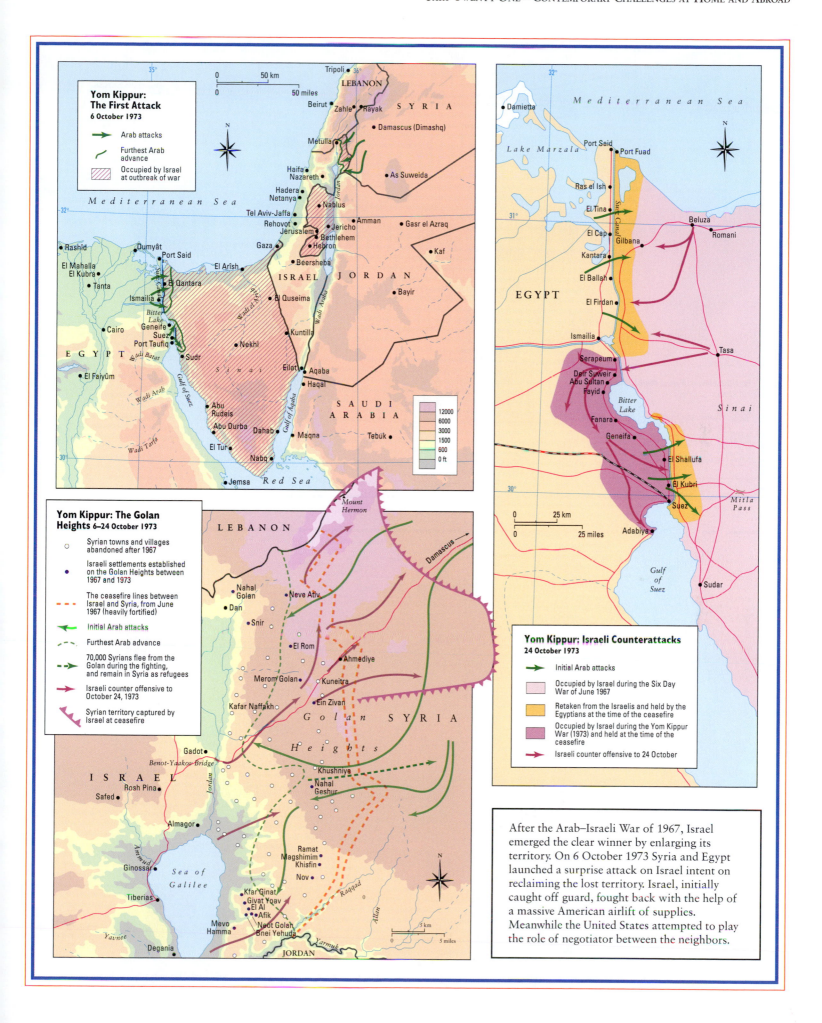

Yom Kippur: The First Attack
6 October 1973

→ Arab attacks

⌐ Furthest Arab advance

▨ Occupied by Israel at outbreak of war

Yom Kippur: The Golan Heights 6–24 October 1973

○ Syrian towns and villages abandoned after 1967

● Israeli settlements established on the Golan Heights between 1967 and 1973

- - - The ceasefire lines between Israel and Syria, from June 1967 (heavily fortified)

← Initial Arab attacks

- - - Furthest Arab advance

- - → 70,000 Syrians flee from the Golan during the fighting, and remain in Syria as refugees

→ Israeli counter offensive to October 24, 1973

➤ Syrian territory captured by Israel at ceasefire

Yom Kippur: Israeli Counterattacks
24 October 1973

→ Initial Arab attacks

▨ Occupied by Israel during the Six Day War of June 1967

▨ Retaken from the Israelis and held by the Egyptians at the time of the ceasefire

▨ Occupied by Israel during the Yom Kippur War (1973) and held at the time of the ceasefire

→ Israeli counter offensive to 24 October

After the Arab–Israeli War of 1967, Israel emerged the clear winner by enlarging its territory. On 6 October 1973 Syria and Egypt launched a surprise attack on Israel intent on reclaiming the lost territory. Israel, initially caught off guard, fought back with the help of a massive American airlift of supplies. Meanwhile the United States attempted to play the role of negotiator between the neighbors.

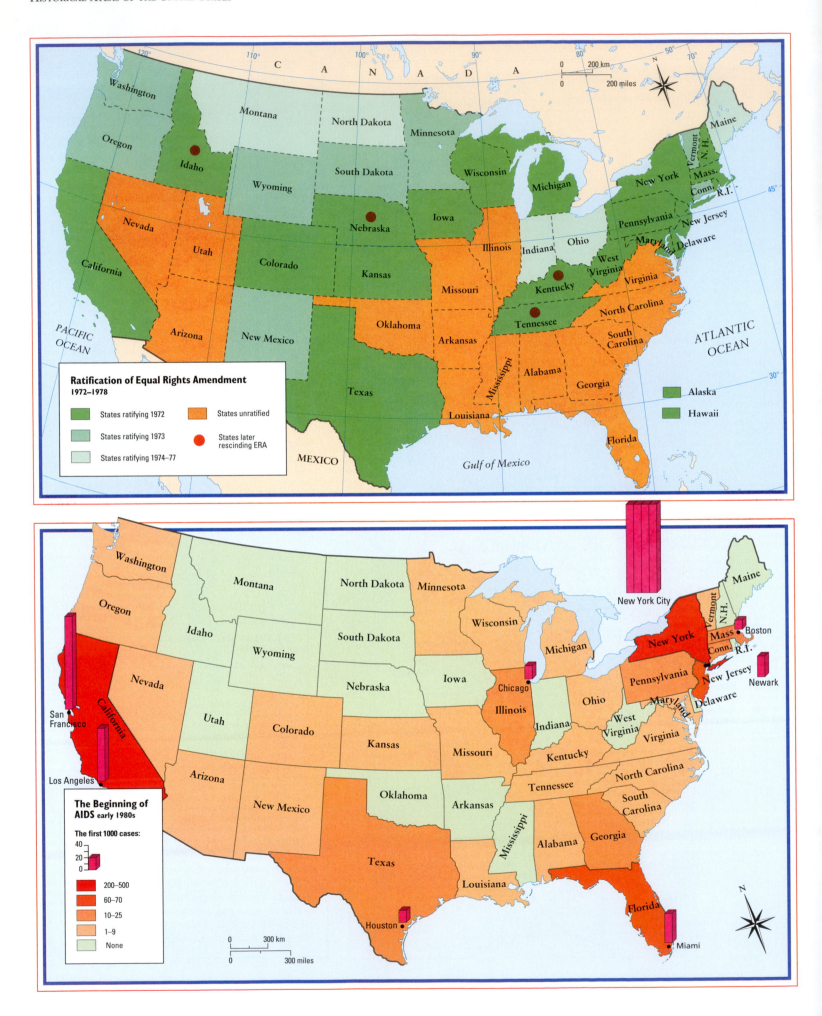

Ratification of Equal Rights Amendment
1972–1978

- States ratifying 1972
- States ratifying 1973
- States ratifying 1974–77
- States unratified
- States later rescinding ERA

Alaska

Hawaii

The Beginning of AIDS early 1980s

The first 1000 cases:

- 200–500
- 60–70
- 10–25
- 1–9
- None

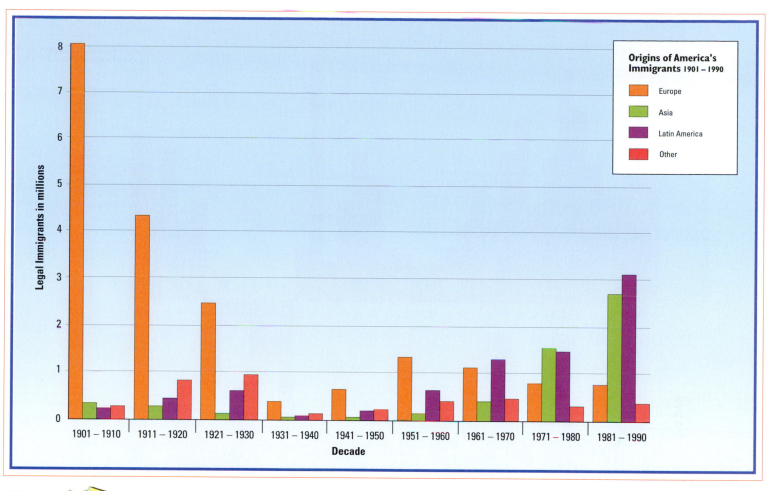

Religious regions reflect, to some degree, the settlement patterns of the U.S. New England, for instance, still has large numbers of Congregationalists and Episcopalians. The midland region stretches westward from the mid-Atlantic states to the Rocky Mountains with Methodists, Presbyterians, and German religious groups. Peninsular Florida is occupied by a diverse religious community who have settled there during the 20th century. The border with Mexico shows large influxes of Spanish Catholics.

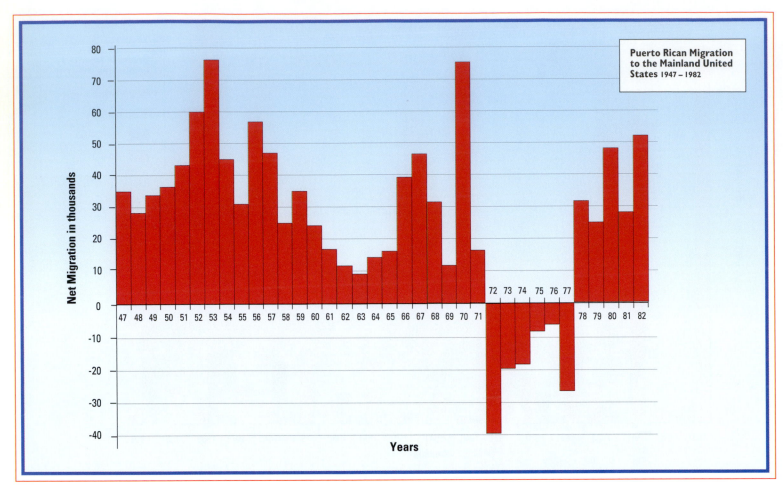

Puerto Rican Migration
to the Mainland United
States 1947–1982

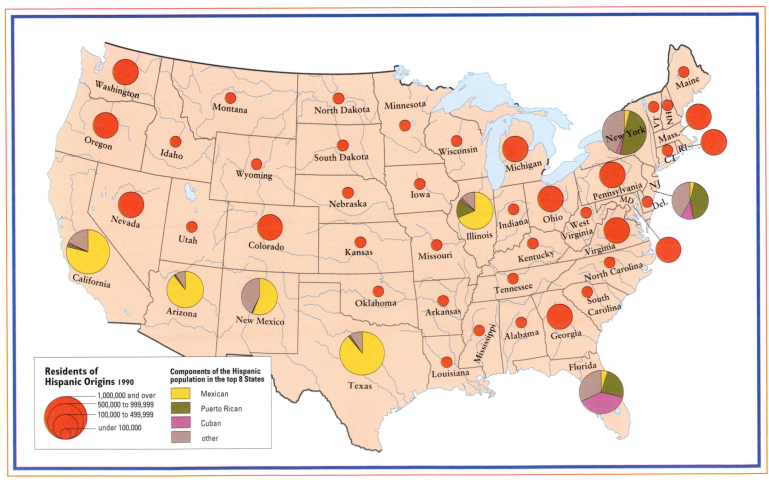

Residents of
Hispanic Origins 1990

1,000,000 and over
500,000 to 999,999
100,000 to 499,999
under 100,000

Components of the Hispanic
population in the top 8 States

Mexican
Puerto Rican
Cuban
other

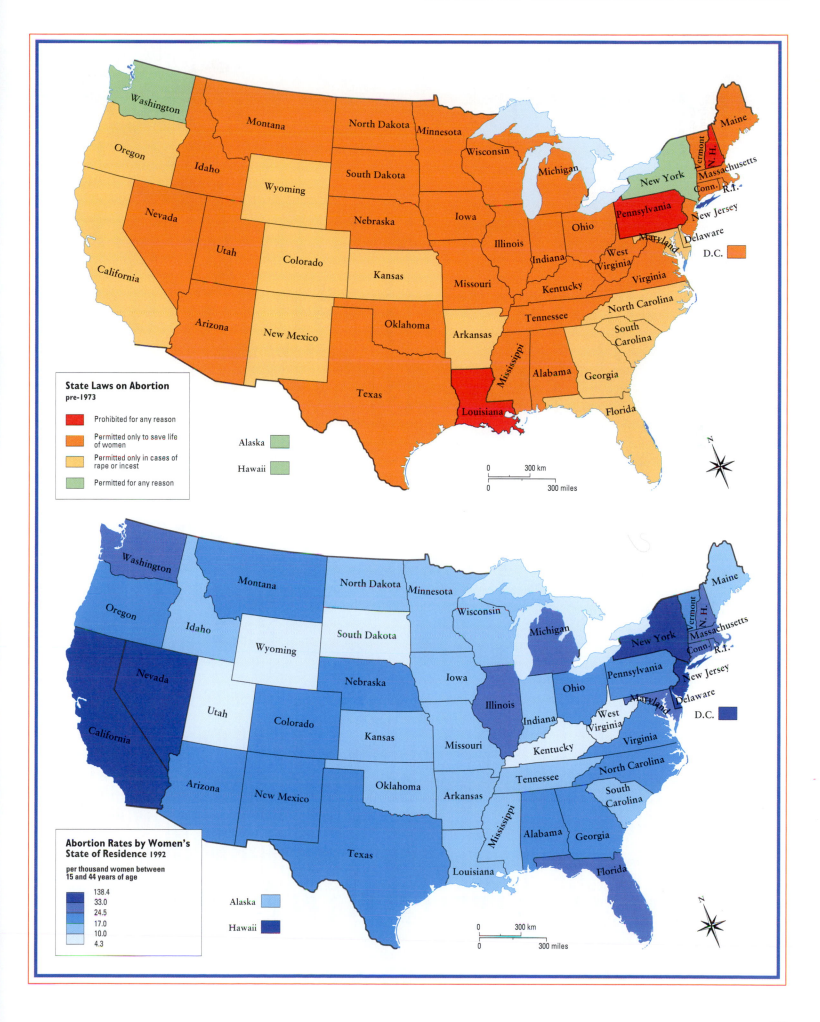

State Laws on Abortion
pre-1973

- Prohibited for any reason
- Permitted only to save life of women
- Permitted only in cases of rape or incest
- Permitted for any reason

Alaska

Hawaii

0 — 300 km
0 — 300 miles

Abortion Rates by Women's State of Residence 1992

per thousand women between 15 and 44 years of age

138.4
33.0
24.5
17.0
10.0
4.3

Alaska

Hawaii

0 — 300 km
0 — 300 miles

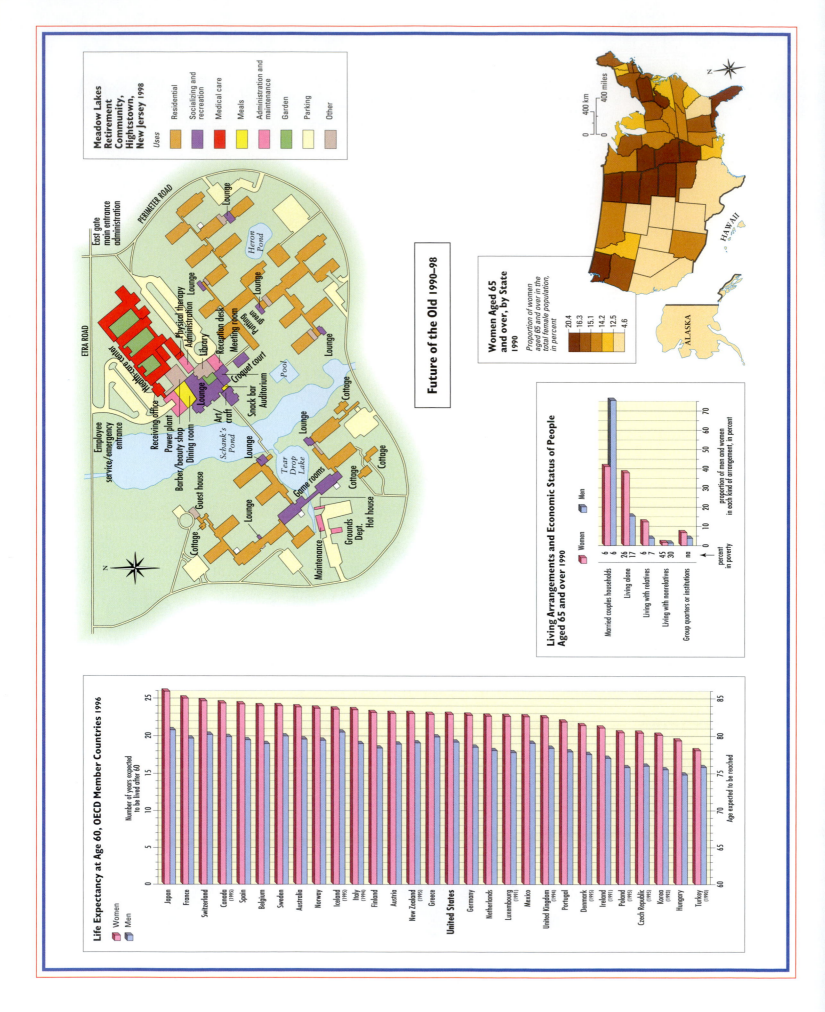

Meadow Lakes Retirement Community, Hightstown, New Jersey 1998

Uses

- Residential
- Socializing and recreation
- Medical care
- Meals
- Administration and maintenance
- Garden
- Parking
- Other

Future of the Old 1990–98

Women Aged 65 and over, by State 1990

Proportion of women aged 65 and over in the total female population, in percent

20.4
16.3
15.1
14.2
12.5
4.6

Living Arrangements and Economic Status of People Aged 65 and over 1990

Women
Men

proportion of men and women in each kind of arrangement, in percent

	Women	Men
Married couples households	6	6
Living alone	26	17
Living with relatives	6	7
Living with nonrelatives	45	30
Group quarters or institutions	no	

percent in poverty

Life Expectancy at Age 60, OECD Member Countries 1996

Women
Men

Number of years expected to be lived after 60

Japan
France
Switzerland
Canada (1995)
Spain
Belgium
Sweden
Australia
Norway
Iceland (1995)
Italy (1994)
Finland
Austria
New Zealand (1995)
Greece
United States
Germany
Netherlands
Luxembourg (1991)
Mexico
United Kingdom (1994)
Portugal
Denmark (1995)
Ireland (1991)
Poland (1995)
Czech Republic (1995)
Korea (1995)
Hungary
Turkey (1990)

Age expected to be reached

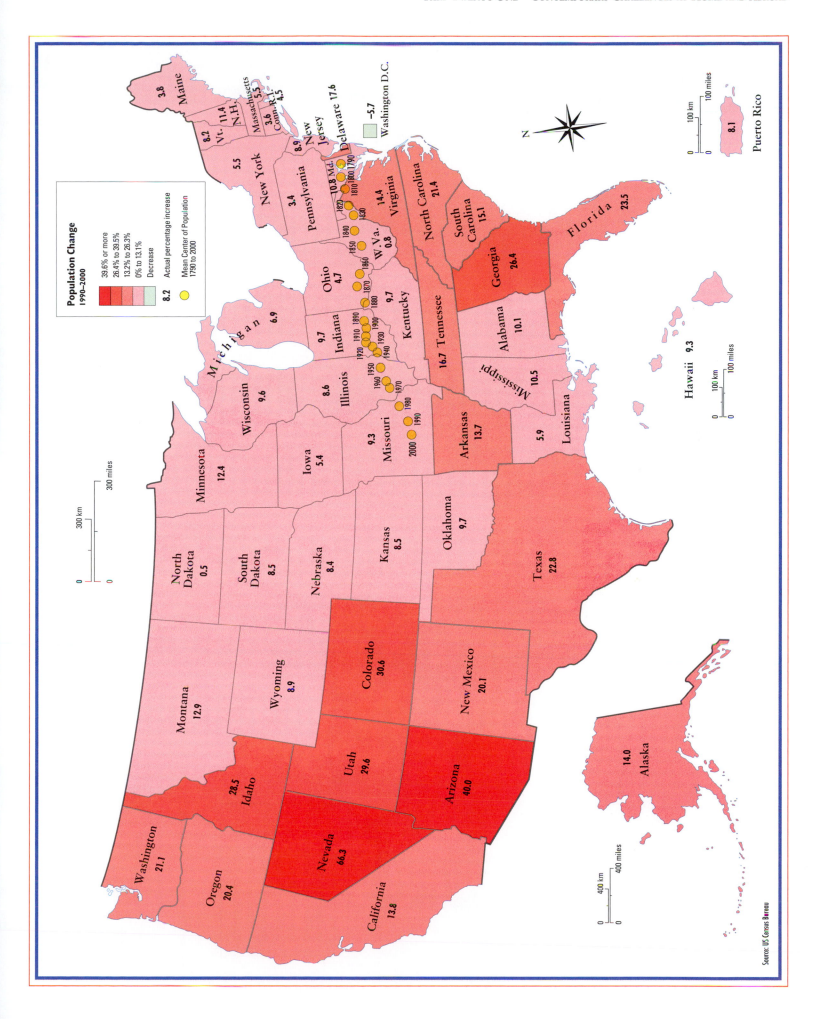

Population Change
1990–2000

39.6% or more
26.4% to 39.5%
13.2% to 26.3%
0% to 13.1%
Decrease

8.2   Actual percentage increase

○   Mean Center of Population
     1790 to 2000

Maine 3.8
Vt. 8.2
N.H. 11.4
Massachusetts 5.5
Conn. 3.6
R.I. 4.5
New York 5.5
New Jersey 8.9
Pennsylvania 3.4
Md. 10.8
Delaware 17.6
Washington D.C. −5.7
Virginia 14.4
W. Va. 0.8
North Carolina 21.4
South Carolina 15.1
Florida 23.5
Georgia 26.4
Alabama 10.1
Mississippi 10.5
Tennessee 16.7
Kentucky 9.7
Ohio 4.7
Indiana 9.7
Michigan 6.9
Wisconsin 9.6
Illinois 8.6
Missouri 9.3
Iowa 5.4
Minnesota 12.4
Arkansas 13.7
Louisiana 5.9
Oklahoma 9.7
Kansas 8.5
Nebraska 8.4
South Dakota 8.5
North Dakota 0.5
Texas 22.8
Colorado 30.6
New Mexico 20.1
Wyoming 8.9
Montana 12.9
Utah 29.6
Arizona 40.0
Idaho 28.5
Nevada 66.3
California 13.8
Washington 21.1
Oregon 20.4
Alaska 14.0
Hawaii 9.3
Puerto Rico 8.1

1790 1800 1810 1820 1830 1840 1850 1860 1870 1880 1890 1900 1910 1920 1930 1940 1950 1960 1970 1980 1990 2000

Source: US Census Bureau

251

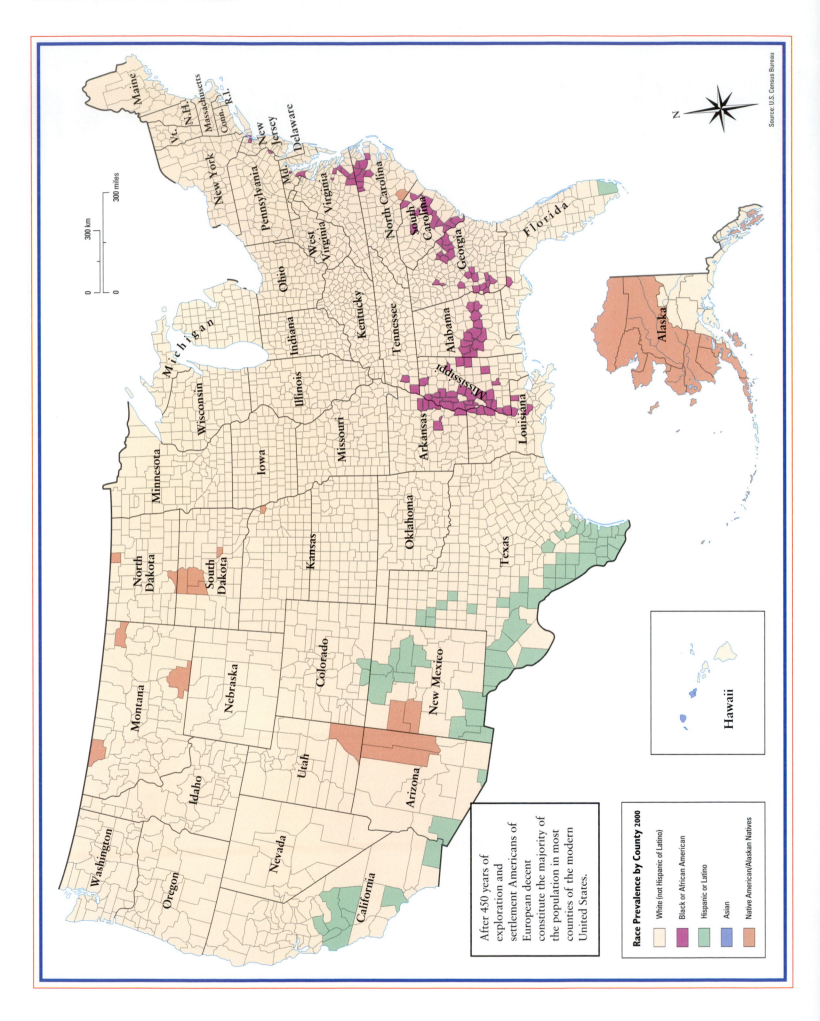

After 450 years of exploration and settlement Americans of European decent constitute the majority of the population in most counties of the modern United States.

Race Prevalence by County 2000

- White (not Hispanic of Latino)
- Black or African American
- Hispanic or Latino
- Asian
- Native American/Alaskan Natives

Source: U.S. Census Bureau

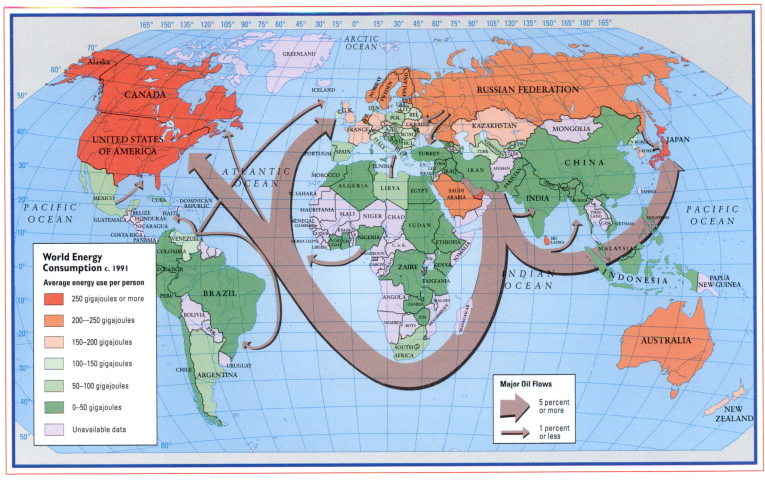

World Energy Consumption c. 1991

Average energy use per person

- 250 gigajoules or more
- 200--250 gigajoules
- 150–200 gigajoules
- 100–150 gigajoules
- 50–100 gigajoules
- 0–50 gigajoules
- Unavailable data

Major Oil Flows

- 5 percent or more
- 1 percent or less

Ethnic Diversity of Former Yugoslavia c. 1990

- Slovenes
- Croatians
- Serbians
- Bosnian Muslims (Slavs converted to Islam after the Ottoman conquest)
- Macedonians
- Germans
- Italians
- Hungarians
- Romanians
- Albanians
- Turks
- Greeks

The potential for ethnic conflict is clearly shown on this map of the former Yugoslavia. These long-standing tensions flared up in the 1990s resulting in savage fighting and ethnic cleansing. Western troops, under UN authority, sought to bring the conflict to an end. The Dayton Peace Accord was approved in 1995, however, sporadic unrest continues.

In December 1904, President Theodore Roosevelt announced that the United States would henceforth function as the "international police power" in the Western Hemisphere. This so-called Roosevelt Corollary to the Monroe doctrine served as the basis for scores of American interventions in the 20th century.

UNITED STATES OF AMERICA

Los Angeles
New York
Philadelphia
Washington

NORTH ATLANTIC OCEAN

Tropic of Cancer

1916
1916
1916
1914
1916
1989
1898–1903, 1906–09, 1917–34, 1994

MEXICO
Mexico City

Miami
Havana

THE BAHAMAS

CUBA
1981–90

1898–1902: U.S. protectorate
1902–58: under U.S. influence
1961: U.S.–supported emigre invasion
1962: Soviet nuclear missiles removed because of U.S. blockade,
O.A.S. membership suspended

DOMINICAN REP.
1905–41: U.S. protectorate
1965: invaded by U.S. forces to restore order

BELIZE

GUATEMALA
1954

1912–19, 1924–25: U.S. protectorate

HONDURAS

EL SALVADOR

NICARAGUA
1912–25, 1926–33: U.S. protectorate

JAMAICA
1972–80

HAITI
1915–36: U.S. protectorate

PANAMA
1903–39: U.S. possession
1968–82

1981–90

COSTA RICA

1903: U.S. possession
1914: Canal opened
Canal Zone leased to U.S
1978: Canal Zone abolished
U.S. personnel withdrawn 2000

Puerto Rico
1898: ceded to U.S.

ST. VINCENT

ANTIGUA

DOMINICA
ST. LUCIA
BARBADOS
GRENADA 1983

Virgin Is.
1917: protectorate acquired from Denmark

TRINIDAD AND TOBAGO

VENEZUELA
1895: under U.S. influence

Caracas

GUYANA
Suriname

French Guiana

Bogotá

COLOMBIA

ECUADOR 1972–76
Quito

Belém

Manaus

PACIFIC OCEAN

PERU
Lima
1968–75

BOLIVIA
1970–71
La Paz

BRAZIL
Brasília
1960: new capital founded

Río de Janeiro
São Paulo

PARAGUAY
Asunción

Tropic of Capricorn

CHILE
Santiago 1973

ARGENTINA

URUGUAY
Montevideo

Buenos Aires

SOUTH ATLANTIC OCEAN

Falkland Is.

N

U.S. Influence in Latin America

→ U.S. military intervention

U.S. expansion, 1898–1945

▪ U.S. possession

▪ U.S. protectorate

▪ Under U.S. influence

U.S. and South America, 1945–85

☆ Overthrow, or attempted overthrow, of left-wing regime by U.S. or U.S.-supported forces

★ Other left-wing regime

◆ Suspended diplomatic relations with U.S., 1960s

✹ Cuban-inspired guerrillas, 1960s

▪ O.A.S. member, 1961

▪ O.A.S. member by 1965

▲ Contributed to Inter-American Peace Force in Dominican Republic, 1965

⊙ Received aid from U.S. under Alliance for Progress program, 1961–70

▪ British Commonwealth

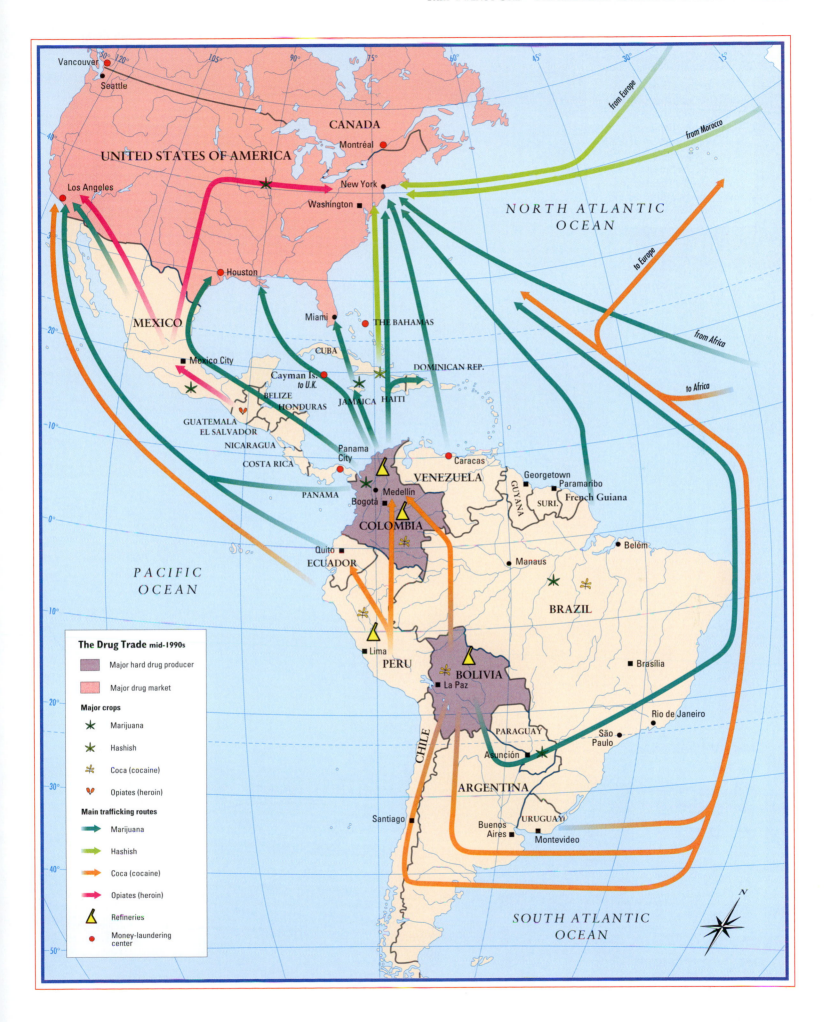

The Drug Trade mid-1990s

Major hard drug producer

Major drug market

Major crops

Marijuana

Hashish

Coca (cocaine)

Opiates (heroin)

Main trafficking routes

Marijuana

Hashish

Coca (cocaine)

Opiates (heroin)

Refineries

Money-laundering center

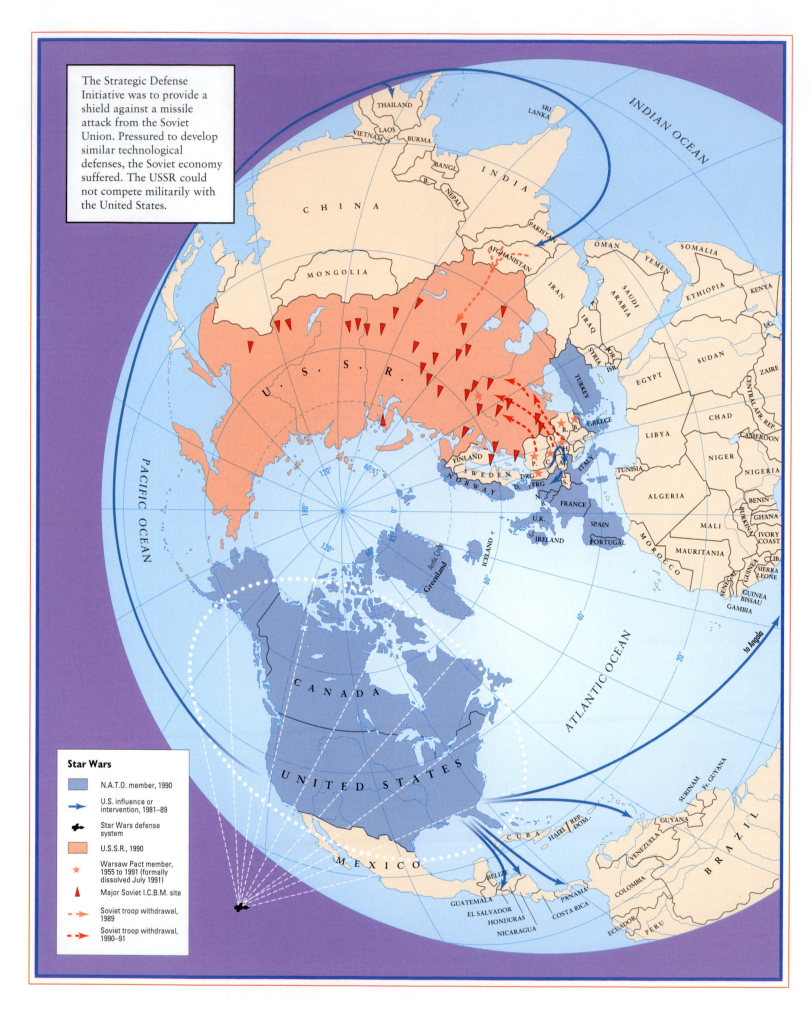

The Strategic Defense Initiative was to provide a shield against a missile attack from the Soviet Union. Pressured to develop similar technological defenses, the Soviet economy suffered. The USSR could not compete militarily with the United States.

Star Wars

N.A.T.O. member, 1990

U.S. influence or intervention, 1981–89

Star Wars defense system

U.S.S.R., 1990

Warsaw Pact member, 1955 to 1991 (formally dissolved July 1991)

Major Soviet I.C.B.M. site

Soviet troop withdrawal, 1989

Soviet troop withdrawal, 1990–91

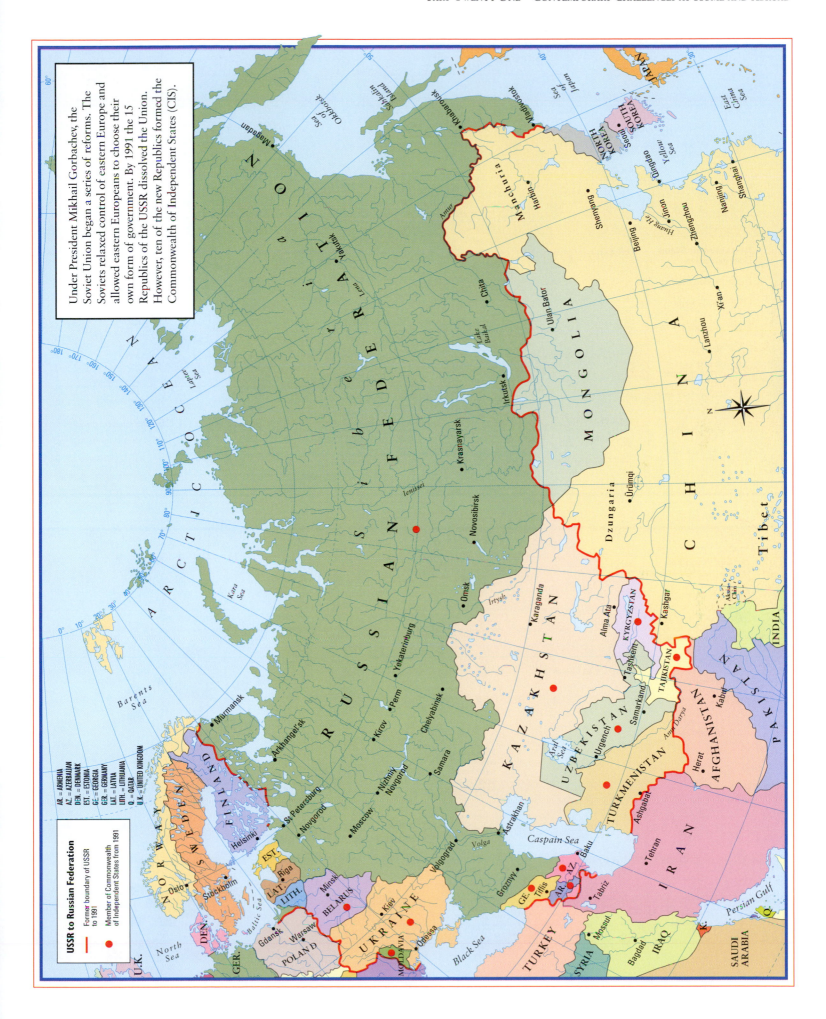

Under President Mikhail Gorbachev, the Soviet Union began a series of reforms. The Soviets relaxed control of eastern Europe and allowed eastern Europeans to choose their own form of government. By 1991 the 15 Republics of the USSR dissolved the Union. However, ten of the new Republics formed the Commonwealth of Independent States (CIS).

USSR to Russian Federation

—— Former boundary of USSR to 1991

● Member of Commonwealth of Independent States from 1991

AR. = ARMENIA
AZ. = AZERBAIJAN
DEN. = DENMARK
EST. = ESTONIA
GE. = GEORGIA
GER. = GERMANY
LAT. = LATVIA
LITH. = LITHUANIA
Q = QATAR
U.K. = UNITED KINGDOM

New European States Emerge 1991–93

- Reunited, 1990
- New state, 1991
- New state, 1992
- New state, 1993
- Area not under control of the new government
- Capital of new state
- Russian Federation
- Border of USSR to 1991
- Ex-Soviet satellite states

1. Serbian backed "Independent Krajina"
2. Serbian and Croatian populations seize control of their own ethnic areas
3. Russian majority form Transnistrian Republic
4. Gagauzian separatist movement
5. Abkhazian separatist movement
6. South Ossetian separatist movement
7. Chechenian separatist movement
8. Armenian population struggle to control Nagorno-Karabakh and adjacent territory to the south

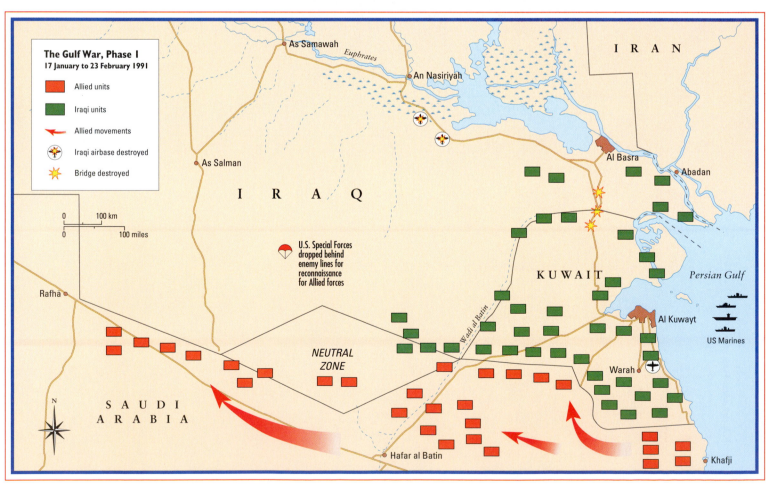

The Gulf War, Phase I
17 January to 23 February 1991

- Allied units
- Iraqi units
- Allied movements
- Iraqi airbase destroyed
- Bridge destroyed
- U.S. Special Forces dropped behind enemy lines for reconnaissance for Allied forces

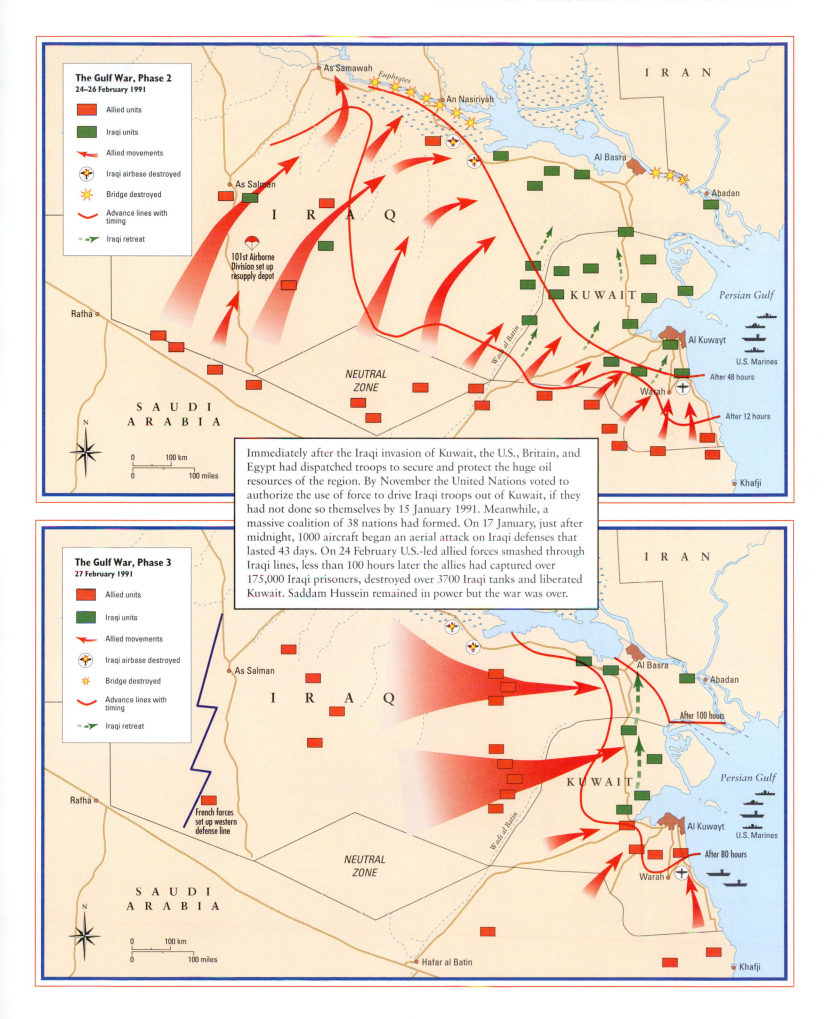

The Gulf War, Phase 2
24–26 February 1991

- ■ Allied units
- ■ Iraqi units
- ➤ Allied movements
- ⊛ Iraqi airbase destroyed
- ✶ Bridge destroyed
- ⌒ Advance lines with timing
- ⇢ Iraqi retreat

As Samawah
Euphrates
An Nasiriyah
IRAN
Al Basra
Abadan

As Salman

IRAQ

101st Airborne Division set up resupply depot

Rafha

KUWAIT

Persian Gulf

NEUTRAL ZONE

SAUDI ARABIA

N

0   100 km
0   100 miles

Al Kuwayt
U.S. Marines

After 48 hours

Warah
After 12 hours

Khafji

Immediately after the Iraqi invasion of Kuwait, the U.S., Britain, and Egypt had dispatched troops to secure and protect the huge oil resources of the region. By November the United Nations voted to authorize the use of force to drive Iraqi troops out of Kuwait, if they had not done so themselves by 15 January 1991. Meanwhile, a massive coalition of 38 nations had formed. On 17 January, just after midnight, 1000 aircraft began an aerial attack on Iraqi defenses that lasted 43 days. On 24 February U.S.-led allied forces smashed through Iraqi lines, less than 100 hours later the allies had captured over 175,000 Iraqi prisoners, destroyed over 3700 Iraqi tanks and liberated Kuwait. Saddam Hussein remained in power but the war was over.

The Gulf War, Phase 3
27 February 1991

- ■ Allied units
- ■ Iraqi units
- ➤ Allied movements
- ⊛ Iraqi airbase destroyed
- ✶ Bridge destroyed
- ⌒ Advance lines with timing
- ⇢ Iraqi retreat

IRAN

As Salman

IRAQ

Al Basra
Abadan

After 100 hours

Rafha

French forces set up western defense line

KUWAIT

Persian Gulf

NEUTRAL ZONE

SAUDI ARABIA

N

0   100 km
0   100 miles

Al Kuwayt
U.S. Marines

After 80 hours

Warah

Hafar al Batin

Khafji

259

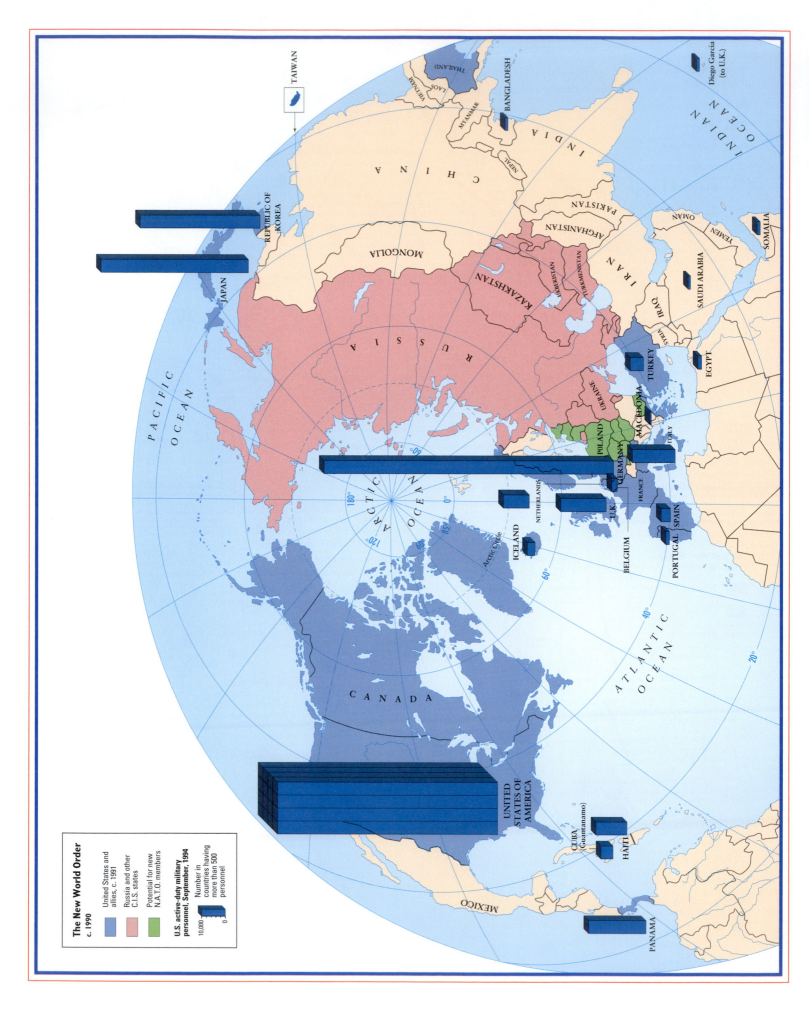

The New World Order
c. 1990

United States and
allies, c. 1991

Russia and other
C.I.S. states

Potential for new
N.A.T.O. members

**U.S. active-duty military
personnel, September, 1994**

Number in
countries having
more than 500
personnel

10,000

0

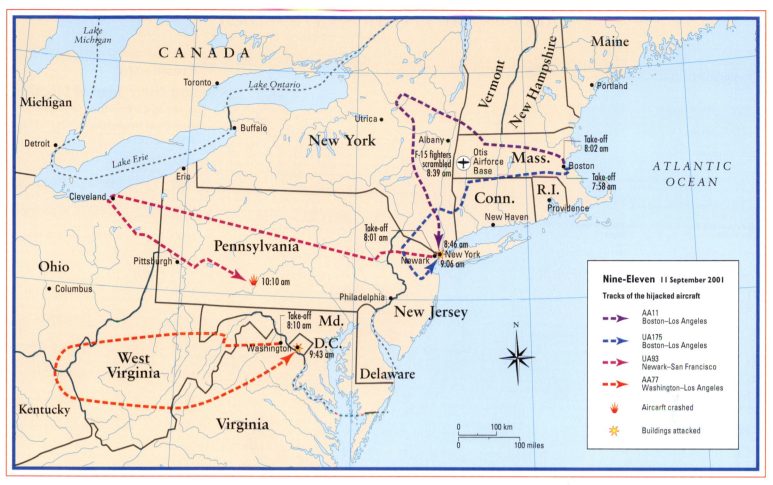

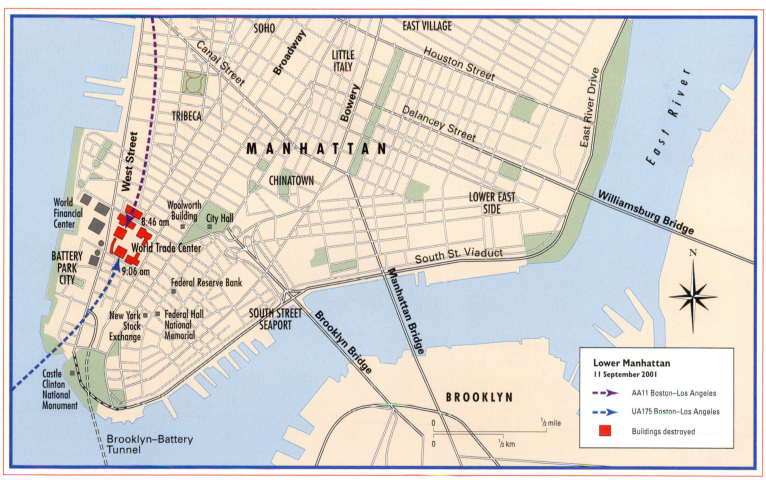

PRESIDENTIAL ELECTIONS 1789–2000

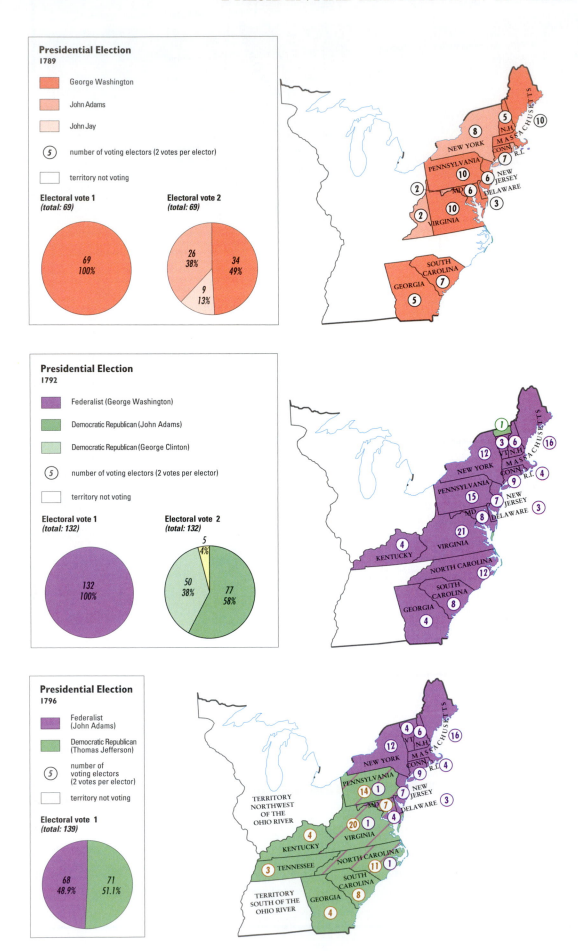

Presidential Election
1789

- George Washington
- John Adams
- John Jay

(5) number of voting electors (2 votes per elector)

⬜ territory not voting

Electoral vote 1
(total: 69)

69
100%

Electoral vote 2
(total: 69)

26
38%

9
13%

34
49%

Presidential Election
1792

- Federalist (George Washington)
- Democratic Republican (John Adams)
- Democratic Republican (George Clinton)

(5) number of voting electors (2 votes per elector)

⬜ territory not voting

Electoral vote 1
(total: 132)

132
100%

Electoral vote 2
(total: 132)

5
4%

50
38%

77
58%

Presidential Election
1796

- Federalist (John Adams)
- Democratic Republican (Thomas Jefferson)

(5) number of voting electors (2 votes per elector)

⬜ territory not voting

Electoral vote 1
(total: 139)

68
48.9%

71
51.1%

Presidents and their Year of Election

Excepting the Presidents serving under exceptional circumstances: 1841, 1865, 1881, and 1974

1789	George Washington
1792	George Washington
1800	Thomas Jefferson
1804	Thomas Jefferson
1808	James Madison
1812	James Madison
1816	James Monroe
1820	James Monroe
1824	John Quincy Adams
1828	Andrew Jackson
1832	Andrew Jackson
1836	Martin Van Buren
1840	William Henry Harrison
1841	John Tyler (Presdient after the death of William H Harrison)
1844	James K Polk
1848	Zachary Taylor
1852	Franklin Pierce
1856	James Buchanan
1860	Abraham Lincoln
1864	Abraham Lincoln
1865	Andrew Johnson (President after the assassination of Abraham Lincoln)
1868	Ulysses S Grant
1872	Ulysses S Grant
1876	Rutherford B N Hayes
1880	James Garfield
1881	Chester A Arthur (President after the assassination of James Garfield)

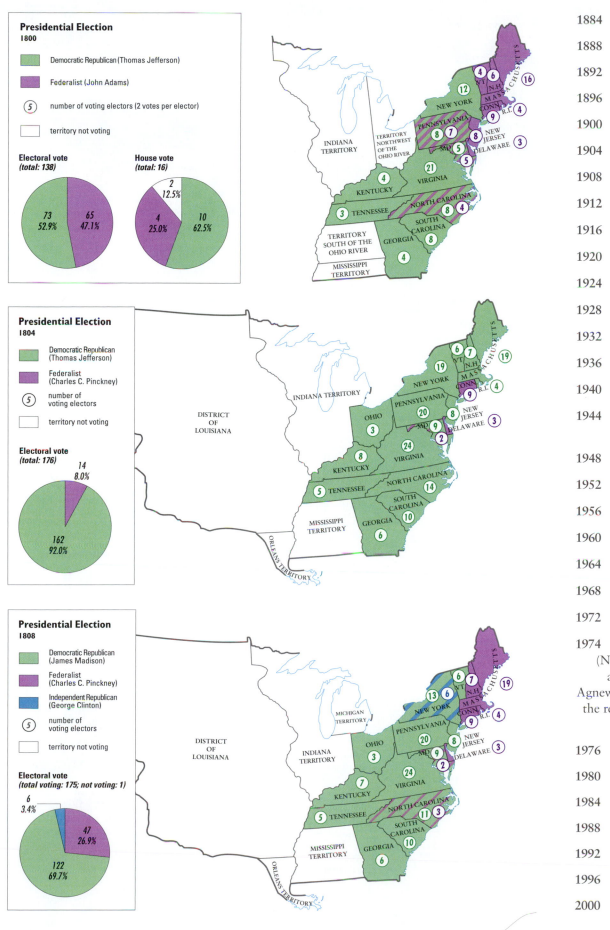

Presidential Election
1800

- Democratic Republican (Thomas Jefferson)
- Federalist (John Adams)

⑤ number of voting electors (2 votes per elector)

☐ territory not voting

Electoral vote
(total: 138)

73 52.9%
65 47.1%

House vote
(total: 16)

4 25.0%
10 62.5%
2 12.5%

Presidential Election
1804

- Democratic Republican (Thomas Jefferson)
- Federalist (Charles C. Pinckney)

⑤ number of voting electors

☐ territory not voting

Electoral vote
(total: 176)

14 8.0%
162 92.0%

Presidential Election
1808

- Democratic Republican (James Madison)
- Federalist (Charles C. Pinckney)
- Independent Republican (George Clinton)

⑤ number of voting electors

☐ territory not voting

Electoral vote
(total voting: 175; not voting: 1)

6 3.4%
47 26.9%
122 69.7%

1884	Grover Cleveland
1888	Benjamin Harrison
1892	Grover Cleveland
1896	William McKinley
1900	William McKinley
1904	Theodore Roosevelt
1908	William H Taft
1912	Woodrow Wilson
1916	Woodrow Wilson
1920	Warren G Harding
1924	Calvin Coolidge
1928	Herbert C Hoover
1932	Franklin D Roosevelt
1936	Franklin D Roosevelt
1940	Franklin D Roosevelt
1944	Franklin D Roosevelt (Died in office)
1948	Harry S Truman
1952	Dwight D Eisenhower
1956	Dwight D Eisenhower
1960	John F Kennedy
1964	Lyndon B Johnson
1968	Richard M Nixon
1972	Richard M Nixon
1974	Gerald R Ford (Nominated to Vice Presidency after the resignation of Spiro Agnew, 1973. Became President on the resignation of Richard Nixon in 1974)
1976	Jimmy Carter
1980	Ronald Reagan
1984	Ronald Reagan
1988	George Bush
1992	William J Clinton
1996	William J Clinton
2000	George W Bush

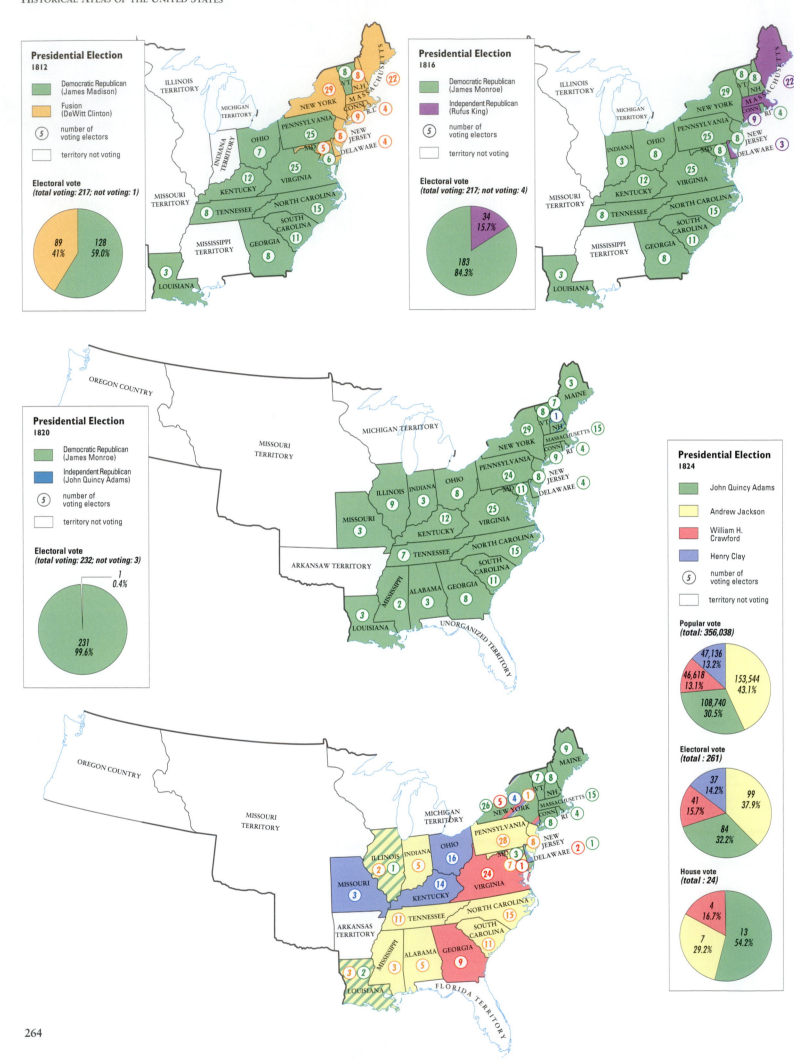

Presidential Election
1812

- Democratic Republican (James Madison)
- Fusion (DeWitt Clinton)
- ⑤ number of voting electors
- territory not voting

Electoral vote
(total voting: 217; not voting: 1)

89 41%
128 59.0%

Presidential Election
1816

- Democratic Republican (James Monroe)
- Independent Republican (Rufus King)
- ⑤ number of voting electors
- territory not voting

Electoral vote
(total voting: 217; not voting: 4)

34 15.7%
183 84.3%

Presidential Election
1820

- Democratic Republican (James Monroe)
- Independent Republican (John Quincy Adams)
- ⑤ number of voting electors
- territory not voting

Electoral vote
(total voting: 232; not voting: 3)

1 0.4%
231 99.6%

Presidential Election
1824

- John Quincy Adams
- Andrew Jackson
- William H. Crawford
- Henry Clay
- ⑤ number of voting electors
- territory not voting

Popular vote
(total: 356,038)

47,136 13.2%
46,618 13.1%
108,740 30.5%
153,544 43.1%

Electoral vote
(total : 261)

37 14.2%
41 15.7%
99 37.9%
84 32.2%

House vote
(total : 24)

4 16.7%
7 29.2%
13 54.2%

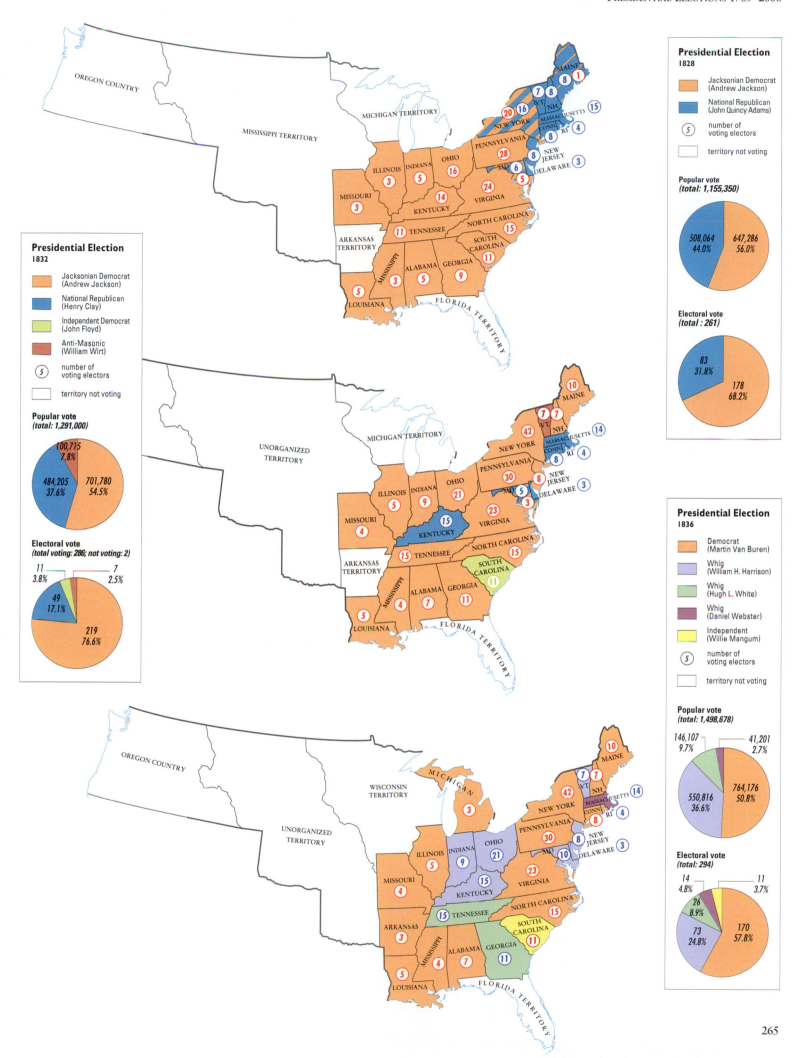

Presidential Election 1828

- Jacksonian Democrat (Andrew Jackson)
- National Republican (John Quincy Adams)
- ⑤ number of voting electors
- territory not voting

Popular vote (total: 1,155,350)
- 508,064 / 44.0%
- 647,286 / 56.0%

Electoral vote (total: 261)
- 83 / 31.8%
- 178 / 68.2%

Presidential Election 1832

- Jacksonian Democrat (Andrew Jackson)
- National Republican (Henry Clay)
- Independent Democrat (John Floyd)
- Anti-Masonic (William Wirt)
- ⑤ number of voting electors
- territory not voting

Popular vote (total: 1,291,000)
- 100,715 / 7.8%
- 484,205 / 37.6%
- 701,780 / 54.5%

Electoral vote (total voting: 286; not voting: 2)
- 11 / 3.8%
- 7 / 2.5%
- 49 / 17.1%
- 219 / 76.6%

Presidential Election 1836

- Democrat (Martin Van Buren)
- Whig (William H. Harrison)
- Whig (Hugh L. White)
- Whig (Daniel Webster)
- Independent (Willie Mangum)
- ⑤ number of voting electors
- territory not voting

Popular vote (total: 1,498,678)
- 146,107 / 9.7%
- 41,201 / 2.7%
- 550,816 / 36.6%
- 764,176 / 50.8%

Electoral vote (total: 294)
- 14 / 4.8%
- 11 / 3.7%
- 26 / 8.9%
- 73 / 24.8%
- 170 / 57.8%

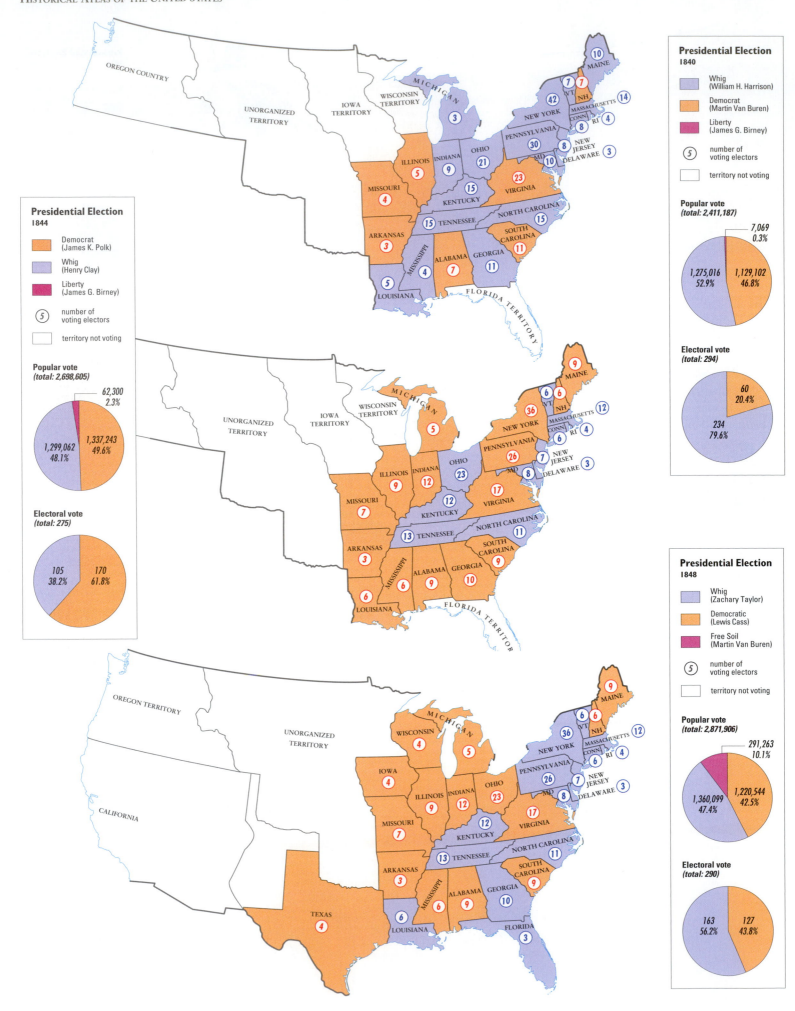

Presidential Election
1840

- Whig (William H. Harrison)
- Democrat (Martin Van Buren)
- Liberty (James G. Birney)
- ⑤ number of voting electors
- territory not voting

Popular vote
(total: 2,411,187)

7,069
0.3%

1,275,016
52.9%

1,129,102
46.8%

Electoral vote
(total: 294)

60
20.4%

234
79.6%

Presidential Election
1844

- Democrat (James K. Polk)
- Whig (Henry Clay)
- Liberty (James G. Birney)
- ⑤ number of voting electors
- territory not voting

Popular vote
(total: 2,698,605)

62,300
2.3%

1,299,062
48.1%

1,337,243
49.6%

Electoral vote
(total: 275)

105
38.2%

170
61.8%

Presidential Election
1848

- Whig (Zachary Taylor)
- Democratic (Lewis Cass)
- Free Soil (Martin Van Buren)
- ⑤ number of voting electors
- territory not voting

Popular vote
(total: 2,871,906)

291,263
10.1%

1,360,099
47.4%

1,220,544
42.5%

Electoral vote
(total: 290)

163
56.2%

127
43.8%

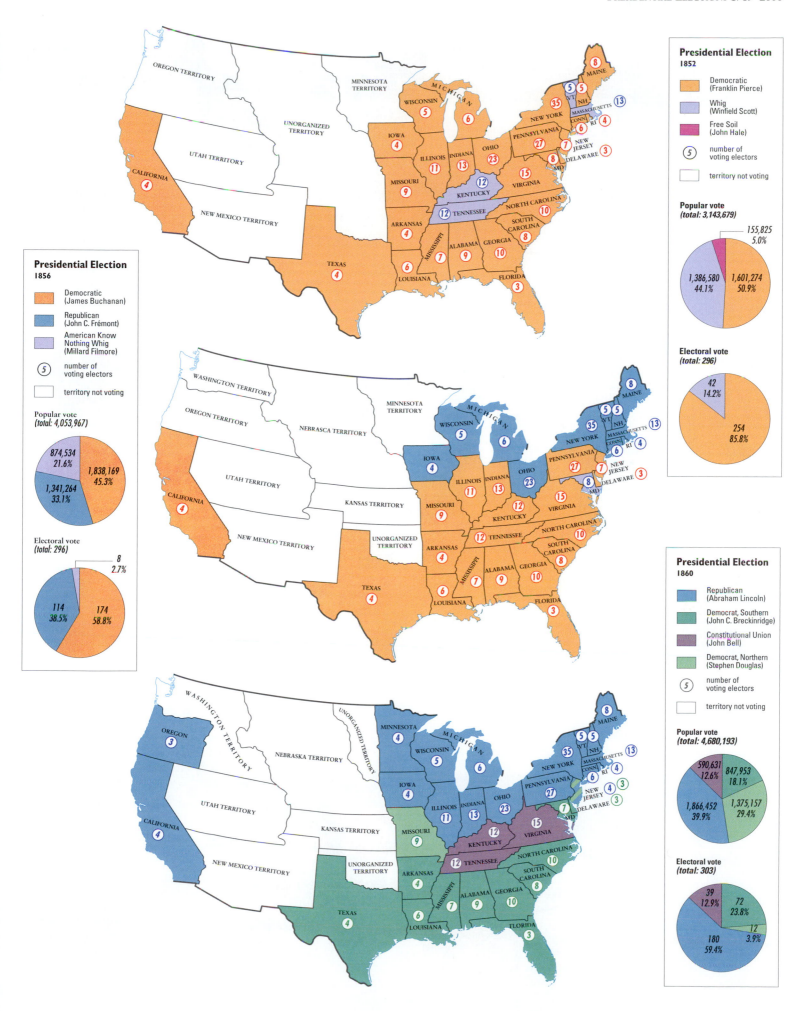

Presidential Election 1852

- Democratic (Franklin Pierce)
- Whig (Winfield Scott)
- Free Soil (John Hale)
- ⑤ number of voting electors
- territory not voting

Popular vote *(total: 3,143,679)*
- 155,825 — 5.0%
- 1,386,580 — 44.1%
- 1,601,274 — 50.9%

Electoral vote *(total: 296)*
- 42 — 14.2%
- 254 — 85.8%

Presidential Election 1856

- Democratic (James Buchanan)
- Republican (John C. Frémont)
- American Know Nothing Whig (Millard Filmore)
- ⑤ number of voting electors
- territory not voting

Popular vote *(total: 4,053,967)*
- 874,534 — 21.6%
- 1,341,264 — 33.1%
- 1,838,169 — 45.3%

Electoral vote *(total: 296)*
- 8 — 2.7%
- 114 — 38.5%
- 174 — 58.8%

Presidential Election 1860

- Republican (Abraham Lincoln)
- Democrat, Southern (John C. Breckinridge)
- Constitutional Union (John Bell)
- Democrat, Northern (Stephen Douglas)
- ⑤ number of voting electors
- territory not voting

Popular vote *(total: 4,680,193)*
- 590,631 — 12.6%
- 847,953 — 18.1%
- 1,866,452 — 39.9%
- 1,375,157 — 29.4%

Electoral vote *(total: 303)*
- 39 — 12.9%
- 72 — 23.8%
- 12 — 3.9%
- 180 — 59.4%

267

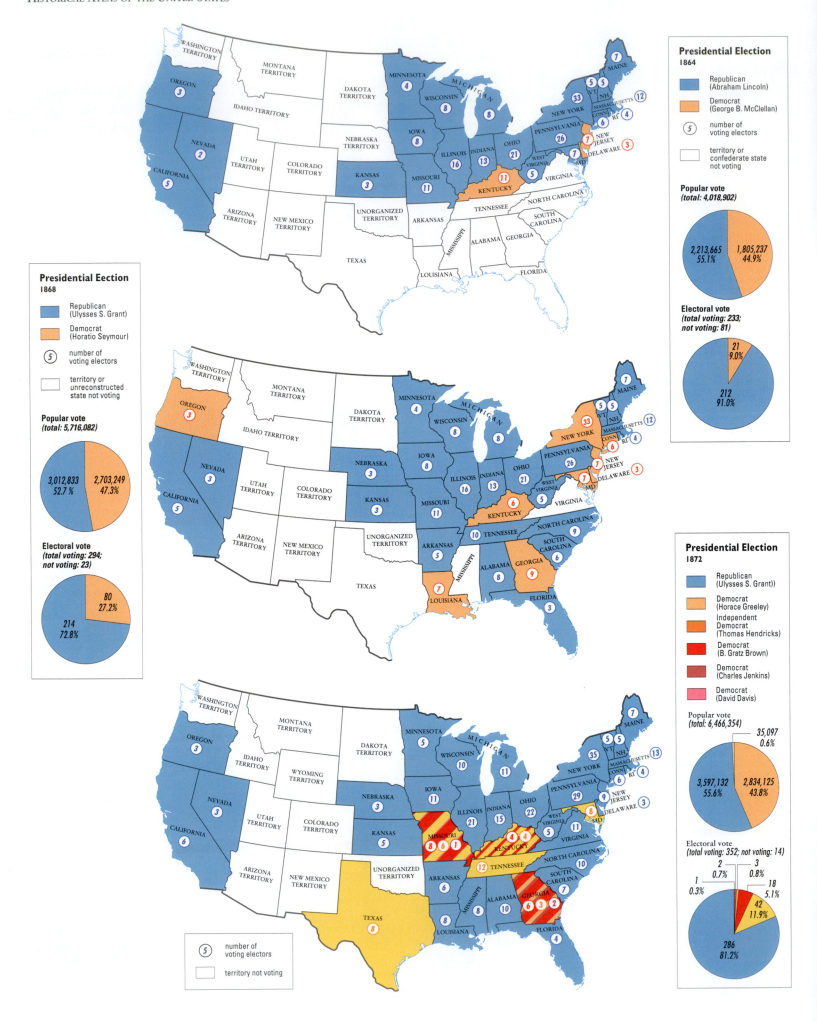

Presidential Election
1864

■ Republican
(Abraham Lincoln)
■ Democrat
(George B. McClellan)
⑤ number of
voting electors
□ territory or
confederate state
not voting

Popular vote
(total: 4,018,902)

2,213,665
55.1%
1,805,237
44.9%

Electoral vote
(total voting: 233;
not voting: 81)

21
9.0%
212
91.0%

Presidential Eection
1868

■ Republican
(Ulysses S. Grant)
■ Democrat
(Horatio Seymour)
⑤ number of
voting electors
□ territory or
unreconstructed
state not voting

Popular vote
(total: 5,716,082)

3,012,833
52.7 %
2,703,249
47.3%

Electoral vote
(total voting: 294;
not voting: 23)

214
72.8%
80
27.2%

Presidential Election
1872

■ Republican
(Ulysses S. Grant))
■ Democrat
(Horace Greeley)
■ Independent
Democrat
(Thomas Hendricks)
■ Democrat
(B. Gratz Brown)
■ Democrat
(Charles Jenkins)
■ Democrat
(David Davis)

Popular vote
(total: 6,466,354)

35,097
0.6%
3,597,132
55.6%
2,834,125
43.8%

Electoral vote
(total voting: 352; not voting: 14)

2
0.7%
3
0.8%
1
0.3%
18
5.1%
42
11.9%
286
81.2%

⑤ number of
voting electors
□ territory not voting

268

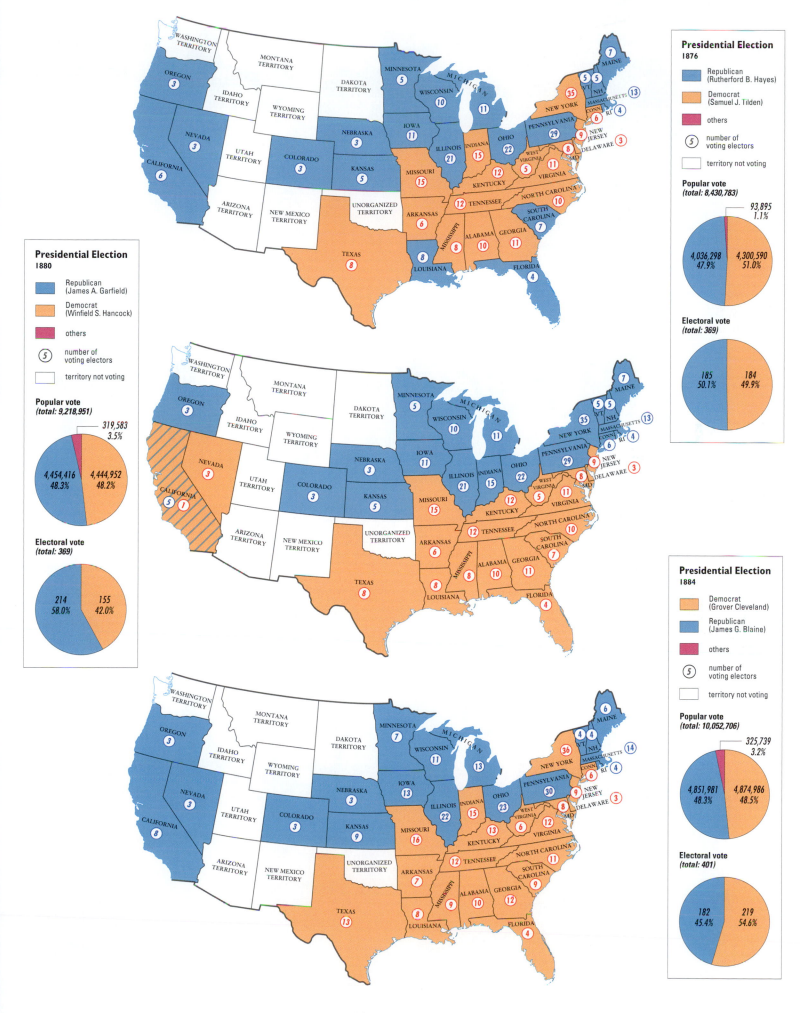

Presidential Election
1876

- ■ Republican (Rutherford B. Hayes)
- ■ Democrat (Samuel J. Tilden)
- ■ others
- ⑤ number of voting electors
- □ territory not voting

Popular vote
(total: 8,430,783)

93,895
1.1%

4,036,298
47.9%

4,300,590
51.0%

Electoral vote
(total: 369)

185
50.1%

184
49.9%

Presidential Election
1880

- ■ Republican (James A. Garfield)
- ■ Democrat (Winfield S. Hancock)
- ■ others
- ⑤ number of voting electors
- □ territory not voting

Popular vote
(total: 9,218,951)

319,583
3.5%

4,454,416
48.3%

4,444,952
48.2%

Electoral vote
(total: 369)

214
58.0%

155
42.0%

Presidential Election
1884

- ■ Democrat (Grover Cleveland)
- ■ Republican (James G. Blaine)
- ■ others
- ⑤ number of voting electors
- □ territory not voting

Popular vote
(total: 10,052,706)

325,739
3.2%

4,851,981
48.3%

4,874,986
48.5%

Electoral vote
(total: 401)

182
45.4%

219
54.6%

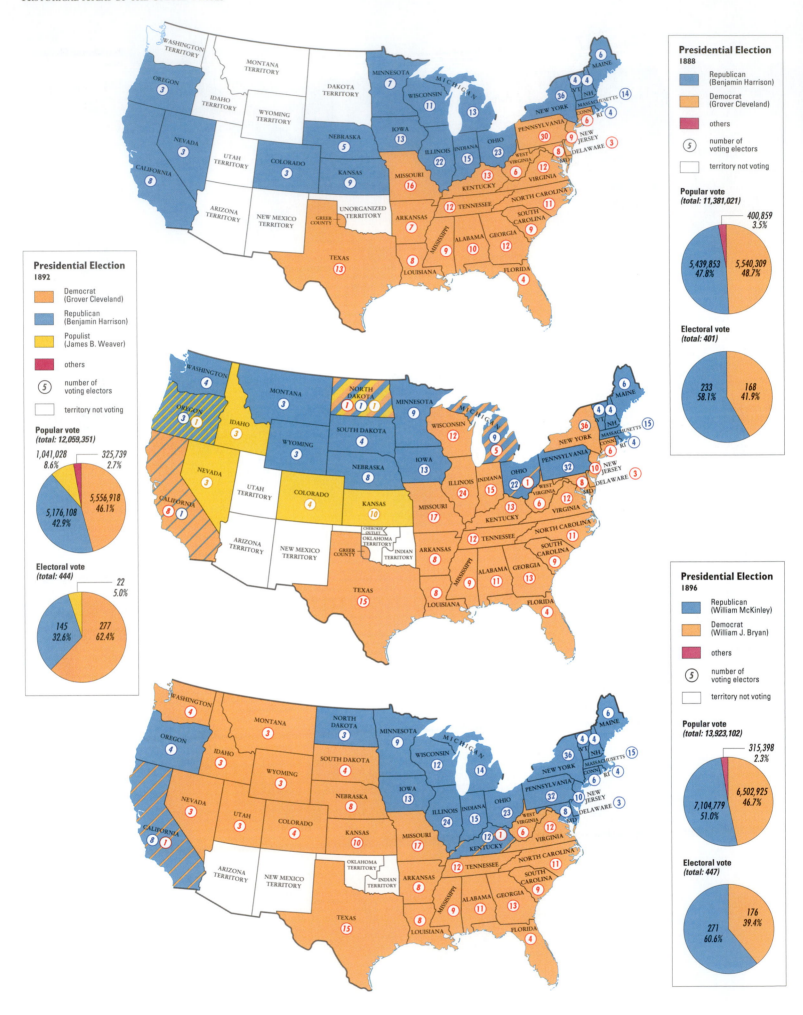

Presidential Election
1888

- Republican (Benjamin Harrison)
- Democrat (Grover Cleveland)
- others
- ⑤ number of voting electors
- territory not voting

Popular vote (total: 11,381,021)

400,859
3.5%

5,439,853
47.8%

5,540,309
48.7%

Electoral vote (total: 401)

233
58.1%

168
41.9%

Presidential Election
1892

- Democrat (Grover Cleveland)
- Republican (Benjamin Harrison)
- Populist (James B. Weaver)
- others
- ⑤ number of voting electors
- territory not voting

Popular vote (total: 12,059,351)

1,041,028
8.6%

325,739
2.7%

5,556,918
46.1%

5,176,108
42.9%

Electoral vote (total: 444)

22
5.0%

145
32.6%

277
62.4%

Presidential Election
1896

- Republican (William McKinley)
- Democrat (William J. Bryan)
- others
- ⑤ number of voting electors
- territory not voting

Popular vote (total: 13,923,102)

315,398
2.3%

7,104,779
51.0%

6,502,925
46.7%

Electoral vote (total: 447)

271
60.6%

176
39.4%

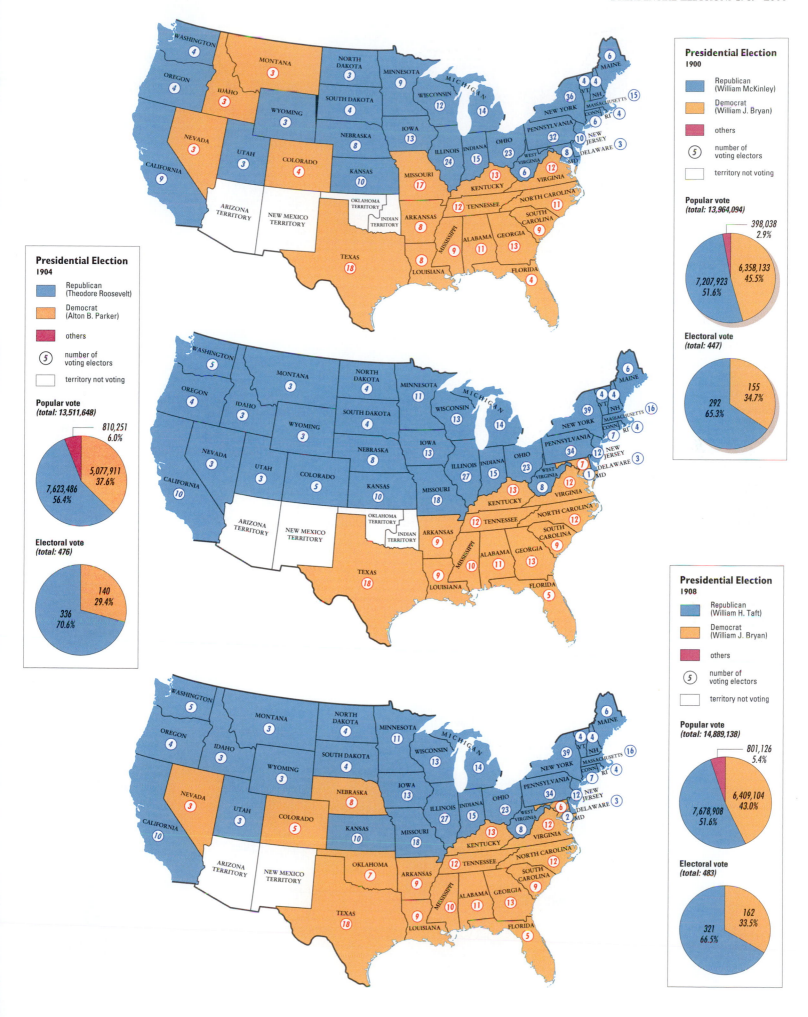

Presidential Election 1900

- Republican (William McKinley)
- Democrat (William J. Bryan)
- others
- ⑤ number of voting electors
- territory not voting

Popular vote (total: 13,964,094)

398,038 2.9%
7,207,923 51.6%
6,358,133 45.5%

Electoral vote (total: 447)

292 65.3%
155 34.7%

Presidential Election 1904

- Republican (Theodore Roosevelt)
- Democrat (Alton B. Parker)
- others
- ⑤ number of voting electors
- territory not voting

Popular vote (total: 13,511,648)

810,251 6.0%
7,623,486 56.4%
5,077,911 37.6%

Electoral vote (total: 476)

336 70.6%
140 29.4%

Presidential Election 1908

- Republican (William H. Taft)
- Democrat (William J. Bryan)
- others
- ⑤ number of voting electors
- territory not voting

Popular vote (total: 14,889,138)

801,126 5.4%
7,678,908 51.6%
6,409,104 43.0%

Electoral vote (total: 483)

321 66.5%
162 33.5%

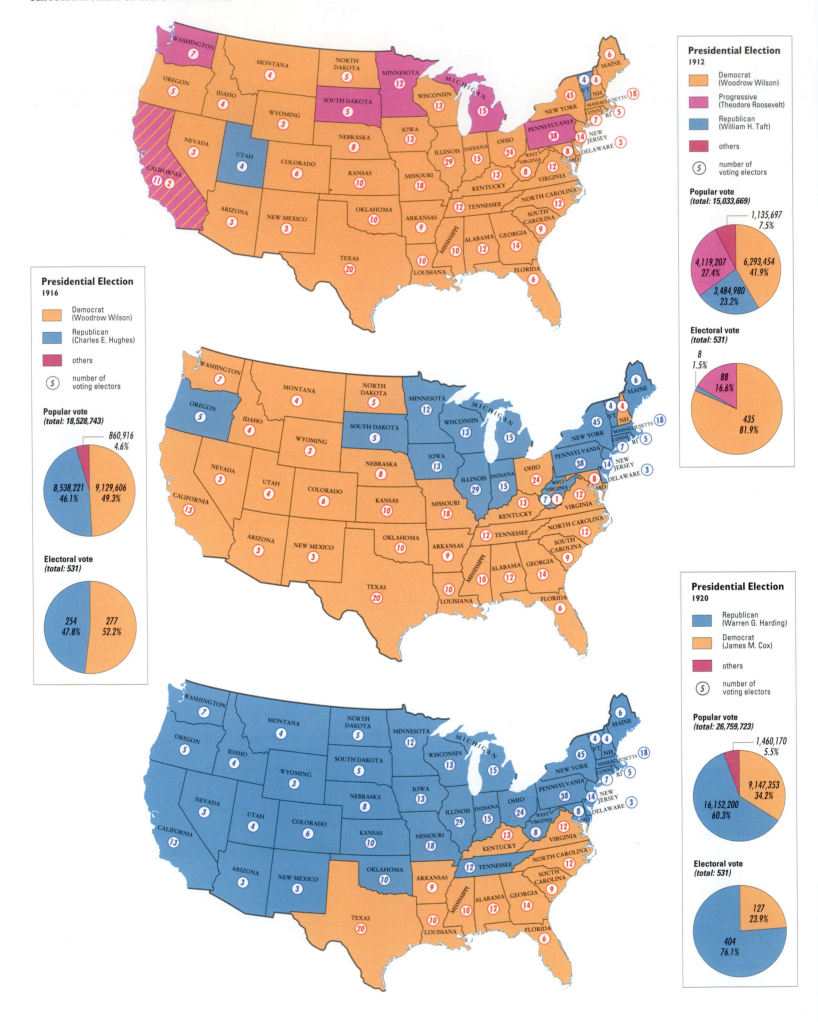

Presidential Election
1912

- ▮ Democrat (Woodrow Wilson)
- ▮ Progressive (Theodore Roosevelt)
- ▮ Republican (William H. Taft)
- ▮ others

⑤ number of voting electors

Popular vote (total: 15,033,669)

- 1,135,697 — 7.5%
- 4,119,207 — 27.4%
- 3,484,980 — 23.2%
- 6,293,454 — 41.9%

Electoral vote (total: 531)

- 8 — 1.5%
- 88 — 16.6%
- 435 — 81.9%

Presidential Election
1916

- ▮ Democrat (Woodrow Wilson)
- ▮ Republican (Charles E. Hughes)
- ▮ others

⑤ number of voting electors

Popular vote (total: 18,528,743)

- 860,916 — 4.6%
- 8,538,221 — 46.1%
- 9,129,606 — 49.3%

Electoral vote (total: 531)

- 254 — 47.8%
- 277 — 52.2%

Presidential Election
1920

- ▮ Republican (Warren G. Harding)
- ▮ Democrat (James M. Cox)
- ▮ others

⑤ number of voting electors

Popular vote (total: 26,759,723)

- 1,460,170 — 5.5%
- 9,147,353 — 34.2%
- 16,152,200 — 60.3%

Electoral vote (total: 531)

- 127 — 23.9%
- 404 — 76.1%

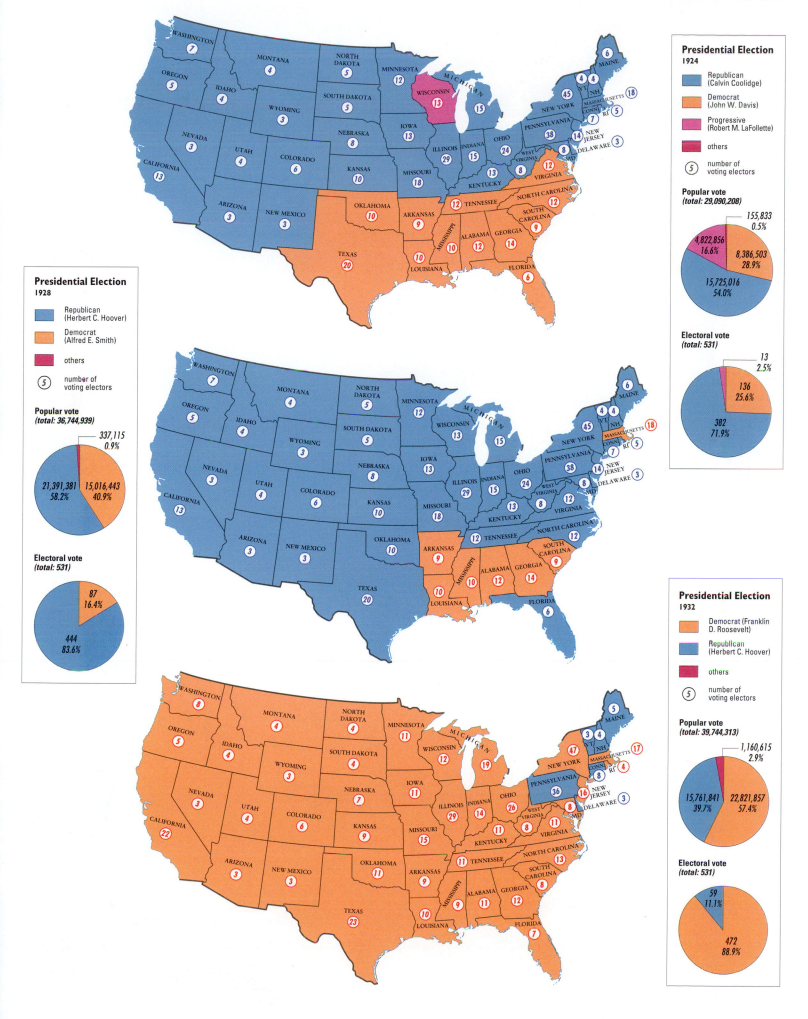

Presidential Election 1924

- Republican (Calvin Coolidge)
- Democrat (John W. Davis)
- Progressive (Robert M. LaFollette)
- others
- ⑤ number of voting electors

Popular vote *(total: 29,090,208)*

- 155,833 0.5%
- 4,822,856 16.6%
- 8,386,503 28.9%
- 15,725,016 54.0%

Electoral vote *(total: 531)*

- 13 2.5%
- 136 25.6%
- 382 71.9%

Presidential Election 1928

- Republican (Herbert C. Hoover)
- Democrat (Alfred E. Smith)
- others
- ⑤ number of voting electors

Popular vote *(total: 36,744,939)*

- 337,115 0.9%
- 21,391,381 58.2%
- 15,016,443 40.9%

Electoral vote *(total: 531)*

- 87 16.4%
- 444 83.6%

Presidential Election 1932

- Democrat (Franklin D. Roosevelt)
- Republican (Herbert C. Hoover)
- others
- ⑤ number of voting electors

Popular vote *(total: 39,744,313)*

- 1,160,615 2.9%
- 15,761,841 39.7%
- 22,821,857 57.4%

Electoral vote *(total: 531)*

- 59 11.1%
- 472 88.9%

273

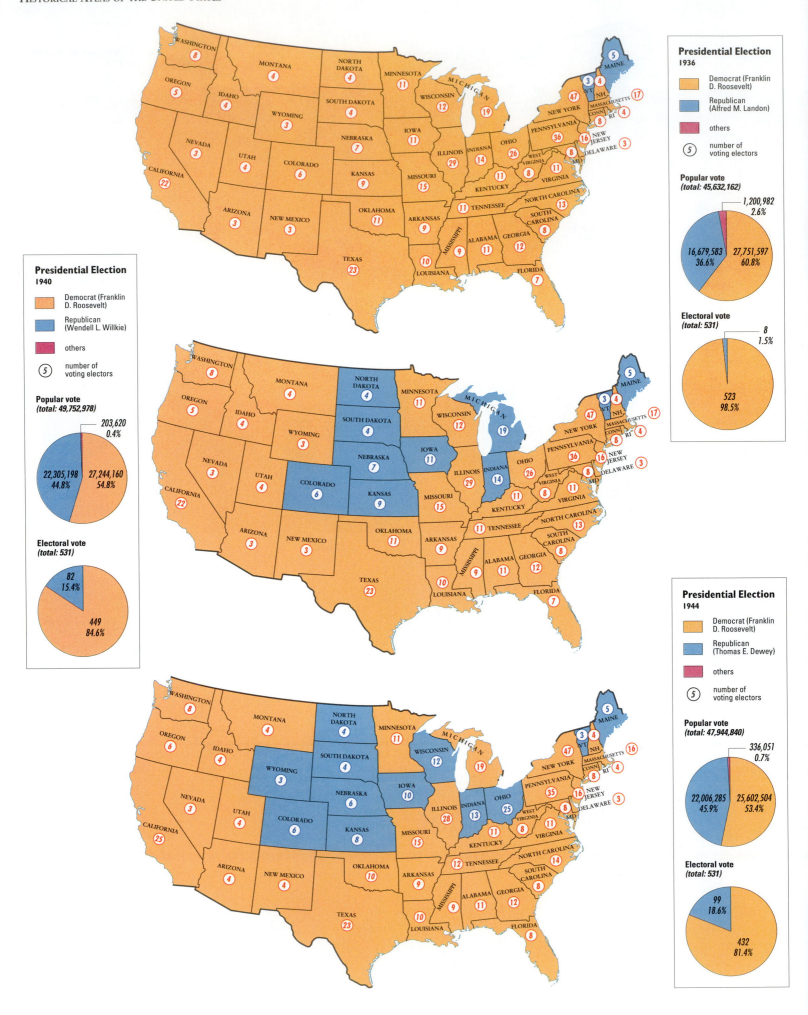

Presidential Election
1936

- Democrat (Franklin D. Roosevelt)
- Republican (Alfred M. Landon)
- others
- ⑤ number of voting electors

Popular vote
(total: 45,632,162)

1,200,982
2.6%

16,679,583
36.6%

27,751,597
60.8%

Electoral vote
(total: 531)

8
1.5%

523
98.5%

Presidential Election
1940

- Democrat (Franklin D. Roosevelt)
- Republican (Wendell L. Willkie)
- others
- ⑤ number of voting electors

Popular vote
(total: 49,752,978)

203,620
0.4%

22,305,198
44.8%

27,244,160
54.8%

Electoral vote
(total: 531)

82
15.4%

449
84.6%

Presidential Election
1944

- Democrat (Franklin D. Roosevelt)
- Republican (Thomas E. Dewey)
- others
- ⑤ number of voting electors

Popular vote
(total: 47,944,840)

336,051
0.7%

22,006,285
45.9%

25,602,504
53.4%

Electoral vote
(total: 531)

99
18.6%

432
81.4%

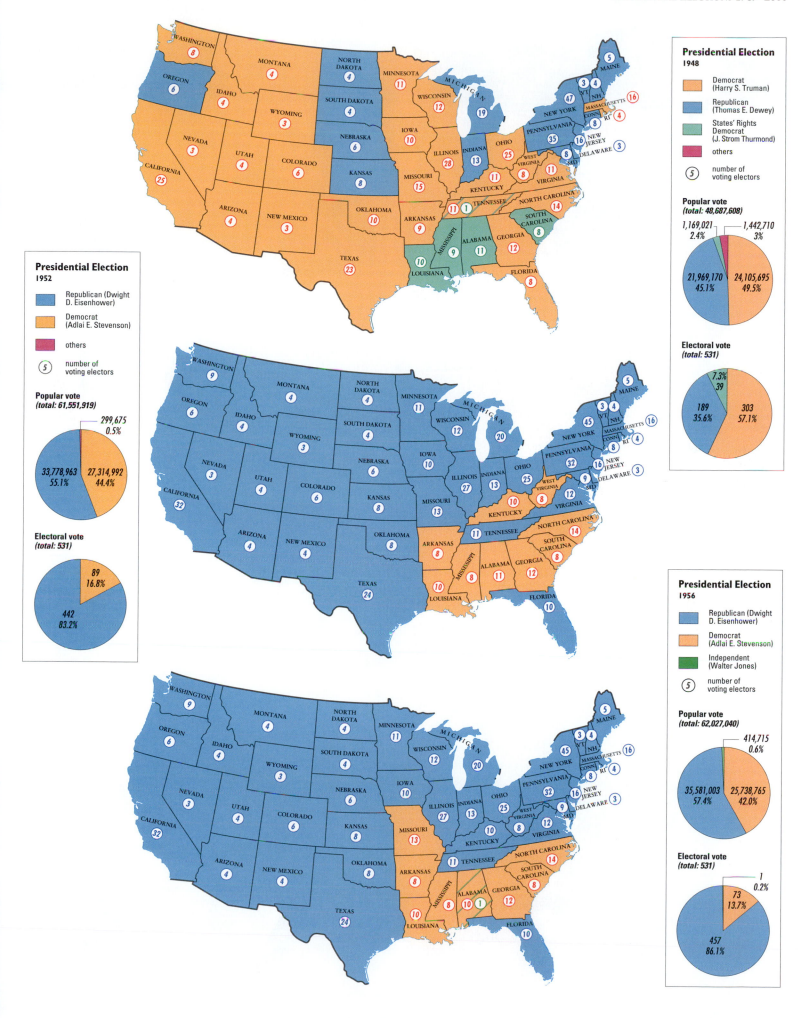

Presidential Election
1948

Democrat
(Harry S. Truman)

Republican
(Thomas E. Dewey)

States' Rights
Democrat
(J. Strom Thurmond)

others

⑤ number of
voting electors

Popular vote
(total: 48,687,608)

1,169,021
2.4%

1,442,710
3%

21,969,170
45.1%

24,105,695
49.5%

Electoral vote
(total: 531)

7.3%
39

189
35.6%

303
57.1%

Presidential Election
1952

Republican (Dwight
D. Eisenhower)

Democrat
(Adlai E. Stevenson)

others

⑤ number of
voting electors

Popular vote
(total: 61,551,919)

299,675
0.5%

33,778,963
55.1%

27,314,992
44.4%

Electoral vote
(total: 531)

89
16.8%

442
83.2%

Presidential Election
1956

Republican (Dwight
D. Eisenhower)

Democrat
(Adlai E. Stevenson)

Independent
(Walter Jones)

⑤ number of
voting electors

Popular vote
(total: 62,027,040)

414,715
0.6%

35,581,003
57.4%

25,738,765
42.0%

Electoral vote
(total: 531)

1
0.2%

73
13.7%

457
86.1%

275

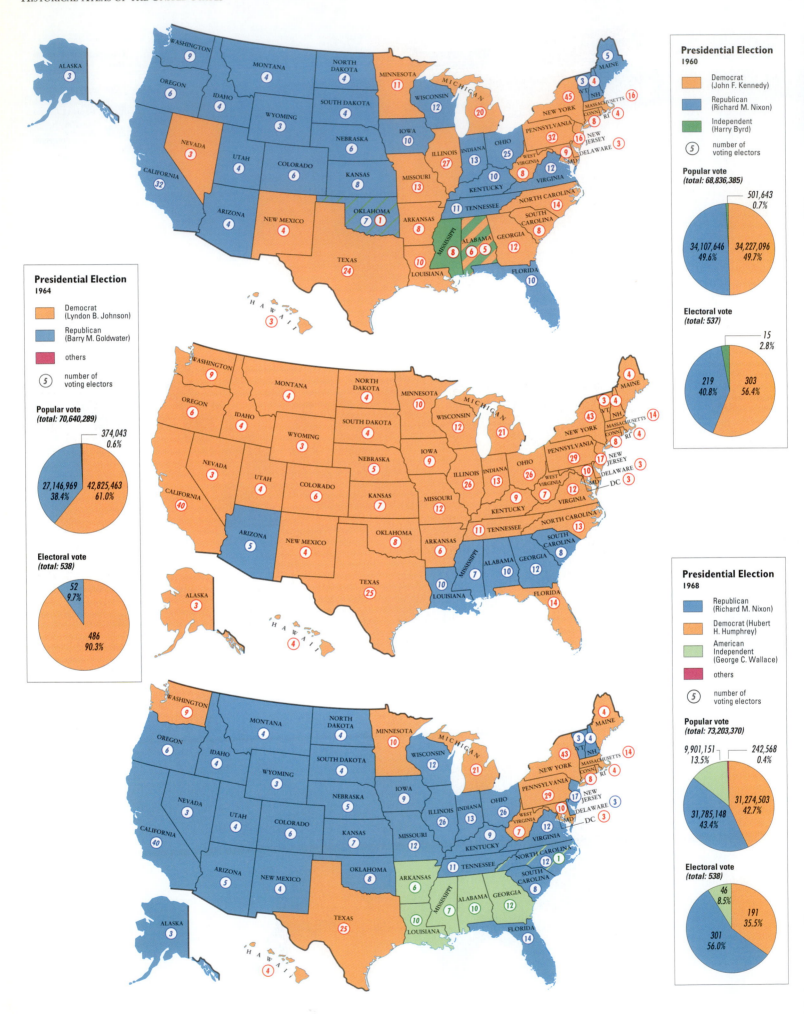

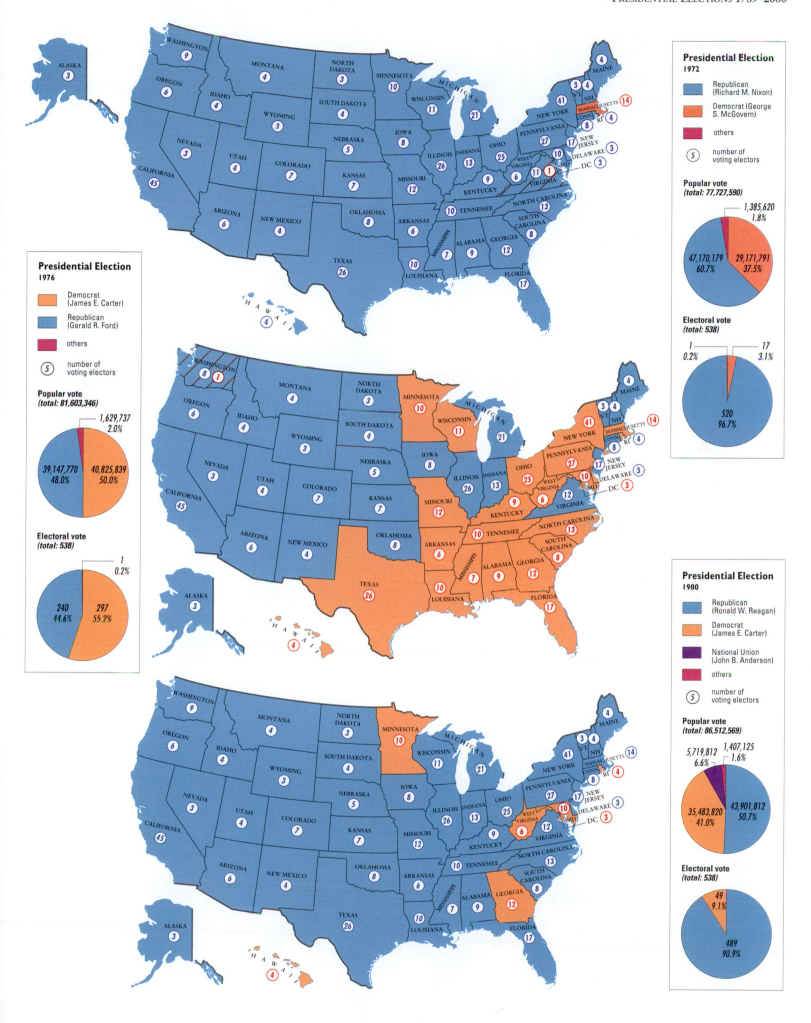

Presidential Election 1972

- Republican (Richard M. Nixon)
- Democrat (George S. McGovern)
- others
- ⑤ number of voting electors

Popular vote *(total: 77,727,590)*

1,385,620 1.8%
47,170,179 60.7%
29,171,791 37.5%

Electoral vote *(total: 538)*

1 0.2%
17 3.1%
520 96.7%

Presidential Election 1976

- Democrat (James E. Carter)
- Republican (Gerald R. Ford)
- others
- ⑤ number of voting electors

Popular vote *(total: 81,603,346)*

1,629,737 2.0%
39,147,770 48.0%
40,825,839 50.0%

Electoral vote *(total: 538)*

1 0.2%
240 44.6%
297 55.2%

Presidential Election 1980

- Republican (Ronald W. Reagan)
- Democrat (James E. Carter)
- National Union (John B. Anderson)
- others
- ⑤ number of voting electors

Popular vote *(total: 86,512,569)*

5,719,812 6.6%
1,407,125 1.6%
43,901,812 50.7%
35,483,820 41.0%

Electoral vote *(total: 538)*

49 9.1%
489 90.9%

277

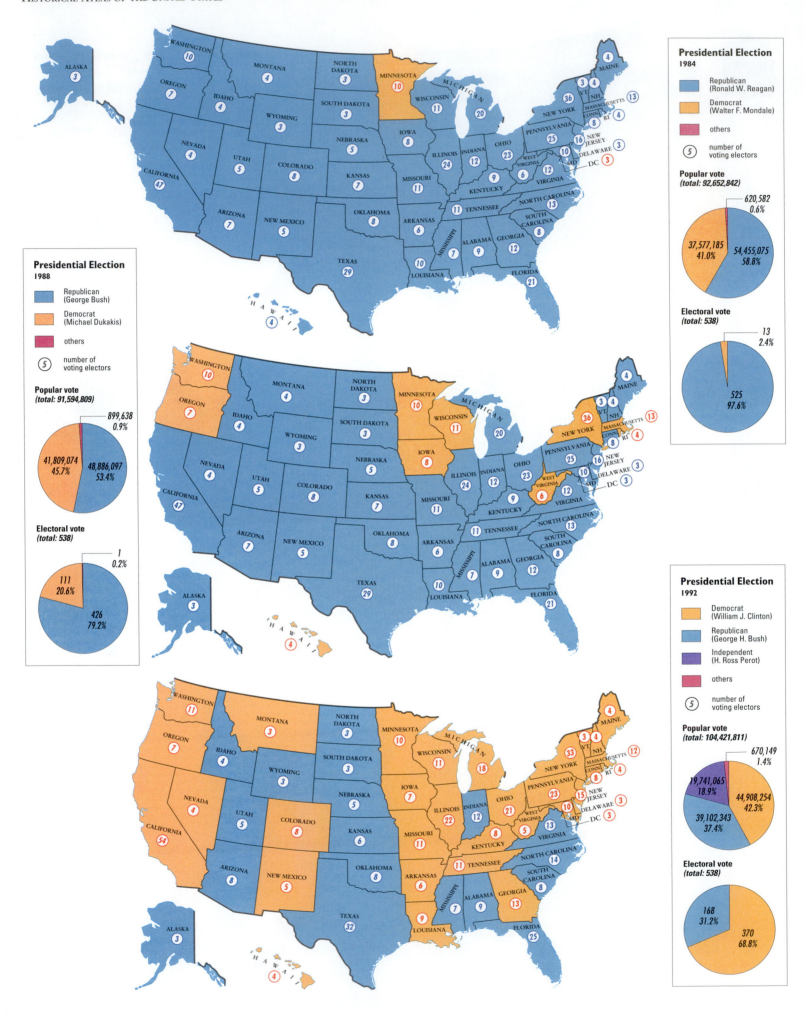

Presidential Election
1984

- Republican (Ronald W. Reagan)
- Democrat (Walter F. Mondale)
- others

⑤ number of voting electors

Popular vote
(total: 92,652,842)

620,582
0.6%

37,577,185
41.0%

54,455,075
58.8%

Electoral vote
(total: 538)

13
2.4%

525
97.6%

Presidential Election
1988

- Republican (George Bush)
- Democrat (Michael Dukakis)
- others

⑤ number of voting electors

Popular vote
(total: 91,594,809)

899,638
0.9%

41,809,074
45.7%

48,886,097
53.4%

Electoral vote
(total: 538)

1
0.2%

111
20.6%

426
79.2%

Presidential Election
1992

- Democrat (William J. Clinton)
- Republican (George H. Bush)
- Independent (H. Ross Perot)
- others

⑤ number of voting electors

Popular vote
(total: 104,421,811)

670,149
1.4%

19,741,065
18.9%

44,908,254
42.3%

39,102,343
37.4%

Electoral vote
(total: 538)

168
31.2%

370
68.8%

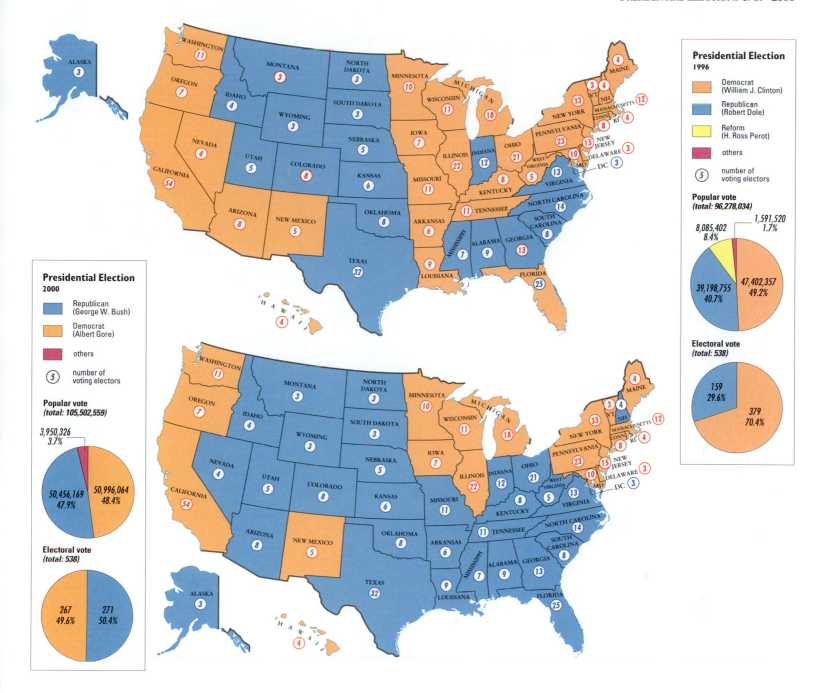

Presidential Election
1996

■ Democrat
(William J. Clinton)

■ Republican
(Robert Dole)

■ Reform
(H. Ross Perot)

■ others

⑤ number of
voting electors

Popular vote
(total: 96,278,034)

1,591,520
1.7%

8,085,402
8.4%

39,198,755
40.7%

47,402,357
49.2%

Electoral vote
(total: 538)

159
29.6%

379
70.4%

Presidential Election
2000

■ Republican
(George W. Bush)

■ Democrat
(Albert Gore)

■ others

⑤ number of
voting electors

Popular vote
(total: 105,502,559)

3,950,326
3.7%

50,456,169
47.9%

50,996,064
48.4%

Electoral vote
(total: 538)

267
49.6%

271
50.4%

Territorial Growth 1775–1970

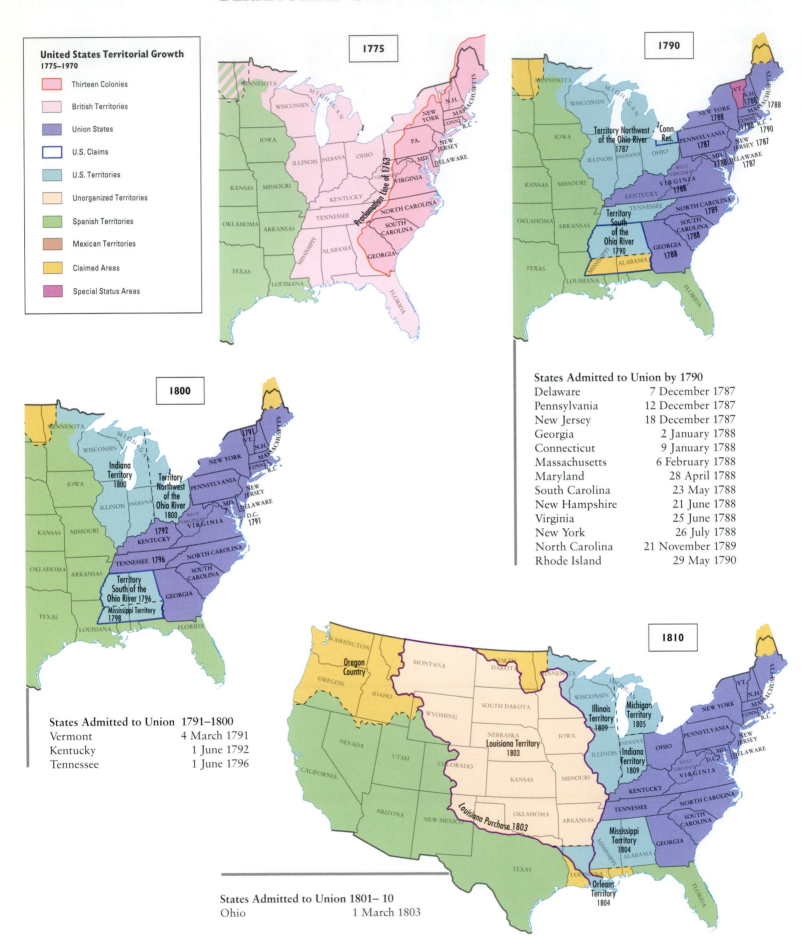

United States Territorial Growth
1775–1970

- Thirteen Colonies
- British Territories
- Union States
- U.S. Claims
- U.S. Territories
- Unorganized Territories
- Spanish Territories
- Mexican Territories
- Claimed Areas
- Special Status Areas

1775

1790

1800

1810

States Admitted to Union by 1790
Delaware	7 December 1787
Pennsylvania	12 December 1787
New Jersey	18 December 1787
Georgia	2 January 1788
Connecticut	9 January 1788
Massachusetts	6 February 1788
Maryland	28 April 1788
South Carolina	23 May 1788
New Hampshire	21 June 1788
Virginia	25 June 1788
New York	26 July 1788
North Carolina	21 November 1789
Rhode Island	29 May 1790

States Admitted to Union 1791–1800
Vermont	4 March 1791
Kentucky	1 June 1792
Tennessee	1 June 1796

States Admitted to Union 1801–10
Ohio	1 March 1803

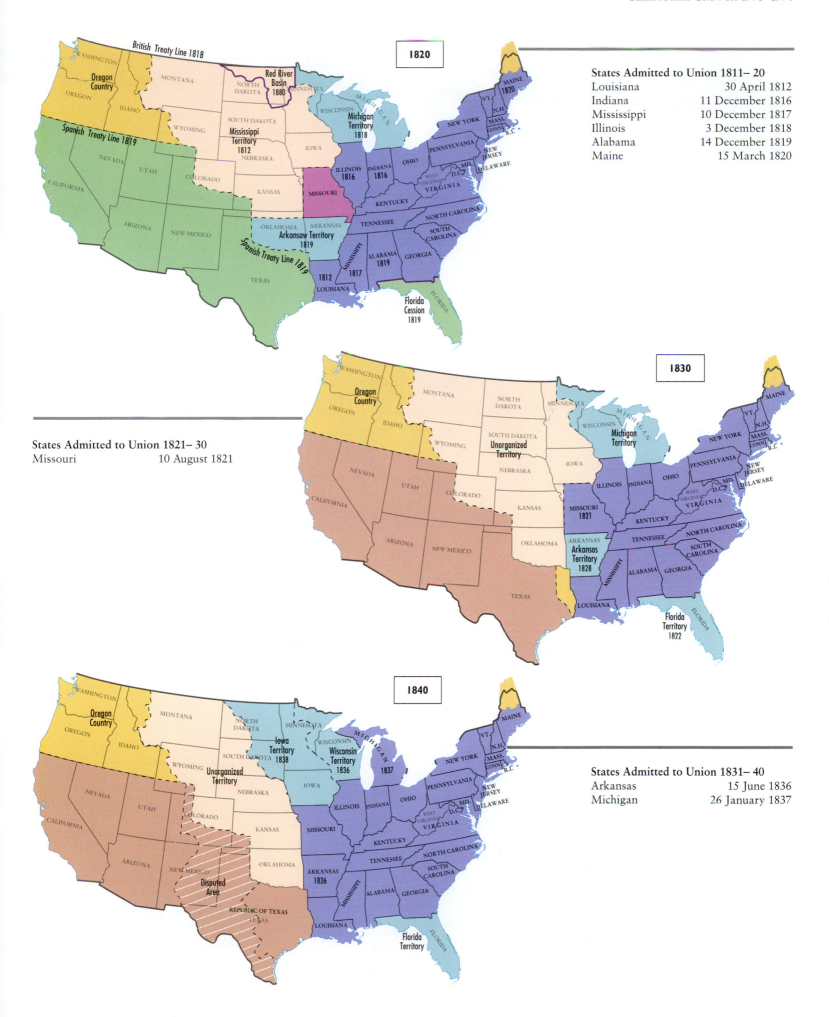

1820

States Admitted to Union 1811– 20

Louisiana	30 April 1812
Indiana	11 December 1816
Mississippi	10 December 1817
Illinois	3 December 1818
Alabama	14 December 1819
Maine	15 March 1820

States Admitted to Union 1821– 30

| Missouri | 10 August 1821 |

1830

1840

States Admitted to Union 1831– 40

| Arkansas | 15 June 1836 |
| Michigan | 26 January 1837 |

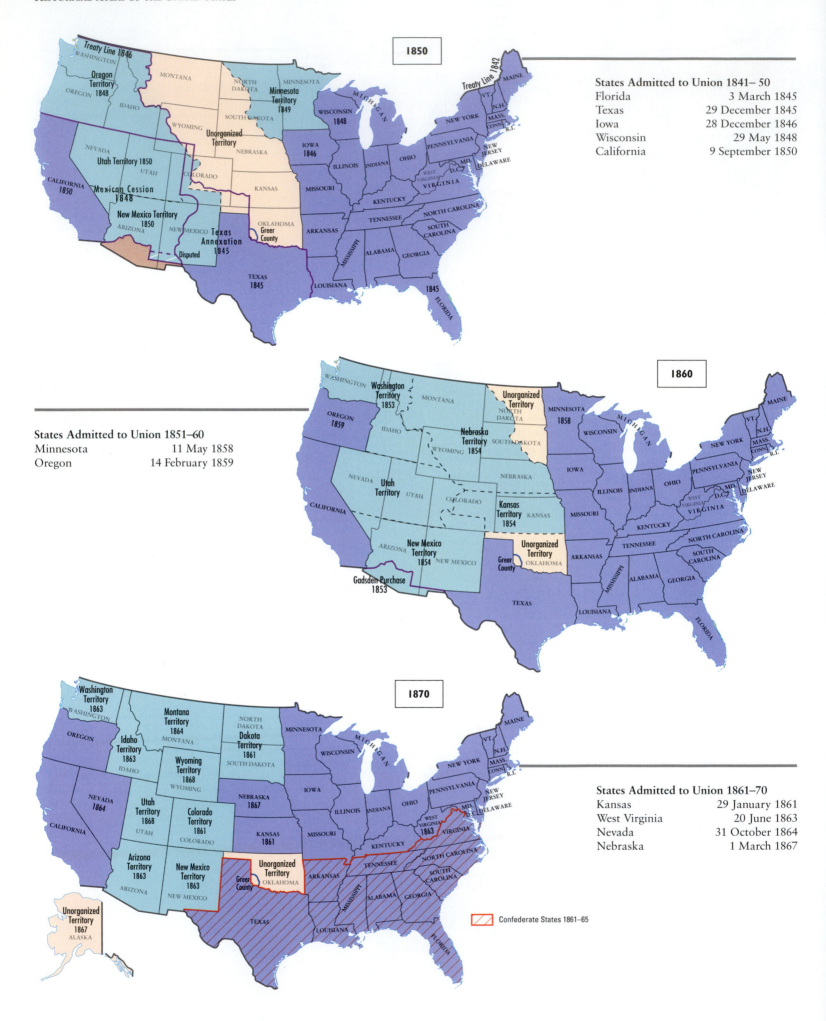

1850

States Admitted to Union 1841–50

Florida	3 March 1845
Texas	29 December 1845
Iowa	28 December 1846
Wisconsin	29 May 1848
California	9 September 1850

1860

States Admitted to Union 1851–60

Minnesota	11 May 1858
Oregon	14 February 1859

1870

States Admitted to Union 1861–70

Kansas	29 January 1861
West Virginia	20 June 1863
Nevada	31 October 1864
Nebraska	1 March 1867

Confederate States 1861–65

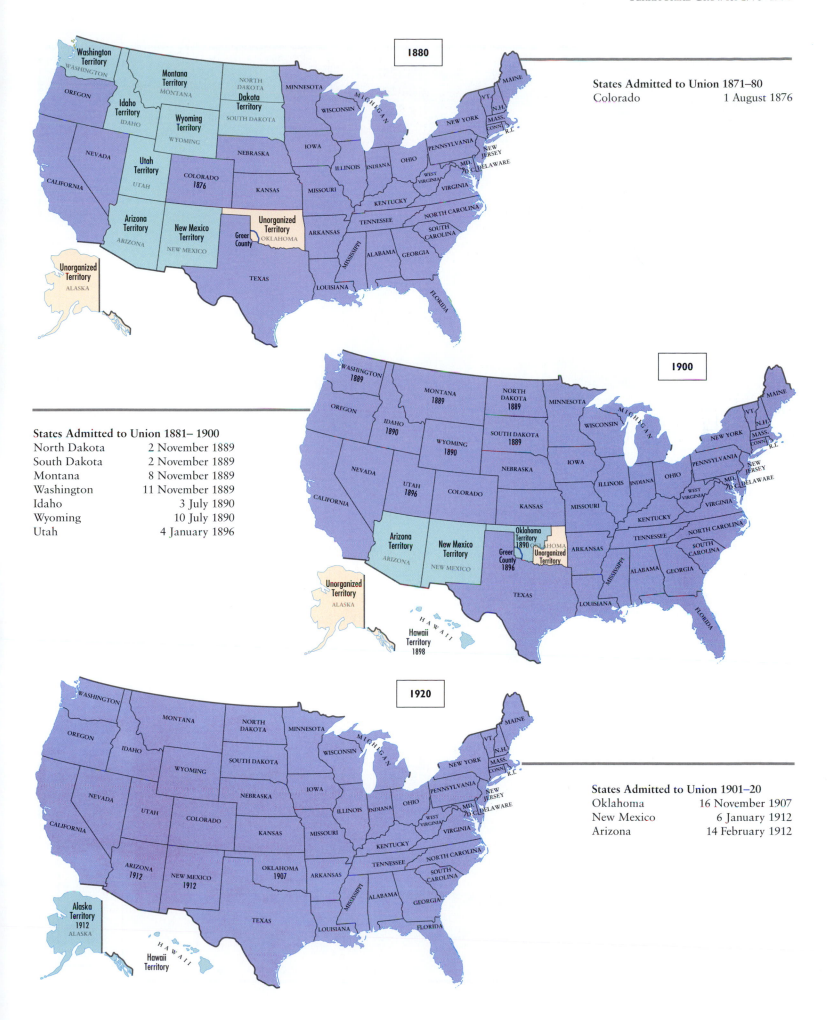

1880

States Admitted to Union 1871–80

Colorado	1 August 1876

States Admitted to Union 1881–1900

North Dakota	2 November 1889
South Dakota	2 November 1889
Montana	8 November 1889
Washington	11 November 1889
Idaho	3 July 1890
Wyoming	10 July 1890
Utah	4 January 1896

1900

1920

States Admitted to Union 1901–20

Oklahoma	16 November 1907
New Mexico	6 January 1912
Arizona	14 February 1912

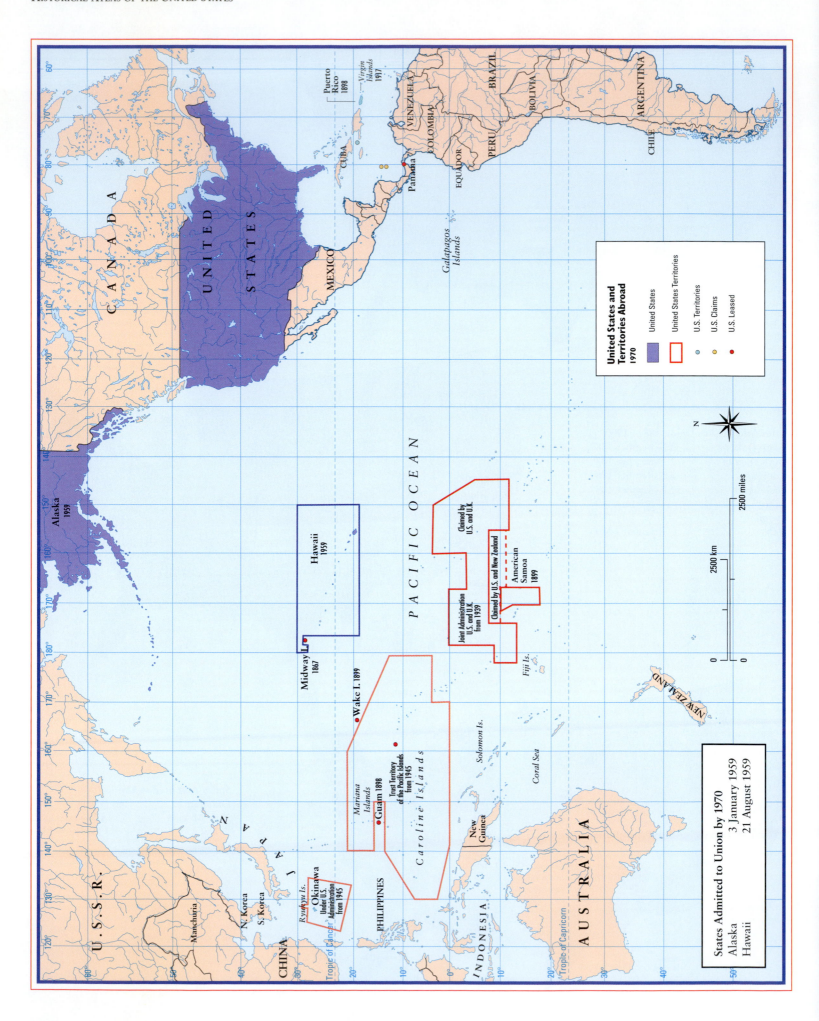

United States and
Territories Abroad
1970

United States
United States Territories
U.S. Territories
U.S. Claims
U.S. Leased

States Admitted to Union by 1970

Alaska   3 January 1959
Hawaii   21 August 1959

SELECTED BIBLIOGRAPHY

The authors and publishers readily acknowledge the work of a large number of scholars and published works, on which they have drawn in the preparation of this atlas. Many of these works remain in print, and can be used as reliable secondary reading on the many topics covered in this atlas. Among them are the following:

Ahlstrom, Sydney E., *A Religious History of the American People*, Yale University Press, New Haven, Conn., 1972.

Allen, James P., Turner, Eugene, J., *We The People: An Atlas of America's Ethnic Diversity* (1st ed.), Macmillan, New York, 1988.

Anderson, Jarvis, *This was Harlem: A Cultural Portrayal*, Farrar, Straus & Giroux, New York, 1982.

Anderson, M.S., *Eighteenth Century Europe, 1713–1789*, Oxford University Press, Oxford, 1966.

Anderson, M.S., *The Rise of Modern Diplomacy, 1450–1919*, Longman, London, 1993.

Andrews, Charles M., *The Colonial Background of the American Revolution: Four Essays in American Colonial History*, Yale University Press, New Haven, Conn., 1924.

Aptheker, Herbert, *The Negro in the Civil War*, International Publishers, New York, 1962.

Bailyn, Bernard, *The Ideological Origins of the American Revolution*, The Belknap Press of Harvard University, Cambridge, Mass., 1967.

Bailyn, Bernard, *The Peopling of British North America: An Introduction*, Alfred A. Knopf, New York, 1986.

Bailyn, Bernard, *Voyagers to the West: A Passage in the Peopling of America on the Eve of the Revolution*, Vintage Books, New York, 1986.

Berkin, Carol Ruth, and Mary Beth Norton, *Women of America: A History*, Houghton Mifflin, Boston, 1979.

Black, Jeremy, *War for America: The Fight for Independence, 1775–1783*, Alan Sutton, Stroud, U.K., 1991.

Black, Jeremy, *Warfare in the Eighteenth Century*, Cassell & Co., London, 2000.

Blanco, R.L., *The American Revolution, 1775–1783: An Encyclopedia*, (2 vols.) Garland Publishing, Inc., New York, 1993.

Blassingame, John, *The Slave Community: Plantation Life in the Antebellum South*, Oxford University Press, New York, 1979.

Boles, John B., *The South Through Time: A History of an American Region*, Prentice-Hall, New York, 1995.

Boller, Paul, Jr. *Presidential Campaigns*. Oxford University Press, New York, 1996.

Brebner, John B., *The Explorers of North America 1492–1802*, London, 1933.

Brogan, H., *Longman History of the United States of America*, Longman, London, 1985.

Brown, R.D., (ed.) *Major Problems in the Era of the American Revolution, 1760–1791*, Houghton Mifflin, Boston, 1992.

Calloway, C.G., (ed.) *The World Turned Upside Down: Indian Voices from Early America*, St. Martin's Press, Knoxville, Ky., 1994.

Cappon, Lester J., et. al., (eds.), Atlas of Early American History: The Revolutionary Era, 1760–1790, Princeton University Press, Princeton, 1976.

Carroll, Bret C., *The Routledge Historical Atlas of Religion in America*, Routledge, New York, 2000.

Congressional Quarterly. *Presidential Elections, 1789–1996*, Congressional Quarterly, Washington, D.C., 1997.

Congressional Quarterly. *Historical Review of Presidential Candidates from 1788 to 1968*. Congressional Quarterly, Washington, D.C., 1969.

Cooper, William J., and Terrill, Thomas E., *The American South: A History*, McGraw Hill, New York, 1991.

Crosby, A.W., *The Columbian Exchange: Biological and Cultural Consequences of 1492*, Greenwood Press, New Haven, Conn., 1972.

Curtin, Philip D., *The Atlantic Slave Trade: A Census*, University of Wisconsin Press, Madison, 1969.

De Lange, Nicholas, *Atlas of the Jewish World*, Phaidon, Oxford, 1984.

DeVoto, Bernard, *The Course of Empire*, Houghton Mifflin, Boston, 1952.

Dittmer, John, *Local People: The Struggle for Civil Rights in Mississippi*, University of Illinois Press, 1994.

Dorr, Robert F., *Air War Hanoi*, Blanford Press, London, 1988.

Dover, E.D. *Presidential Elections in the Television Age, 1960–1992*. Greenwood Press, Westport, Conn., 1992.

Earle, Jonathan, *The Routledge Atlas of African American History*, Routledge, New York, 2000.

Fagan, Brian M., *The Great Journey: The Peopling of Ancient America*, Thames & Hudson, New York, 1987.

Foner, Eric, *Reconstruction: America's Unfinished Revolution, 1863–1877*, Harper and Row, New York, 1988.

Foster, Gaines M., *Ghosts of the Confederacy: Defeat, The Lost Cause, and the Emergence of the New South, 1865–1913*, Oxford University Press, New York, 1987.

Frank, Andrew K., *The Routledge Historical Atlas of the American South*, Routledge, New York, 1999.

Freedman, Lawrence, *Atlas of Global Strategy: War and Peace in the Nuclear Age*, Macmillan, London, 1985.

Freedman, Lawrence, *The Cold War*, Cassell & Co., London, 2001.

Gallagher, Gary W., *The Confederate War*, Harvard University Press, Cambridge, Mass., 1997.

Garraty, John A., *The American Nation* (2 vols.), Addison-Wesley Educational Publishers, New York, 1998.

Gerlach, Arch C., (ed.) *The National Atlas of the United States of America*, Washington, D.C., 1970.

Goetzmann William H., *Exploration and Empire: The Explorer and the Scientist in the Winning of the American West*, Alfred A. Knopf, New York, 1967.

Goetzmann William H. and Williams, Glyndwr, *The Atlas of North American Exploration*, Prentice Hall General Reference, New York and London, 1992.

Greene, J.P. and Pole, J.R. (eds.) *The Blackwell Encyclopedia of the American Revolution*, Blackwell, London, 1994.

Grun, Bernard, *The Timetables of History*, (3rd Edition), Simon & Schuster/Touchstone Books, New York, 1991.

Hans-Erich Stier et al., eds., *Großer Atlas Zur Weltgeschichte,* (8th Edition), Westermann, Braunschweig, 1972.

Harrison, Alferdteen, ed., *Black Exodus: The Great Migration from the American South*, University Press of Mississippi, Jackson, Miss.,1991.

Hastings, Max, *The Korean War*, Michael Joseph Limited, London, 1987.

Haywood, John, *The Historical Atlas of the Vikings*, Penguin Books Limited, London, 1995.

Henri, Florette, *Black Migration: The Movement North 1900–1920*, Garden City, New York, 1976.

Henwood, Doug., *The State of the USA Atlas*, Penguin Books Limited, London and New York, 1994.

Heren, Louis, *The Story of America*, Times Books, London, 1976.

Heyrman, Christine Leigh, *Southern Cross: The Beginnings of the Bible Belt*, University of North Carolina Press, 1997.

Homberger, Eric, *The Historical Atlas of New York City*, Henry Holt and Co., New York, 1994.

Huggins, Nathan I., *Harlem Renaissance*, Oxford University Press, New York, 1973.

Israel: The Historical Atlas, various correspondents of the *New York Times*, Macmillan, New York, 1997.

Johnson, James Weldon, *Black Manhattan*, (preface by Allan H. Spear), Atheneum, New York, 1930 and 1975.

Kalb, Marvin and Abel, Elie, *Roots of Involvement: The U.S. in Asia 1784–1971*, Norton, New York, 1971.

Kupperman, K.O., *Major Problems in American Colonial History*, Houghton Mifflin, Boston, 1993.

LaFeber, Walter, *The New Empire: An Interpretation of American Expansion 1860–1898*, Cornell University Press, New York, 1971.

Lawson, Steven F., *Black Ballots: Voting Rights in the South, 1944–1969*, Columbia University Press, New York, 1976.

Livesey, Anthony, *The Viking Atlas of World War I*, Penguin Books Limited, London, 1994.

Mackesy Piers, *The War for America 1775–1783*, University of Nebraska Press, Lincoln, 1992.

Marsden,George, *Religion and American Culture*, Harcourt Brace Jovanovich, San Diego, Ca., 1990.

McGillivray, Alice and Richard Scammon. *America at the Polls: Harding to Eisenhower; A Handbook of Presidential Statistics*. Congressional Quarterly Press, Washington, D.C., 1998.

McPherson, James M., ed. *The Atlas of the Civil War*, Macmillan, New York, 1994.

Meinig, D.W., *The Shaping of America* (2 vols.), Yale University Press, New Haven, Conn., and London, U.K., 1986.

Merriam Webster's *Geographical Dictionary* (3rd Edition), Hopkins, Daniel J., (ed.), Merriam Webster Inc., Springfield, MA., 1997.

Mieczkowski, Yanek, *The Routledge Historical Atlas of Presidential Elections*, Routledge, New York, 2001.

Miller, J.C., *The Fedalist Era, 1789–1801*, Harper & Row, New York, 1960.

Milner, Clyda A., et al., *Oxford History of the American West*, Oxford University Press, Oxford and New York, 1994.

Morison, S.E., *The European Discovery of America: The Northern Voyages AD 500–1600*, Oxford University Press, New York, 1871.

Nalty, Bernard C., *Strength for the Fight: A History of Black Americans in the Military*, Free Press, New York, 1986.

Namias, J., *White Captives: Gender and Ethnicity on the American Frontier*, The University of North Carolina Press, Chapel Hill, N.C., 1993.

Natkiel, Richard and Preston, Antony, *The Weidenfeld Atlas of Maritime History*, Weidenfeld & Nicholson, London, 1986.

Norton, Mary B.; Katzman, David M.; Escott, Paul D.; Chudacoff, Howard P.; Peterson, Thomas G.; Tuttle, William M. Jr., and Brophy, William J., *A People and Nation*, Houghton Mifflin, Boston, 1995.

Opdycke, Sandra, *The Routledge Historical Atlas of Women in America*, Routledge, New York, 2000.

Oxford Regional Economic Atlas. The United States and Canada (2nd ed.), Oxford University Press, Oxford, 1975.

Palmer, R.R., and Colton, Joel, *A History of the Modern World*, (8th Edition), Alfred A. Kopf, Inc., New York, 1995.

Parish, P.J., *Slavery: The Many Faces of a Southern Institution*, British Association for American Studies, Keele University Press, U.K., 1979.

Pimlott John, *The Historical Atlas of World War II*, Henry Holt and Co., New York, 1995.

Porch, Douglas, *Wars of Empire*, Cassell & Co., London, 2000.

Prange, Gordon W., *At Dawn We Slept: The Untold Story of Pearl Harbor*, McGraw-Hill Books Co., New York, 1981.

Reps, John W., *The Making of Urban America: A History of City Planning in the United States*, Princeton University Press, Princeton, 1965.

Reps, John W., *Town Planning in Frontier America*, Princeton University Press, Princeton, 1969.

Reynolds, Clark G., *Command of the Sea*, William Morrow and Co. Inc., New York, 1974.

Rink, Oliver A., *Holland on the Hudson: An Economic and Social History of Dutch New York*, Cornell University Press, New York and London, New York Historical Association, Cooperstown, N.Y., 1986.

Roberts, J.M., *History of the World*, Helicon Publishing Limited, Oxford, 1992.

Roseboom, Eugene. *History of Presidential Elections*. The Macmillan Company, New York, 1985.

Sauer, Carl O., *Sixteenth Century North America: The Land and its Peoples as Seen by the Europeans*, University of California Press, Berkeley, 1971.

Segal, Aaron, *An Atlas of International Migration*, Hans Zell Publishing, London, 1993.

Silverberg Robert, *The Pueblo Revolt*, Weybright & Talley, New York, 1970.

Simmons, Edwin H., *Marine Corps Operations in Vietnam, 1968*, in *The U.S. Marines in Vietnam 1954–1973*, History and Museums Division, U.S.M.C., Washington, D.C., 1974.

Sowter, T.W.E., *Indian Trade, Travel, and Transportation*, in *Archaeological Report*, Ontario Provincial Museum, Ontario, 1916.

Spector, Ronald H., *The United States Army in Vietnam: Advice and Support: The Early Years, 1941–1960*, Center of Military History, Washington, D.C., 1984.

Spector, Ronald H., *After Tet: The Bloodiest Year in Vietnam*, The Free Press, New York, 1993.

Steel, Ian K., *Warpaths: Invasions of North America*, Oxford University Press, Oxford and New York, 1994.

Stover, John F., *The Routledge Historical Atlas of the American Railroads*, Routledge, New York, 1999.

Summers, Harry G. Jr., *On Strategy: A Critical Analysis of the Gulf War*, Dell, New York, 1992.

Summers, Harry G. Jr., *The New World Strategy: A Military Policy for America's Future*, Simon & Schuster/Touchstone Books, New York, 1995.

Summers, Harry G. Jr., with Karnow, Stanley, *Historical Atlas of the Vietnam War*, Houghton Mifflin, Boston, 1995.

Swagerty, William R., *Indian Trade in the Trans-Mississippi West to 1870*, pp. 351, in *History of Indian-White Relations*, ed. W.E. Washburn in *Handbook of North American Indians*, (vol. 4), gen. ed. W.C. Sturtevant, Smithsonian Institute, Washington, D.C. 1988.

Takaki, Ronald, *Strangers from a Different Shore: A History of Asian Americans*, Little, Brown, Boston, 1989.

Tanner, Helen Hornbeck, et al., (eds.), *The Settling of North America*, Macmillan, New York, 1995.

Thomas, Hugh, *The Slave Trade: The Story of the Atlantic Slave Trade, 1440–1870*, Simon and Schuster, New York, 1997.

Udall, Stewart L., *To the Inland Empire: Coronado and Our Spanish Legacy*, Doubleday & Co., Garden City, New York, 1987.

Weber, David J., *The Spanish Frontier in North America*, Yale University Press, New Haven, Conn., 1992.

Weigley, Russell F., *The American Way of War: A History of United States Military Strategy and Policy*, Macmillan, New York, 1973.

Wentz, Richard E. *Religion in the New World: The Shaping of Religious Traditions in the United States*. Fortress Press, Minneapolis, 1990.

Wetterau, Bruce, *World History*, Henry Holt and Co., Inc., New York, 1994.

Wright, D.R., *African Americans in the Colonial Era: From African Origins through the American Revolution*, Harlan Davidson, Arlington Heights, Ill., 1990.

Wright, L. Leitch, Jr., *The Only Land They Knew: The Tragic Story of the American Indians in the Old South*, Free Press, New York, 1981.

Zelinsky, Wilbur, *Cultural Geography of the United States*, Prentice Hall, Englewood Cliffs, N.J., 1973.

We also made extensive use of information published by the U.S. Bureau of the Census.

INDEX

ACKNOWLEDGMENTS

For Cartographica Limited:

Design: Malcolm A. Swanston

Cartography: Elsa Gibert, Isabelle Lewis, Jeanne Radford, Ian Robbins, Peter Smith, Malcolm Swanston and Jonathan Young.

Typesetting: Jeanne Radford and Isabelle Lewis

Additional Research: Heather Swanston

For Routledge (a member of the Taylor & Francis Group):

Editor: Mark Georgiev

Production: Dennis Teston

Printed in the United States by R.R. Donnelly & Sons, Willard, Ohio.